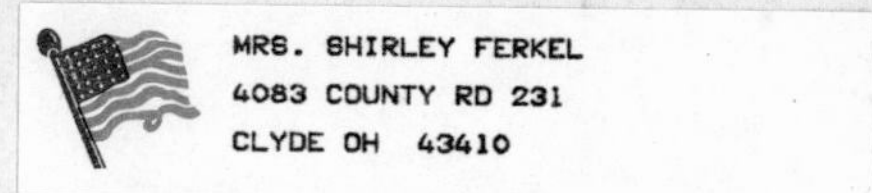

AIDS/acupuncture - 142 Nov. 1992

N. age med. confuses the divine and demonic

* The power of belief - 132 acupuncture, homeopathy and reflexology } p. 105, 139

Yogic Kundalini arousal, dangerous - 140

Herbal medicine - 140

CAN YOU TRUST YOUR DOCTOR?

* altered States of Consciousness 145

Conclusion: p. 408

naturopathy, homeopathy, reflexology } alternate health care

Therapeutic Touch - 391

Other Books By John Ankerberg And John Weldon

Cultwatch: What You Need to Know About Spiritual Deception (Eugene, OR: Harvest House).

When Does Life Begin? And 39 Other Tough Questions on Abortion (Brentwood, TN: Wolgemuth & Hyatt).

The Secret Teachings of the Masonic Lodge: A Christian Perspective (Chicago: Moody Press).

The Facts on the New Age Movement (Eugene, OR: Harvest House).

The Facts on Spirit Guides (Eugene, OR: Harvest House).

The Facts on False Teaching in the Church (Eugene, OR: Harvest House).

The Facts on the Last Temptation of Christ (Eugene, OR: Harvest House).

The Facts on Astrology (Eugene, OR: Harvest House).

The Facts on the Jehovah's Witnesses (Eugene, OR: Harvest House).

The Facts on the Masonic Lodge (Eugene, OR: Harvest House).

The Facts on Mormonism (Eugene, OR: Harvest House).

The Facts on the Occult (Eugene, OR: Harvest House).

Astrology: Do The Heavens Rule Our Destiny? (Eugene, OR: Harvest House).

Christianity and the Secret Teachings of the Masonic Lodge: What Goes on Behind Closed Doors? (Chattanooga, TN: John Ankerberg Evangelistic Association).

The Case for Jesus the Messiah: Incredible Prophecies That Prove God Exists (Eugene, OR: Harvest House).

Do The Resurrection Accounts Conflict? And What Proof Is There That Jesus Rose from the Dead? (Chattanooga, TN: John Ankerberg Evangelistic Association).

1992

JOHN ANKERBERG

CAN YOU TRUST YOUR DOCTOR?

JOHN WELDON

The Complete Guide to New Age Medicine and Its Threat to Your Family

Wolgemuth & Hyatt, Publishers, Inc.
Brentwood, Tennessee

The mission of Wolgemuth & Hyatt, Publishers, Inc. is to publish and distribute books that lead individuals toward:

- A personal faith in the one true God: Father, Son, and Holy Spirit;
- A lifestyle of practical discipleship; and
- A worldview that is consistent with the historic, Christian faith.

Moreover, the Company endeavors to accomplish this mission at a reasonable profit and in a manner which glorifies God and serves His Kingdom.

Published March 1991. First Edition.
Printed in the United States of America.
97 96 95 94 93 92 91   8 7 6 5 4 3 2 1

Wolgemuth & Hyatt, Publishers, Inc.
1749 Mallory Lane, Suite 110
Brentwood, Tennessee 37027

Library of Congress Cataloging-in-Publication Data

Ankerberg, John, 1945–
Can you trust your doctor? : the complete guide to New Age medicine and its threat to your family / John Ankerberg and John Weldon. — 1st ed.
p. cm.
Includes bibliographical references.
ISBN 1-56121-065-X
1. Alternative medicine. 2. Holistic medicine. I. Weldon, John. II. Title.
R733.A58 1991
615.5'3—dc20   90-24698
CIP

To
Dr. William T. Jarvis,
professor of Public Health and
Preventive Medicine,
Loma Linda University Medical School;
President, National Council
Against Health Fraud,
for his commitment
to medical integrity and patient care.

Contents

FOREWORD

Maurice S. Rawlings, Sr.,* M.D., F.A.C.P., F.A.C.C.

Eighty percent of patients seen in the medical doctor's office today have emotional components in their illness or disease.

Medicine for the new age portends to answer this problem by treating not only the body, but the mind and spirit as well. Thus, the whole body is approached by this Holistic Medicine, a rejuvenated practice actually as old as history itself.

Unfortunately, M.D.'s have no degrees in spiritism, no more than the spiritists have in the body or elsewhere. Concerning the mind, there are those with degrees, although neither Psychology or the Metaphysical have achieved scientific status by laboratory reproducibility. Hence, the diversity of practices. Yet occasionally each claims the realm of the other, sometimes with disasterous results, from inappropriate medication on the one hand to induced demonism on the other.

---

* Maurice Rawlings is a graduate of the George Washington University Medical School and a specialist in internal medicine and cardiovascular diseases. He has served as physician to the surgeon general and joint chiefs of staff, Pentagon, and is a fellow of six medical associations and past governor for the state of Tennessee of the American College of Cardiology. He is a member of the International Committee on Cardiovascular Diseases, on the National Teaching Faculty of the American Heart Association, and author of *Beyond Death's Door* and other books relating to patients' near death experiences resulting from his clinical practice in resuscitation.

In a thorough and scholarly fashion, John Ankerberg and Dr. John Weldon have condensed vast research into chaptered categories for the various disciplines of medical practice, ranging from the scientific to the occult, from homeopathy to acupuncture, from chiropractic to crystal healing, from meditation to divination, meticulously concentrating upon those modalities offered in the renaissance of the new age.

Because of subtle Biblical revisions required by some of these groups—massaging verses so people could allegedly see what Holy Writ was really all about—the authors went further and measured each group against Biblical standards.

All you didn't know about new age medicine is now available in textbook form.

FOREWORD

Paul C. Reisser,* M.D.

Several years ago John Weldon and I co-authored a study of the new age movement's efforts to influence health care. Because this subject encompassed such a bewildering array of theories and therapies, our book was primarily a survey, with a few selected topics covered in detail.

Now John Weldon and John Ankerberg have taken the bull by the horns, so to speak. Their new book grapples, in considerably more detail, with the entire realm of alternative medicine and its relationship to mainstream scientific medicine, society, occultism, and the church. The picture is often not pretty, especially when the authors delve into the checkered histories and spiritual pedigrees of some of our country's most popular therapies.

Undoubtedly some feathers will be ruffled by this material. But those who are involved in the practices reviewed here, either as therapists or patients, should read carefully and then do some serious soul searching. All of us desire physical and spiritual health—but a number of self-proclaimed pathways to healing and wholeness actually point in the wrong direction. This book will help many take some important bearings.

---

* Paul Reisser, a graduate of the U.C.L.A. School of Medicine, is a family physician in private practice in southern California. He is a diplomat of the American Board of Family Practice and member of the Physicians Advisory Council for Focus on the Family as well as medical commentator for the national radio broadcast, "Family News in Focus." He is co-author of *New Age Medicine* and the author of *Energy Drainers—Energy Gainers*, a book on healing chronic exhaustion.

(Note: References in the text are keyed to the section entitled Bibliographic Notes. The system includes a number for a title in the bibliographic notes and then, if needed, corresponding page numbers for each title. For example, if the reference is cited as 123:15 then it refers to page 15 of Kurt Koch's *Occult Bondage and Deliverance* [entry 123 in the bibliographic notes].)

PREFACE

Norman Cousins, of the U.C.L.A. medical faculty, observes that perhaps the major medical problem facing America is that Americans don't know how to think properly about health and illness. He sets forth the following argument:

> The main impression growing out of twelve years on the faculty of a medical school is that the No. 1 health problem in the U.S. today, even more than AIDS or cancer, is that Americans don't know how to think about health or illness. Our reactions are formed on the terror level. We fear the worst, expect the worst, thus invite the worst. The result is that we are becoming a nation of weaklings and hypochondriacs, a self-medicating society incapable of distinguishing between casual, everyday symptoms and those that require professional attention. (309:49)

Cousins argues that early in life we become "seized with the bizarre idea that we are constantly assaulted by invisible monsters called germs" and that we must be on constant duty to protect ourselves against them. He points out that the problem is not that germs can cause disease, but that emphasis is not given to an equally important fact that our bodies "are superbly equipped to deal with the little demons, and that the best way of forestalling an attack is to maintain a sensible life style" (309:49).

What Norman Cousins says is true. Our bodies are superbly equipped to deal with disease. As the psalmist observes, we are "fearfully and wonderfully made" (Psalm 139:14). And the truth is that most illnesses are self-limiting. In other words, our bodies are able to handle them without outside intervention.

An exhaustive study was recently released by the U.S. Department of Health and Human Services Task Force in conjunction with the American

College of Physicians. This study suggests that for adults that are symptom free, the annual physical is largely a waste of time. Further, routine blood tests are even less useful for healthy people even though they may account for the largest chunk of our medical bill (310:70).*

The Guide to Clinical Preventive Services, published by the Health and Human Services Task Force, concluded that one of the most important facets in personal health was lifestyle: "After reviewing thousands of screenings and study methods, the study concludes that doctors should reduce blanket testing and spend most of their time counselling their patients on healthy life styles" (310:73). One reason for the burgeoning crisis in health-care, financially and otherwise, is that we are often our own worst enemies. Millions of people live life styles that damage or ruin their health. †

But with a renewed emphasis on life style and personal responsibility for one's health has come another danger, new age medicine. People are generally more health conscious today, but that does not necessarily make them more health-wise. Because of our growing health consciousness and also the expanding influence of the new age movement in our society, America is ripe for influence by new age medicine. As more and more people retreat from the problems of conventional medicine, they are turning in droves to more "natural" methods of healing, those that do not rely on drugs, surgery, or other "invasive" methods.

---

* Of course, for patients with physical symptoms, specific tests and checkups are important. But in healthy people, the only useful tests are those that can catch undetected illness which is also treatable. Of all the common diagnostic blood tests available, only three meet this condition. One is for glucose or blood sugar which may signify diabetes; another test is for creatinine which may suggest kidney disease; and the third is for cholesterol which may increase the chance for heart disease. Regardless, a checkup every two to three years is still wise, and specific yearly or regular tests for prostrate and other cancer or serious conditions is important.

† A good illustration is AIDS. This disease alone has the capacity to swamp and destroy our national health-care system. Several million people are now infected; without a cure, millions will die. And yet AIDS is almost exclusively a preventable disease. Apart from the small if growing number of innocent victims, whether or not a person ever gets AIDS is largely a matter of his or her own personal choice. If a person is sexually chaste and avoids intravenous drugs, chances of getting AIDS are miniscule.

Further, because tens of millions probably will die, something must be said about the cause of this plague: sexual immorality. Homosexuality and fornication are not solely to blame; also to blame is the permissive attitude of society toward sexual behavior in general. We have not upheld moral standards and even now, in the face of this disaster, continue to promote sexual immorality. Sexual sanity may sooner or later be forced upon us; one only wonders how many lives could be saved if we chose it.

In this text our goal is to examine new age medicine critically and in some depth. In part 1 we will investigate the general orientation and beliefs of new age medicine. The overall theme of these chapters is helping the readers to determine if their physicians are practicing scientific medicine or new age occultic practices.

Chapter 1 evaluates how the two approaches of scientific and new age medicine differ. We show why the limits of modern science do not disqualify it from evaluating new age medicine. Chapter 2 supplies specific guidelines for discerning modern versus occultic health practices. We also explain why the problems of modern medicine do not require that people accept new age medicine by default. Chapter 3 discusses the common features of new age medicine. Chapter 4 examines why new age medicine can "work" and still be false. Chapter 5 looks at the underlying premise of much new age medicine, the manipulation of supposed life energies. Chapter 6 documents the reliance of new age medicine on the spirit world and why these spirits are not the enlightened entities they claim to be, but rather deceiving spirits the Bible identifies as demons. In chapter 7 we disclose why a person who seeks out a new age therapist may also be treated with other methods he never requested. In chapter 8 we summarize four reasons why new age medicine should not be trusted.

In part 2 we will individually analyze some of the most common new age forms of health practice and philosophy. Before each chapter we have supplied a brief "summary sheet" for quick access to needed information. The major topics we have evaluated in this volume include acupuncture, altered states of consciousness, applied kinesiology, attitudinal healing/*A Course in Miracles*, channeling, chiropractic, crystal healing, herbal medicine, homeopathy, iridology, meditation, and therapeutic touch.

In any project of this nature, facing budget, space, and other restrictions, there are bound to be shortcomings. Some chapters are more lengthy due to the importance of the subject treated or its complexity; others are too brief. Indeed, several volumes could be written on each of these topics. But whatever the deficiencies, the authors hope that each chapter has sufficient information for the reader to understand the basic issues involved and why a particular practice cannot be recommended.

Collectively, literally tens of millions of people trust and employ the methods cited above. If there is one conclusion to be derived from our research, it is that, by and large, the American people need to be reeducated about their health practices.

❧ ❧ ❧

Due to space considerations many subjects could not be presented even though extensive research was completed on them. Both author and publisher regret these materials could not be included. The subtitle of this book is to be considered in general terms, not exhaustive ones. The present text constitutes a complete guide in that it evaluates most of the major issues raised by new age medicine, including many of its principal therapies. Unfortunately, even if the original sixteen-hundred-page manuscript were published, this text would still be far from exhaustive. Nevertheless, the following list is noted so the reader may understand that citations to and comments about the topics excluded from this text are based upon the author's documented research.

- Acupressure
- Anthroposophical Medicine
- Behavorial Kinesiology
- Astrologic Medicine
- Biofeedback
- Bodywork Methods/the Somatic Arts
- Color Healing (Chromo theraphy)
- Chakra Healing
- Dowsing
- Dream Work
- Edgar Cayce Methods of Healing
- Hypnosis
- Intuition
- Martial Arts
- Muscle Testing
- Naturopathy
- Osteopathy
- Polarity Therapy
- Psychic Anatomies
- Psychometry, Radionics, Radiesthesia, Psionic Medicine
- Psychic Diagnosis, Psychic Healing, Psychic Surgery
- Reflexology
- Self Help Therapy
- Shamanistic Medicine
- Touch for Healthy
- Visualization
- Yoga/Kundalini Yoga

INTRODUCTION

THE ISSUE OF NEW AGE MEDICINE

Some years ago, a three-year study of the Stanford Research Institute International revealed that over twenty million Americans had an active interest in "ideas ranging from astrology to yoga, to Transcendental Meditation to parapsychology . . . to the study of the occult" (430:59–60). More recent Gallup, Roper, and Greeley polls have found equal or much higher levels of involvement in the occult, contact with spirits, and new age topics in general (303). Indeed, the new age movement is a multi-billion-dollar enterprise with influence in many sectors of society (132; 430; 44).* A spiritual vacuum has existed for decades. To a degree it is now being filled with the spiritual content of the new age movement, which is no longer a passing fad, but a growing segment of our culture.

What is the new age movement? Let us give you a brief definition from our book, *The Facts on the New Age Movement:*

> The new age movement (NAM) is a title that refers to a world view or philosophy of life that many people hold. The NAM can also be properly called a religion because it is based on religious views; for example, New

---

* A Gallop poll conducted June 14–17, 1990, revealed that belief in paranormal and new age phenomena (eighteen categories of experience) is widespread in American society and that such beliefs are almost as common among those who are "deeply religious in a traditional sense" even though such beliefs contradict the teachings of more traditional religions.

> Agers hold to pantheism, a belief that everything is a part of God. That is, God is all, and all is God. They believe that every man is part of God, even though those outside of the New Age might not realize it.
>
> Through mystical experiences, or while participating in techniques which alter one's state of consciousness, people are powerfully persuaded that the religious world view of the New Age is true.
>
> An example of this is Shirley MacLaine. During a mystical experience in a hot tub, here is what she said she was led to believe, "My whole body seemed to float. Slowly, slowly I *became* the water . . . I *felt* the inner connection of my breathing with the pulse of the energy around me. In fact, I *was* the air, the water, the darkness, the walls, the bubbles, the candle, the wet rocks under the water, and even the sound of the rushing river outside."
>
> Such mystical experiences have led New Agers to believe they truly are one with the universe and are part of God. It has also led them to believe they have uncovered "human potential," an alleged divine power within themselves that, they think, exists in all men. New Agers want to help everybody discover this power and experientially realize they are one with God. Once people have the mystical experience, New Agers expect that people will live out their new world view. This would mean striving for world unity and peace and then using their new powers to bring it about.
>
> Many New Agers describe encounters with spirit guides or spirit beings. These spirit beings depict themselves as good spirits who claim to be people who have died and now reside in the spirit world to guide and help others spiritually. (304:7–8)

One key aspect of the new age movement is new age medicine, also known as the holistic health movement. New age medicine accepts the philosophy and practices of the new age movement and applies them to the field of health. This is why new age medicine plays an important part in our culture's renewed interest in the occult. Often through new age medical practices, people become interested in new age topics in general.

Marilyn Ferguson is a leader in the new age movement. In her best-selling book, The *Aquarian Conspiracy*, she observes how those treated with new age medicine easily become new age converts:

> Illness, as [consciousness researcher Kenneth] Pelletier and many others have said, is potentially transformative because it can cause a sudden shift in values, an awakening. . . . For many Aquarian Conspirators, an involvement in health care was a major stimulus to transformation. Just as the search for self becomes a search for health, so the pursuit of health can lead to greater self-awareness.

> All wholeness is the same. The proliferating holistic health centers and networks have drawn many into the consciousness movement. A nurse said, "If healing becomes a reality with you, it's a lifestyle. Altered states of consciousness accompany it, increased telepathy. It's an adventure."
>
> One woman sought biofeedback instrumentation to see if she could lower her intraocular pressure and cure her glaucoma. She succeeded, but more importantly, she discovered that her states of consciousness affected her entire life, not just her vision. An M.D., concerned about the abusive doses of Valium he was taking for his headaches, tried biofeedback . . . which led to inner attention . . . which led to meditation and wrenching change, including a far different career in medicine. (149:257–58)

Ferguson also observes how, in order to gain converts to their cause, promoters of new age medicine may attempt to hide the religious nature of their disciplines by carefully speaking in scientific language:

> A psychologist, a national leader in holistic medicine, wandered into the field by way of a T'ai Chi instructor who interested him in acupuncture. He has now successfully integrated alternative medical approaches into the curriculum of a major medical school and has arranged lecture series on holistic approaches for a group of medical schools. "When you develop liaisons," he said, "it's critical that you speak the right language. If I talked yin and yang to most neurosurgeons, they wouldn't hear me. I talk the sympathetic and parasympathetic nervous systems. If we want to help people change, it's important that we don't push them or pull them—just walk together." (149:258)

Philosophers Douglas Stalker and Clark Glymour are the editors of *Examining Holistic Medicine* (3). They also note the proselytizing efforts in new age medicine:

> The goals of the American Holistic Medical Association are bald enough. They want patients to ask their doctors "Are you a holistic physician?" and presumably to take their business elsewhere if the answer is negative. Their proselytizing fervor is equally plain: if each year every member of the AHMA would bring in another member, says a past president of that association, then in ten years every medical doctor in the United States would be among the holists. What kinds of institutions, practices, and science of medicine would this bring us? We think they would be utterly daffy. (3:17)

Nor has the church escaped the influence of new age medicine. Christian practitioners and clients are found in the ranks of most holistic health techniques, but especially in chiropractic, homeopathy, dowsing, applied kinesiology, therapeutic touch, iridology, dream work, hypnosis, and visualization.

For example, in 1986 Dr. Weldon, one of the authors of this book, received a letter from a member of one Baptist church who was concerned because "over forty families are involved in applied kinesiology [muscle testing] and iridology, including our pastor, deacons, and Sunday School teachers." Since the publication of *The Holistic Healers* (356) in 1982, many such letters have been received. By the time the revised edition appeared in 1988, matters had not improved.

Why is this issue important? Why does the influx of new age medicine into the church require that the issue be addressed? In 1988, co-authors Paul Reisser, M.D., Teri Reisser, and Dr. Weldon observed:

> Although awareness of this movement has grown, discernment among Christians has remained marginal in the area of health care practices which are at one level or another hostile to biblical teaching.
>
> More than half of the headquarters personnel of a highly-respected, worldwide evangelical organization have been treated with applied kinesiology, homeopathy and other holistic therapies. Guests on national Christian TV shows have endorsed similar practices. A best-selling Christian author uses and promotes a "Christian form" of acupressure, iridology, etc. The promoter of a healing program whose textbook was dictated by a "spirit guide" [*A Course in Miracles*] was given a friendly interview on Sunday morning at a well-known California church. We have continued to hear . . . stories of churches embroiled in controversy, divided and quarreling after an alternative therapist wins some enthusiastic converts. A large midwestern Baptist church has been split down the middle over the practice of iridology.
>
> Believers who would never dream of promoting the New Age movements are still capable of winning recruits to practices which express New Age thinking. Unfortunately, even when evidence indicates that a practice is incompatible with biblical teaching, not to mention scientific facts, the New Age therapy all too often gets the benefit of the doubt.
>
> An example: segments of *The Holistic Healers* were reprinted in three consecutive issues of the *Journal of Christian Nursing* in 1986. Our critique of Therapeutic Touch . . . elicited a significant amount of mail from Christian nurses who saw nothing wrong with this practice. (1:iv–v)

Brooks Alexander, co-founder of the Spiritual Counterfeits Project in Berkeley, California, observes that one reason pagan spirituality has found a reception in the church is that "the church has become so paganized already that the connection is actually a natural one" (429:6).

In particular, the pragmatism of the modern church is responsible for the adoption of the new age philosophies and practices. In pragmatism, every concern is bypassed except whether or not something works. Important questions are excluded by definition. Whenever pragmatism influences the church, discernment evaporates and new age practices and therapies become acceptable methods of spiritual practice or healing (429:6–7).

Thus, many people are simply unable or unwilling to critically examine the roots, teachings, and consequences of these new age health practices and techniques. They have adopted them on the basis of ignorance, false pretenses, or mere appearance. They have wrongly assumed that merely because a therapy or practice *sounds* medical or scientific, it probably is. Or, when a new health program is enthusiastically recommended by a friend or one's pastor, people incorrectly think the recommendation itself validates the program. Or, when any of these techniques are tried, even skeptically, and found to "work," the person mistakenly concludes they are true and work on the basis of their stated principles—which is rarely the case. Many things in life can "work" and still be false or dangerous.

How influential is new age medicine in modern society? Influential enough. Although holistic health methods have largely remained outside mainstream medical practice, organizations such as the American Holistic Medical Association and The Academy of Parapsychology and Medicine reveal that literally thousands of doctors do employ new age medical techniques in their practices. For example, in the chapter on channeling, we have cited illustrations of the influence of holistic health practices among the medical profession.

But perhaps more significant is the influence of new age medicine within modern nursing. For millions of people, the nursing profession is their first and/or only exposure to health care. In fact, nursing plays an increasingly important role in modern health practice. Among the 1.5 million nurses in this country, literally tens of thousands have turned to new age medicine (431). Unfortunately, discernment among these nurses appears to be marginal. This point is well illustrated by one leader in the nursing profession, Susan M. Williams, R.N., M.S.N., assistant clinical professor of Adult and Critical Care Nursing in the Department of Graduate

Studies and Research of the College of Nursing, Northwestern State University of Louisiana:

> Acceptance of holistic nursing by the profession is evident from the extensive inclusion of holism in the curricula of schools of nursing, from frequent references in the nursing literature, and from the increasing use of holistic jargon by nurses of all persuasions. Further evidence of this acceptance is supplied by the ever-increasing number of "holistic" seminars, workshops, and courses offered to nurses across the country. These programs deal with a wide range of subjects, including wellness lifestyles, acupuncture, visualization, massage, therapeutic touch, and biofeedback. (432:49)*

Williams proceeds to cite specific illustrations of the impact of new age medicine in the modern nursing industry (cf. 431):

> How successful have the holists been in incorporating the concepts and modalities of holistic care into nursing literature, education, practice, and research? The evidence is impressive. . . .
>
> Several nursing books are devoted entirely to holistic nursing. Common to these texts is a denunciation of what are seen as the deficiencies of the biomedical model of health care, a review of the Eastern concepts of healing as an alternative, a belief that nursing is the ideal profession to incorporate holism within its practice, and a discussion of various holistic therapies. As an example, in one text, multiple techniques are suggested as ideas for referral by nurses. Included among them are Rolfing, polarity, psychic healing, iridology, and chiropractic practices. . . .
>
> Even a cursory look at catalogs and program descriptions from university schools of nursing, both undergraduate and graduate, will reveal the widespread adoption of holistic conceptual models, philosophies, and courses. . . .
>
> Holism has become one of the most frequently offered subjects for continuing education seminars and workshops for nurses. . . .
>
> A partial list gathered from textbooks and literature written by nurses for nurses lists all of the following as being holistic practices that nurses

---

* The American Holistic Nurses Association has an active membership and publishes a journal. Numerous textbooks for nurses are written from a holistic perspective and some are entirely devoted to the subject. Nursing schools in particular embrace the concepts of holism by incorporating them into curricula and by teaching such holistic techniques as therapeutic touch and visualization. . . .

The nature of holistic nursing as enunciated by its adherents ranges from what any reasonable person would regard as the common sense practices of good nursing care, to unorthodox and unproven treatments that are the practice of quackery.

> are encouraged to become familiar with: tai chi, homeopathy, acupuncture, acupressure, clairvoyant diagnosis, human auras, Rolfing, applied kinesiology, bioenergetic analysis, therapeutic touch, iridology, polarity, psychic reading and psychic healing, therapeutic massage, reflexology, color therapy, visualization, biofeedback, hypnosis, the Alexander technique, aikido, Feldenkrais method, Lomi body work, and dance therapy. (432:52–54)

Finally, Williams discusses the reasons nursing has been influenced by new age medicine. Among those cited is nurses' traditional belief that nursing alone cares for the whole person—body, mind, and spirit. This widespread, if undemonstrated, idea is promoted in nursing education and makes the profession susceptible to the holistic orientation of new age medicine. Another reason for nursing's acceptance of new age medicine is the desire to distinguish itself as a separate entity from that of medicine. Nursing is more of a "caring" profession, than a "curing" one; it is more concerned with prevention and helping patients to heal themselves than medical treatment; it accepts an intuitive approach far more readily than a scientific one. Further:

> In its attempt to be recognized as a profession distinct from the medical model, nursing has increasingly looked to the behavioral and social sciences for its theoretical base and research decisions rather than to the biological sciences. . . . Nursing is actively engaged in developing its own diagnostic classification and has adopted its own euphemistic jargon different from that of medical terminology. (432:59)

Holistic medicine is accepted among nurses because they are insufficiently trained in basic research and critical skills:

> Many nurses have been swayed by holistic arguments due to a lack of sophisticated scientific skills and an inability to evaluate the quality of the research presented. In spite of serious attempts to be recognized as members of a scientific profession, nurses as a group lack a rigorous background in traditional science and its criteria for research. . . .
>
> Intuitive knowledge and faith are fine, but they should not be confused with scientific reason. We would do well to refer to the ANA Code for Nurses, which clearly admonishes nurses to protect the public from misinformation and misrepresentation and to maintain the integrity of nursing.
>
> Nursing is healing, but it is not sorcery. Most of all, beware of those who label themselves holists. Good nursing can include all the worthy elements of holistic nursing without the label. (432:59–60)

Nevertheless, the influence of new age medicine is not only felt among physicians and nurses; it is also seen in areas as diverse as psychology and business or in unexpected areas such as education and dentistry (refs. 285; 286).

For example, one secular dental textbook observes with concern how occultic medicine is infiltrating its own discipline via nutritional counseling:

> Some dentists utilize pyramid power, divining apparatus (i.e., pendulums, muscle testing, etc.) and other occultic practices in connection with food selection, supplementation assessment, and related activities. Unable to find adequate scientific support for their practices (charging that scientific methods of evaluation are too reductionistic), they turn to traditional methods used by witch doctors, mystics, and shamans, presuming them to better measure "wholeness."
>
> One of the most bizarre dental practices, combining food faddism and occultic practices, involves the use of a pendant (amulet) the patient wears around the neck for treating gum disease. The fob contains a quartz crystal, allegedly "vibrating at the proper frequency" for that particular individual.
>
> This type of magical divination is identical to what is done in witchcraft with the use of amulets, talismans, and charms. (433:310–12)

These authors proceed to show that dentistry can be assimilated by specific new age medical theory and practice:

> Certain so-called holistic dental practitioners write and speak about working with the "life force," which they describe as the "Bio-Energy which holds everything together." Since bio is Greek for life, and energy is synonymous with force, such a description is merely a circular definition that repeats itself and says nothing meaningful.
>
> Some of these so-called holistic dentists also deal with nutrition in terms of balancing body chemistry, utilizing applied kinesiology, hair analysis, and homeopathic and Chinese medicine techniques. (433:312–13)

That new age medicine has influenced even dentistry is only one indication of its modern appeal.

In this text we will ask some hard questions of new age medicine. We will show why almost all new age medicine can be placed in one of two categories and often both: New age medicine is typically either quackery or occultic; this is why it is consequential. We will show that when it "works," it is not working on the basis of its stated principles but on the basis of psychological or spiritistic power. We will reveal that the true source of much new age medicine is the spirit world, and show that even when it does work, it is still dangerous, both physically and spiritually.

Placing new age medicine in a broader perspective can help us to understand some of the issues involved. In the end, there are four basic categories of healing:

- *Natural healing*: The body heals itself, arguably the most frequent kind of healing.
- *Medical healing*: The physician assists the body with various medical treatments.
- *Quack healing*: The unproven claim to heal the body is on the basis of false or questionable methods.
- *Divine or spiritual healing*: God heals the body.

Unless the illness is serious, most people will usually recover, whether or not they go to the doctor. Indeed, a great many healings falsely claimed by various new age therapies are actually the result of the body's unassisted healing ability, not the therapy itself. Doctors themselves will admit that much of their practice simply strengthens or amplifies the body's own healing capacity.

Unfortunately, new age healers often take credit where credit is not due.

But the topic of divine healing is also important. If a personal and caring God exists, then divine or spiritual healing is logical. However, *spiritual* healing per se can either be legitimate or illegitimate, that is, either divine or demonic. In the Scriptures, we discover that God does heal supernaturally according to His will and wisdom (Psalm 103:3; Exodus 4:11). Jesus repeatedly healed people out of compassion for their illnesses and disease (Matthew 4:23–24; 8:16). We also discover that God may give a divine gift of healing to some of His people (1 Corinthians 12:9, 28, 30).

But there are also demonic miracles and healings. God Himself warns that genuine spiritual miracles can occur and yet still be false (Deuteronomy 13:1–5). Such miracles are described as false miracles and lying wonders (e.g., 2 Thessalonians 2:9) because they lead people to worship false gods. Some people may think or claim that they are worshiping the true God, but their practices and philosophy prove this cannot be.

Jesus Himself warned that many people who claimed to perform miracles in His name would depart from Him into eternal judgment for being those "who practice lawlessness" (Matthew 7:22–23). He further warned that false christs and false prophets would perform "great signs and wonders" to try to lead even God's elect astray (Matthew 24:24).

The Apostle Paul spoke of the one who comes "in accord with the activity of Satan, with all power and signs and false wonders, and with all the deception of wickedness for those who perish, because they did not receive the love of the truth so as to be saved" (2 Thessalonians 2:9–10, NASB).

God sternly warned against the false prophet who would work genuine miracles and then counsel rebellion against Him by enticing people to worship a false god:

> If a prophet or a dreamer of dreams arises among you and gives you a sign or a wonder, and the sign or the wonder comes true, concerning which he spoke to you, saying, "Let us go after other gods (whom you have not known) and let us serve them," you shall not listen to the words of that prophet or that dreamer of dreams; for the Lord your God is testing you to find out if you love the Lord your God with all your heart and with all your soul. You shall follow the Lord your God and fear Him; and you shall keep His commandments, listen to His voice, serve Him, and cling to Him. But that prophet or that dreamer of dreams shall be put to death, because he has counseled rebellion against the Lord your God . . . to seduce you from the way in which the Lord your God commanded you to walk. (Deuteronomy 13:1–5, NASB)

Unfortunately, the above verses underscore much of what occurs in modern new age medicine: spiritual claimants performing "miracles" and then counseling people to follow other gods. At its heart, new age medicine is fundamentally idolatrous.

In fact, the reality of spiritual deception within the new age movement is the reason that even practitioners of scientific medicine may become converted to new age beliefs. After they encounter an occult miracle which undermines their faith in scientific medicine, they may join forces with occult medicine and its false gods. Many illustrations are cited in this volume.

Some people have told us that they do not think the issue of new age medicine is important. But new age medicine is important, both to us individually and to our society because:

1. Our health and our family's health is important.
2. The physical and spiritual health of the nation is important.
3. It is important to know if our doctor is using a method that may be quackery or occultic, whether or not it works.

4. New age medicine is a major vehicle for spreading the occult in the United States. We will document that occult practices and philosophies are individually and socially consequential. (See chapter 20)
5. New age medicine is undergirded by a new age world view which is anti-Christian.
6. New age medicine often promotes an irrational attitude toward not just medicine but other areas in life as well.

All of this is why the topic of new age medicine is important to us individually and to our culture. These vital issues which may decide the physical and spiritual health of millions of people and perhaps those of your own family are worth examination.

Part One

THE NEW AGE HEALTH MOVEMENT

ONE

NEW AGE MEDICINE VERSUS MODERN SCIENTIFIC MEDICINE

People concerned about their health or their family's health cannot afford not to distinguish between new age medicine and scientific medicine. It may not only be a matter of health and disease; it may also be a matter of life and death. In addition, new age medicine is full of spiritual implications that can dramatically change a person's life.

The general difference between new age medicine and scientific medicine can be seen in the following chart. We stress that the chart below is for purposes of general contrast only (see chart 1).

New age medicine applies the philosophy and practices of the new age movement, as well as Eastern and Western occultism to medicine. To answer the question of whether new age medicine is scientific or not, we must define what the occult is and then define what science is. According to *Webster's Third New International Dictionary*, the occult is defined as: "something mysterious or supernatural" and "of, relating to, or dealing in matters regarded as involving the action or influence of supernatural agencies or some secret knowledge of them" (305:1560). In other words, the occult by definition involves "the action or influence of supernatural agencies."

How does this differ from science? Natural science does not deal with the supernatural or its agencies at all. It restricts its investigation to the physical realm. Also, science deals in the gathering of reproducible facts.

	Scientific Medicine	New Age Medicine
Premise	Disease operates at the physical level and should be treated physically. (In many disorders there are emotional components that must be treated as well.)	Disease begins at an energy level and should be treated energetically.
World View	Holds most or all premises of materialism and/or naturalism although it is not incompatible with the world view of Christian theism.	Holds many premises of general occultism, pantheism (all is God; God is all) and/or philosophical spiritualism—that all reality is, in essence, spiritual.
Medical Orientation	The scientific disciplines: anatomy, physiology, chemistry, pharmacology.	The metaphysical disciplines: a) Eastern occultic philosophy and practice: Chinese (e.g., Taoism; acupuncture), Hindu (e.g., Vedanta; ayurvedic medicine), Buddhist (e.g., Mahayana; vipassana meditation), Shamanistic (e.g., American Indian; ritual possession); b) Western occultic philosophy and practice (e.g., anthroposophical medicine; homeopathy).
Basis for Methodology (why its methods are used)	Rational scientific inquiry (techniques are used because they are scientifically shown to work on the basis of their stated principles.)	Pragmatic, empirical inquiry (techniques are used primarily because they seem to work, not because they have been demonstrated to work on the basis of their stated principles).
Safeguards	Pre-existing scientific database of confirmed medical testing; double-blind clinical trials; peer review, skeptical attitudes toward research findings; methods not adopted until validated for their effectiveness.	Little or no database; no safeguards against irrational and scientifically unproven methods; uncritical attitudes often permit a variety of false therapies to be accepted.
Medical Findings	Generally consistent by discipline and consistent across discipline.	Often contradictory by disciplines (e.g., iridology, reflexology charts) and across disciplines.
Diagnostic Methods	Physically based; consistently used.	Psychically based; contradictory use.
Status re: Effectiveness	Scientifically validated.	Scientifically disproven or unproven.

Chart 1: Differences Between Scientific and New Age Medicine

Michigan State University Science Professor John N. Moore provides a good definition of science:

> An interconnected series of concepts and conceptual schemes that have been developed as a result of experimentation and observation and are fruitful of further experimentation and observation; or the body of knowledge obtained by methods based upon the authority of observation. (Science is limited to the study of nature: that is, study of matter and energy, because of limiting principles of being empirical, quantitative, mechanical and correctable.) (308:367)

Any definition of science will have its problems, but for our purposes we will use the term *science* to indicate a systematic approach to the study and classification of natural phenomena based upon a healthy skepticism involving regular adherence to what is called the scientific method.

The Scientific Method

What is the "scientific method"? The scientific method is like a road map. A road map will not tell us everything we want to know, but if we read it correctly, it will tell us how to get to our destination and prevent us from getting lost. It will tell us which routes are correct and which are false, and in the long run it will save us time and effort. Simplified, the scientific method in medicine can tell us which "roads" (medical approaches and methods) are valid and which are not. It can tell us if we are on the road we must be on to reach our destination, or if we are on a wrong road leading elsewhere, or nowhere!

How does the scientific method do this? It makes certain that medical procedures of diagnosis and treatment work on the basis of their stated principles. If particular methods do work on the basis of their stated principles, then we are guided safely and can know what to expect.

But if the methods we use do not work on the basis of their stated principles, then we are not guided safely in any manner and can know little or nothing. For example, iridology claims it can diagnose the condition of the body through examination of the eye's iris. Acupuncture claims it can effectively treat high blood pressure. But if these methods can do neither, then the person who relies on them is not guided safely and places his or her health at risk.

Let us illustrate why a scientific approach to medicine is important and the difference it can make to us personally when compared with new age medicine.

Let's say you or your child has a persistent sore throat.

How does the diagnosis based on scientific medicine prove its usefulness? First, you go to the doctor and tell him your symptoms. He examines you, and because he is medically trained, he suspects it may be more than an ordinary sore throat. How does he find out whether his suspicion is true or not? First, he takes a blood sample which reveals a high white cell count. He now suspects you may have strep throat. How does he determine whether you are infected with the streptococcus bacteria and which kind of streptococcus bacteria it is? He determines this by a simple culture which proves the existence of the bacteria and identifies it.

Because your doctor knows that antibiotics, such as penicillin, will kill the strep bacteria, he will write you a prescription. If you take the drug according to his instructions, in a few weeks you will no longer have strep throat and you will feel fine once again.

Now, let us say you or your child has a sore throat and you go to a new age healer. Because he is not medically trained, he wrongly assumes you have a simple cold or flu. He decides that your supposed life energy (*prana*, *chi*) is blocked or slightly out of balance, producing your cold or flu symptoms. By acupuncture treatment or applied kinesiology, he "unblocks" your life-energy and prescribes rest and herbal tea. No blood test is given to determine infection level. No culture is taken to determine if bacteria are present.

In a few days your sore throat subsides, and you conclude new age medicine is wonderful. Not only are you cured, but you did not have to pay for any expensive medical tests.

But two months later you feel tired and feverish and have painful, swollen joints. You go back to your new age therapist. By "muscle testing" or reflexology, he or she again concludes your life energies are blocked. Using therapeutic touch, he claims to transfer his own life energy into your body to assist your own *prana* (life energy) to heal your illness. He also prescribes homeopathic remedies. You go home, still feeling lousy.

One month later you are no better; your speech is slurred, and you experience involuntary, jerking movements of the hands, arms, and face.

You decide it is time to visit a conventional doctor. To your horror you discover that you have streptococcus induced rheumatic fever and chorea; you also have valvular heart disease, a condition you will live with for the rest of your life.

You (or your child) learn a hard lesson about new age medicine. Your new age therapist never knew that an untreated streptococcal infection (which may have no more symptoms than a common sore throat) could temporarily damage your brain and permanently damage your heart. (Indeed, the strain that alledgedly killed Muppet's inventor Jim Henson can be deadly within forty-eight hours.) Your new age therapist had neither access to a medical lab to test your blood levels nor interest in doing so. He had no medicine to prescribe. In fact, he had little interest in scientific medicine at all and was more concerned with manipulating your supposed life energies.

What then is the difference between scientific medicine and new age medicine? The difference is this: Do you have a reliable and accurate road map, and can you interpret it properly so you know where you are going? Or are you driving blindly without any directions and not really concerned about where you may end up?

This illustration reveals the value of the scientific method. It is an important "road map" in health matters.

Because the scientific method involves careful testing of a theory, based on observation and experiments to determine if the theory is valid, it can determine if particular health practices are helpful or harmful. A doctor can suspect that a normal sore throat may be a more serious infection, and he can determine the kind of infection because of previous scientific research based on the scientific method. Without such research, he could tell you little or nothing.

Usually, a theory is based upon information already gathered. For example, scientific data led researchers to theorize that AZT might slow down the progress of the AIDS virus. Careful laboratory experiments confirmed the hypothesis. Then, it was given to people with AIDS. When it was given to people with AIDS, it was discovered that AZT was, in fact, a useful treatment.

But AZT could only be given to people after its effectiveness had been proven. Establishing the effectiveness of a treatment is vital because no one with a real health problem wants to be treated by a method whose effectiveness is either unsure or disproven. Prescribing laetrile for cancer will not help people, and it may even harm them. This is the fundamental problem with new age medicine. Its treatments are characteristically unproven or disproven.

When it comes to the area of health practices, the safeguards of the scientific method are that before a given treatment can be offered to the public, it must have undergone intense scrutiny in order to ensure that the treatment is effective based upon its stated principles. Penicillin must really have been proven to kill streptococcus bacteria. It's not good enough to think it does this, or to simply *claim* it does this; it must really be proven to kill the bacteria. Scientific medicine works because it is based upon proven facts.

New age medicine is not based upon proven facts and, therefore, does not work on the basis of its stated principles. As we will see, the reason some sick people get well while using new age treatments has little or nothing to do with the new age treatment itself. Just because a method seems to work does not prove that it does work, or that it works as claimed.

Thus, we may define scientific medicine as the modern practice of diagnosis and treatment by a medically qualified, scientifically oriented specialist using methods for which effectiveness has been established by rigorous and independent clinical testing. Again, when doctors diagnose and treat their patients today, the methods they use to diagnose and the treatments they offer have already been scientifically proven to be effective.

The New Age Method

How then do we define new age medicine? We may define new age medicine, generally, as the modern practice of diagnosis and treatment by a medically unqualified and often psychically oriented practitioner using methods for which effectiveness has never been established or has been scientifically discredited (see reference 403). Even when a practitioner is medically qualified, this does not in itself validate a new age treatment.

Nevertheless, those who practice new age medicine do not usually have the medical skill of a regularly trained physician.

Further, their methods will neither diagnose accurately nor cure disease. Thus, acupuncturists, iridologists, psychic healers, chromotherapists, applied kinesiologists, practitioners of astrologic medicine, etc., rarely have four years of rigorous post graduate medical education, nor will their techniques diagnose or cure illness.*

The U.S. House of Representatives Select Committee on Aging defines a *quack* as "anyone who promotes medical remedies known to be false, or which are unproven, for a profit" (434:411). But one does not have to promote techniques or remedies for a profit to be a quack. The essence of *quackery* is false or unproven remedies. And this is the essence of new age medicine. *The Oxford American Dictionary* defines a quack as "a person who falsely claims to have medical skill or to have remedies that will cure disease" (186:732).

Is new age medicine really quackery? The definition of *quack* or *quackery* varies slightly from one medical dictionary to the next. To the extent the definition includes the idea of *deliberate* misrepresentation concerning diagnostic and healing ability, an individual new age practitioner is not necessarily a quack. Many of them sincerely believe that their diagnostic and healing treatments work. But if these methods do not work, practitioners are still engaging in misrepresentation, deliberate or not. And misrepresentation of a remedy's effectiveness is the heart of quackery.

New age treatments do not make claims for themselves; the people who practice them do. Because enough new age therapists have made false claims for these treatments, there is little doubt they are quackery. Below we present various definitions of quack or quackery from authoritative medical dictionaries and encyclopedias:

> Quack—"One who misrepresents his ability and experience in diagnosis and treatment of disease or the effects to be achieved by his treatment." (435:947)
>
> Quackery—"A false claim by someone to have both the ability and the experience to diagnose and treat disease." (313:842)
>
> Quack—"Charlatan." (311:619)
>
> Quack—"A pretender to medical skill: an ignorant or dishonest practitioner." (436:596)

---

* When genuine spiritistic power is present, accurate diagnosis or healings can be produced, but they are produced by the spirits, not the method. Further, they are not true healings (see chapter 3). For a discussion of the legitimacy of our acceptance of genuine spirit entities, their prevalence in new age medicine, why belief in them is not inconsistent with a scientific perspective, along with some of the evidence for their identity see chapter 3 and chapter 6.

Quackery—"The practice of medicine by unlicensed persons or the application of treatments which are not generally recognized as appropriate by the [medical] profession." This same text reveals that false "testimonials [are] the main stock and trade of the quack." And that "one of the most dangerous forms of quackery is the advertisement that tells the truth as far as it goes but which by artful devices misleads the reader or viewer into believing that the drug [or treatment] is a cure. The reader's unwarranted inferences are the cause of self-deception." (314:1224–1225)

Quack—"One who fraudulently misrepresents his ability and experience in the diagnosis and treatment of disease or the effects to be achieved by the treatment he offers." (437:1399)

Quackery—"The fraudulent misrepresentation of one's ability and experience in the diagnosis and treatment of disease or of the effects of the treatment offered." (437:1399)

The above definitions include the following items:

- misrepresentation of diagnostic or treatment ability.
- false claims regarding experience in diagnosis and treatment.
- ignorance or dishonesty concerning medical skill.
- the practice of medicine by unlicensed individuals.
- the use of methods not generally recognized by the medical profession.

In light of such definitions, there is little doubt that new age medicine in general should be classified as quackery.

But isn't it true that many people report being cured by holistic therapies? And doesn't this prove new age medicine cures disease? No, because even when these healings are genuine, they are not produced on the basis of the new age techniques themselves, operating on the basis of their stated principles. New age medicine does not work on the basis of its stated principles but upon psychological factors or through the body's natural ability to heal itself over time or through spiritistic powers.

The above differences between scientific and new age medicine are why Drs. Stalker and Glymour observe in their excellent text, *Examining Holistic Medicine*, that ". . . holistic medicine is not a scientific tradition. It has no paradigmatic work, no recognized set of problems, and no shared standards for what constitutes a solution to those problems; it also lacks the critical exchange among its practitioners that is characteristic of the sciences" (3:26).

These authors further discuss how the very existence of new age medicine is undermining medicine in general and, to that extent, the nation's health. They observe,

> The shared aims that tie so many diverse people together are to institutionalize holistic medical practices, and, furthermore, to loosen the demands of evidence that we, as a society, impose on those who claim to cure or prevent disease. The first aim requires the second. . . . Only by abandoning the usual criteria of scientific evidence, and even the usual demands of rational thinking, can the claims of holistic medicants be established and made legitimate. . . .
>
> [However,] the science of holistic medicine is bogus; . . . The philosophical views championed by this movement are incoherent, uninformed, and unintelligent; . . . Most holistic therapies are crank in the usual sense of that word: they lack any sound scientific basis. (3:10)

To cite one example, Dr. Thomas Chalmers is Distinguished Service Professor of Medicine, as well as president emeritus and dean emeritus of the Mount Sinai School of Medicine. He is the author of over two hundred and fifty publications and head of the Clinical Trials Unit at the Mt. Sinai Medical Center. Dr. Chalmers examined the scientific quality of articles found in the most scientifically oriented new age medical journal, *The Journal of Holistic Medicine*. This is the official journal of the American Holistic Medical Association founded by neurosurgeon and new age practitioner Dr. Norman Shealy, author of *Occult Medicine Can Save Your Life* (50).

After examining forty-seven articles from four different volumes, Dr. Chalmers discovered only nine trials of therapies, and of these only two were randomized controlled trials, both by the same author. Yet AHMA proponents have claimed that their journal published empirical studies similar to those in standard medical journals. But the scientific tests were few and far between and "generally not well done." They suffered from errors such "as a lack of adequate control with regard to measurements and separation of investigative agents" (3:14).

This is why Dr. Chalmers concluded that the "*Journal of Holistic Medicine* has a long way to go to achieve the same standards of scientific reporting as the more orthodox medical journals. . . ." (408:163).

This journal leaves much to be desired. And yet it is the premier scientific publication in the field of new age medicine.

When we examine the only other credible new age medical journal we know of, the *Journal of Holistic Health*, matters deteriorate rapidly. After examining one hundred fifty-three articles from all nine journals (the journal ended with Vol. 9), it became obvious that we were not dealing with science at all, but religion—Eastern occultic religion. Consider a few titles:

"Applying Edgar Cayce Readings to the Daily Clinical Practice of Medicine" (88:47–55)

"Cancer Research Based on Readings Given by Cosmic Awareness" (88:84–95)

"The Qabalistic Model of Wholeness" (88:96–101)

"Clairvoyant Diagnosis" (89:37–42)

"Altering Consciousness" (89:93–100)

"Death Does Not Exist" (89:60–65)

"An Electronographic Study of Psychic States Obtained by Yoga" (90:57–59)

"Psychic Diagnosis" (90:90–94)

"The Yoga of Holistic Health" (91:18–21)

"Hypnosis and Altered States of Consciousness in the Holistic Process" (92:94–104)

"Scientific Research on Psychic Energies at the Department of Kinesiology, U.C.L.A." (93:46–54)

"Holistic Health at the Bhagwan Shree Rajneesh Ashram" (93:112–117)

"Parapsychology, Kirlian Photography and Creative Healing" (94:58–62)

"Awakening the Energies of Transformation" (95:72–79)

The articles in this journal may have been written by M.D.'s or Ph.D.'s but they have little to do with scientific medicine.

Susan M. Williams, R.N., M.S.N., reveals that the fundamental problem inherent to all new age medicine is also characteristic of holistic nursing: the unjustified promotion of unproven methods.

> Unproven therapies are presented as alternatives to established medical practices and treated with equal preference to proven ones. There is a notable absence of qualifying statements for the use of these practices. In fact, they are made to appear universally efficacious. Nurses are even reassured that if they use holistic techniques and fail to achieve the desired

> results (certainly a possibility), it is probably because they don't understand *or practice* the philosophy behind them. . . .
>
> Characteristically, the [nursing] holists are prepared to offer an excuse for the lack of evidence, stating that "physiological signs of healing are not a necessary component of the healing episode." How tidy. Results of the few well-designed, double-blind studies that have been done have been transient, of no statistical significance, in need of replication, and have not adequately addressed the very real issue of the placebo effect. . . .
>
> The preponderance of superficial reports from poorly designed studies with no double-blind controlled methods, inexact measurements, inadequate baseline data, an absence of follow-up, and subjective findings simply do not lend credibility to holistic nursing claims. (432:54–57, emphasis added)

The Limits of Modern Science

Science is not infallible, nor should anyone expect it to be. In various ways, science and its methods are always subject to limitations. Our knowledge of the universe will never be infinite and therefore, in some ways, always deficient. Further, scientists are not perfect, nor are the instruments and theories they work with (362). For example, science works by approximation; science never has been and probably never will be a single, consistent, coherent method. One scientific method or theory may have internal inconsistencies or be at variance with another scientific method or theory. When scientists attempt to resolve a theoretical problem by proposing better theories, these may create even more problems.

Science may also be bound by limiting and unnecessary assumptions, such as naturalism or materialism—assumptions that sometimes force the deriving of false conclusions from scientific data. For example, one false assumption derived from materialism (the idea that matter is the ultimate reality in the universe) is the equally false assumption that all life has evolved from inorganic matter to its present form (the theory of chemical and biological macroevolution). In spite of its popularity, this theory was never tenable and is increasingly questioned even in scientific circles (349).

In his *Christianity and the Nature of Science* (302), philosopher of science J. P. Moreland examines some of the limits of modern science. For example, when science claims a uniqueness and power it does not possess, it is really "scientism," the idea that if something cannot be tested by the scientific method, it cannot be true or rational. Moreland comments:

> According to this view, science is the very paradigm of truth and rationality. If something does not square with currently well-established scientific beliefs, if it is not within the domain of entities appropriate for scientific investigation, or if it is not amenable to scientific methodology, then it is not true or rational. Everything outside of science is a matter of mere belief and subjective opinion, of which rational assessment is impossible. . . . But however widely this opinion may be held, it is nonetheless a cultural myth that is patently false. (302:104)

Moreland also shows why even a definition of science is problematic by concluding that "a generally agreed on set of necessary and sufficient conditions for something to count as science has not been found" (302:42). He discusses why the common components of science are not exclusively related to that discipline, including dependence on natural law, empirical testability, falsifiability, measurability, predictability, and repeatability (302:22–43).

He concludes with the following assessment:

> There is no clear-cut definition of science. Neither are there any generally accepted necessary and sufficient conditions for drawing a line of demarcation between science and nonscience. It is foolish to say, with popular opinion, that science by definition rules out theological or philosophical concepts. (302:56–57)

Thus, science and the scientific method or methods such as inductivism, adduction, conventionalism, pragmatism, falsificationism, justificationism, etc., are not exclusive ways of determining knowledge (302:60–101). Theology, for example, is just as rational and truth-seeking a discipline as science (357). In fact, modern science is more indebted to theology than it realizes and, to a significant degree, owes both its origin and its general success to presuppositions that are basically Christian. As several researchers have demonstrated, modern science is in good part a product of the influence of Judeo-Christian religion on Western thought* (see refs. 358; 364; 365).

---

* Eugene M. Klaaren (Ph.D. Harvard) cogently argues for this viewpoint in (358); R. Hookyas is the author of over 125 science publications and professor of the History of Science, University of Utrecht; he argues similarly in (364). Robert E. D. Clark (Ph.D. organic chemistry, Cambridge University) is an honors scholar at St. John's College, Cambridge. He emphasizes, "Christianity has contributed profoundly to the development of modern science" and "scientific development has occurred only in a Christian culture." (365:11, 21)

Because of the Christian belief that a rational God had created a real, ordered, rational universe, Christian men concluded it was capable of fruitful, scientific investigation. This is why most of the early great scientists were Bible believing men (401). In fact, to the extent that science departs from Christian presuppositions and entertains fruitless speculations concerning the reality and orderliness of the universe, it suffers.*

Nevertheless, the general method by which science proceeds is both legitimate and useful; it is the only way science can be done. In fact, in the modern world, science is necessary. Without it, each of our lives and the world as a whole would be vastly different and probably quite worse. We don't think that anyone who understands how people lived in earlier periods of human history would wish to return to a truly pre-scientific age.

Merely because science as a discipline is not unique or because the scientific method has limits and problems is no reason to discard scientific methods or findings when they are true. And proper science has a great deal to say about new age medicine.

The Application of Scientific Principles To New Age Medicine

Each one of us must assume certain things to live in this world: (1) The world exists, is real and ordered. (2) The world can be accurately measured and evaluated to derive useful information. Anyone who does not make such assumptions could not live in this world for even a moment. All men do make such assumptions. Even those who think the world is an illusion never step in front of a bus or car. Without an ordered world subject to accurate measurement and evaluation, nothing could be known and life would be chaotic.

In our evaluation of new age medicine, we have utilized the principles of applied, operational science, which, in turn, assume numbers 1 and 2 above. Those who remind us that this is only an assumption should recog-

---

* For example, when the antirealist presuppositions of Hindu and Buddhist metaphysics enter the domain of science, the skepticism produced has far reaching consequences (360). Further, when the phenomena of theoretical physics (i.e., quantum mechanics) are falsely cited as "justification" for new age medicine, let alone an Eastern view of the world, the result is both confusion in the popular mind and ultimately the betrayal of science (361).

nize it is an assumption based on premises they themselves must live by, regardless of personal beliefs.

The real problem in new age medicine is not a controversy between philosophical and applied science. The real problem is the claims of new age medicine. Often there is simply nothing concrete for applied, operational science to investigate. For example, often new age medicine claims that its techniques work on the basis of mystical life energies (*chi, prana, mana*) and related psychic concepts that can never be scientifically examined or measured. It claims that diseases are not ultimately physical but "astral" or "etheric" in nature. It offers "medicines" such as homeopathic substances that do not even have one molecule of the "remedy" in them.

Advocates of new age medicine may respond to the charge that their practice is not scientific by claiming that traditional medicine has refused to test its methods from either fear or bias. If science would only test their methods, they would be proven true. But such claims are incorrect.

First, some new age methods have been scientifically tested and have been proven false, such as iridology, homeopathy, and astrologic medicine.

Second, one reason why other new age medical techniques have never been tested is their sheer number. The time and effort required to scientifically test scores of new therapies is immense. Another problem is methodological; these therapies may be based on occultic theories which science cannot directly test. For example, therapeutic touch, acupuncture, and psychic healing all claim to manipulate invisible, undetectable energies. Science may be able to test the diagnostic and healing success of these therapies, but it cannot examine the basis on which they claim to operate. Other methods may claim to exclusively influence the astral or etheric "body" which is something science cannot investigate—period.

Third, new age methods may claim to work on the basis of principles that are at such variance with known scientific facts they could not possibly be true. For example, chromotherapy, astrologic medicine, the Edgar Cayce method of healing, muscle testing (such as applied and behavioral kinesiology), reflexology, iridology, and homeopathy each claim to work by methods which, if true, would require throwing out all standard medical texts.

Should science waste valuable time and scarce funding to prove what must be true: that a therapy is false? Scientists do not spend time refuting flat earth theories for the same reason.

Having something to test and measure, such as real physical disease, real test methods and variables, and real medicine, is far more valuable than having nothing to test and measure. If there is nothing to examine or test, then we must become agnostics and skeptics, and little can be known. The only basis in which to accept any claimed medical treatment is blind faith. Then no science is possible, and the witch doctor's magic is just as valuable as the methods of modern medicine.

Nevertheless, while it is true that science cannot fully test occultic ideas, there remains much in new age medicine that is testable, even in methods that employ mystical energies or other unscientific ideas. For example, energy manipulators claim their methods improve health or cure disease, and these claims can often be tested. Iridology claims it can accurately diagnose disease by examining the iris of the eye, and reflexology claims that massaging particular sections of the foot can influence "corresponding" body systems and organs. These claims can be investigated.

Conclusion

When new age medicine claims it is "scientific," we should not be fooled. Rather, we should realize that more often than not new age medicine is really a religion and that it treats its patients on the basis of religious (usually occultic) principles—not scientific ones.

Science has its problems and will always have problems. But when examining new age medicine, science is not the problem. The problem is new age medicine.

TWO

YOUR PHYSICIAN AND HIS PRACTICE OF MEDICINE

Can the average person assume that his physician practices only scientific medicine?

As noted, for the most part, holistic health practices have remained outside the mainstream of medical practice. Nevertheless, the modern breakdown of culture, the revival of mysticism and the occult, the rise of hundreds or thousands of new Eastern and occultic religions and cults, and the growing cultural drift from materialism to pantheism have all had an impact on medicine. In light of this, we can be thankful that most medical doctors remain within the confines of scientific medicine.

But again, literally thousands of other M.D.'s have turned to new age philosophy and practices.* Organizations such as the Academy of Parapsychology and Medicine, with two thousand members, most of whom are

* We may note that some M.D.'s, entirely without new age sympathies, may occasionally employ acupuncture or biofeedback as adjuncts to their medical practice. But this does not qualify them as new age physicians. First, these methods are not employed in a new age manner with new age philosophy or practice. Second, their limited effectiveness is recognized. Some physicians use acupuncture, principally for analgesia, on the assumption it may be working on as yet unknown principles; they reject any associations to mystical life energies. Biofeedback works on known principles and some physicians find it useful for certain physical conditions. However, the explanation for acupuncture analgesia can be found in known principles as well, and even the medical use of biofeedback (see chapter 9) can oftentimes have new age implications. Our point is that the responsible scientific use of acupuncture or biofeedback does not, by definition, make an M.D. a new age physician.

M.D.'s, and the American Holistic Medical Association with seven hundred members, prove that thousands of doctors have opened the doors of their medical practice to new age ideas.

Put bluntly, we do not think such physicians should be trusted by their patients. To the extent that untested or unsound medical techniques are employed, they endanger the patient's physical health. Further, the occultic trappings of many of these new age medical techniques may endanger the spiritual health of the patient.

Questions to Ask Your Physician

How can a person tell whether or not his doctor is practicing scientific medicine? We will supply some specific guidelines below, and certainly, we think that reading this book will be helpful. But informed and attentive listening is also important. Ask your doctor to explain things in simple English; critically think through what he or she says. If you believe it is necessary, do not hesitate to bring up the subject of new age medicine. What does he or she think about it? Why? Has he or she ever considered adopting various new age medical treatments in his/her practice? Which one(s)? Why? What is your doctor's religious world view? Does he have a spiritual leader or guru? Does he follow an Eastern religion or practice a form of Western occultism? Is he frustrated with the problems of conventional medicine and looking for alternate ways of treating his patients? Has a personal crisis in his life led him to explore alternate spiritual lifestyles?

Certainly if you suspect any unusual or unorthodox method or therapy being employed by your physician in his treatment of your problem or condition, you should investigate the matter before treatment begins or continues.

Unfortunately, the occultic nature of new age treatments may be camouflaged by scientific, neutral, or spiritual sounding euphemisms. Because of this, it is often necessary to thoroughly investigate the background of a given treatment before placing one's physical or spiritual health at risk.

How did the practice originate? Who was its founder? What was his world view and spiritual orientation? Is the method or practice accepted in the medical community—if not, why not? Does a method require a psychic sensitivity to operate successfully? Is there any evidence that the method functions on the basis of its stated principles? If it claims to function on spiritual principles, do you understand the world view tied to those principles and how they may be related to the occult? Does accepting the method require adopting a new world view? Does the method "work" only if one believes in it?

Preventive medicine is important not only in our lifestyle but in our choice of health treatments as well.

Let the Patient Beware

Reisser, Reisser, and Weldon's *New Age Medicine* discusses principles for determining which therapies or techniques to avoid. We have reproduced these principles below, added additional ones, and provided illustrations with various new age therapies. In recognition of the ancient Latin phrase "caveat emptor," that is, "let the buyer beware," they are listed as "caveats" (1:147–152).

Caveat 1. Beware of therapies that are energy based and claim to manipulate "invisible energies" or rely on psychic anatomies. Examples are acupunture, muscle testing, reflexology, and color therapy. Nor does a practice that appears entirely innocent, such as passing a hand over all or part of the body, actually prove the innocence of the practice. Therapists who claim to manipulate invisible energies may harm a person spiritually by such a method (123:42–56; 124:104–130; 125:142–154. See also chapters 5, 6).

Caveat 2. Beware of those who utilize psychic knowledge, power, or abilities. Examples are clairvoyant diagnosis, psychic healing or surgery, crystal healing, therapeutic touch, radionics and psychometry, channeling energies, and shamanistic medicine. Those having psychic abilities are ultimately linked to the spirit world, and their methods and practices are consequential (396; 132. See chapter 6).

Caveat 3. Beware of a practitioner who has a therapy that almost no one else knows of. As an example, we could cite something called Terpsichoretrancetherapy or TTT. This is a "hypnopsychotherapeutic" method which claims that "the ritual kinetic trance existing in primitive Afro-Brazilian spiritual [spiritist] sects may be used therapeutically" noting that "under [both] TTT and during a ritual [spirit] possession, the subject undergoes [allegedly therapeutic] regression" (316:131).

Caveat 4. Beware of any technique that is promoted to the general public before it has been validated by mainstream science. This includes new age medicine in general. To accept such practices is unwise because responsible persons do not publicly promote techniques whose value and safety is undemonstrated. Such practices are typically quack methods resulting in the patient's loss of funds, not to mention the sacrifice of responsible health care.

Caveat 5. Beware of anyone claiming that his therapy will cure almost anything, as in chiropractic, color therapy, acupuncture, and homeopathy. Those who maintain their therapy will cure almost anything will probably cure almost nothing. (See chapters 9, 14, and 17.)

Caveat 6. Beware of someone whose explanations are bizarre or don't make sense. For example, a practitioner of astrologic medicine may tell you that the influence of Jupiter or Pluto has affected your nucleic acids. A homeopathist may claim that the more diluted a medicine is the greater its power to heal. A color therapist may ask you to drink water bathed in "yellow rays" to cure indigestion. Further, never hesitate to ask your doctor to explain in simple English or to offer scientific evidence that the therapy works on the basis of its stated principles.

Caveat 7. Beware of therapies whose primary proof is found in the testimonies of satisfied clients. Again, this includes new age medicine in general. Satisfied clients are found in everything from con schemes to witchcraft, but that does not validate a method or practice. Therapies can seem to work and still be false. (See chapter 4.)

Caveat 8. Beware of therapies that rely upon entering altered states of consciousness, such as hypnotic regression, meditation, and many visualization programs. Altered states of consciousness are notoriously deceptive, unreliable in health matters, and frequently open the doors to spiritistic influences. (See chapter 10.)

Caveat 9. Realize that a practitioner's sincerity is no guarantee of scientific or medical legitimacy. This holds true for all practitioners, including Christian ones. Noted evangelical new age health therapists and even pastors have both employed and endorsed questionable or quack medicine.

Caveat 10. Beware of any technique which has been scientifically disproven, such as iridology, homeopathy, astrologic medicine, radionics, and many aspects of chiropractic. (See chapters 14, 17, and 18.)

Caveat 11. Beware of a therapist or physician who claims to diagnose or treat patients on the basis of intuition. In new age medicine intuition is often just a euphemism for psychic/spiritistic inspiration or ability.

Caveat 12. Beware of spiritual imperialism. Avoid any therapist who thinks his or her methods are specially connected to God. For example, many of these therapists will attempt to treat clients psychically without their knowledge or permission. Such therapists assume the divine "right" to do so because "divine" intuition tells them such treatment is "needed."

Further, it is always wise to make certain one's physician has attended an accredited medical school. This is no guarantee that he or she will practice legitimate medicine, but it will weed out those who are medically untrained. Thus, you may determine whether or not the therapy they offer is commensurate with their educational background.

In addition, be wary of a practitioner who will not directly answer your questions or seems evasive. Even some physicians are what we might term "closet psychics." When directly asked if they are practicing energy manipulation or have spirit guides, they will evade the issue in order to retain credibility. Or, they will redefine their occultic beliefs and practices so that they sound scientific. Continue to pursue the issue until you have a definite answer concerning their orientation.

Finally, if the buyer is to beware, the seller of questionable therapies should also beware. Those who deal in the realm of health, not to mention the human spirit, have a responsibility to others not to promote therapies which may endanger the physical, emotional, or spiritual health of their clients. Those who offer therapies which are not scientifically established and/or which may harm their patients need to realize they can be held accountable for their actions.

The Problems of Conventional Medicine

A frequent claim of new age therapists is that conventional medicine has so many problems that it is actually dangerous to your health. They claim that intelligent people should abandon normal medical practices and seek out the more "natural" methods of new age medicine.

No one argues conventional medicine has problems. Because our approach to new age medicine is largely critical does not mean the authors are unaware of the problems in conventional practice. But in almost every area that new age medicine is critical of conventional medicine, it has similar or worse problems. Let us examine some major criticisms of modern conventional medicine and compare them with the problems of new age medicine.

Not "Holistic"*

Critics allege that modern medicine only considers the body, while ignoring the equally important issues of the human mind and spirit. But is this charge really true? Physicians usually do consider the "whole" person; any-

---

* This text is primarily a *critique* of new age medicine: it is not an evaluation of a "neutral" or Christian holistic medicine which would attempt to assess the relationship between illness and health from the perspective of the whole person—physical, emotional, spiritual, social. (Biblically, it seems evident that there is some basis for a relationship between one's spiritual/emotional condition and one's health, e.g., Psalm 38:3-8; Proverbs 3:7-8, 14:30, 16:24, 17:22; As someone once said, "God may forgive your sins, but your nervous system will not.")

Good physicians have often been "holistic" in recognizing multiple factors in the cause and outcome of illness—but they have kept the respective categories in proper balance, concentrating on the physical dimension.

New research in psychoneuroimmunology (PNI) has recently given some apparent scientific support to the idea that the mind may, in certain ways, influence or manipulate the intricate biochemistry that may determine the course of illness. This area of study (cf. behavioral medicine, medical psychology and neuroimmunomodulation) is still in its infancy—and being challenged by skeptics. Nevertheless, there are fruitful areas of research now being undertaken.

The issue of new age medicine is not simply the issue of whether or not attitudes may affect the course of disease. The issue is the *kind* of attitude new age medicine asks us to adopt—and whether such attitudes are really as healthful as claimed. We don't think it is wise in any sense that the advances of scientific medicine be abandoned and occultism be substituted in its place. Nor should the often marginal role played by mental attitudes cause anyone to neglect the crucial role played by biology and physiology.

Nevertheless, one unfortunate consequence of legitimate PNI research is that it may be misappropriated or prostituted by new age medicine as evidence for the "effectiveness" of their occultic methods. If medical science should increasingly recognize non-physical factors in health and disease, new age medicine will claim "scientific" support for its ideas and methods. But occultic methods may "work" for any number of reasons—spiritual (occult), emotional or physical. The real question is: At what cost do they work? It is our view that the philosophy and "cure" offered in new age medicine often has more consequences than the illness itself.

thing that affects their patients' physical health, whether mental or spiritual, e.g., depression does concern a doctor. Good physicians care about people, not bodies. Although the mind and spirit are not a doctor's primary responsibility, a physician will do what he can personally or, when needed, make referrals to a mental health professional or pastor. Good doctors are more "holistic" than proponents of new age medicine are willing to concede.

But, on the other hand, when new age medicine claims to treat the mind and spirit, can they justify the manner of treatment recommended? Questionable fringe psychotherapies and occult practices are not mentally and spiritually healthful or helpful; in fact, they are often harmful.

The problem isn't that conventional medicine ignores mental or spiritual issues; it's just that these areas are of far less importance to physical health than new age medicine claims. In essence, not only is new age medicine largely unqualified in the one key area a physician must be concerned with (physical health practice); its mental and spiritual "treatments" are questionable, quack, or occultic.

The High Cost of Modern Health-Care, Including Insurance Premiums

In part this cost is due to bureaucracy and the high price of technological advances in specialized health-care. In part it is due to a dramatic, if largely unnecessary, increase in medical lawsuits. The phenomenon of AIDS will also greatly increase health costs.* But regardless, if a person truly needs treatment they should get it. It may be expensive, but it is worth the price.

In new age medicine, treatments may cost less, but they will not cure anything either. One is usually just throwing one's money away. This is not rational.

An Overreliance upon Drugs and Surgery

Some drugs are overprescribed, and some surgeries are really unnecessary. This is why being an informed patient and seeking a second opinion is always wise when faced with an important medical decision. But even a

---

* Also, up to 1/4 to 1/3 of the $500 billion spent each year on health is apparently wasted from 1) unnecessary illness (often the patient's fault; the leading killers, stroke, cancer, and heart disease are often preventable) or 2) unnecessary operations (often the fault of society: MD's, the general public, and insurers cooperating). Further, given their cost/benefit ratio, some medical technologies may not be socially affordable.

problem here is better than no drugs and no surgery. When new age therapists criticize drugs and surgery as "unnatural," they forget these methods have saved thousands of lives for every one they have lost. Further, new age medicine's own acceptance of altered states of consciousness, manipulation of occult energies, sometimes bizarre treatments, spirit contact, etc., can hardly be considered "natural."

Limited Self-Policing

Estimates are that up to five to ten percent of physicians have a drug or alcohol problem and that up to five to ten percent more are incompetent. But this represents only a minority of physicians; eighty to ninety-five percent of all M.D.'s are competent.

In comparison, by modern medical standards, almost all new age therapists are not competent, but rather incompetent. Further, do we suppose that new age therapists never have drug or alcohol problems? Finally, in new age medicine there is almost no self-policing whatever; some is better than none at all.

Patient-Related Problems

Patients may treat physicians as if they were infallible on the one hand or refuse to follow their medical advice on the other. If patients never ask questions, never become involved in their own health care, or take no responsibility for their lifestyle, their doctor is not the only one at fault if problems arise.

But we should not think the same problem is nonexistent in new age medicine. When therapists claim to use a divinely instituted practice or to manipulate divine energies, granting them "divine authority" is easy. On the other hand, the treatment and explanations given by new age health practitioners may be so poor that a patient has serious doubts about following their advice.

"Iatrogenic" Illness

This involves illnesses produced by medical treatment itself, such as staph infections in hospitals or the occasional unforeseen consequences of certain prescription or experimental drugs.

But the problem is also found in new age medicine. How many improperly diagnosed and treated illnesses in new age medicine have progressed to more serious complications or death? No one knows because no one is keeping records. Nevertheless, they do occur as subsequent chapters will document.

Technological Advances That May Outstrip Or Outwit Man's Moral Capacity

There are the ethical and social consequences of biomedical engineering. For example, through genetic engineering, scientists may one day allow parents to choose the physical and mental characteristics of their children. But do parents have either the right or the wisdom to do so? Does the state?

But for every potential technological problem of modern medicine, new age medicine offers an equally serious moral or spiritual concern because its methods are so influenced by the world of the occult.

The Validity of Conventional Medicine

Even with its problems, there are at least four reasons why conventional medicine is better for your health than new age medicine.

Proven Methods

The methods of conventional medicine have been proven effective, and in general, new age therapies are either not proven or disproven. Thus, those who use such methods are paying for questionable or quack treatments.

The authors have no necessary preconceived bias against alternate therapies per se. Our position is that before unproven methods are used by anyone, let alone thousands or millions of people, they should be critically examined. If electro-acupuncture really is an effective treatment for heroin addiction, or if homeopathic remedies really do work, fine. But proponents must prove their claims before they can expect people to logically accept their methods. To operate on any other basis is, quite literally, nonsense.

No one would ever think of driving an untested, experimental car on the freeway, especially if the manufacturer's reputation was suspect. The same should hold true for new age medicine. No one should use experimental methods or forget the personal and social consequences of quackery or occult medical practices.

If these methods really are legitimate, then let their proponents subject them to stringent scientific research and then seek confirmation by independent testing. Advocates of new age medicine seem to have avoided a scientific approach for one principle reason: they know or suspect their methods would fail the test and be proven false.

Until new age methods are proven, people who use them place their health at risk.

Circumscribed Health Care

Conventional medicine won't harm anyone spiritually by involving them in occultic healing. Conventional medicine does not employ occultic methods of treatment, nor does it seek to influence a person's spiritual world view, as is often the case in new age medicine.

Graver Inherent Problems

Contrary to new age medicine, the "in house" problems of conventional medicine are less formidable, incidental to its larger effectiveness, and do not annul its value. As we have indicated, almost every problem faced by conventional medicine has a similar, equivalent, or worse problem in new age medicine, whose value is doubtful.

Unique Specialization

Finally, one valuable characteristic of conventional medicine lies in its approach to diagnosis and treatment. The essence of conventional medicine is seen in three related specialties—diagnosis, pharmacology, and surgery, practices which are almost entirely absent from new age medicine:

1. Diagnosis: highly accurate diagnosis by a trained medical specialist with access to a scientific laboratory.
2. Pharmacology: the use of effective, generally safe drugs for a wide variety of illnesses and diseases (antibiotics for bacterial infections, insulin for diabetics, diuretics for high blood pressure, digitalis for heart patients, etc.)

3. Surgery: highly effective surgery or other specialized treatment for serious, life threatening disease or other problems (radiation and surgery for cancer, gallbladder removal, knee surgery, by-pass surgery, etc.)

New age medicine has none of these and often prides itself on rejecting "impersonal" medical technology, drugs, and surgery which it may view as unnecessary or harmful. Yet the importance of each of these three categories is beyond doubt. For example,

> The opposition by orthodox physicians to alternative therapies is based on the principle that the first step in the treatment of any disorder is accurate diagnosis, which itself requires extensive medical knowledge.
>
> Treatment of symptoms without knowing their cause may be disastrous if an underlying remediable but progressive condition has not been recognized. (313:89)

Conclusion

No profession on earth is perfect, and it should not be expected of the medical profession. What should be expected is medical competence and ability—which unfortunately are sorely lacking in new age medicine.

We are not surprised that in any comparison of conventional and new age medicine, conventional medicine wins "hands down."

But what does surprise us is the general lack of response from the medical profession to new age medicine and particularly the lack of response by the Christian medical profession. Only a handful of books exist on this important subject, and most of them are not written by qualified M.D.'s.* Furthermore, those written barely scratch the surface in dealing with this topic. To require medical laymen to respond to these issues reveals a problem that we hope will be corrected in the future.

New age medicine is being accepted by millions of people. Because it really is mostly quackery, one would think professional medical organizations would be more involved in responding to its influence. In part, the problems of standard health care and people's fear over health issues have resulted in people turning to new age medicine. This fact not only neutralizes the positive impact conventional medicine can have in a person's life, but it also leads to a greater acceptance of the irrational and the occult in society.

---

* Exceptions are references 1–4.

THREE

COMMON FEATURES OF NEW AGE MEDICINE

Despite the large number and variety of new age health practices, common themes emerge on a regular basis. Below we present some general characteristics of holistic health procedures. Not every technique fits every characteristic, but the following features are frequently encountered.

Hostility to Modern Science

New age medicine is opposed to modern science for one simple reason: Modern science rejects its premises, invalidates its findings, and shows it to be unproductive. In our chart contrast between scientific and new age medicine in chapter 1, we saw that the two systems of health practice were totally distinct and contrary.

New age medicine can operate only by ignoring scientific facts, and many practitioners know it. If they don't know it, they may at least suspect that scientific testing and evaluation of their particular technique would invalidate it. Such persons may claim that science is too "reductionistic" or "biased" to fairly evaluate their method. But perhaps such persons fear science because if their techniques were tested, they could no longer practice their methods in good conscience.

Incredibly, some new age practitioners act as if the scientific method were a conspiratorial plot developed by Western medicine or the AMA solely to attack new age health methods. The scientific method, however, is an invaluable procedure for sifting the true from the false and is universally accepted and applied around the world in all areas of scientific investigation.

It is rarely applied in new age medicine because to do so is to commit suicide. As a result, new age medicine lives within the confines of a world of its own making with its own special rules. In this "magical" world anything is possible, no matter how implausible or irrational. For example, "medicines" can heal even though not a single molecule of the "medicine" is taken (homeopathy); the iris of the eye can diagnose kidney disease even though this is anatomically impossible (iridology); a physician can diagnose his patient's problem by consulting a psychic a thousand miles away (clairvoyant diagnosis); another physician can diagnose his patient by consulting dead objects *millions* of miles away (the stars and planets of astrologic medicine). Goodness, even ordinary rocks and stones can heal (crystal and amulet healing). Once we believe such things, we can believe anything.

New age medicine is irrational precisely because it refuses to accept demonstrated facts—facts concerning how the body operates and facts concerning how the world operates. But if people refuse to believe in facts, the only thing left is to believe in falsehoods—or fantasies.

Acceptance of Spiritism and Mysterious Body Energies

Because new age medicine is essentially an Eastern and occultic form of medical treatment, the predominance of spiritistic influence is not surprising. Just as spiritism is at the core in the revival of pagan religions and cults in America (317), it is also at the core of new age medicine (chapter 6). Spiritistic influence is found in new age health practices as diverse as acupuncture, dream work, meditation, psychic diagnosis and healing, hypnotic past-life regression, color healing, radionics, rod and pendulum dowsing, visualization, homeopathy, and crystal healing, to name a few.

At this point, some of our readers may be unprepared for a discussion of "spirits." Isn't our emphasis on the importance of science in conflict with an inquiry into spirit entities? Isn't this just as unscientific and bizarre as the mystical "energy fields" of new age medicine?

In fact, we are not abandoning our commitment to the scientific method when we discuss the possible existence of spirits; but neither are we materialists. We are just as convinced there truly is a spiritual realm—a dimension where spiritual realities exist such as God, angels, and devils. In several earlier books the authors have cited sufficient evidence for this viewpoint (132; 366; 396). Our perspective coincides with the belief of most people in almost all cultures and many of the greatest human intellects throughout history. Further, when we speak of the existence of a spiritual reality—God and spirits—we adopt a perspective that nothing in the sciences has shown to be false.

But can we accept the reality of spirits and deny the reality of new age energies? This question raises two concerns. First is the issue of evidence: What genuine evidence exists to substantiate the particular spiritual claims of new age medicine? Second is the issue of interpretation: How do we know the interpretation new age medicine places on spiritual phenomena is correct? On the one hand, more than sufficient evidence exists for the fact of a spiritual world, and we have cited some of this evidence in chapter 6. On the other hand, no evidence exists to substantiate the particular claims of new age medicine concerning the function and nature of its alleged mystical energies. We do not reject the possibility of spiritual energies; we reject the claims, interpretation, and use/abuse of them by new age medicine.

Why are the spirits interested in medicine? They always have been. Researchers have chronicled the dramatic influence of the "gods" in ancient medicine, such as Walter Addison Jane, M.D., in his *The Healing Gods of Ancient Civilizations* (98). In mediumism and much other spiritism of the past and present, "The spirit-guides supply constant medical advice . . . and even give treatment in case of illness" (178:235).

Throughout history the spirit world has sought to gain an influence in the affairs of men through areas over which men have little or no control. Men have no control over the future, so endless systems of divination exist. Men have little control over disease and death, so occultic healing is found everywhere.

But what is significant is how spiritistic manifestations are increasingly relabeled as supposedly latent human powers or psychological phenomena, or hidden under the guise of the alleged "energies" of creation: powers from "the higher mind," "inner teachers," "archetypes," "bioplasma," "*prana*," "life energy," etc., (396).

Perhaps the concept of a cosmic, universal, mystical, or "divine" life energy (supposedly uniting man and God or the universe) is most frequently associated with spiritistic phenomena. Thus, new age medicine believes that in order to really understand health and disease, we must switch our thinking from a model of health based on matter to one based primarily on energy. But in the end, this is an open door to spiritism under another name. It is difficult, if not impossible, to distinguish the use of "energy" in most new age techniques from the manipulation of "energy" found among psychic healers and possessed mediums and spiritists, or in occult magic rituals where the magician is possessed by his familiar spirit.

This energy is invariably associated with pagan religion and occultic practitioners and has up to sixty different designations depending upon the time and culture. In ancient and modern Hinduism, it is called *prana*; in Taoism and ancient Chinese medicine, *chi*; in Japanese culture, *ki*; in Hawaiian Shamanism and Polynesian religion, *mana*.

The developer of modern hypnotism, Franz Anton Mezmer, called it *animal magnetism*; D. D. Palmer, the founder of chiropractic, *innate*; Wilhelm Reich, founder of orgonomy, *orgone* energy; the American Indians, *orinda*. Parapsychologists give it a variety of different designations, for example, *psi*; Samuel Hahnemann, the founder of homeopathy, *vital force*; in yoga theory, *kundalini* energy. Various modern psychics and mediums, such as spiritist Ambrose Worrall and radionics leader George de LaWar, define it as paraelectricity, biomagnetism, psi plasma, or by other terms. Occult magicians define it as *elemental* energy, and the list could go on and on. It is, essentially, psychic energy, as many psychics will admit. *The Psychic Energy Workbook* observes, "We refer to this substance as pyschic energy. The same substance is called 'Prana' by yogi's, 'chi' by practitioners of the martial arts and 'bio-energy' by therapists" (119:9).

Certain aspects of these variously named energies are influenced by the broader context of the system in which they occur. They are not, therefore, necessarily strict equivalents in the sense that all characteristics of one energy will fit those of another. For an examination of its general characteristics, see chapter 5. But again, distinguishing the manifestations of this energy from the manifestations of spiritistic energy in general or the spirits themselves can be virtually impossible.

Eclecticism

New age healers often utilize different techniques in their treatment programs. Although a given practitioner may specialize in one area, additional methods are easily employed by the same therapist. An individual with back pain may visit a chiropractor for chiropractic treatment and also be treated with acupressure, applied kinesiology, iridology, radionics, rolfing, or other methods. In chapter 7 we have cited illustrations of this crossover characteristic of new age medicine by listing some twenty different methods and the additional therapies or adjuncts that may be employed.

Reliance upon Altered States of Consciousness And Psychic Anatomies

Altered states of consciousness are used in therapeutic touch, psychic diagnosis and healing, hypnotic regression, shamanism, radionics, dream work, crystal healing, visualization, and other practices. They may be used in health training, diagnosis, treatment, and health maintenance after treatment (see chapter 10).

Altered states have played a vital role in occult medicine since the dawn of history. They are believed to help "properly" orient the healer or the patient for optimum physical, mental, and spiritual health.

In diagnosis and healing, altered states help a therapist to develop psychic abilities so that the "healer" can receive information from his "higher mind," "cosmic wisdom," or spirit guides. These states can be used to develop clairvoyant vision so a person can allegedly "psychically" see within the body and diagnose the patient's physical condition. They can also be used to diagnose the patient "spiritually" by supposedly psychically examining the "aura" or "astral/etheric bodies."

They may be used in conjunction with almost any new age health technique as a means of developing "intuitive" abilities in diagnosis. In addition, altered states are often recommended to the patient as part of an ongoing treatment program for health maintenance and spiritual growth.

Psychic anatomies are also important in new age medicine. Indeed, through altered states of consciousness the alleged psychic anatomies were first discovered—such as the *chakra* system in Hinduism or the meridian system in Chinese acupuncture. Thus, numerous new age healers, from mediums and spiritists, to psychics and yogis, to energy manipulators and acupuncturists, claim to psychically see the invisible anatomy and its energy "blockage." The particular technique employed is supposed to "realign" or "unblock" the energy, thereby permitting it to flow freely through the body, restoring health.

Development by Suspect Methods

The spiritistic or occultic origin of many new age health practices is undeniable. Examples include psychic diagnosis, healing and surgery, anthroposophical medicine, astrologic medicine, the Edgar Cayce method of healing, *chakra* healing, crystal healing, psychometry and radionics, shamanistic medicine, dreamwork, color therapy, and many more (see chapter 6). In addition, other new age health techniques began solely as the result of simple misobservation or by misinterpretation of bodily responses. As examples, we can cite acupuncture, iridology, chiropractic, and homeopathy.

Homeopathy began when Samuel Hahnemann misinterpreted an apparent allergic reaction as symptoms of malaria, thereby producing the fundamental principle of homeopathy, "like cures like" (2:62, 65); chiropractic began when D. D. Palmer incorrectly concluded that spinal adjustments had cured deafness and a heart problem (26:18–19); iridology resulted from both a misobservation and a false conclusion concerning an owl's iris by Ignaz Peczely (2:89). Acupuncture may have begun by misinterpreting the phenomena of counter-irritation and trigger point analgesia (see appropriate chapters).

Whether their origins involve spiritistic revelations or human error, more complex diagnostic and treatment systems are built around the core "data." Furthermore, because the origins of these systems are not based in scientific medicine but rather in spiritism and human folly, the practices of these methods are far more amenable to occultism and quackery.

Use of Radionic Devices

There are an endless variety of useless machines and gadgets found in new age medicine; we have probably encountered forty different devices. They are used by homeopathists, chiropractors, acupuncturists, in radionics, and by those more "scientifically" oriented. But the device itself has no power and is worthless. What it can become is a scientific-looking apparatus through which spirits may operate.

The world of the occult has many parallels to this phenomenon. Idols, amulets, crystals, Ouija boards, Tarot cards, rune dice, the *I Ching*, and dowsing sticks have no magical powers. They are nothing more than a vehicle through which spiritistic powers may work.

How do we know this? First, this is the conclusion of some practitioners themselves. Second, although the instrument itself is first thought to be the source of psychic power and healing, time and again the mechanism is dispensed with—but the power remains. This reveals that the instrument itself was only a tool or vehicle through which spirits operate behind the scenes, while an individual develops psychically in conjunction with the spirit's help. Not all new age gadgets are disguises for spirits, but many are; the rest are simply quack devices.

Desires for Scientific Respect

This is not a contradiction to the first characteristic; new age medicine simply desires what it cannot obtain. It cannot have the prestige of the term "science" while simultaneously rejecting what science stands for. As a result, it may redefine science to fit its own perspective. Thus, when new age medicine claims to be "scientific," the reference may be to *spiritual* science, *mental* science, *occult* science, etc.

However, it is also true that respected M.D.'s, Ph.D.'s, and scientific researchers are attempting to integrate mainstream science and new age medicine. Usually these men have scientific reputations to uphold and for whatever reason have become enamored with new age medicine. The general result seems to be that science is put on the back burner while occultic practices are utilized and through redefinition made "respectable." For example, mystical occult energies are promoted and supposedly justified or explained by recourse to the discoveries of quantum mechanics, and the *yin* and *yang* of Chinese medicine are magically transformed into the sympathetic and parasympathetic nervous system.

Evasion Concerning Its Spiritistic Associations

Some new age practitioners will deliberately conceal their occult orientation or spirit contacts if they think this would hinder a patient from visiting them. Most are so convinced of the importance and effectiveness of their techniques that they are willing to treat individuals through occult means even without their clients' knowledge. If they think a client would object to their occultism, the client will never know of it.

Because new age medicine is fundamentally an occultic movement, people may not only be treated through spiritistic power, they may also be led into occult practices. Such practices are both physically and spiritually dangerous because they involve one in the realm of demonic spirits (see chapter 6).

Pragmatism

"We don't know how it works, it just works," is the defense of homeopaths, acupuncturists, iridologists, crystal healers, and an endless variety of new age health practitioners.

Because these practitioners cannot justify their methods on the basis of scientific principles, their only recourse is to adopt a pragmatic approach. The problem with this approach—appealing to people's experiences as a means of validating new age medicine—is that it is false (see next chapter).

Many claim that the successes of new age medicine, the satisfied customers, validate the entire movement. If something works, nothing else matters, including an explanation. They point out that all of us benefit from things we don't understand, from TV's and stereos to microwaves and automobiles.

Not knowing how these items work does not prevent us from using them effectively. Space probes, holograms, laser technology, and personal computers work, and no one doubts their effectiveness. But how many can describe the principles on which these items work? Millions of aspirins were used before anyone understood the reason for their effectiveness. New age medicine, they say, is no different. But as Paul Reisser, M.D., explained:

> Unfortunately, this logic does not hold water. The workings of automobiles and stereo sound may be mastered by anyone with ordinary intelligence, given enough time and some straightforward instruction. Likewise, the mechanism by which aspirin relieves headaches was unraveled using straightforward logic and experimentation. No one has swallowed a Bufferin assuming that it contained vital life forces or friendly spirits.
>
> Classical Chinese medicine stands in sharp contrast, in that the observations of the ancients—that pricking the skin in certain areas had specific results—were incorporated into the prevalent religious thinking of that era. (If similar thinking had been applied in Western culture, we might find ourselves hearing that Contac contains angels who dry the nose or Tylenol exorcises pain demons.) Not only does classical acupuncture

> come with its metaphysical baggage intact, but its promoters actively proclaim its religious foundations and implications as well. (1:73–74)

The danger with this approach—satisfied customers—is that it fails to answer the real reason *why* a technique is working and thus makes discernment impossible. To know why something works is often *more* important than knowing *that* something works.

The problem with employing a pragmatic standard which rejects scientific evidence is that it ignores two vital facts. First, the mere fact that something works or seems to work does not answer the moral question of whether or not one should employ dubious medical practices. One should ask himself, *Can my use or recommendation of a fringe treatment harm myself, my family, or another person?* Or, *If the treatment does not work based on its stated principles, am I being dishonest or self-deceived by believing that it does?*

Many of these methods do not need to be true in order to work, and the fact that most of them are false underscores the danger. Psychic healing may work, but that doesn't prove that it works because it claims to employ divine energy. Occult healing may work, but that does not prove the practice is either acceptable or benevolent.

The second fact is that more credible alternate explanations exist for the alleged effectiveness of a fringe treatment than the ones commonly given by practitioners. We live in a technological age of miracles, and most people are naturally conditioned to accept that a wide variety of things work without ever knowing why they work. Thus, the average person accepts a great deal of what he does not understand. The problem is that a mind so conditioned has little problem accepting the fact that fringe medicine works without being too concerned about why it works. In the area of proven technology this is not of great concern, but when we move into the area of the psychic, the mystical, and the occult, it must be of concern.

This is why it is important to examine the issue of *how* new age treatments work or can seem to work and to understand that they do not operate on the basis of their claimed mechanics (see chapter 6).

Obduracy

The scientific testing of new age medicine is still in its infancy, but testing has already invalidated some practices. This includes iridology, astrologic medicine, muscle testing, radionics, homeopathy, and much chiropractic.

But promoters rarely concede defeat because experience tells them their practices "work." In general, the response of new age practitioners to the scientific disproof of their methods has not been a responsible admission of failure or a confession of employing quack methods in healing. New age medicine largely refuses to correct itself or confess to deceiving people on a very important issue, that of health. When confronted with facts, it is facts that suffer, not new age medicine.

Nevertheless, we must admit that some new age healers may be practicing their techniques in relative innocence. We would expect and hope that once they discover the facts and implications of their practice, they would take appropriate action.

Because their techniques have not been proven, the ultimate question faced by new age practitioners is one of ethics in their client relationships. Health practitioners must maintain a high level of social and personal conscience. But how many new age practitioners are ready to view their practices as quackery? Far too few.

Physical and Spiritual Danger

Unproven or occultic practices that masquerade as medical treatments are rarely beneficial. By luck or circumstance, they may not harm but they will not help. Furthermore, new age medical practices may be both physically and spiritually harmful.

Physical Harm

New age medicine is reminiscent of certain cultic views of medicine. Cultic medicine deliberately withholds vital medical treatment on the basis of antiscientific prejudice or irrational religious doctrines. For example, Jehovah's Witnesses prohibit blood transfusions and Christian Scientists avoid orthodox medical treatment altogether. Because of these practices, thousands of people have placed themselves at risk or died—unnecessarily (461).

Something similar may occur in new age medicine. To the degree a holistic health technique misdiagnoses a serious illness or prescribes ineffective treatments for a serious condition or otherwise delays proper medical care, it can be and has been deadly (176:4).

The physical dangers of new age medicine can be illustrated by a report of the British Medical Association in 1987. It warned concerning acupuncture: "The 365 traditional [acupuncture] points run near, some perilously so, to vital structures, and complications ranging from minor to the serious and the fatal have been reported." In addition, "acupuncture [may be] yet another all-too-often possible way of transmitting the AIDS virus." The report also listed serious complications from use of herbal medicines, chiropractic treatments, and osteopathic manipulation (121:67).

Even some promoters of new age medicine are concerned. Dr. Jeanne Achterberg, writing in *Imagery in Healing: Shamanism and Modern Medicine*, observes, "Any current thrust toward romanticizing shamanistic medicine or folk medicine in general should be tempered with the knowledge that often the remedies that were prescribed were clearly wrong and harmful from the standpoint of physical well-being" (59:18–19).

Spiritual Harm

New age medicine is also hazardous because it easily leads people into the world of the occult. In our introduction, we quoted Marilyn Ferguson's observations in *The Aquarian Conspiracy* that new age medicine often results in clients becoming interested in new age philosophy and practices.

Abundant documentation exists concerning the dangers of new age occultism; the works of a dozen researchers can be cited (396; 123–128; 130; 132). The various texts circulating which attempt (quite incorrectly) to treat what are termed "spiritual emergencies" indicate the scope of the problem (127).

Occultists themselves warn of the dangers here, noting that various practices can lead to physical disease, mental illness, demon possession, suicide, or death (131).

New age medicine is dangerous spiritually for another reason. The philosophy of the occult is characteristically anti-Christian and amoral. Occultic philosophy leads people away from salvation in Christ and justifies a variety of sinful behaviors (396; 131; 132).

There is also spiritual danger when healing occurs through spiritistic power which may only reflect a transference of the condition. The lifetime research of Dr. Kurt Koch may be cited to illustrate the problem. Dr. Koch personally counselled thousands of individuals involved in occultic, new age healing and similar practices. His observation is that no genuine healing occurs, but rather merely a transference of the condition from the physical to the emotional or the spiritual realm. In other words, in exchange for a physical healing, the illness is brought to a higher level. Dr. Koch explains:

> Demonic healing always results in an engramm taking place, i.e. a transference from the lower to the upper levels. The original organic illness is shifted higher into the psychical realm, with the result that while the physical illness disappears, new disorders appear in the mental and emotional life of the person concerned, disorders which are in fact far more difficult to treat and cure. . . .
>
> Firstly, one does not realize the force with which these transfers are accompanied.
>
> Secondly, the transfers cannot be reversed, the wheel cannot be turned back, except through the power of Christ.
>
> And thirdly, these magical transfers act as a blockage to a person's spiritual life. (124:121)

Furthermore, people may be led into spiritistic entanglements which may or may not be discernible and may eventually be deadly. Dr. Koch also observes that numerous cases of suicides, fatal accidents, emotional disorders, diseases, strokes, and insanity are to be observed among occult practitioners and that "anyone who has had to observe for forty-five years the effects of spiritism can only warn people with all the strength at his disposal" (300:238; cf. pp. 261–282; and 123:30–31; 126:184–187).

By leading a person into the occult, new age medicine may eventually result in their being demon-possessed (cf. 141, and chapters on meditation and channeling). This process can happen gradually and almost imperceptibly as revealed by specific case histories (318). For those involved in the occult, spirit influence is not always obvious. The authors' research into spiritism indicates that spirits have the ability to operate invisibly behind the scenes in such a way that occultly involved individuals often cannot distinguish their influence from the workings of their own mind. What an individual thinks are his own thoughts or "intuition" is really the influence of a spirit who is a demon and who is seeking to guide a person deceptively. This is one of the consequences for those who enter the world of the occult.

This ability of the spirits to operate invisibly is evident and admitted in the lives of many involved in the occult from parapsychologist Dr. Andrija Puharich and famous psychic Uri Geller to clairvoyant Robert Leichtman, M.D., and many others (133).

These are some of the dangers of new age medicine. No one knows the extent of physical and spiritual damage resulting from new age medicine. We are not alarmists, but with literally millions of people adopting the practices evaluated in this text, we do not think the casualties are few. The paradox is that many discount the possibility of danger altogether; they think new age medicine is a divine movement.

These people need to realize that initial appearances can be deceptive. The full consequences of an activity may only be felt years or decades later, as in the physical impact of smoking or the psychological impact of abortion (460) or the spiritual impact of a religious cult.

❧ ❧ ❧

New age medicine is physically dangerous in two ways: (1) New age medical practices are ineffective medically, can easily misdiagnose a serious ailment, and may prevent a serious ailment from being treated such that the condition progresses toward permanent injury or death; (2) New age medical practices are also physically dangerous because to the extent they involve someone in the world of the occult, they bring the same kinds of physical dangers associated with occultic involvement (131).

New age medical practices are spiritually dangerous in two ways: (1) They may bring people into the realm of spiritism so that the spirits gain some degree of physical or moral influence or control over their lives, whether this is perceived or not; (2) New age philosophy is strongly anti-Christian and therefore may permanently insulate one against salvation in Christ, thereby insuring the loss of eternal salvation.

Conclusion

Consider late nineteenth-century America as an illustration. Cocaine use was legal, and it could even be bought in grocery stores.

At first, everyone thought the drug was wonderful and use was widely encouraged. Thomas Edison enjoyed it. Freud called it a "miracle drug" which he said could be used to stave off fatigue and bring energy. Even Pope Leo XIII gave it an unofficial Catholic blessing, claiming that it facilitated "creativity." Some medical men marvelled at its anesthetic properties, announcing that it enhanced "patient wellbeing."

Thus, in the 1870s the U.S. began to import cocaine. Fifteen years later a wide variety of cocaine products could be found on the shelves, and these products were purchased by millions of satisfied customers. One major drug company alone was selling over a dozen different products.

There were coca-leaf cigarettes, cocaine inhalers for hayfever sufferers, and cocaine crystals. Cocaine flavoring was popular in soft drinks, including Coca-Cola; it was also found in Rocco Cola, Kocanola, Nervola, and one soft drink appropriately called Dope.

Thus, at first, cocaine use was widely heralded and used by millions because it "worked" and seemed to help them. Satisfied customers everywhere provided glowing testimonials concerning its effectiveness.

Of course, it was all a delusion. Within two decades, its real impact was visible: Cocaine addiction and violence had become so unbearable, the drug was finally outlawed. In 1910, President William Howard Taft said cocaine was "more appalling in its effects" than any other drug in the country (134:B6).

In many ways, the use of new age medicine is similar to the use of cocaine. It works. It cures what ails you or seems to. It makes you feel good. Everyone recommends it. The glowing testimonials by satisfied customers are endless.

The only problem is that in the long run it is just as deceptive as cocaine. Not only can new age medicine harm you physically, it can also harm you spiritually. With millions of people following treatments that are irrational and ineffective, which may delay normal medical treatment or interest people in the occult, the collective damage cannot be insignificant.

FOUR

THE EFFECTIVENESS OF NEW AGE MEDICINE

Perhaps the strongest endorsement for new age medicine is the claim by thousands of its followers that it "works." Glowing testimonies can be multiplied for the diagnostic and/or curative powers of a given technique. This claimed effectiveness of its methods is a central issue in new age medicine. Do its therapies really work? How do we know? What does it mean if they don't work? In the field of holistic health practices, we must be careful to determine *why* something works or why something seems to work.

The Nature of Its Success

As we have emphasized, new age medical techniques do not work on the basis of their stated theories and principles. For example, iridology claims that it can diagnose a person's physical condition based upon an examination of the person's iris. But this is scientifically proven to be impossible. If iridology is scientifically disproven, then it cannot work on the basis of its stated principles. When people claim that an iridologist has successfully diagnosed and treated a given problem, what then is really at work?

Whether it is iridology, homeopathy, reflexology, therapeutic touch, applied kinesiology, astrologic medicine, or any other new age medical technique, three very important facts need to be recognized: (1) success is guaranteed for all quack treatments—to a degree; (2) new age health practices may operate as a placebo; and (3) pragmatism is not the only issue: there may be hidden costs in new age therapies. We will discuss these in turn.

Results Guaranteed Only to a Degree

Any quack treatment will "work" most of the time. Why? Because most all ailments, given sufficient time, will go away naturally. The simple fact is that most people do not die from their pains and illnesses. Thus, virtually any treatment, no matter how irrelevant—say, adding pulverized tree bark to one's cereal—is certain to have its "success" stories. All a therapist has to do is make a treatment *sound* good. When a quack method is "packaged" correctly—with charts, machines, and scientific sounding explanations—people attribute a cure where none is deserved, and the quack treatment gets credit for the body's natural recuperative power.

If we "packaged" the treatment correctly, and maintained "science" had discovered a new fever cure—that eating ice cubes at seventy-five minute intervals for fifteen days would lower body metabolism 1 percent, reverse cell dehydration, and cure inflamation, how many people do you think might believe us? Surely some. But because people treated with quack remedies would have gotten well regardless, the time, effort, and money spent on the particular technique were unnecessary.

Hardly insignificant is the fact that new age therapists often tell their clients that in order to cure a given problem, a period involving weeks (or even months) of treatments may be needed. Because these healers are granted authority they usually do not deserve, most people will agree and begin treatment, not realizing that in the same amount of time the problem would disappear naturally.

The Placebo Effect

Patients who believe that a given treatment will work and therapists who are good counselors account for an endless variety of "healings" that have nothing to do with a given new age practice. Therefore, health techniques that do not work on the basis of their stated principles may nevertheless work on the basis of other principles. If a physical problem is emotional or psychological in nature, such as tension headaches, it may respond to psychological treatment, regardless of which new age technique is employed.

Psychosomatic medicine and placebo research indicate that nonorganic complaints will respond to virtually any treatment that either helps a person believe they will be cured or otherwise relieves the psychological or emotional conditions which produced the ailment. Anything from aromatherapy to Zen could be "effective," if the patient believes the "medicine" will work.

Some people may respond by saying that as long as a person's symptoms are relieved, nothing else matters. If these methods act as placebos, then, in their own way, they are still effective. But this misses the point. To promote placebos as legitimate *medicine* is consumer fraud: It is unethical to *know* a technique is a placebo and still sell it to the public as effective medicine.

When a product is marketed, the public has the right to be assured of its quality. When we purchase a cereal for its vitamin content we should expect a nutritious product, not sawdust manufactured to look and taste like cereal. No one would purchase a cereal labelled "one hundred percent sawdust." Likewise, no one would pay fifty dollars a bottle for sugar pills—unless they really believe the pills were effective medicine. To sell them as effective medicine would be a lie. When no one pays good money for known sugar pills, who thinks that new age therapists could effectively market their products merely as placebos? As a result, the therapies are sold on the basis of various claimed principles which make them sound legitimate. And that is the problem.

If we are only tricking people into believing a therapy is effective, what are we really doing? We are deceiving people about the therapy itself and perhaps about our own ethical standards. Furthermore, it is one thing for people to employ placebos for normal aches and pains; it is another to court disaster by employing them in serious illness.

Hidden Costs in New Age Therapies

Many things work and yet are still dangerous. We could cite such things as terrorism, heroin and cocaine, nuclear bombs, consumer fraud such as land swindles, prostitution, abortions, etc. All these are effective. They "work," but they are also dangerous. Whether drug addiction, jail terms, or death, someone pays a price.

The same is true for new age medicine. It may "work" and still be dangerous; a delayed diagnosis or a misdiagnosis may cost permanent injury or even death, although initially, the technique seemed to be working. Also, new age medical practitioners are typically involved in the occult and often have spirit guides. When new age therapy treatments work on the basis of spiritistic power or when they encourage people to explore the occult or to actually adopt occultic philosophy and practices, then these techniques are dangerous. Finally, widespread use of these methods not only endangers the nation's health quality and health standards, but it also promotes an irrationalism that can spill over into other areas of people's lives.

Realizing that the essence of new age medicine is comprised of highly questionable techniques, irrational methods, and occultic philosophies (Taoism, pantheism, etc.) and practices (psychic development, spiritism, etc.), the fact that new age medicine "works" is irrelevant. What one receives in exchange for the "cure" may simply not be worth the price. The gist of new age medicine is illustrated in the following chart:

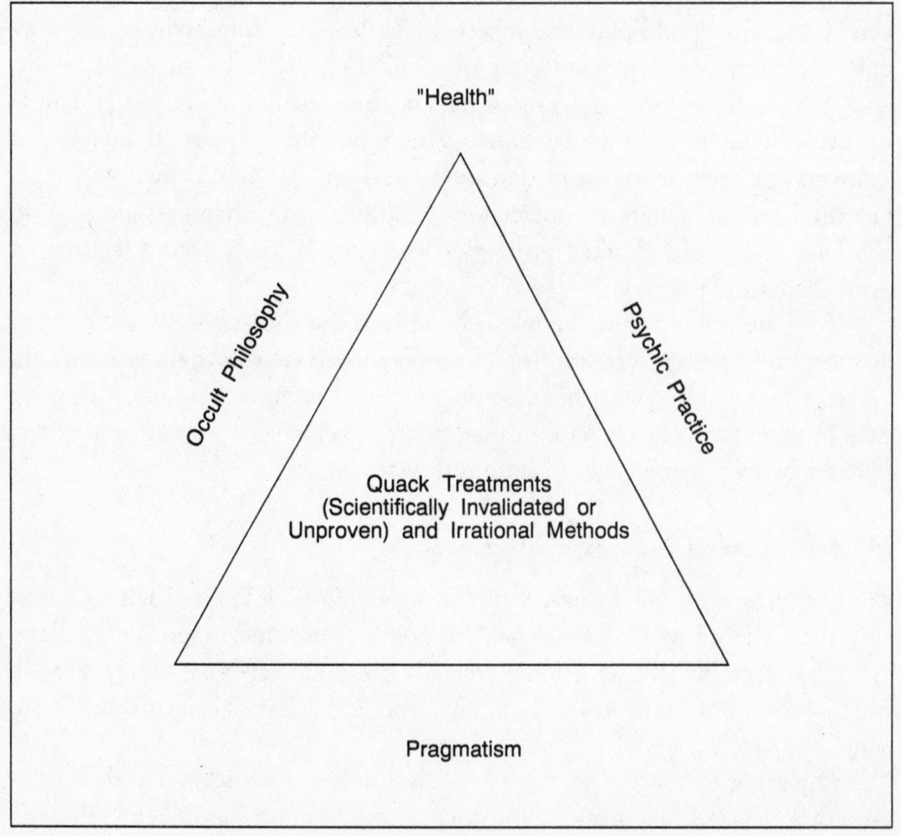

The Essence of New Age Medicine

Scientifically, almost no new age method has ever been proven effective and in all probability never will be. That a treatment claims to be scientific is insufficient; it must really be demonstrated by standard research. Medically, any treatment that does not work on the basis of its stated principles is quackery, and one is asking for trouble if one's illness is of a serious nature. One becomes a guinea pig for those without proper medical training who utilize unproven methods. And rationally, to employ methods of diagnosis and treatment that are unproven does not make sense and may be dangerous.

The Problem with Pragmatism

Let us illustrate why we are concerned. Because new age medicine is undergirded by pragmatism ("it works"), this forces an irrational and often self-justifying approach to new age treatments.

Since publication of *New Age Medicine* (ref. 1), Weldon has received numerous letters from Christians and non-Christians alike taking issue with the critical approach expressed toward fringe treatment methods such as chiropractic, homeopathy, iridology, therapeutic touch, applied kinesiology, etc.

The common elements in most of these letters is instructive. First, people accepted the irrational aspects of a method without asking whether or not it could be effective on the basis of its stated principles. Second, they ignored scientific information which disproved the medical effectiveness of the treatment. Third, they redefined the occultic aspects of a practice as something divine, or they appealed to supposedly unknown "scientific" laws or phenomena of the creation. And fourth, they claimed they knew the treatment was sound because it worked for them personally, and they appealed to alleged miraculous cures that even conventional scientific medicine was unable to effect.

These typical responses indicate four false approaches to new age medicine: (1) an unwillingness to research a practice before adopting it—laziness; (2) the will to believe in spite of contrary scientific data—blind faith; (3) a rationalizing and legitimizing of the mystical and the occult on the basis of entirely unknown factors—speculation; and (4) a personal bias in favor of the method merely because it "worked"—pragmatism.

A recent article by Karl Sabbagh, author of *The Living Body*, discusses the issue of why fringe medicine "works". Some of the information he presents parallels information we have already given; however, this issue is important enough to bear some recapitulation. In his article, "The Psychopathology of Fringe Medicine," he correctly affirms, " . . . when it works, it works for none of the reasons given by fringe practitioners themselves" (120:155).

He proves how this can be true by discussing a specific method whereby literally anyone can set up a new treatment (it doesn't matter what the treatment is, even something like ritualized flower picking) and be guaranteed enough successes to make people believe that the treatment is successful, when, in fact, this is not the case.

We only need to understand three undeniable facts: (1) the relative benign nature of most illnesses treated; (2) the natural variability of disease; and (3) the psychosomatic aspect of many ailments that respond to a placebo factor. If we understand these, we can understand how anyone could, almost overnight, be guaranteed a successful new age healing practice, regardless of the method used or its effectiveness.

First, as we observed, the majority of ailments and problems that cause people to seek practitioners are of a relatively minor nature and will get better no matter what happens. The new age therapist wins.

But second, even with genuinely serious disease, every disease has periods of remission where a patient feels better and is actually improved. This is true even for fatal diseases like cancer whose overall trend is usually downward. But this fact of disease variability can be used to great benefit by new age practitioners, *regardless* of the short- or long-term outcome. The new age therapist wins again.

If the patient begins to improve from natural remission, the therapist can claim the treatment is effective. If the patient remains stable and doesn't get worse, the therapist can claim the treatment has arrested the disease. If the patient gets worse, the therapist can claim that either the treatment or dosage must be increased or revised—or that the patient hasn't been treated long enough for the treatment to work. After all, unless it is a fatal illness, the patient will get better sooner or later anyway. But even if the patient dies, the therapist can claim that he started the treatment too late or even that the patient must not have been following his instructions properly. The new age therapist always wins.

Due to the very nature of the disease process, virtually any treatment would be able to boast at least some success, and fringe medicine gets credit for what would have occurred anyway.

Sabbagh also observes that there is a natural tendency in each of us to ascribe cause-and-effect where none exists. This may be related to simple ignorance of the nature of disease, which in turn can lead to a false perception about the nature of a cure.

> People often get better or go into remission for no discernible reason when they have not been given acupuncture or homeopathic remedies. Most of us are just not familiar enough with probability figures or the natural history of disease to make the sort of informed judgments that apply in the assessment of therapeutic effectiveness. (120:158)

Third, the relation between psychology and medicine indicates how new age medicine can "work" even though the treatment itself is worthless. Again, the majority of illnesses treated in fringe medicine are not serious; they include problems such as headaches, insomnia, various discomforting sensations, constipation, irritability, etc. Many of these ailments are emotional in origin; obviously, if they are psychologically induced, they can be psychologically alleviated. Thus, the positive results of new age medicine are related more to faith in the practitioner or the method than any inherent effectiveness of the method itself.

Drs. Krippner and Villoldo provide a good example of the potential power of belief. This is certainly a rare case, but it illustrates the point. A cancer patient had been resistant to all treatment. He was completely bedridden and had a life-expectancy of a few weeks. Despite the prognosis, the patient heard of an anti-cancer drug called Krebiozen and discovered that this drug was to be tested at the hospital where he was. He requested the drug on an experimental basis; the request was reluctantly granted.

The response was amazing. After only one day of treatment, the tumors melted to half their original size. Within ten days, virtually all signs of the disease disappeared and the patient was discharged. But after two months, conflicting reports appeared in the newspapers about the effectiveness of Krebiozen. The client lost faith in the treatment—and the tumors returned.

The patient's physician told him not to believe what he read and insisted that a new, more powerful, and more effective form of Krebiozen was to arrive the next day. With the patient's optimism restored, he was given a placebo treatment of water injections. Recovery was more dramatic than before. He was discharged and continued to be free from symptoms for two months. The second remission continued until just after newspapers published an announcement from the American Medical Association that a nationwide test had proven that Krebiozen was worthless. Within a few days, the patient was readmitted to the hospital, and he died within forty-eight hours (46:196).

The above is allegedly a true story. No one doubts that the ailment dealt with here, cancer, was serious. No one doubts that Krebiozen was worthless; it had been scientifically proven to be ineffective. This means that the treatment the patient received was basically a placebo, a sugar pill. But it dramatically reveals the effect that a person's mental state may have on his physical condition. As long as the patient thought the treatment worked, that he would be cured, he was apparently able to stimulate his own immune system to stave off the onslaught of cancer. But as soon as his faith in the treatment subsided, the cancer returned. Many people have experienced significant but temporary remission of serious illness (multiple sclerosis, etc.) from almost any treatment (bogus or not), if they believe in it. The problem is that these are characteristically temporary remissions suggesting that whatever the value of the power of belief, its limits must be recognized.

What this means is that virtually any new age treatment could be "effective" because each acts in a similar manner: They create the same psychologically therapeutic environment fostering psychosomatic improvement through the belief in the therapy or the therapist. This is reinforced by the usual complex charts, devices, pseudoscientific terminology, and the concern and empathy shown by the therapist for the patient.

If, as the above illustration shows, it is rarely possible for something as serious as cancer to enter remission from psychological factors, how much more possible is it that a wide variety of common ailments such as headaches, anxiety, depression, and back pains can go into remission based on psychological factors?

By now it should be obvious that any given person with any given ailment could walk into the office of a reflexologist, homeopathist, acupuncturist, iridologist, applied kinesiologist, chiropractor, or shaman, and all methods employed could be "effective." But because each of these techniques claims to work on entirely different and conflicting principles, it must be obvious that the method itself is not producing the cure.

The Danger in Its Methods

Why then are we so concerned about new age medicine? If human faith is what is operating in many of these cures, and new age medicine stimulates faith, what is the harm?

By and large, the "faith" that is stimulated by new age medicine involves faith in the world of the occult. New age medicine carries spiritual trappings along with its physical treatments. People who think they are healed on the basis of a specific treatment such as therapeutic touch, acupuncture, or applied kinesiology tend to become interested in what it was that cured them. Thus, they become interested in the mystical life energies that these methods claim to manipulate. They become interested in the world of the occult. They come to trust in occultic principles.

Furthermore, to say that the power of the mind operates sometimes is not to say it operates at all times. And the more serious the illness, the greater the risk in using ineffective techniques. Many of these methods are irrational; they reject scientific medicine and operate on the basis of known falsehoods.

We must remember that thousands of people have died as a result of some irresponsible faith healer or new age therapist who has assured them that their lifesaving medical treatment can now be dispensed with and all that is needed is for them to follow the new program. When we support the irrational in one area, such as medicine, this tends to spill over into other areas of life.

When a child with leukemia is taken off chemotherapy and placed under the supervision of a homeopath or a chiropractor, and the child dies as a result, who can be unconcerned? When a man with a highly infectious form of tuberculosis refuses hospital treatment, goes to a new age practitioner who diagnoses constipation and supplies a herbal remedy, and then dies after a period in which he distributed T.B.-laden sputum to those around him, who can be indifferent (120:163–164)?

Conclusion

When a treatment works or seems to work, it is vital to know why it works. If we fail to answer that question, we may waste valuable time and money, encourage an irrational approach to medicine, support a form of institutionalized dishonesty, encourage dangerous forms of occultic practice and philosophy—or even cause our own death or that of another.

That is why it is vital to understand why something works.

Five

THE IMPORTANCE OF "MYSTERIOUS ENERGY" IN NEW AGE MEDICINE

What is the connection of new age medicine to spiritism? As discussed in chapter 1, acceptance of a genuine spiritual world is not inconsistent with commitment to the scientific method. In fact, new age medicine cannot correctly be evaluated without giving sufficient attention to these categories: Both the scientific method and a Biblical evaluation of spiritistic phenomena play a key role in the proper evaluation of holistic health practices.

Many new age therapies claim to balance, unblock, restore, infuse, or otherwise manipulate invisible energies which allegedly exist or circulate within the human body. These invisible energies are often associated with psychic anatomies in the body, such as the Chinese meridians or the Hindu *chakra* system.

The concept of energy is important in new age medicine because of the claim that a disorder of these energies' "natural flow" is the root cause of illness and disease. Unless the energy flow is properly restored, health is impossible. Hence, in much new age medicine, the manipulation of energies and health care are inseparable.

Examples of therapies which claim to manipulate invisible energies include acupuncture and acupressure, applied kinesiology, behavioral kinesiology, therapeutic touch, shiatsu, Do-in, Jin Shin Do, foot and hand reflexology, polarity therapy, G-jo, orgonomy, dowsing, homeopathy, chiropractic, psychic healing, yoga, many of the martial arts such as aikido and Tai Chi Chu'an, much naturopathy, crystal healing, and some body therapies such as neo-Reichian bioenergetics.

Consider that traditional and much modern chiropractic teaches a divine energy, which founder D. D. Palmer called "innate intelligence," resides within the body. This "innate intelligence" is said to be connected to the "universal intelligence" [God] through the nervous system. Spinal manipulation allegedly restores "innate's" ability to heal the body and maintain health.

Similarly, traditional and much modern homeopathy teaches that human illness and disease begin at the level of the body's "vital force" and that it is this force, and *not* the body disease per se, that must be treated by homeopathic medicines. But to treat an "energy" disease with *material* medicines is useless. Thus, homeopathists claim that their medicines have been magically converted into dynamic energy by homeopathic rituals, a process of repeated diluting and shaking called potentization.

The Nature of Its Existence

The crucial issue is whether this energy really exists as claimed. If this energy does *not* exist as claimed, then no energy imbalance exists to cause disease—and the "manipulation" of nothing at all will cure nothing at all. Energy manipulators are then only guessing when they claim to treat a psychic anatomy within the body. They really have no idea what they are doing.

Does this mean that energy manipulators are doing absolutely nothing at all when they claim to manipulate invisible energies in order to heal? Certainly this is sometimes true; it may be frequently true. But it is not always true: New age therapists may indeed be involved with real occult energies. What is important to realize is that this energy does not exist or function in the manner *claimed* by new age healers. Divine energy does not circulate within the body through psychic pathways whose imbalance causes disease. Cosmic energy does not connect man's essential nature to "God" or the universe. But if some new age healers legitimately claim to manipulate invisible energies, what then is this energy?

We believe that the energy that does exist is spiritistic or spiritistically-used energy; that is, various natural energies either used by the spirits or the energy manifestations of the spirits themselves are falsely interpreted as the workings of completely "natural," "human," or divine energies.

The history of spiritism shows that in order to produce physical manifestations, spirit entities have the ability to extract energy from the surrounding environment or even from people. When the energy is extracted from healers, or seance participants, the result is a drained, depleted feeling. After a seance, mediumistic exhaustion is a common result. When energy is extracted from the environment, it is often manifested as a heat loss; the environment becomes colder.

The discussions under "ectoplasm," "materialization," and "mediumship" in Dr. Nandor Fodor's *An Encyclopedia of Psychic Science* offer numerous illustrations and theoretical discussion (178:113–117, 216–229, 232–238). He states, "As a rule most mediums require assistance for the production of their phenomena. The sitters of the circle are often drained of power. . . . Some mediums draw more of the sitters' vitality than others. . . . In one instance in Mme. d'Esperance's mediumship the draw on the sitter proved fatal" (178:236–237). When energy is placed into a person, the result may be a feeling of euphoria or being energized. But whether the energy is extracted from people, the environment, or is itself the spirit's own energy, it is not the omnipresent divine energy claimed by new age medicine. This energy is used by demons primarily to secure hidden agendas such as spiritual deception or occult bondage. People who experience this energy are often powerfully influenced to accept new age teaching or to become active in occult practices.

Essentially, modern new age health methods have only adopted the energy concepts of various pagan cultures and/or traditional occultic theories, such as the *chi* energy of ancient Chinese Taoism, the *prana/kundalini* energy of Hinduism, the *mana* energy of Polynesian shamanism, and the psychic force of the occultist and parapsychologist.

In theory, anyone can argue that some form of mysteriously structured energy might exist "within" the human body as in the flow of *chi* through the meridians, or *prana* through the chakras. It can be argued that no one, for example, knows the internal "structure" of the human spirit. Christian promoters of new age medicine often argue that *chi, prana, mana,* etc., are unknown and unidentified natural components of God's creation which circulate within the body through invisible channels.

But these energy systems are theoretically suspect because of contradictory teachings, and in practice, too closely associated with occultism for us to be comfortable with the idea of "neutral" or natural life energies. And not even Christians would accept them as part of the divine, pantheistic energy of new age medicine. Therefore, we believe it is unwise to uncritically accept the existence of such energies within the human body. We arrive at this conclusion for two reasons.

Not Proven, but Assumed to Exist

First, this energy is not proven to exist in the manner claimants suggest; it is merely assumed to exist.

No one can demonstrate its existence as taught by new age healers; the assumption is merely on the basis of characteristically suspect pagan and occultic theories.

In terms of the claims made, not a shred of scientific evidence exists for either these energies or the psychic anatomies of Hinduism, Taoism, Buddhism, or the occult—not that one can expect direct scientific evidence for psychic energies or anatomies. However, some reasonable evidence should be forthcoming concerning the *results* of alleged energy balancing.

If all disease is simply the product of energy blockage or imbalance, then those who have their "energies" maintained in normal balance should be qualitatively much healthier than the rest of us. In fact, they should be disease free. This is something that can be tested, but no one in new age medicine seems anxious to do so.

"Energy balancing" has existed for millenia in pagan cultures, yet no evidence exists that it works in the manner claimed. After thousands of years one might expect some results. Therefore, it is natural to be skeptical of such practices and the underlying theories on which they are based.

Associated with Spiritism

Second, whenever this energy *is* clearly manifested and demonstrated, it is connected with the spirit world. This can be proven by an examination of psychic healing, psychic surgery and other psychic powers (psychokinesis, etc.), shamanism, channeling (spirit possession), *shaktipat diksha* (energy transmission from a spirit-possessed guru to his disciple), meditation or yoga induced *kundalini* arousal, and other occultic phenomena. These are all demonstrable spiritistic manifestations (see refs. 6; 58; 111; 132).

Thus, there is no doubt that often these energies are either the manifestations of the spirits themselves or the spirits' uses of natural (e.g., electromagnetic), human (e.g., physical or psychological), or occult energies for their own purposes.

Again, it is true that when a practitioner claims he is balancing *chi* energy, as in acupuncture or muscle testing, that he may be doing nothing at all. But who can tell? People who practice new age medicine are typically open to the psychic realm and the world of the occult. They are often psychics and occultists themselves. If the practitioner is psychic or has spirit guides, then he or his spirit guide may indeed be manipulating or inputting energies into the body.

However, the consequences may not be small: such energy transmission can result in occultic personality transformation, the development of psychic powers, spirit possession, and other forms of occult bondage. Who knows what really happens in such energy transfers? Can the occult input of this energy into a person influence or harm the human spirit in any manner?

For example, consider only two possibilities. First, that the input of this energy into the body can dramatically change a person's view of reality, typically along non-Christian lines:

> the healing process [i.e., energy influx] . . . changes their structure of reality and the way they view the rest of life. Life is not the same after such a shift as this. (250:103)

The results of such a life change can be seemingly positive—or confusing, painful, and even terrifying (250:103).

Second, many energy channelers, psychic healers, "aura" scanners, and "chakra" healers claim that this energy input actually produces the dangerous phenomenon of *kundalini* arousal. Medium and new age healer Rosalyn Bruyere "runs" energy into her patients, with both physiological and spiritual effects.

> One of the results of running energy on a person is vasodilation, which is why people flush when they undergo a healing treatment. Another result is an increase in blood perfusion. Both these phenomena are related to the movement of red [chakra] energy in a body. One of my mentors channeled red [chakra] energy between the first and second center to stimulate the system. In other words, he used his kundalini energy to tap into another's. When the system is stimulated in this way, kundalini energy flows from

> the point of stimulation directly into the heart chamber. Since blood perfusion is increased, the heart muscles relax. This rising kundalini flow also causes one to go into an altered state of consciousness, and the heart chakra opens. (250:204)

And,

> The healer channels from his or her own particular chakra into the corresponding chakra of a client. . . . The actual sensation of transmitting energy is like flowing water, like a force moving through the healer's body. (250:98–99)

Those familiar with the supernatural energy manifestations in the world of the occult understand how dramatically and powerfully they can manipulate both the human mind and body. Again, who knows what they may do to the human spirit? The radical "god-possession" phenomena in some guru cults, such as Da Free John's spiritual community (188:3–169), the terrible phenomenon of yogic *kundalini* arousal (103:27–106, 254–290, 298–340), the raw power of genuine psychic surgery (6:113–146), the dramatic and dangerous energy manifestations in the kabbalistic master ritual (104:120–134), the energy manifestations in Hindu and Buddhist Tantrism and the Rajneesh cult (111:39–49, 100–152, 174–208), are only a few illustrations. All of these are frightening manifestations of demonic power. And it is this power that is often employed in new age medicine.

Because the energy concepts of new age medicine are so closely intertwined with these dramatic and clearly spiritistic manifestations of energy found in the world of the occult, we believe it is dangerous to assume these energies are human, neutral, or divine. But this is exactly the teaching of new age medicine.

The bottom line is this: Because new age medicine (1) rejects the safeguards of scientific investigation and conclusion; (2) accepts occultic theories and spiritistic phenomena; and (3) hopes to manipulate vaguely defined energies, it has little safeguard against demonic deception. For us, this is the key to deciding personal involvement.

Characteristics of Its Energy

Below we present some key characteristics of this energy which collectively establish its connection to the world of spiritism and demonism.

Unidentifiable

No one knows what this energy is or even how it works. When new age therapists claim such energy works in a particular way, they are guessing. It has never been scientifically established either to exist or to work as claimed.

Amoral, Not Divine

Those familar with this energy, such as many new age health therapists and virtually all practicing occultists, admit it can be used for evil purposes just as for (allegedly) good purposes. The same energy by which so-called "white" witches perform their "good" deeds is used by black witches for evil (105:102). Even though this energy is often used for evil purposes, new agers think this energy is part of God and that it is one essence with their true inner nature. Therefore, they wrongly conclude they too are part of God. But in all forms of black magic, satanism, voodoo, human sacrifice, witchcraft, and the occult, the energy is used for overtly evil purposes (see 111:165–208). Because it does not distinguish moral concerns, this energy cannot be labelled as divine.

Not an Impersonal or Neutral Part of Nature

Christian holistic healers have often claimed that this energy (*prana*, *chi*, etc.) is a neutral aspect of God's creation, a gift of God to be explored and used to His glory, especially in healing. They believe that as yet unknown scientific laws will one day explain what is currently unknown or which even seems magic now. The discoveries of modern quantum physics are often cited as an illustration of genuine but unexplainable phenomena.

Evangelical Christian and holistic healer Monty Kline asserts:

> What natural laws that explain various wholistic health practices are yet to be elucidated? Dare we assume that we know all that is to be known about the Creation?
>
> To say that invisible energy forces are the common denominator of all creation is not scripturally heretical; it's only offensive to our traditionally accepted world view.
>
> Thus, the Ch'i energy of acupuncture, auras, and chakras [are] . . . just another part of God's creation, only unknown. . . . Acupuncture, acupressure, applied kinesiology, iridology, reflexology, biofeedback, or most other

> common "wholistic health" practices [are not condemned in Scripture as occult activities]. . . . Practices such as acupuncture or applied kinesiology [are] based upon principles of God's creation. (135:3–6)

But we are not at all convinced that quantum physics will ever be able to prove that acupressure, homeopathy, reflexology, psychic healing, and various occultic energies are simply operating on the basis of currently unknown *natural* laws. Quantum physics is often misapplied by new age therapists (319:107–125; cf. ref. 252). Further, to say most holistic health practices are to be accepted as non-occultic simply because they aren't listed in Scripture is a bit too convenient. Many activities which everyone accepts as occultic are not listed in Scripture, from voodoo and black magic to Ouija boards and palmistry to various automatisms (automatic writing, etc.). The only issue is whether or not a practice is occultic or potentially occultic. Scripture condemns all occultism whether or not the specific practices themselves are listed.

Finally, because of their clearly occultic nature or strong occultic ties, we believe no one should assume these energies are divine, natural, or neutral without proof. And proof can probably never be had.

But as revealed in occultic magic ritual (such as that found in David Conway's *Magic: An Occult Primer*), this energy is indistinguishable from the occult power that occultists claim is given by demons in magic ritual. It is even indistinguishable from demons themselves (122:129–131).

Personal and Intelligent

Further, this energy can act independently, display intelligence, enter a person, and cause the development of psychic powers, radical occultic personality transformation, and spirit possession. This is documented in numerous texts such as Swami Muktananda's spiritual autobiography, *Play of Consciousness* (187), or Da Free John's *Garbage and the Goddess* (188).

Mary Coddington's *In Search of the Healing Energy* correlates a variety of these energy concepts, including the *huna* (Polynesian shaman) energy called "mana," Paracelsus' "archaeus" (life force), Mesmer's "animal magnetism," Cayce's "psychic energy," Hahnemann's homeopathic "vital force," D. D. Palmer's chiropractic theory of "innate intelligence," Reich's "orgone energy" and the energies in kundalini yoga, and psychic healing. She observes that by whatever name it is called "the healing energy always displays a remarkable similarity" and is frequently "portrayed as having an intelligence of its own" (65:11–12).

Transferable

This energy is often transferred into a person during new age healing practices. But when the energy is transferred, the process may be indistinguishable from a person who claims he is being filled with occult energy manipulated by his spirit guide or being filled (possessed) by the spirit itself. Possessed gurus, psychics, and occultists transfer energies into people in the same way new age healers do (see refs. 47; 219; 229; 269; 284; 287–290; 293; 322).

Further, people who confess to being voluntarily possessed by spirits or demons universally claim to be "channels" for this energy. They claim that miracles performed by them are a result of their use of this energy. Spiritist Barbara Brennan's *Hands of Light: A Guide to Healing Through the Human Energy Field* proves that the energies of the spirits or those energies the spirits claim to manipulate are generally indistinguishable from the energies of new age medicine (47:169–230; see also chapter 6).

Linked to Unbiblical Doctrines

This energy provides the theoretical and practical foundations for unbiblical doctrines and occultic theories. Most new age therapists and occultists link the alleged energy in the body to cosmic, universal, or divine energy. This is the basis for pantheistic doctrines which teach that because everything is a manifestation of divine energy, that therefore everything is divine.

This becomes the basis for asserting that all men are part of God. As Dr. Jack Gibb, a leader in new age psychology and consultant to numerous top U.S. corporations, observed at a major new age health conference, "The absolute assumption that a lot of us are making in the holistic health movement is that . . . I believe that I am God and I believe that you are [God]" (89:44). Medium and new age chakra healer Rosalyn Bruyere asserts, "In the new age the idea [is] that each of us is an expression of Deity . . . a part of God" (250:181).

This energy is the basis not only for pantheistic doctrines. It is also the basis for everything from the study of parapsychology, to individual psychic development, to the so-called experience of "enlightenment" in Eastern religions and Western occultism. In fact, this "enlightenment" is often demonization (111:165–208; refs. 317; 294).

Associated with the Occult

By a brief review of relevant literature, we may prove how frequently this energy of new age medicine is linked to a variety of occult practices and how extensively new age health practices are dependent upon them.

Psychic Jack Schwarz is the author of *Human Energy Systems* (63). Schwarz is considered a leader in the field of new age medicine. His book incorporates naturopathy, homeopathy, Tarot healing, herbal medicine, aura reading, color/*chakra* healing, energy channeling, aspects of shamanism, past lives, yoga, auric fields, and psychic development. His book is recommended by several new age healers as an important tool for establishing contact with the spirit world (47:171).

Aubrey Westlake, M.D., in his *The Pattern of Health: A Search for a Greater Understanding of the Life Force in Health and Disease* (62), joins radionics, Bach flower remedies, pendulums, medical dowsing, mesmerism, orgonomy, psychic healing, Hawaiian (huna) shamanism, anthroposophical medicine, homeopathy, and Reichenbach's odic force.

Dr. Victor Beasley's *Your Electro-Vibratory Body: A Study of the Life Force as Electro-Vibratory Phenomena* (61) (Vol. 1 of 6) discusses *pranic* energy magnetism, radionics, *chakra* energies, altered states of consciousness, auric bodies, and others.

Chiropractor David V. Tansley's *Radionics and the Subtle Anatomy of Man* (56) incorporates radionics, color healing, Bach flower remedies, amulet healing, auras, *chakras*, homeopathy, etc.

Occultist Douglas Baker's *Esoteric Healing* (53, 54) discusses spiritism, *chakra* healing, *prana*, auras, astral energies, altered consciousness, etheric bodies, Bach flower remedies, astrology, psychic rays, acupuncture, radionics, etc.

Christopher Hills, an occultist yogi and psychic researcher, is author of the multi-volume *Supersensonics: The Science of Radiational Paraphysics* (57). He examines radionics, dowsing, altered consciousness, esoteric rays, astrology, mandalas, I Ching, Tantra, *kundalini* energy, Taoism, pyramid energy, etc.

Victor Beasley's *Dimensions of Electro-Vibratory Phenomena* (70) incorporates *chakras*, radionics, and various psychic energies.

Radionics researcher Edward Russell's *Design for Destiny: Science Reveals the Soul* (69) joins reincarnation, parapsychology, life fields, and various psychic powers.

MacIvor and LaForest's *Vibrations* (64) discuss color healing, homeopathy, radionics, and the astral body.

Occultist Bernard Gunther's *Energy Ecstasy and Your Seven Vital Chakras* (67) incorporates psychic healing, energy meditation, yogic breathing, chanting, visualization, meridians, Tantra, *prana*, and auras.

Corinne Heline's *Occult Anatomy and the Bible* (72) blends etheric bodies, alchemy, higher consciousness, and general occultism.

Noted parapsychologist Thelma Moss' *The Body Electric* (68) discusses acupuncture, magnetic passes, psychic healing, bioenergy manipulation, Kirlian photography, the energy (astral) body, and more.

Outward Bound: The Spiritual Basis of the New Age Self-Integrative Therapies (66) reveals connections between Tantric shamanism and many new age therapies and practices, in particular new age psychotherapy such as Reichian orgonomy and bioenergetics.

Gallimore's *The Handbook of Unusual Energies* (71) combines odic energy, orgone energy, acupuncture, theosophy, Edgar Cayce, crystal energy, radionics, pyramid energy, and other methods.

In conclusion, this energy is (1) unidentified by modern science; (2) amoral; (3) apparently not a part of Nature, that is, not a natural part of the material creation. Further, this energy is (4) often intelligent, personal, and powerful; (5) transferable; (6) the theoretical and practical basis for unbiblical doctrines and occultic theories; and (7) strongly associated with occultic practices. Perhaps it goes without saying that although we have just described the energies of new age medicine, we have described common characteristics of demons as well.

Conclusion

Once again, a foundational premise of much new age medicine is that this universal energy is the basic fabric of everything in the universe. Disease results from a blockage, deficiency, or imbalance in the flow of this energy within the body. This energy can be activated or channeled by a healer who unblocks, restores, or balances this energy.

Because much new age medicine assumes the existence of "natural" energy blockages within the body, it therefore *requires* the manipulation of, or the flow of additional energy into a person from an outside source, usually the healer, as the primary or only means to produce healing.

But, this would seem to be a cruel hoax on the part of the spirit world. Who can say that the movement or influx of this energy could never be the influx of a spirit itself, or some manipulation of the human mind or spirit for ulterior motives? The result of such energy channeling and manipulation can be occult bondage. Thus, in the guise of promoting physical health, the spirits produce spiritual seduction and even ruin (123:42–56; 124:75–131).

The body does, of course, have a natural healing potential; as we noted earlier, each of us will recover from the majority of our illnesses without any treatment at all. By giving our own immune system sufficient time, and ourself sufficient rest, care, and nutrition, we will heal ourselves.

New age medicine, however, often makes this natural process of healing the basis of an occultic principle: that the body's "healing force" is really part of some form of universal/divine cosmic energy. In other words, new age medicine uses the concept of a natural healing force within the body, the *vis medicatrix naturae* (the healing power of nature), as a basis for the idea of an inherent occultic energy, allegedly divine, which, properly manipulated, will heal disease. This is why so much of new age medicine is fundamentally occultic in nature: It associates a natural process with a supernatural one and thereby opens the doors to the occult.

In essence, new age medicine assumes the body's natural capacity to heal itself is accomplished through occult energy which it labels as universal and divine. Therefore, if the physician would heal, he must learn to understand and cooperate with this energy. This opens the door of medicine to the occult, and the spirit world is free to operate under the mask of an alleged universal divine energy. Consequently, how we interpret the body's healing abilities may determine our approach to medicine. Consider the division in medical history between the vitalist (e.g., occultic) approach to health and the materialistic (or scientific) approach to health.

Dr. Richard Grossinger in *Planet Medicine: From Stone Age Shamanism to Post-Industrial Healing* observes:

> Vitalism is, at once, a science, a religious philosophy, and a doctrine which radically alters all other theories of matter and being. . . . In some versions, even inanimate matter contains a slumbering vital force that can be

> aroused by a form of [occultic] hermetic chemistry or pharmacy. There is perhaps no more succinct way to define vitalism than to say it is everything which modern science is not. (78:116)

And that is the problem of new age medicine: The rejection of science and the dependence on manipulating mysterious occultic energies are simply invitations for the spirit world to become involved in new age health practice.

SIX

THE ASSOCIATION WITH THE SPIRIT WORLD AND DEMONIC ACTIVITY

We have discussed the importance of energy manipulation for new age medicine and suggested that this energy manipulation could be tied to spiritistic manifestations. In this chapter we will present evidence directly linking the spirit world to new age medicine as documentation for our concerns.

How is new age medicine associated with the spirit world? What does Scripture say about this? What evidence exists to show that the spirits who operate through new age medicine are really demons?

The Invisible Operation of Spirits

Can spirits really operate invisibly behind the scenes through new age health therapists? The author's research on new age "intuition" reveals that a person can unsuspectingly be dramatically influenced by a spirit entity.

Spirits work through many new age healers, often without their recognizing it, because new age health practices are so often occultic. Spirits and the occult go hand in glove. New age medicine fulfills numerous spiritistic goals, such as the dissemination of occultic philosophy and practice in society. To think that the spirits would not be involved in that which promotes the moral and spiritual disintegration of society is to be ignorant of the mechanics of spiritual warfare, such as deception and camouflage.

We will cite one illustration of a new age healer who, although often aware of her spirit guides, nevertheless cannot always determine when they work through her. She observes, "There are times when my guidance is more obvious than other times" (47:15).

Barbara Brennan has an M.S. in physics and has been a research scientist for NASA at the Goddard Space Flight Center for five years. She spent two years in neo-Reichian bioenergetic counselling, one year in massage therapy, two years studying and experiencing altered states of consciousness, one year in homeopathy, three years in Core Energetic training (a radionic-based analysis of "astral/etheric" bodies based on the psychic work of Dr. John and Eva Pierrakos), five years in "Pathwork Helpership Training," and several years studying privately with psychic healers and shamans. She is founder and director of the Gaiabriel Foundation in New York City and lectures and conducts workshops throughout North America and Europe.

Barbara Brennan channels the spirit guide, Heyoan, among many others.

> As my life unfolded, the unseen hand that led me became more and more perceptible. At first I vaguely sensed it. Then I began seeing spiritual beings, as if in a vision. Then I began to hear them talking to me and felt them touch me. I now accept that I have a guide. I can see, hear, and feel him. . . . "He" says that his name is Heyoan, . . . His introduction to me was slow and organic. The nature of our relationship grows daily, as I am guided to new levels of understanding. (47:14)

Her *Hands of Light: A Guide to Healing Through the Human Energy Fields* (47) links auras, *chakras*, opening acupuncture meridians, etheric/astral bodies, chiropractic, yoga, reflexology, homeopathy, herbal cures, energy balancing, past lives, psychic surgery, meditation, color therapy, visualization, and other methods.

Yet the text connects all these disciplines to spiritism: She believes spirits can operate behind the scenes through all these methods—indeed any method—to psychically influence the patient. Furthermore, she shows that those who visit new age healers may pick up a spirit guide in the process. Because she can "see" her patients' guides, she assumes the guide came in the door with the client. But who can say the person had a guide before they entered her office? She says:

> I usually have about three [spirit] teachers that guide me. The person who has come to me for help will usually be accompanied by his guide or guides. (47:171)

Later in the book, she confesses:

> The guides of the patient always come to healings and assist. If you are alert, you will see them walk into the healing room with the patient. At this point in the healing they usually pull the patient out of his body and care for him so that a deep relaxation can take place and allow for the template [occult] work to be done. Usually the patient's experience is that of floating in a peaceful state. He usually is not aware of how deeply he has moved into an altered state of consciousness until he gets up or tries to stand up at the end of the healing. . . . The guide's hands work directly through the healer's hands in an overlay manner. The guides come down over the shoulders and into the hands and arms of the healer. (47:222)

She also describes how her guide(s) heal through her; for example, in verbal channeling:

> I feel it kinesthetically. I see the guide behind my right shoulder, and I hear the first few words from that direction. When I and the guide are ready to begin, I lift my hands and hold [my] fingertips together in front of my solar plexus or my heart. . . . At this point, I usually begin to channel verbally. At first the words come from the right shoulder area. The more connected to the channelling process I become, the closer-in the words are. The guide also appears to come closer. Soon, there is no lag time between hearing and speaking the words, and the apparent direction they are coming from moves to above and inside my head. The guide also visually appears to fit over me like a glove. The guide begins to move my arms and hands in coordination with the conversation. "He" also uses my hands to balance my energy field and to run energy into my chakras while "he" is talking. This keeps the energy high and focused. My personality self seems to be floating off and above, listening and watching it all. At the same time, I feel merged with the guide, as if I am the guide. As the guide I feel much bigger than the personality me, Barbara.
>
> At the end of the conversation, my experience is one of the guide lightly disconnecting and lifting off, while my consciousness sinks downwards into my body and my personality self. (47:172)

Later, Brennan discusses the immediate healing process where the spirits heal directly through her while inside of her. She supplies several illustrations using various healing methods.

Reflexology:

> In channelling for the healing itself, you allow the guides to utilize more of your energy field . . . allow the guides to partially come into your field and do work on the patient's field through direct manipulation. In both case[s], allow your hands to be guided by the spiritual teacher. In the first case, the guidance and hand movements are general and may begin as soon as you put your hands on the patient's feet. In the second, they are both very intricate and very precise and are usually done on the higher levels of the field (5–7). Many times the guide will reach his hand through the healer's hand and beyond, going right into the body of the patient. (47:203)

Auric/chakra healing:

> As the energy is flowing, clearing, charging, and generally rebalancing the energy field of the patient, you will probably feel it flowing through your hands. . . . You can direct energy like a beam of light deep into the body. It can fill, or it can knock things loose. The guides will direct you as to what is needed and run the appropriate energy through. (47:206, 217)

Crystal healing:

> A crystal is a very powerful tool . . . it goes in, cuts and collects the energy which, . . . the guides turn to white light. . . . The healer can scan the auric layers to see if the *chakras* or organs need restructuring. . . . If the guides decide to do ketheric template work (seventh layer), the healer must take the crystals away from the patient. . . . (47:218)

But in all of this, the patient may never know the healing was performed spiritistically. All the client may experience is a relaxed condition with or without various energy sensations:

> The patient . . . will be curious as to what you did. At this point, it is important not to go back to the linear mind too much since that would pull her out of the altered state of consciousness. Explain in brief terms what you did, just enough to satisfy her, but not enough to disturb her relaxed state. (47:230)

Barbara Brennan is not unique. In America there are literally thousands of healers like her. Throughout the world there are millions. These "healers" openly admit that spirit guides work through them in healing. Yet they confess that they cannot always determine when this is occurring, that the spirits can work through them undiscerned.

Our question for new age healers is this: How can you be certain a spirit is not working behind the scenes in your own practice?

The True Source of Power

Is the spirit world the true source of power behind much new age medicine? We can not say that every new age medical technique has its origin directly in the spirit world. But we do know that occult practices, philosophy, and religion are in large measure dependent upon spiritistic revelations. To the extent that new age medicine is comprised of occultic philosophy and practice, one can logically expect to find spiritistic involvement.

Thus, if we examine the founders and leaders in modern new age medicine, we characteristically find occult involvement. The following are representative illustrations, some of which are further documented in part 2 of this book.

The founder of anthroposophical medicine was the occultist Rudolph Steiner who practiced and encouraged necromancy, or contacting the spirits of the dead (342:232–233; 343:35; ref. 341). Astrologic medicine is replete with spiritistic influence (44:201–255). Attitudinal healing has been dramatically influenced by the spirit-written texts, A *Course in Miracles*, and medium Jane Roberts' *The Nature of Personal Reality: A Seth Book* (see chapter 12).

Modern leaders in the field of biofeedback, such as Elmer and Alyce Green, are often scientific investigators and promoters of occultic phenomena; Elmer Green has a spirit-guide he calls "the Teacher" (22:289–90). The Edgar Cayce methods of healing were developed by medium Edgar Cayce, through whom the spirits dictated thousands of pages of information on health issues, alleged past lives, and other aspects of the occult (see refs. 180–185). D. D. Palmer, the founder of chiropractic, was involved in psychic practices and interested in spiritism (26:17; 30:33; 31:48–49). Many leaders in the field of color healing are spiritists and occultists (ref. 23; 47; 251; 335).

Many leaders in crystal healing have spirit guides (83:v, 2, 22; 82:1; 85:8, 23). Some leading dowsers are spiritists (259:44; 298:151). Many leaders in dreamwork also have spirit guides (332:116–119; 32:85, cf. refs. 33, 34). Shamanistic medicine is spiritistic by definition. But many other founders and leaders of new age medicine have spiritistic contacts or are variously involved in the world of the occult.

Naturopath Bernard Jensen, the modern founder of iridology, is a member of an occult sect encouraging spiritistic contact, the Rosicrucians (136:226–229); chiropractor George Goodheart, the modern founder of applied kinesiology, is a psychic (433:310); Wilhelm Reich, the founder of orgonomy, was involved in the occult and the spirit world (75; 438:279; 74:161–201); sources tell us that Samuel Hahnemann, the founder of homeopathy, was apparently a spiritist (189, see chapter 17). He was also a follower of the famous spirit-medium Emanuel Swedenborg, as well as a Mason (17:14; 2:67). Leaders in the field of radionics, such as George De la Warr and its founder Albert Abrams, have been involved in spiritism or the occult (190:5; 6:53–63). Randolph Stone, founder of polarity therapy, was an occultist and a member of the spiritistic Hindu sect Radhasoami (137:314–324; 80:99). The founder of psychosynthesis, Robert Assagoili, was an occultist and a leader in Alice Bailey's Lucis Trust/Arcana workshops in Italy (138:224–25); Dolores Krieger and Dora Kunz, the founders of Therapeutic Touch, are both psychics; Dora Kunz is a spiritist and the president of the spiritistic Theosophical Society (60:13; 45:111). One prominent leader in modern visualization, Mike Samuels, M.D., is a confessed spiritist and author of the text *Spirit Guides* (139). (For additional information, see the respective chapters in part 2.)

Time does not permit us to list or research the personal history of every founder of a new age therapy. But nearly 100 percent of those we did examine were in some way involved in the occult.

That so many founders or leaders of new age medical techniques are psychics, spiritists, and occultists is one reason why new age medicine is so permeated with occultism. Yet, the history of occult practice is littered with human wreckage; it is, therefore, ironic to see it so thoroughly linked to human *health*. If the Bible did not state that the spirits of the occult world were demons, one would almost be forced to that conclusion based upon its history.

The Warnings of Scripture

The Bible does clearly teach that the spirits who operate in the world of the occult are not what they claim to be—enlightened spirits sent from God—but demonic spirits bent on the deception and destruction of human beings.

What are some of the Scriptures relating to spiritism and the occult that warn men against occultic involvement? The following Scriptures prove that God considers occultic involvement a serious matter and that it is better avoided wherever it is found.

God warned ancient Israel not to adopt the occult practices of the pagan nations surrounding her:

> When you enter the land which the Lord your God gives you, you shall not learn to imitate the detestable things of those nations. There shall not be found among you anyone who makes his son or his daughter pass through the fire [human sacrifice], one who uses divination, one who practices witchcraft, or one who interprets omens, or a sorcerer, or one who casts a spell, or a medium, or a spiritist, or one who calls up the dead. For whoever does these things is detestable to the Lord; and because of these detestable things the Lord your God will drive them out before you. (Deuteronomy 18:9–12, NASB)

God also judged the ancient kings of Israel when they disobeyed Him and practiced occultism. This reference is to King Manasseh of Judah:

> And he did evil in the sight of the Lord according to the abominations of the nations whom the Lord dispossessed before the sons of Israel. For he rebuilt the high places which Hezekiah his father had broken down; he also erected altars for the Baals [evil gods of human sacrifice] and made Asherim, and worshiped all the host of heaven and served them [astrology]. And he made his sons pass through the fire in the valley of Ben-hinnom [human sacrifice]; and he practiced witchcraft, used divination, practiced sorcery, and dealt with mediums and spiritists. He did much evil in the sight of the Lord, provoking Him to anger. (2 Chronicles 33:2, 3, 6, NASB)

As this verse suggests, in ancient Israel the occultic practices so often associated with idolatry (worship of false gods and spirits) inevitably led to human sacrifice, as is increasingly occurring in the Western world today (363).

> But they mingled with the nations, and learned their practices, and served their idols, which became a snare to them. They even sacrificed their sons and their daughters to the demons, and shed innocent blood, the blood of their sons and their daughters, whom they sacrificed to the idols of Canaan; and the land was polluted with the blood. Thus they became unclean in their practices, and played the harlot in their deeds. Therefore the anger of the Lord was kindled against His people, and He abhorred His inheritance. (Psalm 106:35–40, NASB)

The Bible further identifies the spiritistic powers behind idolatry as demonic:

> They made him jealous with their foreign gods and angered him with their detestable idols. They sacrificed to demons, which are not God—gods they had not known, gods that recently appeared, gods your fathers did not fear. You deserted the Rock, who fathered you; you forgot the God who gave you birth. (Deuteronomy 32:16–18)

> But the sacrifices of pagans are offered to demons, not to God, and I do not want you to be participants with demons. (1 Corinthians 10:20)

At the time of Isaiah, the people had become practitioners of various sorceries which God condemned:

> They [judgments] will come upon you in full measure, in spite of your many sorceries and all your potent spells. You have trusted in your wickedness and have said, "No one sees me." Your wisdom and knowledge mislead you when you say to yourself, "I am, and there is none besides me." Disaster will come upon you, and you will not know how to conjure it away. (Isaiah 47:9b–11a)

In the New Testament, the practitioners of the occult are seen as those who lead people astray from the faith:

> There they met a Jewish sorcerer and false prophet named Bar-Jesus, who was an attendant to the proconsul, Sergius Paulus. The proconsul, an intelligent man, sent for Barnabas and Saul because he wanted to hear the word of God. But Elymas the sorcerer (for that is what his name means) opposed them and tried to turn the proconsul from the faith. Then Saul, who was also called Paul, filled with the Holy Spirit, looked straight at Elymas and said, "You are a child of the devil and an enemy of everything that is right! You are full of all kinds of deceit and trickery. Will you never stop perverting the right ways of the Lord? Now the hand of the Lord is against you. You are going to be blind, and for a time you will be unable to see the light of the sun." (Acts 13:6b–11a)

> Many also of those who had believed kept coming, confessing and disclosing their practices. And many of those who practiced magic brought their books together and began burning them in the sight of all; and they counted up the price of them and found it fifty thousand pieces of silver. So the word of the Lord was growing mightily and prevailing. (Acts 19:18–20, NASB)

The New Testament also reveals that when the spirit is cast out from one with occultic powers, the powers are lost, revealing that psychic powers are not human (i.e., natural and innate) but given by demons. The Apostle Luke reports on one spiritist who was apparently seeking to validate her own practices by linking them with the apostle's ministry.

> Once when we were going to the place of prayer, we were met by a slave girl who had a spirit by which she predicted the future. She earned a great deal of money for her owners by fortune-telling. This girl followed Paul and the rest of us, shouting, "These men are servants of the Most High God, who are telling you the way [*hodon*; lit. "a way"] to be saved." She kept this up for many days. Finally Paul became so troubled that he turned around and said to the spirit, "In the name of Jesus Christ I command you to come out of her!" At that moment the spirit left her. When the owners of the slave girl realized that their hope of making money was gone, they seized Paul and Silas and dragged them into the marketplace to face the authorities. (Acts 16:16–19)

Finally, we present below a selected list of additional Scriptures relating to the existence of spiritual warfare:

> The Spirit clearly says that in later times some will abandon the faith and follow deceiving spirits and things taught by demons. (1 Timothy 4:1)

> Finally, be strong in the Lord, and in the strength of His might. Put on the full armor of God, that you may be able to stand firm against the schemes of the devil. For our struggle is not against flesh and blood, but against the rulers, against the powers, against the world-forces of this darkness, against the spiritual forces of wickedness in the heavenly places. (Ephesians 6:10–12, NASB)

> Be of sober spirit, be on the alert. Your adversary, the devil, prowls about like a roaring lion, seeking someone to devour. (1 Peter 5:8, NASB)

> I [Jesus] am sending you [Paul] to them [the Gentiles] to open their eyes and turn them from darkness to light, and from the power of Satan to God, so that they may receive forgiveness of sins. (Acts 26:17b–18a)

> The god of this age has blinded the minds of unbelievers, so that they cannot see the light of the gospel of the glory of Christ, who is the image of God. (2 Corinthians 4:4)

> The coming of the lawless one will be in accordance with the work of Satan displayed in all kinds of counterfeit miracles, signs and wonders, and in every sort of evil that deceives those who are perishing. They perish

> because they refuse to love the truth and so be saved. (2 Thessalonians 2:9, 10)
>
> For such men are false apostles, deceitful workmen, masquerading as apostles of Christ. And no wonder, for Satan himself masquerades as an angel of light. It is not surprising, then, if his servants masquerade as servants of righteousness. Their ends will be what their actions deserve. (2 Corinthians 11:13–15)
>
> But for the cowardly and unbelieving and abominable and murderers and immoral persons and sorcerers and idolaters and all liars, their part will be in the lake that burns with fire and brimstone, which is the second death. (Revelation 21:8, NASB)

Some people scoff at the idea of a personal devil and demons; however, a powerful reason for accepting the reality of a personal devil is the testimony of no less an authority than Jesus Christ.

No one denies that Jesus accepted the Bible as the literal word of God. Because the Bible is God's Word and not merely the opinions of men, what it says about the existence of a personal devil is true; therefore, in light of the abundance of data supporting its claim to divine inspiration (324), we may assume its statements about Satan are reliable. If one believes in the truth of the Bible, then to doubt the reality of the devil is impossible. Jesus Christ Himself believed in the reality of Satan and demons and had many encounters not only with the devil, but also his demons (Matthew 4:1–10; 8:28–34; 12:22–28).

No one else in human history can speak with more authority than Jesus Christ. No one else in all history ever directly claimed to be God (John 5:18; 10:30; 14:9) and proved the truth of His claim by literally rising from the dead (Matthew 20:18,19; John 20:24–28; Acts 1:3). In our book on the Resurrection we have detailed the persuasive logical, historical, and legal evidence for the fact of Christ's rising from the dead (348). If He rose from the dead, something unique in all human history, then He is both Lord and God and what He says is true, including His statements about the devil, demons, and spiritual warfare.

Unfortunately, for many people, the testimony of the Bible is insufficient to prove that these spirits who are so active in new age medicine are really demons. For such people, we present the following additional evidence.

Proof of Demonic Activity

How do we further know these spirits are really demons? Proof that the spirits who claim to be benign entities are really demons can be seen in the consensus of history and religion; the testimony of active occultists; the testimony of former occults and spiritists; the well-documented phenomenon of spirit possession where spirits possess people and speak lies through them or injure them in various ways; in the consistent prejudice against historic Biblical Christianity displayed by virtually all spiritistically inspired and occult literature; and in the history of the occult and modern psychic research which has left a trail of shattered, ruined lives.

The Consensus of History and Religion

Belief in a world of literal evil spirits has been with man throughout his history. It has been an accepted truth for most people in most times and cultures, whether ancient or modern (Assyrian, Babylonian, Celtic, Egyptian, Greek, Hebrew, Indian, African, Muslim, Roman, Tibetan, Persian, Chinese, Buddhist, Hindu, Christian, Jain, Japanese, Slavic, etc.) (140:565–636). In light of so vast a testimony from history, culture, and religion, can anyone credibly remain skeptical about the reality of spiritual evil in the world?

The Testimony of Practicing Occultists of an Awareness of Evil

Whether magicians, psychics, channelers, gurus, mediums, witches, or Satanists, innumerable testimonies indicate they are very much aware of the reality of spiritual evil, however they may choose to define it. Many of them believe in literal evil spirits and have had personal encounters with them. Such encounters leave little doubt as to their malevolent nature (e.g., 354:70–72; 122:196–99). For example, spiritist Sri Chinmoy discusses the deceptive nature of spirits, that even allegedly "good" spirits will turn on a person and then "they try to cut your throat" if the individual attempts to declare independence from them (355:19).

He also observes, "The hostile forces [can] take the form of a particular spiritual Master and ask the disciples to commit suicide. 'If you commit suicide, I will be able to give you liberation sooner' it would say. . . . These hostile forces are very clever" (354:94).

Testimony About the Reality of Demons from Former Spiritists

The testimony of many former spiritists and occultists is that the spirits they once completely trusted were really demons who were seeking to deceive them. Their once friendly spirit guides turned on them and/or attempted to destroy them. These frightening accounts are reported by Raphael Gasson (106), Victor Ernest (108) and Ben Alexander (110), all former long-standing spiritistic mediums. Doreen Irvine was a leading European witch (105). Mike Warnke was a Satanic high priest (322); Johanna Michaelsen was a former psychic and assistant to a Mexican psychic surgeon (107). All of them agree that spirit guides they once considered divine or enlightened entities were actually demons.

The Experience of Demon-possession

Another line of evidence involves the experience of demon-possession, which occurs in nearly every culture and religion, ancient or modern (refs. 141; cf. 140:565–636). Former witch Doreen Irvine declares, "Demon-possession is real, very real, and is increasing at an alarming rate in this present day and age" (142:138). Naturally, the very act of a spirit invading and controlling a person implies, even demands, hostility and malice. And it is usually the occultist who gets possessed. In his text *People of the Lie*, psychiatrist M. Scott Peck, author of the best-selling *The Road Less Traveled*, observes, "It seems clear from the literature on possession that a majority of cases have had involvement with the occult—a frequency far greater than might be expected in the general population" (143:190).

Opposition to Biblical Teaching

In addition, the teachings of the spirits themselves universally oppose the teachings of the Bible. There has never been a genuine spiritistic revelation that was not anti-Biblical and which failed to oppose the teachings of Christ. The most logical explanation for the spirits' single-mindedness is that they are the very spirits that Jesus Christ and the Bible expose as demons.

Damage and Destruction

Finally, the damage and destruction revealed in the history of the occult is strong evidence that occult activity links one to a world of evil spirits

(131). In addition, some of the most astute minds of our modern era have accepted the reality of demons. The brilliant Christian apologist C. S. Lewis said in regard to their existence,

> It seems to me to explain a good many facts. It agrees with the plain sense of Scripture, the tradition of Christendom, and the beliefs of most men at most times. And it conflicts with nothing that any of the sciences has shown to be true. (144:VII)

Trial lawyer, philosopher, and theologian Dr. John Warwick Montgomery holds eight earned degrees including two doctorates. He asserts, "The problem involved in determining whether demon-possession occurs and whether witchcraft works is absurdly simple. The documentation is overwhelming" (145:146). He also states, "There is overwhelming extra-Biblical data and empirical confirmation of the scriptural claims" regarding the existence of a personal devil and demons (141:232).

When one considers not only the divine authority of the Bible and the testimony of Christ who, as God, was also an infallible authority, but also the consensus of history and religion, the testimony of active and former occultists, the phenomenon of spirit possession, the hostility to Biblical revelation displayed in spiritistic literature, and the personal wreckage in the history of occultism, one is hard-pressed to maintain simply that demons do not exist.

In the end, one either trusts the spirits and ignores the facts or one trusts the facts and ignores the spirits.

For those who wish additional information, we suggest they consult *The Facts on Spirit Guides*, from which most of the above was excerpted (132), and our *The Facts on the Occult* (396).

Conclusion

Why is it logical to assume demons are interested in new age medicine? Almost every war fought on earth has employed deception or camouflage in battling the enemy. In 500 B.C. a Chinese general remarked, "All war is deception." In our modern age, from the super-secret stealth bomber to "thermal imagers" that display near and far infra-red energy (e.g., body heat), camouflage and deception continue to be a key aspect of war strategy.

Being invisible or otherwise confusing the enemy will always supply an advantage in combat. Consider a few illustrations: First, less than 1 percent of all "dazzle painted" ships were hit in World War I. Second, in both World Wars decoy or false shadows often protected real airplanes on the ground. Sometimes, airfields were so well camouflaged they not only escaped bombing, their own pilots had difficulty finding them.

Thousands of wars have been fought throughout human history, but the Bible teaches that there is also a spiritual war (Ephesians 6:10–18). If spiritual warfare exists, should we assume the enemy never employs deception or attempts to confuse his targets? Death is by far the most profound reality anyone faces; people's interest in their health is natural. The claim of this book is that the field of health has become a target of demonic deception—spiritual warfare, if you will—that Satan and his demons are using people's concern over their health as a way of fooling them spiritually. Of all created beings, the demon is the master of camouflage. As Dr. Kurt Koch explains:

> The devil is a many-sided and versatile demagogue. To the psychologist he says, "I will give you new knowledge and understanding." To the occultist, he will say, "I will give you the keys to the last secrets of creation." He confronts the religionist and the moralist with a mask of integrity and promises them the very help of heaven. And finally to the rationalist and the liberalist he says, "I am not there. I do not even exist."
>
> The devil is a skillful strategist. He is the master of every tactic of the battlefield. He befogs the front. He hides behind a camouflage of empty religious talk. He operates through the use of the latest scientific method. He successfully fires and launches his arguments on the social and human plane. And his sole aim is to deceive, to entice, and to ensnare his victims. (155:7)

Again, the Bible itself warns:

> And no wonder, for Satan himself masquerades as an angel of light. It is not surprising, then, if his servants masquerade as servants of righteousness. Their end will be what their actions deserve. (2 Corinthians 11:14–15)

As a former new age writer told us,

> It was new age medicine which influenced me more than anything previously and catapulted me into the world of the occult. I wasn't looking for anything supernatural. I only wanted to cure the pain in my neck. When the treatment worked, I became fascinated with the entire subject of holistic medicine. Before I knew it, I was converted to paganism. I had

> abandoned my Christian upbringing, adopted a pantheistic world view, and was active in various occult practices. I began writing articles on higher consciousness and mystical energies and how they could be related to "God" and new age medicine.
>
> Looking back, I can see how my initial fascination over supposedly being healed by muscle testing and homeopathy became a compelling seduction urging me to adopt the philosophy that underlay my alleged healing. But personally, I paid a price. I was never physically healed, but my spiritual life was derailed for years.
>
> I don't think anyone should underestimate the deceptive power of new age medicine (456).

Artists who play with the foreground and background of their paintings can make almost any object invisible, say a zebra or tree,—at least until the item is pointed out. Once the hidden object in the painting is pointed out, the observer never again loses it.

That is why the goal of this book is to "point out" some of the spiritual deceptions in the field of new age medicine. We hope that for many people what was once hidden will now become evident.

SEVEN

THE ECLECTIC NATURE OF NEW AGE MEDICINE

Clients of new age medicine may be treated with additional methods than those they expected or sought. In this chapter we will examine why new age health practitioners use a variety of methods.

Why a Variety of Methods?

First, the philosophy of new age medicine encourages such an approach. New age medicine claims to be "holistic," which means it can supposedly treat the "whole" person—body, mind, and spirit. Thus, it does not restrict itself to treating only a physical problem, but rather sees mind, body, and spirit as interrelated. Therefore, to treat a mental or physical problem, a spiritual treatment may also be required. To some degree, then, new age health practitioners claim they are physician, psychologist, and priest wrapped into one.

Most new age techniques claim to be holistic treatments because by themselves they work to influence the whole person—body, soul, and spirit. But if a problem is more spiritual than mental or more mental than physical, then more than one approach may be required.

For example, a person with headaches may be treated with chiropractic spinal manipulation for his physical problem (pain in the head), while yoga meditation may be prescribed for the more serious condition of emotional tension causing the headache. But because mind, body, and spirit are all interrelated, treating a given illness by emotional and physical means only may be deemed ineffective. Physical illness may be a symptom of a deeper spiritual illness requiring spiritual treatment. Headache may not only result from stress; it may supposedly result from a "blockage" of one's "life energy." Thus, applied kinesiology, acupuncture, or therapeutic touch may be prescribed to unblock the flow of energy and thereby "cure" the "root" problem.

This new age approach to medicine radically changes how people are treated. While a conventional physician may simply prescribe penicillin for a viral infection, a new age practitioner may think it necessary to prescribe astrological counselling along with healing by crystals and hypnotic regression into a past life.

The second reason a variety of techniques may be employed is that the methods of diagnosis one may choose are as abundant as the methods of treatment. Thus, in addition to a variety of possible *treatment* practices, new age medicine can employ a variety of different *diagnostic* methods, such as iridology, applied kinesiology, clairvoyant diagnosis by a spirit guide, or diagnosis through a radionics instrument.

Third, employing a variety of treatments may be a financial necessity. Concentrating on one particular therapy, such as reflexology, may not pay the bills. Thus, the more treatments one can advertise, the greater the number of clients, the greater the income, and the better the chance one will remain in business.

Fourth, by using different methods of diagnosis and treatment, new age practitioners think they can improve their public image as effective healers. The more methods used, the more "holistic" or "comprehensive" one appears. Anyone who employs so many different "medical" practices must be all the more "medically" competent.

Consider how treating a person "holistically" may require the use of all the following different methods:

- *Iridology*: diagnoses the problem; e.g., asthma.
- *Astrology*: determines the correct time for treatment.
- *Herbal teas*: treats the physical symptoms.
- *Occult meditation*: treats the mental symptom; e.g., anxiety, depression.
- *Acupuncture*: treats the spiritual problem; unbalanced or blocked life energy.

- *Hypnotic "past life" regression*: treats the ultimate cause; e.g., "karma" from the past life where the patient had lung cancer.

In fact, any number of different techniques could be used in diagnoses and treatment of any given problem. Because almost all new age therapies work at least to some degree on the basis of the placebo effect (people's faith and trust in the therapy or therapist), almost any techniques will work for some people some of the time, so all methods are equally valuable. They can even be combined in an unusual manner.

To illustrate, an acupuncturist may employ what is known as "homeoacupuncture," a combination of homeopathy and acupuncture.

In this process, homeopathic solutions are injected into acupoints. Acupuncture may also involve auricular acupuncture, which is also termed "earology" by some. The idea is that the external human ear corresponds section by section or point by point to the inner organs and functions of the human body. In the same way, the iridologist assigns different organs and functions of the human body to the iris of the eye, and the reflexologist assigns them to sections of the hand or foot. In fact, throughout history, the human body has been miniaturized and stuffed into numerous parts of the body: the eye, the ear, the head, the face, the foot, the hand, even the nose and anus! (115:26, 39, 59, 65, 84, 101).

Cross-Pollenization of Techniques

The following chart of twenty alternate therapies is intended to show how easily a given new age therapist can incorporate other techniques or methods. All the following were encountered in the literature. The most common additions are the use of altered states of consciousness, occult meditation, and some form of psychic diagnosis or healing. But regardless, if you seek out a practitioner in the left-hand column, you may also be treated with a therapy from the right-hand column.

Principal Method:	Additional Therapy or Adjunct:
Therapeutic Touch	Occult Meditation Altered States of Consciousness Radiesthesia/Rod & Pendulum Dowsing Yoga Psychic Energies Psychic Diagnosis & Healing

Principal Method:	Additional Therapy or Adjunct:
Color Therapy	Radiesthesia/Rod & Pendulum Dowsing Astrology Psychic Diagnosis & Healing Occult Meditation
Biofeedback	Altered States of Consciousness Occult Meditation Psychic Diagnosis Yoga
Chiropractic	Applied Kinesiology Iridology Reflexology Crystal Healing Radiesthesia/Rod & Pendulum Dowsing Acupressure Psychic Diagnosis Kundalini Yoga Rolfing
Homeopathy	Radiesthesia/Rod & Pendulum Dowsing Psychometry Astrology Psychic Diagnosis
Acupuncture & Acupressure	Homeopathy Kundalini Yoga Astrology Occult Meditation Spiritism Psychic Diagnosis & Healing
Endogenous Endocrinotherapy (A naturopathic method to allegedly "normalize" a malfunctioning endocrine gland.)	Acupuncture Homeopathy Osteopathy Applied Kinesiology Herbal Treatment Short Wave Irradiation
Astrologic Medicine	Chiropractic Homeopathy Radiesthesia Muscle Testing Occult Meditation, Yoga Spiritism Rod & Pendulum Dowsing Psychic Diagnosis & Healing Iridology Crystal Healing
Body Work (This is general term for such disciplines as Rolfing, the Alexander method, Functional Integration, Orgonomy, Bioenergetics, Arica, and dozens more. Also known as Somatics.)	Yoga Psychic Diagnosis & Healing Occult Meditation Altered States of Consciousness

Principal Method:	Additional Therapy or Adjunct:
Psychic Healing	Radiesthesia/Rod & Pendulum Dowsing Spiritism Occult Meditation Altered States of Consciousness
Reflexology	Astrology Radiesthesia/Rod & Pendulum Dowsing Occult Meditation Altered States of Consciousness Psychic Diagnosis
Herbal Medicine	Astrology Radiesthesia/Rod & Pendulum Dowsing Psychic Diagnosis & Healing Spiritism Homeopathy Occult Meditation
Yoga, Visualization	Spiritism Occult Meditation Altered States of Consciousness
Naturopathy	Iridology Acupuncture Herbal Medicine Radiesthesia/Rod & Pendulum Dowsing Homeopathy Biofeedback Chiropractic Astrology
Dowsing	Altered States of Consciousness Radiesthesia/Rod & Pendulum Dowsing Occult Meditation Psychic Diagnosis & Healing
Polarity Healing	Psychic Diagnosis & Healing Spiritism
Applied Kinesiology & Touch for Health	Aromatherapy Reflexology Yoga Psychic Healing Iridology Shiatsu
Iridology	Astrology Psychic Diagnosis Naturopathy Applied Kinesiology Radionics Rod & Pendulum Dowsing
New Age Osteopathy	Homeopathy Iridology Radionics Color Therapy Edgar Cayce Methods Occult Meditation

This list reflects only some of the associations gleaned from the literature and is not exhaustive. In theory, almost any new age practice could incorporate almost any other practice.

The reason for the above situation is obvious. New age medicine is not based upon scientific medicine. It is based on occultism, Eastern disciplines, quackery, guesswork, intuition, etc. New age practitioners often employ a variety of methods because each method is potentially compatible with another; because the more methods one offers, the greater the financial remuneration, or because employing a variety of methods makes the practitioner appear more "holistic."

Conclusion

But there are dangers in such extensive cross-pollenization. First, a practitioner whose primary treatment method is relatively harmless may incorporate additional treatment methods which are positively harmful. Second, the more exposure to a variety of treatments, the greater the chance something will work, thereby converting the person to new age philosophy as well as practice. Third, most of these methods are designed to work on not only the body but the mind as well. For example, in *Mind Therapies Body Therapies,* shaman-instructed author and naturopath George Feiss examines some fifty alternate or unconventional new self-help therapies such as autogenic training, Silva mind control, reflexology, polarity therapy, the Alexander technique, bioenergetics, aikido, etc. Many of them are based on the mystical life energy concepts of the East. Feiss observes, "In actuality there are no hard and fast boundaries for any of these disciplines; all of them affect the whole (mind-body) organism to varying degrees" (73:vii).

The world view of these therapies and the openness to the psychic realm evident in many of them bring subtle, if negative, spiritual implications. Any systematic technique that is seriously pursued and that works on the mind-body system within an Eastern or occultic context may become the vehicle for spiritual warfare. One may become more open to the psychic realm; one may actually be treated psychically; one may develop psychic powers; or one may develop an alien world view that insulates against Christian truth. One may even be demonized.

EIGHT

CAN YOU TRUST NEW AGE MEDICINE?

Trust between a doctor and patient is essential; it forms the very heart of the practitioner/client relationship. Without it, a relationship is impossible. But by and large clients cannot trust new age practitioners/medicine for at least four reasons.

First, new age medicine is largely quackery. New age health practices almost never work on the basis of their stated principles. Iridology, muscle testing, acupuncture, reflexology, homeopathy, and all the rest—each claims to work on the basis of certain (more or less) clearly stated principles. Yet none of them do. When treatments are successful, they are so for reasons unrelated to the given therapy.

Furthermore, new age medicine is not scientific medicine; its techniques are almost never scientifically validated and many are potentially dangerous. But every health practitioner is morally and legally responsible to know that the methods they employ are safe and effective. Put bluntly, any health practitioner who is ignorant of his own methods is either uninformed, incompetent, deceived, or a charlatan.

Is it acting responsibly to place our trust in persons who, for whatever reason, employ quack treatments, even while claiming they are safe and effective? No one trusts deceived persons, because deceived people cannot be relied upon. Quackery and deception should not form the basis of health care.

Second, innumerable false claims are made in new age medicine. The public is routinely supplied with misinformation, not facts. When methods are widely promoted as working on the basis of principles that are not established and when false claims are made concerning the curative powers of these techniques, the public has legitimate reason for suspicion.

New age practices or techniques are often said to be scientific practices or to be scientifically validated when this is not true. With the lone exception of biofeedback (and even here significant misinformation is broadcast), no new age health practice discussed in part 2 has been scientifically validated in the normal sense.* In fact, most new age therapies actually treat people on the basis of *religious* principles, not scientific ones.

In addition, the information cited in support of the supposed factual or scientific nature of a practice or belief is often misinterpreted, misquoted, or simply bogus. For example, Kirlian photography often claims to prove the existence of the human aura or astral-etheric body. One new age health encyclopedia asserts that "high voltage Kirlian photography has shown the existence of energy waves and currents around all living things: That is, we now have photographs of what apparently are auras" (80:100). But this is not true. There is no evidence that Kirlian photography scientifically reveals a human aura (151:403–409).

Acupuncturist Sidney Rose-Neil claims acupuncture theory has been scientifically demonstrated:

> A Korean Professor, Kim Bong Han, has demonstrated photographically the existence of the meridians as a separate physiological system. He has also shown that the meridians contain DNA and RNA—two substances basic to life and reproduction. His work, documented with histological, pathological, and photographic evidence, is now available in English. (76:60)

But this is also not true as we will show in the chapter on acupuncture (see part 2). As Paul Reisser, M.D., points out:

> Unfortunately, none of these results have been replicated in the West. . . . It seems unlikely, however, that such an elaborate system would have escaped the notice of Western anatomists over the past five centuries. Felix Mann, an experienced English acupuncturist, cites evidence that the Bong

---

* Osteopathy, as practiced by osteopaths with a scientific approach, would be an exception, subject to certain possible qualifications. But like conventional physicians, a significant portion of osteopaths have turned to new age medicine.

> Han structures are based on distortions of tissue occurring in the preparation of microscope slides. Even if the Bong Han system is eventually verified, it remains in the realm of physical structure and offers no support for the circulation of invisible life energies. (1:75)

False claims are also routinely made regarding the number and kind of problems a treatment will cure. Most new age practitioners wrongly think their method will cure almost anything. But quack treatments will cure nothing. One acupuncturist claims:

> Conditions which can be successfully treated include migraine headaches, ulcers and digestive troubles, lumbago, arthritis, fibrositis, neuritis, sciatica, rheumatism, dermatitis, eczema, psoriasis and other skin conditions, high blood pressure, depressions and anxiety states, asthma and bronchitis and many others. (76:57)

But again, this is simply false.

Third, new age medicine promotes irresponsibility; it rarely polices its claims or its methods. The reason why is easy to see. Those who use unproven methods themselves cannot judge others who do the same without being hypocritical. Thus, new age practitioners routinely defend not only the bogus methods they personally employ but new age medicine in general.

> Writers on holistic health are curiously reluctant to tell their readers how to separate the wheat from the chaff in the alternative techniques of health care. Many do not admit that there is any chaff at all, and the few who do (such as LeShan) stop short of telling us how to spot it. (409:150)

But what if new age medicine is entirely chaff? Then, separating the wheat from the chaff is not even possible.

Fourth, new age medicine confuses the divine and the demonic. New age health techniques are often based upon Eastern or occultic philosophies, their religious traditions or practices, or easily incorporated with them. Yet new age therapists claim their methods are associated with things truly divine and spiritual.

But philosophies and practices which are occultic, Eastern, or spiritistic have nothing to do with the divine. They have everything to do with the demonic. (Refs. 292; 304; 105–109; 111; 123–128; 130–132; 145)

For the above reasons and more, new age medicine cannot be trusted. Those who visit health practitioners need to be assured that they can trust those who treat them. And despite its claims, new age medicine cannot provide those assurances.

PART TWO

NEW AGE HEALTH PRACTICES

ACUPUNCTURE

Definition: Acupuncture is the practice of ancient Chinese needle stimulation based upon the occultic religion of Taoism.

Founder: Unknown; the traditional Chinese text is *The Yellow Emperor's Classic of Internal Medicine.*

How Does It Claim to Work? Acupuncture claims to work by stimulating acupuncture points with needles, supposedly permitting the cosmic energy of the universe (*chi*) to flow freely through the body organs and systems, maintaining health.

Scientific Evaluation: Disputed, but largely discredited; while its Taoism is ignored in scientific studies, these studies have yet to demonstrate acupuncture's effectiveness scientifically. A definitive three-year study released in 1991 concluded acupuncture was nothing more than, at best, a powerful placebo (462).

Occultic Potential: Taoist practice and philosophy; psychic practitioners; meditative programs and other occultic practices used in conjunction with acupuncture therapy.

Major Problem(s): Acupuncture works on the basis of psychological, religious or occultic principles, not scientific ones or its own stated theories.

Biblical/Christian Evaluation: Classical acupuncture involves the practice of an ancient pagan medicine inseparably tied to Taoism.

Potential Dangers: Needle stimulation has occasionally produced physical complications and injuries, some serious; misdiagnosis of a serious illness; occult influence.

NINE

ACUPUNCTURE

In China today, over a million doctors practice acupuncture. In Japan there are some sixty thousand, and almost three million more practice throughout the East (76:60). In France and Germany treatment can be obtained under national health programs where it is used in hospitals. In Russia several universities reportedly teach it. Some ten thousand practitioners exist in Europe (76:60).

In America there are an estimated sixteen hundred to two thousand practitioners nationwide, with numbers growing, and at least twelve hundred residing in California alone (191:27). If each practitioner sees only ten patients per day, at least one million people per year receive acupuncture treatments, assuming they visit their therapist six times a year.

In spite of the comparatively low numbers of therapists in the U.S., acupuncture is one of the most visible alternate new age therapies. It has found adherents among American presidents (John F. Kennedy), movie stars (the late Lorne Greene), sports stars (Roman Gabriel), and among statesmen and royalty (Winston Churchill, Prince Bernard of the Netherlands).

The Nature of Acupuncture

Acupuncture is an ancient Chinese treatment using needles to allegedly stimulate the flow of *chi* (mystical life energy) in the body. In order to diagnose the condition of the *chi* flowing through invisible body channels called meridians, the therapist will usually examine twelve major "pulse" points, six on each wrist. After allegedly learning where the flow of *chi* is blocked or deficient, he will stimulate the proper acupuncture points. This stimulation of the "acupoints" will restore the flow of *chi* and maintain inner balance in the body. This supposedly keeps the body healthy.

The practice of acupuncture varies considerably among practitioners. In addition to different methods of pulse diagnosis and needling, patients' acupoints may also be injected with various substances, such as water, saline solution, lidocaine, or vitamin B^{12}. Moxibustion may also be used; here, a cylindrical cone of the plant *mugwort* is placed upon an acupuncture point and then lit, allegedly to stimulate the *chi* energy.

Another method is ear acupuncture (sometimes known as earology) where practitioners find all the acupoints they require in the organ of the ear. Or scientifically-oriented acupuncturists may stimulate acupuncture points with electricity, ultrasound, or even laser beams. A popular variation on acupuncture is known as acupressure where finger pressure replaces stimulation by needles. In fact, our evaluation of acupuncture applies equally to accupressure since both are based upon the same principles.

Underlying Philosophy: Taoism

One cannot understand classical acupuncture apart from a basic knowledge of its religious and philosophical foundation.

Essentially, acupuncture involves a medical/religious practice based upon an ancient Chinese philosophy known as Taoism. Taoism is a traditional occultic philosophy stressing the idea that one must live in harmony with the universe and its forces. Its religious practices incorporate occultic techniques and rituals, including alchemy, spiritism, geomancy, sorcery, etc.

One religious dictionary observes Taoism as,

> a series of organized religious movements that worship the Tao ('the Way') and its emanations and observe magical, physical, alchemical and meditative practices aiming at immortality. . . . The movements claim frequent direct communication with the divine powers [gods or spirits] and have repeatedly announced powerful new revelations. (150:742)

The dictionary further observes that the spirits and gods of Taoism "can also be considered [e.g., bodily] energies to be refined, harmonized, and combined" (150:743).

Acupuncture, acupressure, and related practices, such as Taoist yoga, have spurred a growing interest in Taoism in America today. This is only one illustration among scores showing how religiously-based new age health practices tend to spur interest in the religions associated with them.

Nevertheless, the ancient Chinese speculated concerning a mysterious force of nature that had generated the entire universe. This force of cosmic energy was called the Tao. Tao precedes even God and is the absolute and universal cosmic energy which lies behind man and nature.

Tao refers primarily to "the Way" or "the Path" and thus is a reference to "the way or path of the universe"—in other words, a reference to how the universe functions or operates. The purpose of man is to live in harmony with the Tao. Therefore, for man, the Tao represents the path of life one is to follow.

The principle manifestations of Tao are explained by the universal energy called *chi* and the opposite forces of *yin* and *yang.*

Yin and *yang* are the activating components of the cosmic life energy or *chi. Chi* circulates through everything in the universe, manifested primarily in its *yin* or *yang* aspect. In its primary nature, everything in the universe is said to be either *yin* or *yang.* Examples of *yin* are death, female, evil, vice, disease; examples of *yang* are life, male, good, virtue, health.

Although *yin* and *yang* are opposed to each other, ultimately they are still one. Thus, Taoism does not distinguish between opposites in any ultimate sense: both life and death, health and illness, God and Satan, good and evil, light and dark, pure and impure are ultimately manifestations of the Tao or universal cosmic energy.

The first concern of Taoist philosophy is harmony between man and the universe, mediated through the Tao. Holding to an ancient occult philosophy depicted by the phrase "as above, so below," the Chinese believed that the macrocosm, or the universe including the stars and planets, influenced the microcosm, or man. (This is why astrology plays an important role in classical Chinese medicine.) Thus, the universe itself, with its flow of Tao, or cosmic energy, influences the physical body of man. The cosmic energy *chi* permeates not only the entire universe, but the mind and body of man as well.

But the universe is not in harmony, and men are not in balance with the Tao. The purpose of Taoist practice and medicine (e.g., acupuncture) is to restore man's harmony with the universal cosmic energies:

> In the unmanifest world (bsien-t'ien) the Tao is the perfect creative harmony; in the manifest world (bou-t'ien) the balance is disturbed, and in the microcosm of the human body there are forces (often personified as demons or worms) that tempt one away from integration in the Tao and the full continuance of vitality. But the death-dealing forces in the human microcosm can be reversed, and the sequence of progression from life to death, yang to yin, can move back from death to life, yin to yang, so that humans can reach the eternal state of potentiality which characterizes the newborn child. (150:742)

But acupuncture is merely one *part* of what is needed to operate in full harmony with the cosmic forces of the Tao; this is why true acupuncture is always part of a larger program of religious instruction and often occultic practice. To separate acupuncture theory (Taoism) from acupuncture practice is to strip it of its real power and efficiency.

In other words, Chinese medicine sees man as one in body and spirit and ultimately as one with the universe. This is why man finds his ultimate value and harmony when he is in unity with the Tao, or the cosmic path. To make acupuncture merely one method of physical cure, as Western scientists do, is a distortion of the nature of the universe itself and the very purpose of man.

Thus, Chinese medicine, including acupuncture, is based squarely on the concept of the Tao, *yin* and *yang*, and the flow of *chi* throughout the universe and the body.

Now we can see how acupuncture blends with ancient Taoist theory. Acupuncture claims to restore the balance of *chi*, the universal "life energy." *Chi* is believed to circulate in the body along twelve or more meridians—non-physical channels that lie beneath the surface of the body. The acupuncture points are located at specific sites along the meridians.

These acupoints are believed to be the actual spots at which the *chi* energy can be influenced by stimulation. This supposedly either releases excess *chi* or corrects a deficiency, thus maintaining harmony in the body between *yin* and *yang* and the Tao.

Furthermore, each meridian is associated with a different body function or organ. If an organ is deficient in *chi*, illness will eventually result. Acupuncture claims it can restore *chi* to body organs and systems, thus maintaining health.

Yin and *yang* forces must be perfectly balanced. Constant interaction between *yin* and *yang* occurs in the body and its organs. If the balance is upset, the flow of *chi* is adversely affected, and we become sick.

Man can only function "properly," that is, properly physically and spiritually, when the *chi* is flowing unobstructed in harmony with the cosmic energy. Thus, acupuncture theory holds that the psychic energy within the body must function in harmony with the psychic or cosmic energy of the universe. When the flow of psychic energy along the meridians becomes obstructed or blocked, organs do not receive their supply of *chi* energy and the end result is the manifestation of illness or disease.

Psychic Hiroshi Motoyama is director of the Institute for Religion and Psychology, an organization seeking to scientifically and psychically investigate the occult anatomies of the ancient Chinese (meridians) and Hindus (*chakras*). He describes the process by which a blockage of *chi* produces illness:

> If the flow of energy is stopped in a meridian, then at the point of stoppage, subjective symptoms (i.e., pain) are likely to appear. . . . If this condition continues for a long time, then one will experience gradually nervous pain, skeletal muscular pain, rheumatism, organic disease. If we can remove the excessive energy from the point and correct the blockage so that the energy can flow smoothly again, then the disease or the subjective symptoms of pain, etc.[sic], will disappear. (12:21)

Origin

The origin of acupuncture is unknown, but similar practices can be traced to ancient shamanism. Dr. Samuel Pfeifer, M.D., a consulting psychiatrist and head physician at a psychiatric clinic in Switzerland, observes:

> Treatment with needles, later termed acupuncture (from the Latin acus—"needle" and punctus—"point") in the west, goes back to the earliest doctors, probably spiritistic shamans. They performed rituals similar to those found in today's voodoo-cults, that attempt to expel evil spirits by sticking needles into the body of the sick. Later scholars abandoned the demonic model and integrated the use of needles into their astrological theories. (2:28)

Another source indicates that in the third to first centuries B.C., acupuncture was used in occultic ritual as a form of blood letting, also permitting the escape of the "evil spirits" related to disease (350:42).

Acupuncture may have had a similar occultic origin in China, or its beginnings could have been more mundane. Pedro Chan is an acupuncture research associate at the White Memorial Medical Center in Los Angeles and author of several texts on acupuncture. He observes that according to tradition, about five thousand years ago the Chinese made the observation that pain could be relieved by rubbing stones against their bodies. They allegedly observed that some soldiers, wounded by arrows, recovered from longstanding illness. The principle was eventually developed that stimulation of various points of the body either by pressure or needle insertion could result in the alleviation of such illness (8:11).

Nevertheless, because of the occultic theories underlying acupuncture and its occult associations historically, some variation on the first theory is probably a more accurate assessment of how acupuncture originated, even in China.

Traditional Text

The traditional acupuncture text is called *The Huang-ti Nei-ching Su-wen* ("Essential Questions from the Classic Book of Internal Medicine"). Popularly known as *The Yellow Emperor's Classic of Internal Medicine*, or simply, the *Nei Ching*, it consists of thirty-four books allegedly compiled between 2,500 and 1,000 B.C., although the best edition available dates from A.D. 762 (15). The *Nei Ching* was inspired largely by the astrological and occultic (e.g., Taoist) religious concepts of the day.

But this text is important for one reason: Traditional Chinese medicine still relies upon this work which combines a mystical view of life and an ancient pre-scientific, occultic medicine based upon it (15:70). In fact, acupuncture practitioners around the world rely upon this volume for theory and practice.

If we wish to understand acupuncture properly then, we must first understand the *Nei Ching*. Henry Sigerist, formerly the director of the John Hopkins Institute of the History of Medicine, observes that it is probably "the most important early Chinese medical book" (15:vi).

The text is composed of a dialogue between the legendary *Huang-ti*, the Yellow Emperor of China, and his physician, *Ch'i Po*. Part 1 discusses the mystical Taoist theory which underlies Chinese medicine, while part 2 describes the various occultic Taoist healing methods:

> The second part . . . describes the actual ways an acupuncturist may heal and prevent diseases. Besides a thorough description of the needle and points, it includes a multitude of recipes and various forms of massage as

> well as magic spells and charms. All of these methods were supposed to restore the balance of cosmic forces in the patient. It was the theory of the first part, and the practical applications of the second part of the *Nei Ching*, which formed the fundamentals of Chinese medicine. . . . Ancient Chinese medicine was governed by the idea that diseases were sent by gods and demons. (2:27)

The first page of the *Nei Ching* sets the tone for the rest of the text. The emperor wonders why in ancient times people lived to be over a hundred years of age and remained in good health but that "today" people only live half that age and become decrepit. His physician Ch'i Po responds, "In ancient times those people who understood Tao [the way of self-cultivation] patterned themselves upon the Yin and Yang [the two principles in nature] and they lived in harmony with the arts of divination" (15:97).

Chinese medicine, then, teaches that true health is based upon living and believing a particular *religious* philosophy. "The only manner in which man could obtain the right Way, the Tao, was by emulating the course of the universe and complete adjustment to it. Thus man saw the universe endowed with a spirit that was indomitable in its strength and unforgiving toward disobedience" (15:11).

True "health" involved the realization that life and death, health and disease, good and evil, male and female were all one:

> The fact that in these contrasts Yang represented the positive and Yin the negative side, must not be interpreted to mean that the Yin was a "bad" and the Yang a "good" principle. It must always be borne in mind that Yin and Yang were conceived of as one entity and that both together were ever present. (15:14)

Balance between *yin* and *yang* was the key. The *Nei Ching* observes,

> If Yang accumulates excessively one will die from the (resulting) disease. If the force of Yang is blocked, the blockage should be dispelled. If one does not drain it thoroughly and guide away the rough matter, there will be destruction. (15:107–108)

Dr. Mary Austin is an osteopath and authority on acupuncture. In *The Textbook of Acupuncture Therapy*, she illustrates how the *Tao* and *yin* and *yang* interrelate:

> The Life-process is activated and maintained by what is called, in Acupuncture, Vital Force or Life Energy. . . . We, in Acupuncture, accept it as

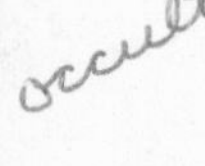

> a basic concept or premise that this Vital Force (Life Energy) is a manifestation of a unitary bi-polar energy that, in living creatures, permeates every cell and tissue of the organism—in form, structure, and process.
>
> The behavior of this Life Force . . . constitutes the Laws of Nature.
>
> For every mode or form of existence, from the largest system or organization to the minutest individual system (macroscopic to microscopic) there is an appropriate normal behavior pattern or complex of natural laws that must be observed. There is no escaping the absolute imperative of Natural Law.
>
> . . . the activity Yang and activity Yin are not two separate or different forces, but represent polarities of the one Force, the Life Force or vital energy. (9:1–2)

Because disease represents an imbalance in this energy,

> An acupuncteur . . . first aims to locate the energy imbalance and ascertain its nature. Having done this he aims to restore the balance to what it should be normally by manipulating the vital energy.
>
> The practitioner thinks and works in terms of vital energy rhythms, polar changes, restoration of proper balance at deep levels. (9:3)

The Relationship Between Theory and Practice

The occultic philosophy of Taoism, involving the universal life energy (*chi*), *yin* and *yang*, plus other beliefs such as astrology and the five elements, are all bound together in the *Nei Ching*, traditional Chinese medicine, and most modern acupuncture.

Why is it important to recognize the religious basis of most modern acupuncture practice? Because in the end, it is doubtful that acupuncture theory and acupuncture practice can be successfully separated. What this means is that those who visit acupuncturists are being treated on the basis of religious principles and that they will be instructed to live their life according to the teaching of Taoism.*

Philosophical Taoism is more nonsectarian, rational, and contemplative while religious Taoism is more esoteric, magical, sectarian, and occultic. For example, a philosophical Taoist would accept death as a natural event and an opportunity to return to the Tao; a religious Taoist would attempt to resist death by practicing alchemy as a means to attain physical immortality.

* Taoism is usually divided into philosophical Taoism and religious Taoism. Although the two groups belong to the same tradition, they are not equivalent.

Nevertheless, even philosophical Taoists can hold to certain occultic philosophies and practices (150:738).

Some Westerners have attempted to separate acupuncture from Taoism. Classical acupuncturists, however, warn that this is a futile approach, destroying the effectiveness and true purpose of acupuncture—harmony with the Tao. They stress that, at best, the results of such practice will be marginal.

The reason for their concern is obvious. The *Nei Ching* itself gives strict warning about separating theory and practice:

> Those who rebel against the basic rules of the universe sever their own roots and ruin their true selves. Yin and Yang, the two principles in nature, and the four seasons are the beginning and the end of everything and they are also the cause of life and death. Those who disobey the laws of the universe will give rise to calamities and [evil] visitations, while those who follow the laws of the universe remain free from dangerous illnesses, for they are the ones who have obtained Tao, the Right Way.
>
> Obedience to the laws of Yin and Yang means life; disobedience means death. (15:104–105)

Thus, according to one introduction to the *Nei Ching*,

> Medicine was but a part of philosophy and religion, both of which propounded oneness with nature, i.e., the universe. . . .
>
> Numerous references [in the *Nei Ching*] impressed the reader that his health, and with it the highly desirable state of longevity, depend largely on his own behavior toward Tao. (15:10,12)

In fact, the first method of treatment in the *Nei Ching* is designed to cure the spirit: "The treatment of the spirit consisted in guiding towards Tao those persons who by infringement 'of the basic rules of the universe [had] severed their own roots and ruined their true selves' " (15:53).

When one understands how deeply Taoism is woven into the practice of acupuncture, one understands why so many practitioners are adamant that *unless one is also a Taoist* in his religious outlook, one cannot successfully practice acupuncture. Consider the following assessments by traditional practitioners:

> Although a western scientifically trained and oriented medical practitioner might achieve a certain amount of technical "know how" he will not be able to become a true physician or healer in the highest traditional sense unless and until he makes a serious attempt to understand and put into practice the Principles of the Way of Life expounded in the *Nei Ching*. (10:13)

> We should see, then, that we are the infinite universe which expresses itself through a form called a body.
>
> If we can identify ourselves with this, our larger self, [then] our will can be as infinite as the supreme will of God.
>
> Until man can identify with his larger self . . . he will never be able to understand the philosophy of the Far East. In particular, he will never be able to practice acupuncture unless he can see it as applying the philosophy of the order of the universe.
>
> In its true spirit, acupuncture cannot be appreciated except by those who have understood the unique principle and applied it in their daily lives.
>
> Without this fundamental understanding . . . the practice of acupuncture could be dangerous. (17:9)

The attempt to separate acupuncture from its Taoist principles is held to be "dangerous" because apart from Taoism one is not living in real harmony with the universe:

> Man should regulate his activity by *yin* and *yang* according to the Tao (or the way) of day and night and to the Tao of the four seasons. If he goes against the order of the universe, his violation will eventually translate itself into sickness and suffering. (17:48)

William A. McGarey, M.D., a leader in the use of the "medical" applications of medium Edgar Cayce, observes:

> If one is going to study acupuncture seriously as a tool in therapy, he should have a considerable background of understanding of the [Taoist] laws, no matter how he intends to apply his knowledge. (14:75)

Genuine acupuncture is far more than merely a needling technique. Acupuncture is based upon the idea that the one who truly desires health must live in a certain manner. He must have a certain religious view. That religious world view is classical Taoism, an occultic philosophy which is deeply anti-Christian (320).

Major Problems

Acupuncture claims to "diagnose" the "*chi* energy" condition of the meridians and their corresponding physical organs or systems. How does one determine the condition of meridians? Acupuncturists claim that the principle method for diagnosing is through evaluation of the radial pulses felt on the forearm just above the wrist. Experienced acupuncturists think they can distinguish literally "hundreds of different variations in the pulses" (76:57). This supposedly informs the acupuncturists which meridians are "improperly" functioning, whether the *chi* energy flow is blocked or unbalanced. Just as iridologists, they even claim to diagnose illnesses and problems before they manifest in physical symptoms (see chapter on iridology).

In order to unblock or balance the energy flow, acupuncture needles are inserted into the acupuncture points which "regulate" the flow of *chi.* Once the practitioner diagnoses which meridians are unbalanced or blocked, he supposedly knows which points require needling. The needles are then inserted into the skin to varying depths and for varying lengths of time to restore the proper flow of *chi.*

But is this a scientific practice, as many promoters claim?

Subjective Diagnosis

The single most important aspect of acupuncture is diagnosis through the pulse. The *Nei Ching* itself observes, "Those who wish to know the inner body feel the pulse and have thus the fundamentals for diagnosis. . . . The feeling of the pulse is the most important medium of diagnosis" (15:163). But this method is very different from the pulse check of the orthodox doctor.

In acupuncture, pulse diagnosis can last half an hour or more. Up to twelve pulses must be examined, one for every major meridian, six per wrist. Again, the pulses allegedly provide the acupuncturist with information telling them which meridians are deficient in *chi* energy and whether *yin* or *yang* is dominant. "The rate of the [pulse] beat is of less importance than the energy flow [of *chi*], strong or weak, regular or irregular" (325:125).

In other words, the acupuncturist claims he can actually detect the movement of *chi,* a psychic, non-physical energy, flowing through invisible non-physical meridians. Not only this, he can distinguish possibly hundreds of different variations in the flow and by this determine the condition of the body. Modern acupuncturists claim, "The truly great discovery made by the Chinese, as regards to the pulse, was that through the pulse it is possible to read not merely the health of the organism as a whole, but that of each inner organ separately." (9:35).

One acupuncturist observes, " . . . it takes a long time and a great deal of practice to become proficient in reading and interpreting the pulses"

(10:40). Even acupuncturist William McGarey, M.D., a follower of Edgar Cayce, observes:

> An important technique in acupuncture therapy—and an absolute must for the traditional Chinese doctor—is the strange, almost unbelievable procedure of diagnosing one's illnesses by sensing the qualities of the pulse.
>
> This gives the doctor the information he is seeking, and he knows from this what energies are out of balance in the body, how the Ch'i is flowing through the meridians and exactly what needs to be done to correct the situation. (14:63)

But, in fact, diagnosing anything objective from the pulse is pure fiction, a physical impossibility. Why?

First, there is no uniformity among Chinese physicians as to the proper methodology:

> I've seen the pulse evaluated differently by oriental physicians, and it appears to me that the difference arises because of the type of acupuncture that they practice. . . .
>
> Acupuncture authority Felix Mann gives a chart in his book which shows how various authors report their use of the pulse and what they think they are evaluating when they do their diagnosis. (14:63,68)

Second, some don't even use the pulse: "Every acupuncturist is encouraged to learn the pulse diagnosis, but not all do" (14:68).

Third, proper pulse diagnosis requires a kind of "meditation." Thus, the diagnostic procedure is supposedly simple " . . . if one assumes the proper meditative, lost-in-posture." (14:65).

How exactly is the body diagnosed through the pulses? Acupuncture authority Mary Austin describes the procedure. In the following citation, the reader should note that the "condition" of the mystical energy *chi* is evaluated by an open and receptive mind. This is reminiscent of the manner in which the practitioner of Eastern or occultic meditation is open and receptive to the phenomena or results of meditation (see chapter 19):

> When feeling pulses the practitioner "listens" to them much as one might listen to an orchestra—each pulse representing one of the instrumentalists.
>
> The Practitioner himself must be *relaxed, calm and receptive*. When he palpates at each position, at each level, he quite deliberately, silently, says to himself, "I am now listening to the pulse of the Small Intestine (for example), to hear and *to try and understand* what it is saying to me."

> This almost ritual approach to the reading of pulses has often been sneered at by Westerners who understand so little of Far East wisdom. It does not matter if it takes a whole hour to feel and to access the pulses.
>
> It is important to *cultivate the ability* to listen to the *vital message* which will become *clearly revealed* to the *calm and* RECEPTIVE mind.
>
> What is the Life Force doing in each of the Organs and Organ Meridians?
>
> The human being will tell you through the pulses, the *inmost secrets* of the Life Force animating it—and its message will be a *truthful* message. If the practitioner *is sincere* and genuinely seeks to understand and receive the message, it will be there.
>
> Accept what you read—*whether your reasoning tells you it ought to be different or not.* It is not up to the practitioner to dictate to the pulses what message they "ought" to be giving and therefore only listen to what he thinks the message should be. The practitioner's task is to read the message as the Life Force in the patient gives it. . . . Never neglect the pulses. Even if you are not "acting on the pulse signs," see what the pulses have to say. In this way you will learn how the pulses alter in response to what you do. (9:49-51, emphasis added)

Calm and receptive minds; personal sincerity and respect for the "life force"; the mystical revealing of the inmost secrets of cosmic energies—this is the essence of acupuncture diagnosis. Do Westerners who visit acupuncturists know they are being diagnosed in this manner, or do they wrongly assume a level of Western medical skill is in operation, however unusual the methods used? One can only guess at the potential hazards of misdiagnosis through such a system.

But Mary Austin also observes that *intuition* plays an important part in pulse diagnosis: "When assessing your patient, do so as far as possible in silence; . . . and do not despise your own intuition. The better your own state of health, the more reliable will be your own intuitive assessment" (9:271).

She observes that one Indian acupuncturist lists no less than 66 different kinds of pulse beats which he claims are only the *major* differences one must learn to recognize in order to diagnose accurately.

> Sensitivity to the pulse so refined as to enable a practitioner to differentiate that number of pulse beats requires years of experience and guidance by a master of the art. [But] In the *Nei Ching* you will find relatively few broad categories of pulses—expressed in terms difficult for a Westerner to visualize. Which of us, in the West, for example, would know when a pulse was like a leaf floating on the water? Or like scraping a piece of bamboo? Or like a string of pearls? (9:270)

Or, how a pulse could determine the "fishiness" of the eyes (325:124)? Indeed, when we examine the directions in the *Nei Ching*, we discover that any accurate, objective pulse diagnosis is virtually impossible (15:42–47, 57, 162–168).

This is undoubtedly the reason for the practitioner's reliance upon subjective *intuition* or hunch in pulse diagnosis. *The Alternative Health Guide* observes: "Some experienced practitioners work largely on hunch. . . . Others require an elaborate accumulation of data relating to Chinese cosmology [e.g., astrology]" (325:124). For example,

> Remember, no one is at your elbow to tell you whether you are "right" or "wrong"; there is no one to prompt you into imagining you are feeling what you think they expect you to feel. All you are asked to do is to be receptive to detect what is, in fact, happening—what this is does not matter—simply try to describe what you feel. (9:40)

Because "the chief means of diagnosis employed in the *Nei Ching* is the examination of the pulse" and "all other methods of determining disease are only subsidiary to palpitation and used mainly in connection with it" (15:42), we can see that the principle method of acupuncture diagnosis is subjective and intuitive or psychic, not objective and scientific.

The *Nei Ching* has said that the pulses are to be used, not only for diagnosis, but also for prognosis and even for divination. Further, even dreamwork is employed: ". . . interrogation as to dreams and their interpretation" can supposedly provide useful information in diagnosis (15:47). Like astrological and other divination, pulse diagnosis can also allegedly reveal the time of death. The *Nei Ching* observes,

> Yin and Yang have their respective periods during which they influence the pulse. From the assistance they give each other during this period one can know the functions of the pulse. These functions fall into certain periods, and thus one is able to know the date of death.
>
> If it were not for excellent technique and the subtlety of the pulse one would not be able to examine it. But the examination must be done according to a plan, and the system of Yin and Yang [the two cosmic principles of nature] serves as a basis for examination. (15:162)

But can we truly believe that pulse diagnosis is an effective method for medical diagnosis, let alone for divination, dream interpretation, and determining the time of death?

Consider the following characteristic description of pulse diagnosis in the *Nei Ching*:

> All those who excel in the art of feeling the pulse find that when it is fine, slow, and short, there is an excess of Yang and when the pulse is slippery like pebbles rolling in a basin, there is an excess of Yin. (15:167)

But how can the sound of "pebbles rolling in a basin" reflect an objective evaluation of mystical energy flow? Consider another description:

> When one feels at the inside the pulse which indicates the outside, and when this inside pulse does not indicate the outside, there is a (harmful) accumulation within the heart and stomach. When one feels at the outside the pulse which indicates the inside, and when it does not indicate the inside, the body is hot and feverish [sic]. (15:167–168)

(No problem of clarity here!) And yet the *Nei Ching* warns that pulse diagnosis must be infallible:

> The most important requirement of the art of healing is that no mistakes or neglect occur. There should be no doubt or confusion as to the application of the term of "complexion and pulse." These are the maxims of the art of healing. (15:57)

Again, anyone who believes that an examination of the pulses, according to traditional acupuncture theory, can reveal the things claimed for it, is not dealing in the realm of scientific medicine but either in quackery or pyschic diagnosis.

Claims of Miraculous Powers

Traditional acupuncture theory is a *religious* doctrine, not a scientific theory. It teaches that if one is living in harmony with the Tao, then one is free of disease. Because virtually all illness and disease is related to some violation of the Tao, acupuncture theory teaches that restoration of blocked energy resulting from personal violations of the Tao and a person's reintegration with the Tao is capable of healing virtually any and all illness.

Theoretically at least, some religious Taoists should be in perfect health, and gain immortality even in this life. This is both the claim of their system and their goal (150:738, 743; 367:40). But if Taoist theory is true, why do they continue to suffer from diseases and die like the rest of us? Why are there never any magical alchemical transmutations into a condition of immortality?

Nevertheless, this belief of Taoism (that living in harmony with the Tao can cure all disease) is why, when acupuncture was first introduced into the West, wild claims were made concerning its ability to treat virtually any illness or disease. And such claims are still being made. Acupuncturists claim they can cure migraine headaches, ulcers, arthritis, high blood pressure, rheumatism, asthma, bronchitis, heart disease, cancer, and anything else one cares to mention (e.g., 76:57; 9:31–32, 46, 62–63).

Even depression, neurosis, other psychological problems, and mental illness can supposedly be cured by acupuncture. Because every disharmony—physical, emotional, or spiritual—is caused by an imbalance of *yin* and *yang* and disharmony with the Tao, the restoration of balance produces physical, mental, or spiritual health. Thus, ". . . in acupuncture we have one of the most powerful of all therapy methods for the treatment of psychological disturbances so far discovered by man" (9:270; cf. 76:57).

Anti-Scientific Treatments

Even if *chi* did exist, it could never be subjected to scientific testing, as acupuncturists have admitted (14:81). Why? Because *chi* is essentially an occultic energy lying outside the realm of scientific testing (14:81).

Like most new age therapies, acupuncture is opposed to modern medicine. Whenever acupuncture is practiced by anyone other than a qualified physician trained in conventional anatomy and physiology (rather than meridians and life energy), acupuncture is either a religious practice, quackery, or occultic. Anyone who doubts this need only read the *Nei Ching*, upon which the vast majority of modern acupuncture treatments are based.

These acupuncture treatments are thus based upon the *yin/yang* duality which assigns certain characteristics and properties to various items based on their "spiritual" (*yin* or *yang*) nature.

Consider the following typical excerpt from one acupuncture text:

> Foods rich in *yin* calories weaken the heart and the kidneys, with a corresponding dimunition of sexuality.
>
> If a person ingests *yin* substances in excess of the requirements of his environment, his interior will become more and more *yin* until it is an excellent setting for many varieties of microbes or germs. As a matter of fact, *it is not these microbes that cause sickness*; they only aggravate or specify a sickness which is already present. (17:44, emphasis added)

But who has scientifically verified the "properties" of *yin/yang* or proven the alleged correlations to different items? To the extent that diagnosis and treatment are regulated by the mysticism of the Tao, *yin/yang*, and the five elements, they can hardly be considered scientific medicine.

Consider the following recommended treatment: "A poultice of immediately-killed carp is marvelous for pulmonary fevers, as this is a very *yin* fish. One can apply this to the chest of the sick person, and even have him drink the blood of this fish" (17:45).

That the majority of acupuncture practices today are not scientific can be seen from the following selected citations:

> All philosophy and *science* should be unified under a single concept of the universe, a cosmology consisting of the unique principle of *yin* and *yang*. Without an understanding of dialectical monism, the acupuncture of the Far East must remain dead. (17:7–8, emphasis added)

> He [the physician] must look at the empiric results. For the practice of medicine is *an art*—not really a science. (14:ix, emphasis added)

Acupuncture deals with energy, not human physiology; therefore, the acupuncturist need not have a particular concern with modern medical science or physiology. Dr. Mary Austin argues as follows:

> Remember always that it is an energy pattern you are dealing with; and it is energy that you are manipulating. You are not concerned to name and to classify disease germs! Your action is not directed toward any single symptom, let us say for example such as "decreasing alkilinity [sic] in the urine" per se—always your mind is focused on the energy pattern and how to alter that. (9:272–273)

Further, all conventional physicians operating on the principles of scientific medicine can treat their patients regardless of their own individual health. But if an acupuncturist is not in good health, he supposedly should not treat patients at all. Why? Because it is his own pulses that he uses to gauge the condition of his patient's pulses. And if his pulses are "unhealthy" (i.e., out of harmony with the Tao), he will never be able to "accurately" gauge the condition of his patients' pulses. Only when the acupuncture therapist is himself properly aligned with the beliefs and practices of metaphysical Taoism, is he capable of making an accurate diagnosis:

> According to Tradition, the practitioner uses his own pulses as the standard by which he assesses those of his patient. No wonder the Far East Tradition demands the healer to be a model of good health himself, and to

set an example to his patient. A practitioner in poor health should not give Acupuncture treatment, let alone diagnose. (9:37)

Another illustration of the anti-scientific nature of modern acupuncture is in its acceptance of traditional bodily "organs" which do not even exist. Thus, concerning the "Circulation meridian," acupuncturists freely confess that "Western physiology does not recognize this as an inner organ. The Far East doctors do" (9:42).

Another non-existent organ according to Chinese medicine is called "the three-heater," the "thermo regulator," the "three burning spaces," and other names. Remember that each organ has its own corresponding meridian. Traditional acupuncture charts have the three-heater meridian clearly laid out; but which physical organ does it correspond to? No one knows. But since meridians "must be related to an organ, the organ must exist" (9:67).

Dr. Mary Austin attempts to resolve the dilemma by first examining the traditional characteristics of the three-heater and then looking in the body for a logical place it might be located:

> If we are going to look for an organ, . . . that could correspond to the three-heater we might just as well form as clear a picture as we can about what such an organ should do: and then look in the most likely place for these requirements to happen. . . .
>
> Being so vital an organ—if such an organ exists—it will need to be almost perfectly protected from all risk of trauma or disturbance from external circumstances. (9:67, 69)

After evaluation, she decided that the organ was behind the eyes and that the organ is part of or related to the hypothalmus, the organ which lies below the brain and controls body temperature (9:72–73 cf. 273).

But other Western acupuncturists have disagreed and either assigned it a different organ or remained silent. Chiropractor and touch for health inventor John Thie claims the organ related to the triple-warmer is the thyroid gland at the front of the neck (20:101).

Contradictory Theories and Practices

Another indication of the unscientific nature of acupuncture is the incredible contradictions in theory and practice one encounters. Dr. William McGarey observes,

> We have been told that knowledge of the meridian and its location is very important in practice—that it is not so bad to miss a [acupuncture] point

> with a needle as long as one stays on the line of the meridian. Yet other teachers insist it is vitally important to hit the acupuncture point itself. The picture remains unclear. (14:29)

Did you ever wonder how the acupuncture points that supposedly reside along the meridians were first determined? Acupuncture points are not uniform for each person; they vary from school to school and also from individual to individual. Austin explains how the Chinese attempted to resolve the problem:

> How are we going to set about describing the exact position of acupuncture points? What standard of measurement can be used that will be valid for a child or adult, for a dwarf or a giant?
>
> Thousands of years ago the Chinese solved this difficulty of accurate description. . . . They devised a flexible unit, a "Chinese inch" which varies from person to person, and from one part of the body to another and yet is always valid.
>
> For any given individual this A.U.M. [acupuncture unit of measurement] will be constant, although even on the individual allowance has to be made for his personal variations. There is, therefore, a standard technique for doing this. (9:26)

But how does one determine the acupuncture unit of measurement? It varies from school to school; for example, some French and German schools make it the width of the last phalange of the middle finger of the patient. Traditionally, however, it is determined by "the distance between the ends of the outer folds (thumb side) formed at the articulations of the first and second, and the second and third phalanges of the fully flexed middle finger" (9:27).

Variations in determing the A.U.M. plus additional considerations leave no objective standard for locating acupuncture points (9:27). This explains why the number of acupuncture points ranges from three hundred sixty-five to two thousand or more.

If a hundred acupuncturists were to determine the acupuncture points on the same individual, do you think they would all agree? If they wouldn't, then how does any acupuncturist know he is doing "proper" acupuncture? There is also the problem of contradictions in diagnosis. Acupuncturists do not always agree on which illnesses or diseases are related to which meridians (9:44). But without an objective standard, accurate diagnosis is impossible.

Consider for a moment how difficult any really accurate diagnosis would be in any acupuncture practice. First, you have the underlying Taoist premise of a mystical life energy flowing through invisible channels called meridians. Acupuncture points supposedly lie somewhere along these meridians, but their position can vary from school to school and person to person. Diagnosis of a patient's physical condition is made on the basis of an "intuitive" examination of the pulse, at least for acupuncturists who use the pulses. After examination, the "proper" acupuncture point must be needled (or maybe not) in order to correct the imbalance of *chi*.

But who can explain how objective physiological diagnosis can be made on the basis of a subjective intuition concerning the pulses, or on the basis of a "proper" location of acupoints? How? Various schools of acupuncture also have different approaches toward their use of the meridians (16:ix–x). Although there are traditionally twelve meridians, some use twenty-six, some use up to sixty (16:ix). Again, the number of acupuncture points varies from three hundred sixty-five to two thousand or more (410:182). If some acupuncturists find all the points they need in the ear, of what relevance are the acupoints along the meridians of the body?

Furthermore, psychics who claim to be able to "see" inside the body allege that they are uncovering many additional meridians and acupuncture points. Where is the line drawn? What does one do when one psychic's clairvoyance contradicts another's, as is often the case?

So what value do the acupuncture points and needling have? Apparently, none:

> Doubts have also been raised concerning the necessity to locate the exact points indicated on the acupuncture charts. Acupuncture stimuli are being given in such a chaotic way in China, writes Professor Wall, that it is impossible to start investigating the practice of acupuncture scientifically on this foundation. Research on volunteers in Toronto have shown that the needle-stimulation of wrong points led to the same pain-relieving effect. (2:43)

With a diagnosis that is entirely subjective, with contrary acupuncture charts, a wide variety of meridians and points, how is it possible for any acupuncturist to claim that he can do accurate diagnosis and treatment based upon precise correlations of meridians and points to organs and treatments? How can acupuncture possibly claim to work on the basis of its stated principles?

Scientific Evaluation

From 1972 on, acupuncture has been subjected to a large number of scientific tests (e.g., 1:172–174). Despite excessive claims, the only symptom for which acupuncture needling initially seemed to have clinical validation was pain relief. But even so, this never verified the traditional interpretation of acupuncture based on the flow of *chi* along alleged meridians. A variety of theories were proposed to explain how acupuncture might work, which had nothing to do with the mystical life energy concepts of Chinese Taoism (1:70–75).

For example, the idea of alleviation of pain through distraction (counterstimulation) is widely known; the intense stimulation of one part of the body may decrease the sensations felt in another. "This concept of *counterirritation* is an extremely old method of pain control and has been verified experimentally" (1:70–71). The body is also known to have a number of "trigger" points. These are small areas of local tenderness usually noted with muscle or joint pain. Stimulation of the trigger point, particularly injecting them with a local anesthetic, can bring about profound and prolonged pain relief (1:71).

An earlier text co-authored by Dr. Weldon had accepted the use of acupuncture, in certain situations, for pain relief. This acceptance, if not recommendation, was based upon the apparent effectiveness of acupuncture-mediated pain relief and upon this only. "Clinical trials have not established the effectiveness of acupuncture in any other area" (1:66–75). We noted that where pain relief is concerned, "cultural conditioning, belief that the procedure will work, friendly surroundings, and mood also appear to affect the results" and that "the duration of pain relief may range from transient to permanent" (1:70).

After an evaluation of possible physiological mechanisms explaining the analgesic effect of acupuncture, we concluded:

> The only by-product of ancient Chinese medicine which has been reasonably validated is a treatment of chronic pain with counter-stimulation therapy, using either needles or electrical pulses. If you are considering receiving such treatment, your pain problem should be evaluated by a qualified physician and the therapist should be someone trained in conventional anatomy and physiology, not in meridians and life energy. . . . The use of acupuncture for treating other medical problems, such as high

> blood pressure, hearing loss, obesity, and so on, has not been validated to our knowledge by any controlled study and is extremely suspect. (1:92)

Notice also that counterirritation therapy is not limited to acupuncture; acupuncture may produce the analgesic effect of counter stimulation, but so may other treatments.

Nevertheless, many researchers became convinced that, Taoism aside, acupuncture needling itself (using traditional acupuncture points) was somehow an effective analgesic. But this conclusion is probably not justified, or justified only in part. Below we will cite reasons for largely rejecting these researchers' conclusions.

Inseparable from Taoism

We have already shown why classical acupuncture practice cannot be separated from its Taoist philosophy. If one is practicing acupuncture apart from Taoism, one is simply not practicing *true* acupuncture. This is why psychological or even occultic factors are so important to the success of acupuncture and why the results are so contradictory when one attempts to use the practice of needling scientifically, apart from Taoist belief.

No one can deny that acupuncture works *best* when both acupuncturist and patient *believe* in ancient Taoism and all that accompanies it. This is a point that must be reemphasized. Referring to the underlying occultic Taoist philosophy of acupuncture, Dr. Pfeifer illustrates its importance by citing a leading practitioner's views:

> What is downplayed by some and explained away by others, is fiercely defended by a third group. The amazing effects of acupuncture can be reached "only when the practitioner follows the principles handed down through the millennia," declares acupuncturist-specialist, Dr. Schnorrenberger. He even rejects the combination of Western diagnosis and Chinese treatment. Never should Western acupuncturists choose their needling sites according to scientific Western medicine. "It is absolutely necessary," he writes, "that acupuncturists follow the theories of ancient Chinese medicine, if they want to see significant success. If they disregard these ancient theories, then they can only practice an unspecific stimulation therapy at best." (2:32)

Similar statements have been made by modern Taoist philosopher, George Ohsawa, the father of macrobiotics. He expressly states, "*Oriental*

medicine cannot be separated from its philosophical underpinnings. Many parapsychologists and psychics, therefore, regard acupuncture as a proof of their occult teachings" (2:32; cf. 439:1–15).

Reliance on Analgesics

Not only is faith in Taoism important to acupuncture success, but much of the pain relief associated with acupuncture appears to originate in the pain relieving medication given during treatment. A 1976 publication of the National Academy of Sciences, *Acupuncture Anesthesia in the People's Republic of China* (Washington, D.C., 1976) noted that fully 90 percent of all operations in China were *not* performed using acupuncture for pain relief, and that, even when it was used, Western methods of anesthesia were employed (2:42).

In another publication Paul Reisser, M.D., observed:

> Some especially interesting commentary was written by Dr. John J. Bonica, chairman of both the department of anesthesiology at the University of Washington and the Ad Hoc Committee of Acupuncture of the National Institutes of Health, and a long-time student of the phenomenon of pain. Bonica's careful observations of acupuncture anesthesia in China illuminated a number of facts which were misunderstood by previous observers.
>
> Initial reports, for example, suggested that this form of anesthesia was used in the majority of surgical operations in China. From statistics supplied by the Chinese, however, Bonica calculated that it is used in less than ten percent of all cases. Furthermore, while apparently reducing the sensation of pain, acupuncture usually does not totally eliminate pain or other uncomfortable sensations. (Some writers have observed that the word anesthesia, meaning "absense of sensation," does not apply to acupuncture, and that the word hypalgesia, meaning "decrease of pain," is more appropriate.)
>
> Nearly every patient receives, in addition to needling, a narcotic or barbiturate injection prior to surgery or a slow "drip" of narcotic (usually Demerol) into a vein during the operation. Local anesthesia is frequently injected into sensitive structures before they are cut or manipulated. . . . Emergency surgery is essentially never done using acupuncture. While in a large series of operations a ninety-four percent rate of effectiveness was reported in a major Chinese publication, Bonica pointed out that a large number of these patients experienced pain to the point where significant supplemental medication was required. (1:66–67)

That the pain medication routinely given in acupuncture treatments is sufficient to control pain is revealed in that needles have sometimes inadvertently fallen out during operations, and yet patients did not feel any pain—because the pain medication alone was sufficient to prevent it (2:43). Dr. Pfeifer recalls, "I have seen for myself, that low doses of analgesics may suffice in individual patients whilst an [surgical] operation is being performed. . . . It takes less analgesic to produce freedom from pain than was assumed before" (2:43).

The Power of Belief

Acupuncture does work in pain relief, but not consistently. More and more researchers are saying that acupuncture belongs in the realm of psychosomatic medicine: The counter-stimulation effect of the needling itself has less power to produce pain relief than a patient's own faith. In essence, when acupuncture works in pain relief, it usually works on the basis of psychological and cultural factors, not biochemical or scientific ones. This is one reason why, "In the last few years the gap between acupuncture practitioners and rational medicine has widened and will continue to do so" (410:191).

Even if a person *doesn't* believe in Taoism, his belief in the acupuncturist or the technique itself may be powerful enough to produce dramatic results.

All of us can remember when we were children and our mother kissed the injury, the pain really did disappear. Attributing special power to the acupuncturist or to acupuncture itself is a bit like attributing magical power to a mother's kiss. No one doubts the mind has the potential to regulate pain control; by sheer willpower every professional athlete has experienced dramatic mental control over pain during vigorous workouts. When people strongly believe in a health practice, something similar is in operation and can account for its success.

The power of belief in a given technique is illustrated by a study done at the University of San Francisco. Fifty patients were to have a wisdom tooth removed. Without medication this is an excruciating procedure; nevertheless, satisfactory pain relief "was reached even with completely ineffectual medications, provided that the patient *believed* in them" (2:42).

Scientific testing has also proved that those who believe in acupuncture are far more likely to benefit from it, so much so that many researchers have concluded the practice is useless without such belief. "The method is not indicated," says German acupuncture professor Dr. Herget, "when patients have a negative attitude toward the procedure" (2:48).

Dr. Christian Klopfenstein observed in a letter to Dr. Pfeifer:

> Personally I believe that acupuncture is not a very accurate science. Even if some aspects have scientific explanations, nothing is very sure. . . . It seems obvious to me that the *spirit of magic and suggestion* have a strong influence on the results. All these unconventional methods demand the *faith* of the patient. (2:50)

Apparently, then, faith in the practice of acupuncture—not acupuncture needling itself—is largely responsible for pain relief.

Does Not Function as Claimed

When acupuncture was first studied in the West, the claim that it was successful only due to hypnosis and suggestion were often ridiculed. After almost thirty years of studies and research, this conclusion may turn out to be the most correct of all.

As far back as the mid-1970s, research was conducted which strongly suggested acupuncture's effectiveness was due to such factors. The *San Francisco Chronicle* for October 14, 1976, cited two controlled research studies done at major American medical centers and reported before a meeting of the American Society of Anesthesiologists.

In one study conducted at the Albert Einstein College of Medicine in New York and at Montefiore Hospital, one hundred ninety-nine patients received eleven hundred acupuncture treatments for chronic pain problems associated with neuritis, neuralgia, arthritis, low back pain, and blocked blood vessels.

The patients were randomly divided into two groups. One group received the standard hand or electrical needling as used in China. Needling was done at the classical Chinese acupuncture points supposed to bring pain relief. The other group had needles inserted at various places in the body where acupuncture texts predicted they would do no good at all. But, as it turned out, "There was no significant difference at all in the results among the various groups of patients." In both groups, some were helped and some were not.

There was, however, one important difference, not relating to acupuncture, but to hypnosis. Every patient was tested beforehand for susceptibility to hypnosis. Significantly, the "excellent to good" results occurred among thirty percent of the patients who were hypnotized easily, but among those who were difficult or impossible to hypnotize, only thirteen percent experienced positive results from acupuncture. The conclusion was that "the limited success of acupuncture in the experiments depended as much as anything else on the 'ceremonial effect' of the treatment and on the fact that most of the patients believed in the method because of the widespread publicity acupuncture had received in recent years" (192).

Another study was conducted at Emory University Medical School in Atlanta which cast further doubt on acupuncture's effectiveness. Increasingly strong electrical shocks were given to a group of paid volunteer subjects; pain threshold and tolerance were determined for each subject:

> Then each received a treatment without knowing what it was: Classical acupuncture needling plus an injection of morphine; needling in a non-classical spot plus morphine; classical acupuncture plus a shot of plain salt water; and fake acupuncture plus a salt water shot.
>
> The result: There was no significant difference at all in the subjects' threshold for pain or their tolerance to it—regardless of whether the acupuncture was orthodox or unorthodox or whether they received morphine or a "placebo." (192)

Other research was described in reports issued in scholarly journals such as *Annals of Internal Medicine* (Vol. 84, 1976, pp. 381–384); *New England Journal of Medicine* (Vol. 293, 1975, pp. 375–378); and *Pain* (Vol. 3, 1977, pp. 3–24) which obtained similar results and also indicated psychological components to acupuncture pain relief.

We cite these mid-1970 studies for a reason. Even fifteen years ago these studies had cast doubt upon the effectiveness of acupuncture. Yet because of all the mystique, misinformation, and hoopla over the practice in the last twenty years, most people today believe it to be an effective treatment for all sorts of ailments—a viewpoint which is clearly unsubstantiated.

This illustrates that we must be very careful to adopt a skeptical view toward new medical claims until they have really been proven. In 1978, one encyclopedia of unconventional medicine reported:

> A Korean Professor, Kim Bong Han, has demonstrated photographically the existence of the meridians as a separate physiological system. He has also shown that the meridians contain DNA and RNA—two substances basic to life and reproduction. His work, documented with histological, pathological and photographic evidence is now available in English. (76:60)

But this just wasn't true. As Dr. Reisser discussed elsewhere:

> Professor Kim Bong Han of North Korea did extensive work with animals and humans which reportedly showed systems of ducts and superficial corpuscles in the skin corresponding to acupuncture points and meridians. Radioactive phosphorus (P32) injected into the points of the abdominal wall of a rabbit was found to disperse along lines toward neighboring points in a manner suggesting a meridian system. (How rabbit points were determined in the first place is not explained.) In other anatomical and histological (that is, microscopic tissue) studies, he claims to have found four systems of ducts and to have determined the electrical, mechanical, biochemical and embryological characteristics of them and the fluid they contain. (Probably this is the basis for Dr. Thie's confident statement about meridians [that they have been scientifically demonstrated].)
>
> Unfortunately, none of these results have been replicated in the West, although one might argue that few scientists have been searching for Bong Han Corpuscles. It seems unlikely, however, that such an elaborate system would have escaped the notice of Western anatomists over the past five centuries. Felix Mann, an experienced English acupuncturist, cites evidence that the Bong Han structures are based on distortions of tissue occurring in the preparation of microscope slides. Even if the Bong Han system is eventually verified, it remains in the realm of physical structure and offers no support for the circulation of invisible life energies. (1:74–75)

Peter Skrabanek is an authority on the physiology of pain. He has authored three books on substance P, a key peptide involved in nociception,* plus over seventy papers, many in the field of the neurotransmitters of pain. He observes in his "Acupuncture: Past, Present and Future":

> There is no denying that acupuncture is effective in some patients with functional and psychosomatic disorders. So is placebo. It is also a fact that the acupuncture effect is unpredictable and unreliable. Results depend on the [person's] faith. Negative findings . . . may reflect negative attitudes on the part of the experimental subject.
>
> The simple explanation for a better average response to acupuncture than to more conventional placebos is its very unconventionality, the mystique surrounding an ancient-Oriental ritual [etc.]. . . . By discussing acupuncture in terms of placebo, distraction, suggestion, and hypnosis, and taking into account the natural history of self-limiting and functional disorders that acupuncture is supposed to cure, it will lose its attraction, its novelty, and its power over the mind of the gullible. The gullible include scientists. (410:190)

---

* A nociceptor is any sensory receptor for painful stimuli.

Some scientists had suggested that needling somehow stimulated the body endorphins. The endorphin hypothesis suggests that pain relief may be produced when the body's natural pain-killers, called endorphins, are released as a by-product of needle stimulation. But, "There is no good evidence that acupuncture-induced pain relief is mediated by endorphin release" (410:189).

Further, Dr. Skrabanek discusses the relationship between hypnosis and acupuncture:

> Kroeger, who is experienced in hypnoanalgesia, pointed out the similarities between acupuncture and hypnosis: conditioning, ritual, indoctrination, autogenic training, misdirection, autosuggestion. In China, the strong traditional belief in the power of needles was further augmented by sociopolitical rewards for good behavior during acupuncture [even if one felt pain].
>
> Moore and Berk wrote: . . . "in demonstrating . . . a possible link between response to treatment and susceptibility to hypnosis, we are challenging those who believe that acupuncture offers a unique approach to pain control." (410:191)

Dr. Skrabanek believes that the search for a physical cause to the successes of acupuncture (such as the theory of endorphin release) is futile and doomed from the start "since the problem is not biochemical but psychological and cultural" (411:191).

Consider the following factors commonly related to acupuncture practice: strong faith, belief, or trust; suggestion, autosuggestion, hypnosis; the standard use of anesthesia; overestimation of surgical pain; conditioning and ritual (indoctrination or other special preparation prior to use); and counter-stimulation and distraction produced by needling.

When the above factors are considered, the effectiveness of acupuncture per se is seen to be non-existent. Why? Because every demonstrated effect of acupuncture can be explained on the basis of other factors. If so, then acupuncture has no scientific validity. This is why an exhaustive review of all the studies done on acupuncture to date (meta-analysis) concluded that acupuncture was at best a powerful placebo (462).

But most acupuncturists are not listening to the scientific challenge to their methods. Rather, they are abandoning science altogether and returning to Taoism, or rationalizing their practices and evading the issue. Let us give you one example: The only apparent "development" in acupuncture for twenty-five hundred years has been the increase of acupoints from the tradi-

tional three hundred sixty-five (corresponding to the days of the year, the human microcosm mirroring cosmic time, the macrocosm) to over two thousand. But,

> This proliferation has been skillfully exploited by the acupuncture apologists who obfuscate negative results from controlled trials—since any random point is more likely than not to be an acupoint, "the impossibility of choosing placebo points" precludes the possibility of an objective evaluation of acupuncture! (410:182)

Consider also the deliberate attempt at misinformation promoted by some leading acupuncturists:

> In the last few years the gap between acupuncture practitioners and rational medicine has widened and will continue to do so. In the keynote address at the founding convention of the American Association of Acupuncturists and Oriental Medicine in Los Angeles in 1981, R. A. Dale announced the coming of the great age of holistic harmony in which acupuncture will play a pivotal role. Since his remarks represent the mainstream of acupuncture ideology, they are worth our attention: "Acupuncture is a part of a larger struggle going on today between the old and the new, between dying and rebirthing, between the very decay and death of our species and our fullest liberation. Acupuncture is part of a new age which facilitates integral health and the flowering of our humanity."
>
> Dale differentiated five attitudes of the medical profession to acupuncture: (1) "the reactionary extreme," which should be ignored, isolated, and exposed; (2) "the conservative opposition," which should be supplied with data and statistics ("although the American Medical Association will not be convinced by such arguments, some of its members will be"); (3) "the liberal support," whose members are "usually cautious not to discuss their views with their colleagues from Groups 1 and 2," but they are "excellent candidates" for Group 4, "the progressive support"; (4) "support by medical heretics," who are "excellent candidates not only for active membership in our association but for leadership roles."
>
> The tactics and strategy to be adopted by the acupuncturists when dealing with the public are, according to Dale's advice, as follows: (1) undermine their faith in modern medicine and science, (2) educate them in their need for alternative medicine, and (3) explain to them that what they need is not a medical specialist but an acupuncture generalist.
>
> The openness of this document is disarming. Let us note, however, that Dale's "New Age" is matched only by the WHO's [World Health Organization] messianic rhetoric of "health for all by the year of two thousand." Unreal promises and false hopes raised by the medical profession, no less

> irrational than the illusions of "alternative" medicine, deserve to be criticized as mercilessly as the deceptive fancies and will-o'-the-wisps of the holistic prophets and quackupuncturists. (410:191–192)

That acupuncture as commonly practiced is not scientific, and therefore potentially hazardous, should be obvious. The acupuncturist who diagnoses by pulses believes that he can diagnose energy imbalances in any given organ, give a prognosis, and even warn of unsuspected future disease. "This miraculous ability of the radial pulses to communicate information about the entire body would seem to require a clairvoyant examiner. It has no basis in physiology" (1:58). There is no known scientific or medical basis on which traditional acupuncture can possibly work. Any acupuncturist who is successfully diagnosing patient conditions on the basis of his pulse work or other methods is more probably involved with psychic/spiritistic diagnosis.

Occultic Potential

Because acupuncture is based on an occultic philosophy involving manipulation of mystical life energies; because acupuncture is traditionally associated with magic, astrology, and the occult; and because many modern acupuncturists are really psychics who operate through occult powers, no doubt some of the successes in acupuncture are also due to spiritistic forces.

The occultic philosophy behind acupuncture is unmistakable. The *Nei Ching* claims that the acupuncturist should be trained in divination (15:97), such as astrology, so that practices may be related to the most opportune times as determined by the heavens. The *Nei Ching* asserts, "All the laws of acupuncture must attend upon the sun, the moon, the planets, the stars, and the four seasons. These are the eight factors of the atmosphere and when the atmosphere is established one can apply acupuncture" (15:217). Astrological and other timing is important because, "according to Far Eastern medicine, man is something like a cybernetic who is under the control of external cosmic influences" (17:37). But as the authors have discussed elsewhere, genuine power in astrology often originates in spiritism (44:201–255).

The *Nei Ching* itself is a magical text which can even divine the time of one's death:

> When two elements of *Yin* attack, death will occur after thirteen days at dusk. When three elements of *Yang* attack, everything swells and death ensues after three days. . . . When two elements of *Yang* attack, the patient's sickness will recur, death cannot be warded off, and the patient will die after ten days. (15:130–131)

The concepts of the *yin* and *yang* are also closely related if not inseparable from the philosophy on which the Chinese system of divination known as the *I Ching* is based. One acupuncturist observes, " . . . we should thoroughly understand that the theory of the five elements, which is the same as the scheme of the *I Ching*, is only an elaboration of the more general and fundamental theory of *yin* and *yang*" (17:26).

Some parapsychologists study acupuncture as a psychic phenomenon (14:xii); the spirit world has encouraged its use through mediums such as Edgar Cayce (14:vii, 13); both traditional and modern application teach the occultic idea that *chi* is divine energy or God (14:123–124) and that man is also God (17:9).

Because acupuncture is based on an occultic philosophy, Taoism, and is traditionally replete with paganism, classical treatment by acupuncture, even in the West, often involves occultic aspects. In addition, in new age medicine today, any given acupuncture practitioner may combine his practice with a wide variety of new age healing techniques, most of which are occultic. Acupuncture may be used with psychic diagnosis, astrologic medicine, kundalini arousal, applied kinesiology, shamanism, reflexology, homeopathy, channeling or spiritism, chiropractic, and virtually any other technique or method an acupuncturist may find useful.

The ease with which acupuncture may be incorporated into other treatments is seen in the following citation:

> It would be evidence of narrowmindedness to reject *a priori* a synthesis of acupuncture and other methods. . . . The ideal therapist is one whose spirit is pliable enough, and his knowledge is broad enough, for him to use at one and the same time, the quintessence of all known reputable methods. There is no need for conflict between adherents of acupuncture schools, or different methods: on the contrary, the ideal is a combining of them all into the one and only valid therapy, namely the one that heals.
>
> As far as I have been able to understand Far Eastern medicine-philosophy and practice, the Far-Eastern practitioner never relied upon acupuncture as the sole means of effecting a cure. (9:267, see chapter 17)

For example, consider the integration of acupuncture and homeopathy:

> The medicine philosophy of Samuel Hahnemann, as expounded in *Organon,* represents the nearest Western medicine philosophy to that of the Far-Orient that I have so far come across. Many passages in this book of his could as easily seem to be imagined as quotations from some Far Eastern text. In support of this there seems to be the fact of the widespread and profound appreciation of Hahnemann in such countries as India. The suitability of a "marriage" between Acupuncture and Homeopathy was envisaged by Dr. de la Fuye, who made what was probably the first attempt to bring these two therapies together. (9:266)

Because acupuncture rejects science and claims to manipulate mystical or psychic energies, the door is left open to spiritistic operations performed under the names of these energies. As Dr. Pfeifer observes,

> The acupuncturists' failure to present scientific evidence has created *a lush culture medium for occult therapies*. Increasingly, authors are not even bothering to explain acupuncture scientifically. They would rather rely on cosmic, spiritistic and occult powers, that are adorned with pseudo scientific labels. . . . (2:43–44)

Thus, an acupuncturist may be no more than a psychic/spiritistic healer who uses psychic abilities to diagnose or treat his patients under the concept of a universal life energy. When acupuncturists employ hand passes over alleged meridians to manipulate *chi,* the practice is indistinguishable from what many psychic healers do. Distinguishing a psychic or spiritistic input of energy from classical acupuncture theory that claims to manipulate invisible energies can be impossible. In acupuncture theory, every invisible power is traced back to *chi.* On what basis then can they be distinguished? Some acupuncturists have spirit guides and some claim to be able to manipulate the invisible *chi* energy merely by touch—again no different than what a psychic/spiritistic healer claims.

Acupuncture treatment may even involve or incorporate the dangerous yogic phenomenon of *kundalini arousal*. A number of psychics claim to have established a connection between *kundalini* energy and the Chinese *chi* energy. They claim that the energies manipulated in acupuncture are the same energies that can be manipulated through the practice of *yoga* to arouse *kundalini.* As one illustration, we could cite the writings of psychic Hiroshi Motoyama (11;13;18). Motoyama claims that the occult anatomies in Chinese medicine, as illustrated in acupuncture, were derived from and in many ways parallel to the occult anatomies of India; just as the Chinese meridians are associated with internal organs, so are the yogic *chakras.*

Finally, courses in learning acupuncture are frequently interrelated with Chinese culture, herbal medicine, Taoist, or other new age meditative practices and philosophy (e.g., 191:31).

Although there are a few practitioners who attempt to retain a scientific approach to acupuncture, most do not. Acupuncture in the main is either quackery, an occult practice, or potentially an occult practice. This is why it is also potentially dangerous.

The Physical Dangers of Acupuncture

Many have claimed that the responsible scientific use of acupuncture is physically safe. But we need to remember that most acupuncture is not practiced scientifically and regulation of the industry is nonexistent. The *American Medical Association Encyclopedia of Medicine* explains: "Currently there are few legal checks on acupuncturists in the U.S. and no formal qualification is necessary to practice" (313:66). This means that anyone can read a few books on the subject and begin practicing acupuncture.

Good practitioners can avoid infection, one of the most frequent side-effects of acupuncture treatment, by proper sterilization methods. But how many are scrupulous in this regard? Furthermore, religious traditions, which incorporate non-physical anatomies and "health" systems based on them, invariably warn of certain physical dangers associated with those practices.

Perhaps because we are dealing with occult energies and spiritistic powers, the physical hazards encountered are merely those that one normally finds in the world of occult practice in general (396; 131). Another possibility is that these practices may have the potential to damage the human organism in an as yet undetermined manner.

Nevertheless, like yoga writings, acupuncture texts do warn of potential dangers. For example,

> Some points are forbidden to the needle because treatment with the needle at the point is dangerous. As an example, a needle inserted at a point known as "blue death" causes death by stopping the heart action. This point is *strictly* forbidden to the needle, and as with other points forbidden to needle, alternative methods of treatment must be used. (10:25)

Another heeds,

> Note this caution: Be very careful indeed about using the heart meridian in cases of heart disease. The acupuncture novice is advised to steer clear of the heart meridian (and the circulation meridian) in heart disease or where heart disease is suspected.
>
> According to the wise masters of acupuncture there is only one safe way to treat heart disease by acupuncture; and that is by what is known as "applying the five elements laws." (9:29–30)

But what does Taoist philosophy have to do with safely treating heart disease? And what about unrecognized and undetected heart disease? Heart disease is America's number one killer; millions of people may not even know they have such a condition. And yet this same text goes on to state that "the heart meridian is of special value for the treatment of certain psychological and/or emotional states" (9:30). Another acupuncturist, who is an M.D., warns, "Acupuncture, at any point, should never be used during normal pregnancy. . . . Use of acupuncture during pregnancy might bring about the loss of the pregnancy" (14:55).

A report of the British Medical Association observed that, besides being a possible way of transmitting the AIDS virus, other problems were associated with normal acupuncture treatments. "The three hundred sixty-five traditional [acupuncture] points run near, some perilously so, to vital structures, and complications ranging from the minor to the serious and the fatal have been reported" (121:67).

Dr. Samuel Pfeifer, M.D., warns:

> Complications and failures are not infrequent but are rarely mentioned. An article in the *Journal of the American Medical Association* (JAMA) describes various severe complications after acupuncture treatment. The list includes infections at the needling sites, misdiagnoses, and even puncturing of the lungs.
>
> Especially tragic is the case of a physician who, while attending an introductory seminar on acupuncture, suffered a heart attack. Instead of rushing him to the hospital, the various "specialists" experimented with their needles on their unfortunate colleague. The ambulance crew who tried to resuscitate him were hindered at their actions as multiple small needles had to be removed from the patient's upper lip to enable a proper oxygen supply to be administered. . . . The physician expired on his way to the hospital. (2:46)

Dr. Pfeifer issues a stern warning saying that controlled scientific studies have repeatedly confirmed the truth that acupuncture treatment is totally ineffective for organic disease, and therefore is worse than useless when it prevents proper treatment from being administered (2:46).

❧ ❧ ❧

As with new age medicine in general, acupuncture is either quackery or occultic. It does not and cannot operate on the basis of its stated Taoist principles.

Altered States of Consciousness

Definition: The deliberate cultivation of abnormal states of consciousness (states not normally experienced apart from a specific technique or program to develop them).

Founder: Unknown

How Does It Claim to Work? Proponents claim that altered states allegedly produce a "higher" state of consciousness or "being," including dramatic revelations and a positive restructuring of the participant's world view.

Scientific Evaluation: Science cannot evaluate subjective claims concerning a particular state of consciousness. Scientific research in this area is a mixture of investigating normal, marginally altered consciousness (e.g., dreams) and occultic and parapsychological exploration of mystical, occultic states.

Occultic Potential: Spirit contact, psychic transformation.

Major Problem: Occultic associations.

Biblical/Christian Evaluation: Forbidden on the basis of occultic associations.

Potential Dangers: Mental illness; occult bondage; spirit possession.

TEN

ALTERED STATES OF CONSCIOUSNESS*

Psychologist and new age consciousness researcher Kenneth Ring of the University of Connecticut observes, "Not since the early days of psychology has there been so much attention devoted to the question of the nature of consciousness, and probably no period in Western psychology has exceeded the present one in the interest taken in manipulating states of consciousness" (374:125). John White's (ed.) *What is Enlightenment?: Exploring the Goal of the Spiritual Path* is illustrative: It contains fifteen essays by some of the world's leading pundits of consciousness extolling "the new global quest for higher consciousness and transcendence" (376). Included are essays by Zen Buddhist Alan Watts; transpersonal psychologist Ken Wilbur, the alleged "Einstein of consciousness research"; guru-spiritists Da Free John, Meher Baba, and Gopi Krishna; drug experimenter and "perennial philosopher" Aldous Huxley; plus noted professors of religion and psychiatry such as Houston Smith and Roger Walsh.

Today, millions of people are purposely altering their consciousness in a spiritual quest having uncertain parameters; "enlightenment" and conscious-

* By altered states of consciousness, we refer to the cultivation of deeper and, by our definition, *abnormal* states of consciousness, i.e., those not normally experienced apart from deliberate cultivation and usually, but not exclusively, developed in conjunction with some religious or occultic practice or goal. We do not refer to those normal but different states of consciousness such as daydreams, reverie, sleep, imagination, etc.

ness experimentation have become big business (304; 337). According to doctors Villoldo and Krippner,

> Anthropologists have estimated that there are at least four thousand societies in the world today; about ninety percent of them have institutionalized at least one set of procedures for systematic cultivation of specific kinds of altered states. (46:198)

But altered states of consciousness, or ASCs, are also widely utilized in the field of new age medicine. First, their use in the development of many holistic health techniques is suspected. Because so many originators of new age health methods were psychics, spiritists, and occultists who routinely practiced entering altered states of consciousness, it is not unexpected that information received in these states influenced the development of these systems (see chapter 6).

Second, altered states of consciousness are employed in numerous holistic health techniques. In most forms of concentrated psychic diagnosis, psychic healing, and psychic surgery these states are considered essential. New age techniques as diverse as therapeutic touch, chromotherapy or auric healing, meditation, biofeedback, hypnotic regression ("past life") therapy, radionics, shamanism, dream work, yoga, crystal healing, visualization, channeling, and many others may utilize altered states of consciousness either for the practitioner in diagnosis or for the patient in treatment.

Today, altered states are seen as a legitimate field of exploration not only in medicine, but also in a variety of schools of psychotherapy, particularly transpersonal psychology, and the multi-disciplinary field of what is termed "consciousness research."

For many people, ASCs are increasingly seen as a "key" to personal development, as a method for unlocking the secrets of the creation, and as the means to secure the higher "evolution" of individual consciousness and thus of humanity. But few have any idea just where this road may take them.

Occultic Potential

Historically the linkage between pagan cultures and the manipulation of consciousness for occult purposes, such as spirit possession, has been strong. This indicates that the spirit world has a vested interest in encouraging the exploration of altered states of consciousness along specific lines, especially those devoted to spirit contact.

The history of Eastern religion, Western occultism, modern parapsychology, etc., constantly reveals the importance of developing altered states of consciousness for contacting other dimensions. Revelations from the spirits themselves often stress their importance for this very purpose (refs. 287–301).

Nobel scientist Sir John Eccles once commented that the human brain was "a machine that a ghost can operate" (285:19). His statement illustrates the truth that given the proper conditions, the human mind can become an open door permitting the influence of spirits. How can the mind be so affected that spirits gain some measure of control over it? Altered states of consciousness are the principal method offering the proper conditions.

Altered states may involve a large variety of subjects—everything from hypnosis and other trance states to possession states (as in mediumism and shamanism) to altered states that are characteristically pathological (as in *kundalini* arousal and shamanism), to directed visualization and imagery, lucid dreaming, drug-induced states of consciousness, meditation and biofeedback-induced consciousness, and many others.

Why do so many different practices have the potential to induce spirit contact? Because nearly all altered states share a degree of common ground, and this common ground is conducive to spirit influences. In essence, almost any altered state is at least capable of producing spirit encounters. When such meetings are deliberately sought, they occur regularly.

For this reason altered states have undergirded virtually all of Eastern and Western occultism (e.g. 253): They are typically prerequisites for the spirit contact necessary for success along the given "spiritual" path. The needed spirit contact and/or manifestation of power (e.g., the development of psychic abilities) typically do not occur apart from the requisite altered state. Thus, virtually all methods which attempt to induce ASCs (and there are scores) have the potential to lead to spirit contact and even to spirit possession (e.g. 111). The individual technique is irrelevant; the altered state itself is instrumental in permitting spiritistic influence.

The research of sociologist Erika Bourguignon indicated that of 488 societies observed, over ninety percent had made trance and spirit possession states socially acceptable (146:16–17). In the West today, trance and possession states are also becoming more acceptable. One only need consider new age promoters like Shirley MacLaine, the vast influence of the modern channeling phenomenon, (e.g., 287–290, see chapter 13) or the millions of followers of Eastern gurus.

The research of Tal Brooke in *Riders of the Cosmic Circuit* offers a detailed examination and critique of Eastern metaphysics including the altered states of consciousness found in the meditative disciplines of endless numbers of gurus. Altered states of consciousness are revealed as typically the means to spirit contact and possession (111:39–50, 107–139, 165–208).

In fact, in many quarters what was once termed "spirit possession" is now often simply called "altered consciousness." Raymond Prince's (ed.) *Trance and Possession States* (1968) and Erika Bourguignon's (ed.) *Religion, Altered States of Consciousness and Social Change* (1973) are only two research studies revealing such connections. The reason much new age literature fails to make any real distinction between the two states is simply because potentially they are so closely associated and difficult to separate. Spirit possession is, finally, just another altered state.

Consider the following further illustrations connecting spiritism and altered states:

- When modern parapsychology began in the late nineteenth century, the subjects examined were typically spiritistic mediums. Yet most of these mediums had become mediums and contacted the spirit world by experimentation with various forms of hypnosis and meditation-induced altered states of consciousness (see chapter 19).

- What some researchers term the "Shamanistic State of Consciousness" (SSC) is considered essential for the shaman to contact his "power animals" or spirit guides.

- Spirit mediums routinely enter a light to moderate trance which permits the spirits to assume control over and speak messages through them (see chapter 13).

- Occultic meditation is acknowledged by almost everyone as an excellent method to contact the spirit world (see chapter 19).

- Spirits can even be contacted through a supervised program of dream work.

- Many new age disciplines offer various techniques of visualization as a help to contacting the spirit world.

- Even drugs, such as psychedelics and marijuana, have been known to foster contact with the spirit world. (374:149; 368; cf. 371:72)

In general, then, altered states of consciousness are potential open doors to the spirit world.

Modern Consciousness Research

Modern "consciousness research" offers the perfect opportunity to blend traditional science (measuring the physical correlates of states of consciousness) and subjective experience (the personal cultivation of altered states for religious purposes). Because these states are so powerful and fascinating, many academic researchers today are blending their scientific expertise with their personal exploration of novel states of consciousness. The end result is one form of the new age scientist—a person academically trained in the field of science who attempts to integrate revelations from altered states and personal occultic development into his respective discipline.

One example is the eminent scientist Dr. John Lilly, perhaps best known for his research with dolphins. Lilly's autobiography, *The Scientist*, and his book, *The Deep Self*, reveal the typical connection between the exploration of altered states of consciousness, spirit contact and guidance, the terrible consequences of these practices, and the blending of scientific discipline with occultic practices and philosophy (369:109, 134–145, 180–198, 207–8). Since Lilly first published his book in 1978, thousands of scientists, strangely, have followed in his footstsps (370).

But the supposedly "scientific" process of "mapping" various states of consciousness is typically drawn from Eastern and occultic traditions which are notoriously dependent upon spiritistic influences (refs. 374; 336; 337; 338).

Further, numerous recent texts on the exploration of consciousness such as Ken Wilbur's *The Atman Project* (336), Stan and Christina Grof's (ed.) *Spiritual Emergencies* (337), Benjamin B. Wolman's and Montague Ullman's (ed.) *Handbook of States of Consciousness* (377), John White's (ed.) *Frontiers of Consciousness* (338) and *What is Enlightenment?* (376), Jeffrey Mishlove's *The Roots of Consciousness* (253) and dozens of others reveal that the modern exploration of altered states of consciousness is merely a sort of euphemism for psychic development, the exploration of the occult, and spirit contact.

Bourguignon observes that, "In traditional societies—and to a considerable extent in modern societies as well . . . altered states tend to be spoken of in connection with supernatural entities such as 'spirits'" (146:3; cf. p. 5).

According to Bourguignon, "the vast majority of societies" have socially institutionalized the phenomenon of altered states of consciousness and these states are typically those associated with spirit contact and spirit possession (146:3–5).

In fact, more than one text exploring altered or mystical states of consciousness has stated that the mystical state of consciousness and the state of spirit possession are one and the same. For example, Cambridge-educated John Ferguson observes in his *An Illustrated Encyclopedia of Mysticism* that spirit "possession . . . is the core of mystical experience" (118:148).

Potential Dangers

There are risks to cultivating altered states. First, they may induce mental illness in unstable individuals, or they may naturally progress to mental illness even with the sound of mind. Because no one can know if this will occur, the risks are similar to those of taking drugs. Exploring altered states is a bit like rushing down to the beach to watch the expected tidal wave. You may or may not be engulfed, but if you are, it will be too late to change your mind.

Arnold M. Ludwig, writing in Charles Tart's (ed.) *Altered States of Consciousness*, observes, "As a person enters or is in an ACS, he often experiences fear of losing his grip on reality and losing his self-control" (372:16). In one of her altered states, modern shamaness and best-selling author Lynn Andrews could not distinguish reality and believed she was going insane. "I was terrified. I began to inhale great breaths of air, gasping. I sobbed uncontrollably. I had finally done it—I had lost my mind" (375:183). Psychotherapist Elsa First comments, "There are risks in cultivating altered states of consciousness. One of these risks . . . may be a permanent alienation from ordinary human attachments" (373:65).

Those new agers who do successfully "integrate," such experiences may come to interpret them positively as an experience of "spiritual emergence" (337). But to redefine ASC-induced psychopathological experiences as some form of "higher consciousness" is simply unwarranted, yet more and more respected psychologists who have become personal explorers of consciousness are blurring the distinction between sanity and insanity. Many actually view insanity as a spiritual blessing (337:77; 374:149–150)! Unfortunately, they rarely seem to ask the right questions concerning the personal, social, and spiritual implications of their experiences.

As we have seen, altered states can open one to the supernatural realm and contact with spirits who are really demons (132; 141). Furthermore, that a legitimate connection exists between spirit-possession and some mental illness is undeniable. Even Kenneth Ring confesses,

> Another common occurrence when functioning at this level of consciousness is encountering "entities." Though sometimes benevolent, they are more often threatening and are intent on gaining control over the individual's body or consciousness. There are many cases of such instances of attempted or successful possession to be found in the literature on spiritualism, magic, witchcraft and madness, but in the West we have typically dismissed these symptoms of possession as hallucinations. . . .
>
> Such visitations are by no means restricted to those who have ingested a psychedelic agent—they are potentially available to anyone who has entered this region of consciousness by whatever means. . . .
>
> In my own view, many of the claims made by 'mental patients' that they are possessed by alien entities are best understood as representing a perfectly accurate assessment of what has happened to them. It is time that we began taking the concept of possession seriously instead of dismissing it as a superstition or an hallucination. (374:142–143, 150)

Another problem with altered states is their ability to profoundly affect the perception of the person who cultivates them. The ultimate goal of most programs to develop altered consciousness is the destruction of the "limited" personal self to "uncover" the alleged divinity of the "true" self. Leading consciousness researcher John White explains:

> But the critical point to be understood is this: the value of mystical and transformative states is not in producing some new experience but in *getting rid of the experiencer*. Getting rid, that is, of the egocentric consciousness which experiences life from a contracted, self-centered point of view rather than the free, unbound perspective of a sage who knows he or she is infinity operating through a finite form. . . .
>
> The perennial wisdom is unchanging; truth is one. That is agreed on by the sages of all major religions and sacred traditions, all hermetic philosophies, genuine mystery schools and higher occult paths. Enlightenment is the core truth of them all. Even more broadly, it is the essence of life—the goal of all growth, development, evolution. It is the discovery of what we ultimately are, the answer to the questions: Who am I? Why am I here? Where am I going? What is life all about? . . .

> *Enlightenment is realization of the truth of Being.* Our native condition, our true self is Being, traditionally called God. (376:xiii)

But significantly, the internal experience of oneself as "God" is often accomplished through possession by a spirit entity who manipulates one's states of consciousness toward such false perceptions (refs. 111; 131; 318; 229; 187; 244; 317).

Indeed, one may watch as the committed explorer of consciousness is slowly consumed by the spirits, the addiction increasing while the individual "self" is slowly dismantled for replacement by its new host. As in shamanism, the "normal, ordinary" world and the personal self are eventually obliterated even while the seeker of consciousness is increasingly linked to a shadowy, underground world of evil spirits whose control increases with each new "adventure" in consciousness. Let us cite one example, exerpted from an earlier text by the authors (132:40–41).

Carl was a qualified psychologist with a degree in physics and a personal interest in religion (especially Christianity) and in parapsychology, or the scientific study of the occult. His personal psychic abilities amazed not only himself but those who knew him. He was enormously excited by Aldous Huxley's *Doors of Perception*; what Huxley achieved by drugs Carl was certain he could achieve by psychic means: that, and perhaps more. Although fascinated by Christianity, Carl was convinced that the modern churches were corrupting the original teachings of Christ; hence, he sought "true Christianity" through occult means.

Consumed with a desire to find "original Christianity," he became personally involved in cultivating altered states of consciousness, reincarnation research, and astral travel. As his studies and involvement in the psychic world continued, he explored realm after realm. He was bright and enthusiastic, not to mention careful. Most of all he was *certain* he was on the road to vast personal discoveries. He had, in his view, all the right motives—and talent, abilities, and opportunities to complement them.

Eventually a midwestern university offered Carl a professorship and allowed him to both teach and continue his experiments, which provided numerous psychic and mystical experiences. Gradually, however, Carl admitted to himself that some deep alteration was taking place inside of him (318:419). He had earlier encountered some gnawing doubts about the fundamental nature of his spiritual path, but he suppressed them because their implications were too uncomfortable. Any doubt as to what kind of spirit was leading him could mean a total revision of his work; it could even mean resigning his professorship and renouncing his parapsychological research (318:418).

Giving up his research would have been costly, but after years of painstaking effort, benevolent motives, and great enthusiasm, Carl became consumed by forces so evil he ended up as an incoherent vegetable requiring exorcism and eleven months of hospitalization.

His eventual renouncement of all study and research in parapsychology was deplored by fellow colleagues who never learned the real reason for his strange disappearance from the community. He finally had to conclude,

> Solemnly and of my own free will I wish to acknowledge that knowingly and freely I entered into possession by an evil spirit. And, although that spirit came to me under the guise of saving me, perfecting me, helping me to help others, I knew all along it was evil. (318:485; cf. pp. 385–488)

Thus, pursuing altered states may result not only in a wholly unexpected but radical transformation of one's world view and even personality, but also in one's demonization (131; 132; 396).

❧ ❧ ❧

The development of altered states of consciousness is not participating in a form of "higher consciousness" or true spirituality, as new age proponents would have us believe. Rather, it involves an abnormal, regressive state of consciousness, one particularly conducive to demonic contact and manipulation. The radically altered world view generated is characteristically occultic and brings consequences from encouraging occult practices or adopting occult philosophy.

The growing acceptance of altered states by increasing millions, their use in psychotherapy, medicine, and many other fields is, unfortunately, only a reflection of the increasing influence of occultism in our society.

Applied Kinesiology (Muscle Testing)

Definition: Applied kinesiology is a method of diagnosis and treatment that combines chiropractic, muscle-testing, nutritional evaluations, and other methods for overall preventive medicine and health maintenance.

Founder: George Goodheart

How Does It Claim to Work?: Applied kinesiology claims to induce proper structural and chemical-nutritional organization in the body, as well as "left-and-right-brain" hemisphere balance. It claims to evaluate and correct problems of the nervous, circulatory, lymphatic, skeletal-musculature, and "meridian" systems, thereby maintaining health. Its practices are believed to permit the even flow of cosmic energy throughout the body, thus nurturing individual organs and systems with the proper supply of *chi* energy.

Scientific Evaluation: Discredited; see chapter on acupuncture and chiropractic.

Occultic Potential: Psychic healing; energy channeling.

Major Problem(s): Unsubstantiated practice with occultic potential.

Biblical/Christian Evaluation: Practices that are quack or potentially occultic should be avoided.

Potential Dangers: Misdiagnosis; quack treatment; occultic influence.

Eleven

APPLIED KINESIOLOGY (MUSCLE TESTING)*

In the early 1980s, a British chiropractor association newsletter carried the headline "Applied Kinesiology—the fastest growing health-care approach in the States" (325:116). In the 1990s, applied kinesiology has continued to attract large numbers of therapists, especially chiropractors, and clients. Practitioners often claim that "AK is in the vanguard of the modern movement of preventive medicine" (129:27).†

The Nature of Applied Kinesiology

Applied kinesiology, a practice often taught in chiropractic schools, is a system of diagnosis and treatment claimed as being more concerned with

* Modern new age muscle testing methods must be distinguished from the scientific discipline of kinesiology proper. *Webster's Third New International Dictionary* and the *Encyclopedia Britannica* both define formal kinesiology as "[the] study of the principles of mechanics and anatomy in relation to human movement" (416:1244). *Webster's New Twentieth Century Dictionary* defines it as "the science or study of human muscular movements, especially as applied in physical education" (415:1002).

† A popular form of applied kinesiology is touch for health, developed by chiropractor John Thie in conjunction with George Goodheart; also, the practice of behavioral kinesiology, developed by John Diamond, M.D., is an extension of the principles of applied kinesiology.

health than illness. The goal of practitioners is allegedly to prevent serious disease (129:14). The approach of the AK therapist is decidedly "holistic":

> Applied kinesiologists are far more interested in health than in disease. Their goal is to prevent serious illness. . . .
>
> Applied kinesiologists look at every person from a "triad of health perspective." This is the three-sided nature of every human being that makes up a healing art's triangle of "*structure*, *chemistry*, and *mentality*." . . . Most applied kinesiologists, being "holistic physicians," attempt to work with all three areas of health, and in some cases they include a "spiritual" dimension. (129:14)

In evaluating a patient's condition, the AK practitioner claims to evaluate five bodily systems—nervous, lymphatic, vascular, cerebrospinal, and "meridian." It claims "all five systems are so intricately interwoven, each with the other, that it is impossible to separate them" (129:16).

The primary diagnostic procedure for the AK practitioner is the muscle test. Applied kinesiology claims it can diagnose the condition of the body by testing various muscles and assessing their relative strength or weakness. Muscle testing is accomplished by, for example, pushing or pulling on an arm or finger muscle while the client resists the force. The therapist "feels" the amount of resistance, enabling him to "diagnose," for example, the condition of the *chi* energy flow. Supposedly, readjusting the *chi* energy may be done by hand passes along so-called meridian lines, touching acupressure points, or other methods. AK muscle testing claims its methods can evaluate the structural, chemical/nutritional, and left-right brain organization of the body (129:103). Thus, "a large portion of the applied kinesiology practice is devoted to evaluating for abnormal body organization" (129:105).

The medical claims made for AK are astounding, to say the least. We are told "a competent AK practitioner may, indeed, perform vital health services unmatched in the healing arts" (129:29). AK "can help the physician determine the major cause of a patient's health problem" (129:135). In fact, AK muscle testing may eventually be proven "infallible," or failing that, "extremely accurate" (129:117).

AK not only has unmatched diagnostic potential, but its increasing acceptance guarantees the public can approach the practitioner with confidence:

> In a brief session, a competent applied kinesiologist can evaluate your various bodily functions by testing your muscles, and then present you with a

> fairly accurate picture of how your glands, organs, lymphatic system, nervous system, circulation, and muscle and bone structures are working. . . .
>
> Applied kinesiology (AK) is a practical and reliable diagnostic tool and holistic therapeutic modality. . . . Today there are hundreds of competent clinical and practical researchers contributing to the ever growing body of knowledge. Since the practice was founded by a chiropractor, it makes sense that most applied kinesiologists are chiropractors. However, over the years other physicians, including dentists, M.D.'s, podiatrists (chiropodists), osteopaths, and even psychiatrists, have learned the art. Today we may approach an applied kinesiologist with confidence. (129:9)

Origin

Applied kinesiology (AK) was developed by chiropractor and psychic George Goodheart who received much of his information on applied kinesiology by psychic means. Drs. Pollack and Kravitz disclose the following information:

> The originator of applied kinesiology is George Goodheart, a Michigan chiropractor, who has worked out elaborate charts showing the effects of specific nutrients and herbs upon specific organs, teeth, acupuncture meridians, and muscles. These are extremely elaborate, and a major question is raised as to how such complex interrelationships could possibly be validated without the efforts of numerous researchers and the production of a great deal of published research. When a major proponent of applied kinesiology was queried on this, he stated that Goodheart was psychic (personal communication) and developed his charts by this means.(433:310)*

In developing his system, Goodheart combined the occultic philosophy of early chiropractic theory (see chapter 14) concerning the body's supposed Innate Intelligence with ancient Eastern practices designed to regulate supposed mystical life energies within the body. From 1964 to 1977, Goodheart produced various applied kinesiology research manuals, such as the applied kinesiology *Workshop Procedure Manuals* for 1964, 1972, and 1973–76 (81:287).

Applied kinesiology is thus a blending of the theory and/or practice of chiropractic and ancient Chinese Taoism: "Combining Eastern ideas about

---

* The authors personally confirmed Goodheart's psychic approach with Dr. William Jarvis, professor of Public Health and Preventive Medicine, Loma Linda University Medical School, Loma Linda, CA; and president of the National Council Against Health Fraud.

energy flow with his own chiropractic techniques and other sources, Goodheart developed his new system" (325:116).

Goodheart developed applied kinesiology for health professionals, but he and chiropractor John Thie invented a less technical, more popular approach for laymen in the practice of touch for health. In this form, applied kinesiology has become one of the easiest to learn and most popular of new age therapies.

Although Goodheart made use of formal kinesiology in the development of his system,

> It should be stated from the outset that applied kinesiology is unrelated to formal kinesiology, the study of bodily movements and the muscles which control them. The latter is a legitimate science with applications to physical therapy and rehabilitation. (1:81)

Classical chiropractic theory teaches there is an alleged spiritual intelligence that controls the body called Innate Intelligence. It is supposedly connected to Universal Intelligence ("God") through the nervous system (see the chapter on chiropractic). Goodheart adopted this philosophy and combined it with the idea that individual muscles display or reflect back the supposed "energy" condition of their alleged corresponding organs by means of the acupuncture meridians. By "testing" the muscles to supposedly determine the organ's "energy" or *chi* level, one is able to "diagnose" the problem and to correct the energy "imbalance" or "blockage" in the respective organs or bodily systems. In essence then, Goodheart combined chiropractic and Chinese Taoist healing methods in order to employ "muscle testing procedures to tap the innate intelligence of the body in order to assess the energy levels of the life forces which control the body" (411:44).

Chiropractic teaches that muscle *spasm* is a problem, but Goodheart thought that muscle *weakness* was the more serious problem. He claimed to have discovered that muscle "weakness" on one side of the body would cause normal muscles on the other side of the body to appear (or become) tight. The key was to find "weak" muscles and "strengthen" them because weak muscles themselves were only symptoms of a deeper problem. "Weak" muscles supposedly reveal that a corresponding illness or disease exists or is developing somewhere else in the body.

Goodheart thus argues that he discovered applied kinesiology ". . . from a simple observation made in 1964, [that] most muscle spasm is not primary, but secondary to antagonistic muscle weakness" (413:77). As a result, muscle "weakness" was the real issue and this became his principle diagnostic method. Divulging similarities to chiropractic and osteopathic theory, he observes:

> Applied kinesiology has led to the recognition that structural integrity [e.g., muscle condition] and body function [e.g., health or disease] are intimately associated. Virtually any disease state of the body will have a structural manifestation, a specific "body language" pattern, represented by specific muscle weakness patterns. Muscle testing, then, becomes a tool with which to read the body's language, and this tool has opened avenues of investigation that lead into nearly every aspect of the diagnostic and therapeutic modalities available to the present-day wholistic physician. (411:77)

Goodheart affirms that, in some manner, every disease state is manifested through the muscles. Once a practitioner learns to "read" the muscles through AK, he can effectively diagnose the illnesses, problems, or diseases they represent. Therefore, practitioners "do not rely on a knowledge of symptoms, in the usual clinical sense, since the patients' muscles provide them with all the information they need" (325:118).

Goodheart further claims that his muscle testing procedure can be used in conjunction with almost any other new age technique, and this is why so many other holistic health methods employ it.

Goodheart therefore accepts the false claims of some chiropractors, osteopaths, and acupuncturists who thought they noted specific muscle function ("weakness") to corresponding organ disease. In his own words:

> Weakness in a specific muscle was found whenever demonstrable dysfunction in a specific organ was identified, and the neurolymphatic, neurovascular, and acupuncture reflex centers for a given organ were all found to be related to this same specific muscle. For example, patients with kidney disease will display concurrent weakness of the psoas muscle; those with gastric disease will show an associated weakness of the pectoralis major, clavicular division, and so on. . . .
>
> Not every weak muscle has an associated organ dysfunction, but every organ dysfunction is accompanied by a weak muscle. (412:78)

How extensively the above beliefs are related to quack medicine can be seen in the associations Goodheart freely lends to them.

Significantly, he proceeds to observe that the same relationships are found in such discredited systems as hand-and-foot reflexology and iridology (412:78). He also claims that applied kinesiology can, through what he calls the "challenge technique," actually "demonstrate" the existence of that which no chiropractor has ever demonstrated—the infamous chiropractic "subluxation" (see the chapter 14). Thus, Goodheart discloses, "This procedure permits identification of subluxations and their distant effects . . . [i.e. on various organs]" (412:78).

"Magical" Properties

AK can even perform "magic"; practitioners believe it has such powers because AK teaches two basic errors. First, that body language is infallible. Goodheart claims that "body language never lies" and "the response of the body is unerring" (412:78–79). Second, that the body is so sensitive that at extremely fine energy levels it can actually detect and respond to the toxicity or efficacy of various substances. As a result, Goodheart and other AK practitioners think they can even perform miracles. "The AK physician [sic] can accurately diagnose with the process of therapy localization . . ." (129:42). "Therapy localization" is a bizarre technique Goodheart calls "the most astounding concept in applied kinesiology" (412:78) because it:

> Is capable of identifying virtually all faults and dysfunctions that have an effect on the nervous system. These encompass everything from subluxations of the spine to imbalances in the body's energy fields. (412:78)

"Therapy localization" is a fancy term for a common, if varied practice, among all muscle testers. Usually, a particular food object or other substance is placed in the hand, or sometimes the mouth; the goal is to use muscles to determine if the substance is good or bad for you. By supposedly determining its effect upon a designated "indicator muscle," the "good" or "bad" (strengthening or weakening) effect of that substance upon the entire body is said to be revealed (21:21).

For example, when a cube of white, refined sugar (which most people think is bad for them) is held in the left hand, the muscles in the right arm supposedly are weakened, thus "proving" sugar is bad for the whole body. And the right arm muscle is considered weakened by a simple muscle test. A person who significantly resisted the downward pull of his outstretched right arm before holding the sugar will "amazingly" discover all resistance is gone when he repeats the "test" while holding white, refined sugar. All kinds of substances can be "tested" in this manner for their supposed effect on the body. This method is also used to allegedly test allergies and nutritional deficiencies.

Needless to say, this practice is pure quackery and is easily disproven by anyone who will themselves test the practice on others. The "positive response" muscle testers find in the general population is explained largely by people's suggestibility.

Nevertheless, Goodheart believes that applied kinesiology can actually be used to test the "toxicity" or "effectiveness" of nutritional and other substances by determining their supposed effects upon the muscles. (A bizarre extension of this idea, called *Behavioral Kinesiology*, applies this theory to an endless array of items and circumstances.) For example, by placing the substance in the mouth, he thinks one can determine its strengthening or weakening effect upon the proper muscle, and thereby prove its good or bad effect on the body:

> Additional advancements in AK [applied kinesiology] revealed that specific nutritional requirements of the body manifest themselves through a specific muscle weakness for each nutrient, and this weakness will be abolished immediately upon ensalivating the appropriate nutritional material. Further, the effectiveness or toxicity of various nutritional products as well as food allergies can be tested by having the patient chew the substance while monitoring the strength of a specific muscle. Obvious food allergens (such as refined sugar to the hyperinsulinism patient) will cause immediate weakening of an associated muscle when the substance is chewed and ensalivated, before any swallowing or usual absorption can take place. (412:78)

In other words, magic. Applied kinesiology teaches that each large muscle is specially and magically related to a specific body organ, and these in turn are related to a specific acupuncture "meridian." When a muscle is "tested" and found to be weak, the level of *chi* or "energy" in that muscle and its associated organ is deficient or blocked; therefore, the muscle is treated in various ways to restore the flow of *chi*. Hand passes are a frequent method employed; a meridian may be traced and retraced from one end to the other with the palm of the hand. This allegedly strengthens the muscles and its related organ. The organ is therefore automatically and magically healed (21:6), as the *chi* energy in both muscle and organ is restored to proper functioning and thereby supposedly producing health.

In addition to muscle testing therapy, other new age practices may be employed: "It is often found that a number of therapies are necessary to obtain optimum balance" (76:44).

Scientific Evaluation

Promoters of AK call their system a "new medical science" (129:130); unfortunately, they exaggerate. We have selected a popular text on the subject to illustrate the real nature of the practice. Thankfully, this text does warn about the quacks in the field (129:13, 41, 65, 132).

A Chicago practitioner "muscle tested" a woman and discovered her tubes were blocked, that she would never have children, and that she had cancer. A medical exam revealed she had no cancer and was pregnant (129:13). Practitioners "demonstrated" the effectiveness of "pyramid-energy pills" by standard AK techniques (129:132). In reference to a common AK practice in California and other states, a person is tested for nutritional deficiencies by placing a tablet on their chest, instead of the tongue, the "proper" location (129:133–134).

Exposing quackery is to be commended, but this book proceeds to claim anyone can easily "distinguish between the competent [AK] practitioner and the quack . . ." (129:131). But after reading the book, we wonder on what basis this determination is to be made.

In all three cases cited above—and there are hundreds of others—the people were apparently sincere AK practitioners. The results achieved were based on standard AK theories, or logical extensions of them. The question is, "Why are these practices thought to be quack and other AK methods legitimate?" If AK is based on mystical energies, how can we say practices are quack merely because they are different, such as placing the tablet on the chest rather than the tongue? Indeed, it is confessed that these "unconventional" practitioners are only "accepting a school of thought that suggests the body detects 'energy patterns' of the substance from the spot on the chest just as well as it does from the tongue" (129:133).

But is *any* "school of thought" ruled out when we claim to detect or manipulate mystical energies? When was it ever proven that the "tongue" method was a legitimate practice? And is there any reason to think that placing the tablet on the nose or any other part of the body isn't just as "legitimate"?

Given the novel claims AK makes, and the fact none are demonstrated, doesn't the real quackery lie with AK itself? (Consider again our discussion of quackery in chapter 1.) For example, how are the above quack methods different from the methods employed by any AK practitioner?

> "Count by fours," Dr. Hetrick repeated as he cradled my leg in the position to test my sartorius.
>
> I did as requested and naturally I had to concentrate to recall the correct sequence. As I concentrated on the count my muscle suddenly tested weak. This body language told Dr. Hetrick that my adrenals needed still more therapy. . . .
>
> "Now, hum the tune to 'Happy Birthday,'" he requested, again poised to test my leg muscle. . . .
>
> This time it tested strong, which indicated that the right hemisphere of my brain, the side responsible for creativity, was evidently not involved in the apparent body disorganization. . . .
>
> The ability to discern diagnostic information from our muscle reactions to left-brain/right-brain activity is simply part of the complexities AK physicians probe in order to be better doctors. (129:112–113)

Consider the following beliefs and "discoveries" of AK:

- Muscle testing reveals if chiropractic manipulation has been successful or not. (129:42)

- "In addition to taste response reactions, the AK techniques can also test reactions to substances that we breathe in. . . . One AK researcher experimented with homeopathic compounds and Bach flower remedies by having a subject inhale specially prepared vapors, then testing the muscle responses." (129:65)

- AK practitioners are taught to use muscle testing "to supplement and double-check blood and urine test information." The AK evaluation of leg "turn-ins" (associated with the "gait mechanism") "has particular value" in metabolic detection. In fact, a standard test chemically assaying the blood has been proven incomplete and that "AK procedures provide more complete data." (129:118)

- "AK researchers have learned that water-soluble vitamins trigger left brain activity and fat-soluble vitamins trigger right brain activity. Since correct body organization requires left-brain activity to affect right-sided muscles and vice versa, manual muscle-testing procedures will be accurate and effective tools only when specific nutrients and vitamins are tested on the proper sides." (129:128–129)

As a final illustration of AK quackery, consider the practice of "temporal tapping." Even leading practitioners such as David Walther, author of the definitive textbook of AK, *Basic Procedures and Muscle Testing*, accepts the practice (129:19, 114). This involves tapping or manipulating the temporal bone (in the temple area), while giving the patient "positive affirmations." It is the unique invention of George Goodheart:

> The founder of applied kinesiology decided to experiment with penetrating the sensory system by transmitting positive and negative thoughts, and other stimuli, while manipulating the temporal bone. At first he was unsuccessful, but after considerable experience, he found success. (129:114)

Not surprisingly, even promoters confess, "AK physicians [sic] are working more in the realm of hypothesis in temporal tapping than they are in hard and fast knowledge" (129:117).

Nevertheless, we are told the process works and that it is an invaluable procedure:

> Like palpating or other aspects of a manipulative physician's practice, temporal tapping is a highly skilled procedure, and its proper use can be yet another diagnostic tool for isolating and ferreting our basic causes of a particular symptom. Walther says "the temporal tap is used to penetrate the sensory filter, influence some types of therapy, control some involuntary activities, and give additional therapy localization information." However, the physician must have already determined the patient's brain hemisphere dominance, or whether the patient is a mixed dominance type, before applying temporal tap procedure.
>
> Temporal tapping seems to be an excellent "audit mechanism" that applied kinesiologists may use to determine whether all of the five systems have been fully explored and possibly corrected. Those five systems, again, include the nervous system, circulatory system, lymphatic system, skeletal-musculature system and the acupuncture meridians. (129:114–116)

Finally, practitioners maintain that we have not yet begun to uncover the miraculous powers of AK: "Most likely, the actual truth of the value of applied kinesiology lies beyond even some of the seemingly improbable relationships only touched on in this book" (129:137). If so, one wonders why it is also confessed, "Therapy localization is a phenomenon for which the current data base of knowledge has no adequate explanation" (129:135) and "you will not find traditional M.D.'s throwing any bouquets in the direction of applied kinesiology" (129:138). If AK is really so marvellous, why aren't physicians even interested in the practice? Furthermore, why have practitioners of AK refused to listen to the medical community when it challenges and refutes their methods? Perhaps AK practitioners are unconcerned with the medical communities' lack of excitement because of their suggestion that when it comes to medical matters, even physicians are pretty much in the dark like the rest of us:

> Bear in mind that the most prestigious medical doctor at the most prestigious medical facility, following the most prestigious and expensive set of diagnostic and exploratory evaluations, including surgery, is still pretty much guessing. (129:137)

Apparently, we are to believe that even eminent medical doctors are "pretty much guessing" while practitioners of AK are at the forefront of preventive medicine and can perform vital health services unmatched in the healing arts, including pure magic. But are these AK claims and practices anywhere close to the practices of careful medicine or science? No, and this is why we think applied kinesiology is quackery.

The fundamental problem of applied kinesiology is the general problem of new age medicine: Methods which are a combination of quackery, Eastern mysticism, and/or occultism will not prove useful or beneficial.

The AK claims concerning "temporal tapping," therapy localization, brain hemispheres, and all the rest do not inspire great confidence in the practice. The quackery is also evident in its claimed associations between muscles and their corresponding organs, which have absolutely no basis in traditional physiology. Applied kinesiology rejects what science has proven true in this field and instead proposes we accept a series of fantasies which have nothing in common with modern medicine or human anatomy. The alleged flow of *chi* along supposed meridians and the claim that applied kinesiology can balance "life energies" reveals the Eastern mysticism in the practice. But this, too, is fantasy and potentially occultic.

For these reasons, even some Christian chiropractors have a problem with applied kinesiology. Chiropractor Glenn Hultgren questions its basic approach and suggests the practice is off limits to Christian chiropractors. He is uncomfortable with its embracing of meridian therapy, suggests it is a form of religious practice, and questions its claim to have any anatomical connection between muscles and internal organs and concludes:

> In Dr. David Walther's notes, he teaches the use of acupuncture, temple tapping (hypnosis), auricular therapy, foot reflexology, pulse diagnosis, and

Palmer [*chiropractic*] therapy all as a part of A.K. What is the definition of A.K.? What limits does it place upon its practitioners? (440:1–12)

Hultgren also observes another entirely irrational procedure, one that is common to applied kinesiologists:

Surrogate testing is a common practice among A.K. practitioners, whereby a baby or small child is placed on the abdomen of the mother and the muscles of the mother are tested to determine dysfunction of the organs of the baby. What is the scientific veracity of this procedure? (440:11–12)

Finally, applied kinesiology muscle testing for the toxicity or effectiveness of various substances is also quackery. Applied kinesiology as a whole violates everything science tells us is true in these areas. Therefore, no basic teaching or practice of applied kinesiology can be scientifically established as true, and scientific testing of AK claims proves they are false. None of these methods ever appear in *Scientific American*, *Science*, the *Journal of the American Medical Association*, or any other reputable periodical—unless it is to repudiate them. For example, the *Journal of the American Dietetic Association* for June 1988 contained an article by James J. Kennedy et.al., "Applied Kinesiology Unreliable for Assessing Nutrient Status." Comparisons between kinesiologists employing normal biochemical testing, placebos, retesting, and the use of a computerized dynameter to measure exact muscle strength proved that applied kinesiology is no better than random guessing to determine nutrient status.

Occultic Potential

Science is not the only problem faced by applied kinesiology; the incorporation of mystical and Eastern concepts can also open the door to the occult. There is no doubt that AK claims it can detect and manipulate mystical energies:

The competent AK physician is trained in understanding the various energy patterns within the body. From the ancient tradition of acupuncture, AK physicians have learned the meridian system's value in diagnostics. It has been discovered that when there is an energy imbalance within the meridian system, the body will reveal this information. (129:39–40)

The term "energy pattern" is used often by AK physicians and it has various levels of meaning. . . . For example, the patterns drawn around the

> body by the acupuncturist are invisible, but can be demonstrated by both the acupuncturist and the AK physician. (129:60–61)

Once the concept of manipulating invisible energies is accepted, a logical outcome is to employ other psychic methods that supposedly do the same, as for example, using occult pendulums. In *Applied Kinesiology*, Tom and Carole Valentine discuss the exciting "ongoing experimentation" by AK researchers with pendulums:

> We have seen demonstrations by persons claiming an ability to "dowse" food or nutritional supplements with a pendulum dangling from their fingers. If the pendulum swings clockwise, the dowsers claim, the substance is "good for you," and if the pendulum rotates counter-clockwise, it is "negative." (129:117–118)

That AK techniques and muscle testing in general clearly *can* be used for occultic purposes is demonstrated in various occultic and spiritistic books which employ them toward that end, such as *The Psychic Energy Workbook* (119:42–51) and *The Perelandra Garden Workbook: A Complete Guide to Gardening with Nature [i.e., spirit] Intelligences* (147:17–18).

In the former book, muscle testing is used for several psychic purposes. Exercise 15 seeks to determine which objects (such as jewelry) have become "psychically contaminated" and need psychic cleaning to stop their deleterious effects upon the body (119:42–43).

Or, in Exercises 15 and 19, the muscle test can be used to psychically gauge the influence of emotional states or physical energy levels (119:43,49). After objects or emotions are psychically cleansed, the person is to engage in the technique of "Flowing Energy Through Your Entire Body" (119:43).

In *The Perelandra Garden Workbook*, medium Machaelle Wright explains how to use the "finger loop" version of muscle testing to receive "yes" or "no" answers from the nature spirits or *devas* (147:17–18). Ms. Wright receives instructions from these spirits in the same manner employed by the founders and leaders of the famous spiritistic Findhorn community in Scotland (226).

That applied kinesiology is used in occult practice is not surprising given the fact that Goodheart himself is a psychic who developed his system by psychic methods.

Applied kinesiology is not a practice that should be trusted or utilized. Those who claim it is a valuable adjunct to health concerns are simply wrong.

Attitudinal Healing

Definition: Attitudinal healing is the regulation or maintenance of physical, mental, and/or spiritual health by learning "proper" mental attitudes.

Founder: Unknown.

How Does It Claim to Work? Because the spirit, mind, and body are interrelated, "proper" mental attitudes may influence the entire person toward desired spiritual, psychological, and/or physical goals.

Scientific Evaluation: Unsubstantiated claims.

Occultic Potential: Adopting new age philosophy; encountering spiritistic revelations and contacts.

Major Problem(s): Mental attitudes are typically restructured to harmonize with new age/spiritistic philosophy.

Biblical/Christian Evaluation: The form of attitudinal healing examined in this chapter is from Jane Robert's *The Nature of Personal Reality* and the three-volume text, *A Course in Miracles*. These materials constitute spiritistic revelations admittedly produced by occultic means, which the Bible forbids (Deuteronomy 18:9–12). Cultivating occultic or unbiblical attitudes toward life is not in harmony with scriptural purposes, but rather is spiritually harmful.

Potential Dangers: Adopting occultic philosophy and practice in the guise of physical, mental, and spiritual health.

TWELVE

ATTITUDINAL HEALING ("SETH": A COURSE IN MIRACLES)

Though often overlooked, attitudinal healing is an important aspect of new age medicine. It reminds us that new age medicine is concerned with more than mere physical health; it is also concerned with a particular spiritual world view of occultic new age philosophy. And new age philosophy teaches that genuine health is "holistic"—incorporating complementary spiritual beliefs, mental attitudes, and physical therapies. Attitudinal healing, then, illustrates the importance of both mental and spiritual belief to physical health.

In one sense, attitudinal healing encompasses a broad variety of traditional and new age groups and methods which claim that a particular mental attitude or world view is important to physical or spiritual health. Some of these include Religious Science (science of mind), Christian Science, various New Thought religions, certain schools of psychotherapy (especially the Transpersonal school), numerous individual standard and fringe psychotherapies, *yoga meditation*, and Buddhist psychology.

One particular form of attitudinal healing, however, is common to new age medicine: Its basic goal reflects new age philosophy that man is inwardly divine. Therefore, as a god, he can powerfully mold and create his own reality, if he chooses. This is also a fundamental premise of much Western magic and Eastern occultism. Man's only problem is to learn how to manipulate his consciousness (see chapter 10) in order to perceive true reality and also mold it according to his wishes. Attitudinal "healing" provides the key.

The Nature of Attitudinal Healing

Two of the most popular modern texts on attitudinal healing were both dictated from the spirit world. Medium Jane Roberts' best-selling *The Nature of Personal Reality: A Seth Book* (346) and Helen Schucman's best-selling *A Course in Miracles* (refs. 163, 166, 167) dominate the field. These two books alone have been read by over one million people and their concepts have influenced additional millions. Our analysis will concentrate on Schucman's text, although the philosophy of both is related.

Seth

"Seth," the spirit guide of the late Jane Roberts, affirms the following fundamental premises of attitudinal healing: (1) "The real work is done in the mind," (2) "The inner self brings about whatever results the conscious mind desires," and (3) "Basically you create your experience through your beliefs about yourself and the nature of reality" (346:11–12, 64, 85; cf. pp. 27, 75). What Seth proceeds to teach is that each person, as a god, literally creates his or her entire physical, mental, and spiritual reality. Even the material world itself is not independent of a person's consciousness. Moment by moment, a person's consciousness actually creates the world and his or her experience in it. Seth explains:

> Your experience in the world of physical matter flows outward from the center of your inner psyche. Then you perceive this experience. Exterior events, circumstances and conditions are meant as a kind of living feedback. Altering the state of the psyche automatically alters the physical circumstances.
>
> There is no other valid way of changing physical events. . . . Your thoughts, feelings and mental pictures can be called incipient exterior events, for in one way or another each of these is materialized into physical reality. . . .
>
> There is nothing in your exterior experience that did not originate within you. (346:10)

In other words, this world is not the independent, fixed creation of an infinite personal God apart from us, as the Bible teaches. It is literally and personally our own creation. As Seth emphasizes, we are God. Seth proceeds to offer specific techniques for attitudinal changes that will allegedly give us the ability to demonstrate our godhood by recreating our reality according to our personal desires. Cultivating altered states of consciousness is particularly important [cf. chapter 10].

> The methods that I will outline demand concentration and effort. They will also challenge you, and bring into your life expansion and alterations of consciousness of a most rewarding nature.
>
> I am not a physical personality. Basically, however, neither are you. Your experience now is physical. You are a creator translating your expectations into physical form. The world is meant to serve as a reference point. The exterior appearance is a replica of inner desire. You can change your personal world. You do change it without knowing it. You have only to use your ability consciously, to examine the nature of your thoughts and feelings and project those with which you basically agree.
>
> They coalesce into the events with which you are so intimately familiar. I hope to teach you methods that will allow you to understand the nature of your own reality, and to point a way that will let you change that reality *in whatever way you choose*. (346:xxii, emphasis added.)

Seth claims people must realize that their beliefs about reality "are just that—beliefs *about* reality, not attributes of it." Therefore, "You must then realize that your beliefs are physically materialized. . . . To change the physical effect you must change the original belief—while being quite aware that for a time physical materializations of the old beliefs may still hold." (346:75)

Indeed. Regardless, we see that Seth teaches we have divine abilities. Not only are we gods who instantly create our reality, we can mold that reality in any manner we choose, a fundamental premise of magic. The relevance of such a philosophy to healing is obvious. If we can literally alter physical reality, we can alter the physical reality of our own bodies. Seth maintains:

> All healings are the result of the acceptance of one basic fact: That matter is formed by those inner qualities that give it vitality, that structure follows expectation, that matter at any time can be completely changed by the activation of the creative faculties inherent in all consciousness. (346:xxii–xxiii)

The only problem is that Seth's own theology and moral teachings, not to mention his views on the nature of reality, reveal him to be a lying spirit, an entity the Bible identifies as a demon (132; see also chapter 6). Not only does Seth lie about God, moral values, and salvation (346:238–242; cf. ref. 132), he also lies about the nature of both reality and humanity itself. If men really had the power Seth claims, surely there would be some evidence for it. Biblically and experientially, we know that men are not powerful gods who literally create the universe; we know, and all history demonstrates, that all the "consciousness raising" in the world will not alter our personal reality in the manner Seth argues for.

Seth is a liar, but he is teaching something that literally millions of people prefer to hear: that they are gods who have the potential to control, regulate, and create reality. Nowhere is this desire for godhood better illustrated than in the text *A Course in Miracles*.

A Course in Miracles

This chapter concentrates on that form of attitudinal healing presented in the best-selling three-volume text, *A Course in Miracles* (1975). To date, the *Course* has sold over 250,000 sets and has had great impact. It has been or is being translated into French, Spanish, Italian, Portuguese, Hebrew, and other languages (157:18).

The printer for *A Course in Miracles*, Coleman Graphics, Inc., publishes over fifty additional book titles, most of them written by students of the *Course*. One example is psychologist Kenneth Wapnick's book, *Christian Psychology in A Course in Miracles*.

According to *New Realities* magazine, even a brief listing of the organizations who recommend the *Course* to their constituents or have incorporated it into their curriculum is impressive—est (The Forum), the Association for Humanistic Psychology; the Center for Attitudinal Healing; the Association for Research and Enlightenment (Edgar Cayce); the Spiritual Frontiers Fellowship, founded by famous trance medium Arthur Ford; The Association for Transpersonal Psychology; The Institute of Noetic Sciences; and Stuart Emery's Actualizations seminar, to name only a few (159:48; cf. ref. 160). From presidents of universities and owners of football teams—"to various researchers and authors that read like a 'Who's Who' of the consciousness movement" (159:48)—the *Course* continues to expand in popularity. Scores of individuals in numerous occupations have also incorporated *Course* teachings into their respective professions.

In light of its sales, the number of teachers of the *Course*, and its indirect influence through other mediums (no pun intended), a conservative estimate would be that at least one to two million people have been exposed to the *Course* teachings, and probably more.

Psychiatrist Gerald Jampolsky is one of the more influential promoters of the text, extolling its virtues throughout the country in lectures and books. He appeared on the "Phil Donahue Show", "Today", and was featured on "60 Minutes". Even Robert Schuller hosted him at his famous Garden Grove Community Church (158:3). Jampolsky's best-selling books, *Good-Bye to Guilt, Out of Darkness into the Light, Love Is Letting Go of Fear*, and *Teach Only Love*, condense basic themes of the *Course*. His Center for Attitudinal Healing was founded in 1975 under the direction of an "inner voice" which instructed him to establish a center where the principles of the *Course* could be taught and demonstrated.

Jampolsky's *Teach Only Love* asserts that the *Course* is "central to attitudinal healing" (161:23). In *Good-Bye to Guilt*, he describes his conversion to the *Course* and its relation to the Center:

> I began to change my way of looking at the world in 1975. Until then I had considered myself a militant atheist, and the last thing I was consciously interested in was being on a spiritual pathway that would lead to God. In that year I was introduced to . . . *A Course in Miracles*. . . . My resistance was immediate. . . . Nevertheless, after reading just one page, I had a sudden and dramatic experience. There was an instantaneous memory of God, a feeling of oneness with everyone in the world, and the belief that my only function on earth was to serve God.
>
> Because of my Jewish background, however, I found that as I got into the course, I developed a great deal of resistance to its Christian terminology. . . .
>
> Nevertheless because of the profound effect the course had on my life, I decided to apply its principles in working with catastrophically ill children. In 1975, my inner guidance led me to help establish The Center for Attitudinal Healing in Tiburon, California, to fulfill that function. (162:4, 11)

He observes that the *Course* itself is not used at the Center (the full *Course* program requires a minimum of a year to complete); however, the staff are expected to "adopt and demonstrate the principles of attitudinal healing" taught by the *Course* (162:11).

The Christian church has also been influenced by the *Course*. Evangelical Christians, such as author Virginia Mollenkott in *Speech, Silence, Action*, attest to its alleged benefits in their lives (158:3). Some churches are even using it as part of their educational programs because it has received glowing endorsements by numerous Catholic and Protestant clergy.

In fact, the *Course* specifically directs itself toward acceptance within the Christian church. The spirit author claims to be "Jesus Christ" Himself and distinctively Christian terminology is utilized throughout. SCP research Robert Burroughs observes:

> It has also found a ready and expanding audience within the Christian Church, which is not surprising either. Biblical illiteracy is rampant and commitment to orthodoxy often less than vigorous and sometimes consciously absent. Those conditions are aggravated by the very nature of the *Course* writings. Couched in Biblical terminology and allegedly dictated by Jesus Christ, they easily confuse and seem designed specifically for that purpose. (156:9)

Of course, many other non-Christian *spiritistic* writings have similar themes, i.e., (1) the Biblical God or Jesus is the alleged author; (2) the writings typically encourage spiritistic contact in one form or another; and (3) they claim to be a message for the Church, (e.g., medium Levi M. Arnold's *History of the Origin of All Things* (1852), the occultic *Oahspe: A Kosmon Bible* (1882), A. J. Russell's evangelical best-seller *God Calling* (1945) (see ref. 330). In each case new revelations seek to deliberately revise and discredit Biblical teachings—often by subtle and spiritual sounding explanations and methods. Nevertheless, the fact remains that in all such revelations, "God" denies His earlier teachings in Scripture (330).

A Course in Miracles was channeled through an atheistic psychologist named Helen Schucman. Dr. Schucman would not permit public knowledge of her role as the medium and eight-year channel for the *Course* until after her death in 1981.

The method of transmission was a clear, distinct inner voice that promised "to direct her very specifically"—and the "voice" did just that. In fact, the same spiritistic direction is promised to the student of the *Course* (163:477–78). Dr. Schucman described the process as the kind of inner dictation common to many other channeled works:

> It can't be an hallucination, really, because the Voice does not come from outside. It's all internal. There's no actual sound, and the words come mentally but very clearly. It's a kind of inner dictation you might say. (164:20)

Dr. Schucman, of course, was the most unlikely channel possible: a respected research psychologist, pragmatic materialist, and a committed atheist at the time of receiving the revelations. She had been associate professor at Columbia University's College of Physicians and Surgeons, and associate research scientist and chief psychologist at the Neurological Institute of The Presbyterian Hospital, among other prestigious appointments. Her Jewish background and commitment to atheism made her very uncomfortable with the "Christian" tone of the messages. Her co-scribe on the project, Dr. William Thetford, was an agnostic teacher and research assistant (to the famed psychologist Dr. Carl Rogers) who held appointments at the Washington School of Psychiatry, Cornell University Medical College, and the College of Physicians and Surgeons of Columbia University. He is currently civilian medical specialist in family medicine at the David Grant USAF Medical Center at Travis Air Force Base, California, as well as director of the Center for Attitudinal Healing in Tiburon, California (162:214).

Robert Skutch, publisher of the *Course*, observes that the power and tenacity of the "voice" was made all the more impressive by Dr. Schucman's obvious reluctance:

> She did know that the material was coming from an unusually authoritative source—one she did not intellectually believe in.
>
> Thus began the actual transmission of the material which Helen would take down in more than one hundred shorthand notebooks over a period of seven-and-a-half years. The situation proved to be tremendously paradoxical. On the one hand, she resented the Voice, objected to taking down the material, was extremely fearful of the content and had to overcome great personal resistance, especially in the beginning stages, in order to continue. On the other hand, it never seriously occurred to her not to do it, even though she frequently was tremendously resentful of the often infuriating interference. . . . (164:20)

The *Course* thus illustrates two characteristics of spiritistic inspiration: (1) whenever possible seek a contact that will provide the most credence for the revelation produced, and (2) force production of the material regardless of personal cost to the channeler.

In Schucman's case an atheistic, skeptical materialist would be quite unlikely to "invent" such revelations while her scholarly standing would provide credibility. Further, the "voice," like the spirits, was merciless and unrelenting:

> The Voice would dictate to Helen almost daily, and sometimes several times a day. . . . She could, and very often did, refuse to cooperate, at least initially. But she soon discovered she could have no peace until she relented and joined in once again. Despite being aware of this, she still sometimes refused to write for extended periods. When this occurred, it was usually at the urging of her husband that she did return to work, for he knew full well that she could only eliminate her distress by resuming her function as *Course* "scribe," and he was able to convince her that to continue fighting the inevitable could only have a deleterious effect on their relationship. . . .
>
> The acute terror Helen felt at the beginning did gradually recede, but part of her mind simply never allowed her to get completely used to the idea of being a channel for the Voice. . . . For the most part she was bleakly unbelieving, suspicious and afraid. (164:20–23)

Indeed. Mysterious powers that take control of one's life are something to be feared. Robert Skutch also recorded Schucman's own perception of the phenomenon:

> Was the Voice that Helen heard dictating the material really that of Jesus? Both Helen and Bill believed the material must stand on its own, regardless of its alleged authorship. At her deepest level, Helen was certain that the Voice was that of Jesus, and yet she still had ambivalent feelings on the subject. In her own words:
>
> "Having no belief in God, I resented the material I was taking down, and was strongly impelled to attack it and prove it wrong . . . .
>
> But where did the writing come from? Certainly the subject matter itself was the last thing I would have expected to write about, since I knew nothing about the subject. Subsequent to the writing I learned that many of the concepts and even some of the actual terms in the writing are found in both Eastern and Western mystical thought, but I knew nothing of them at the time. Nor did I understand the calm but impressive authority with which the Voice dictated. It was largely because of the strangely compelling nature of this authority that I refer to the Voice with a capital 'V.'" (165:78)

Dr. Schucman goes on to admit her complete bafflement: "I do not understand the [control of] events that led up to the writing. I do not understand the process and I certainly do not understand the authorship. It would be pointless for me to attempt an explanation" (165:78).

Her co-scribe on the project, Dr. Thetford, records his observations in an interview in *New Realities*,

> The material was something that transcended anything that either of us could possibly conceive of. And since the content was quite alien to our backgrounds, interests and training, it was obvious to me that it came from an inspired source. The quality of the material was very compelling, and its poetic beauty added to its impact. . . .
>
> I think that if it had not been for many of the extraordinary experiences that occurred during the summer of 1965, neither Helen nor I would have been willing to accept the material she scribed. (165:18)

The *Course* teaches that for physical and spiritual health, people must accept "proper" attitudes toward themselves, life in general, and the world. These attitudes, in essence, constitute the *rejection* of Biblical teachings, such as sin, guilt, and atonement, and the *acceptance* of new age occultic teachings, such as pantheism (all is God; God is all) and psychic development. Specifically, the *Course* offers a Westernized Hinduism with the distinct goal of changing its readers' perceptions into conformity with the non-dual (*advaita*) school of Vedanta Hinduism. This school maintains that the world is ultimately a dream or illusion and that all men are inwardly God. Another major goal of the *Course* is to encourage the student to accept psychic (spiritistic) guidance.

Volume 1 is the "text" itself, presenting the spiritual (metaphysical) and theological teachings, including heretical treatments of Jesus Christ, His death on the Cross (vicarious atonement), the Holy Spirit, and the doctrine of salvation, to name a few. (We document this below.)

Volume 2 is a "Workbook for Students" which offers three hundred sixty-five spiritual lessons and exercises to help the participant personally assimilate the new world view, while also cultivating openness to psychic and spiritistic guidance. Volume 2 has two specific goals: (1) learning new age Hinduism and (2) unlearning orthodox Christianity. Thus, part 1 of volume 2 offers an extensive indoctrination into the religious philosophy of new age Hinduism, although couched in Christian terminology.

Part 2 of volume 2 provides a specific theological "reindoctrination" for unlearning the "errors" taught by orthodox Christianity. Some fourteen doctrines are covered, including "What is forgiveness?"; "What is Salvation?"; "What is the world?"; "What is sin?"; "What is the Body?"; "What is the Christ?"; "What is the Holy Spirit?"—on through "The Real World"; "The Second Coming"; "The Last Judgment"; "Creation"; "The Ego"; "Miracle"; and "Man."

The "Workbook for Students" has very specific goals in mind. For example,

> It is the purpose of this workbook to train your mind to think along the lines the text sets forth. . . . The training period is one year. The exercises are numbered from 1 to 365. . . .
>
> The workbook is divided into two main sections, the first dealing with the undoing of the way you see now, and the second with acquisition of true perception. . . .
>
> The purpose of the workbook is to train your mind in a systematic way to a *different perception* of everyone and everything in the world. . . .
>
> Be sure that you do not decide for yourself that there are some people, situations or things to which the ideas are inapplicable. . . .
>
> The overall aim of the exercise is to increase your ability to extend the ideas you will be practicing to include *everything*. This will require *no effort* on your part. The *exercises* themselves meet the conditions necessary for this kind of transfer. . . .
>
> Remember only this; you need not believe the ideas, you need not accept them, and you need not even welcome them. Some of them you may actively resist. None of this will matter, or decrease their efficacy. But do not allow yourself to make exceptions in applying the ideas the workbook contains, and whatever your reactions to the ideas may be, use them. Nothing more than that is required. (163:1–2, emphasis added)

Below we present some of the titles describing the mental exercises offered in the *Course*:

> God is in everything I see.
> I have invented the world I see.
> My mind is part of God's. I am very holy.
> My holiness blesses the world.
> My holiness is my salvation.
> I am the light of the world.
> Forgiveness is my function as the light of the world.
> My salvation comes from me.
> I am entitled to miracles.
> I am among the ministers of God.
> I walk with God in perfect holiness.
> There is no death. The Son of God is free.
> Salvation of the world depends on me.
> I am the holy Son of God Himself.

God has condemned me not. No more do I.
The glory of my Father is my own.
Fear is not justified in any form.
Let me not see myself as limited.
The Son of God is my identity.
My Self is ruler of the universe.
Let me remember there is no sin.
My holy vision sees all things as pure.
The Word of God is given me to speak.
The Holy Spirit speaks through me today.
The holy Christ is born in me today.
I came for the salvation of the world.
My Father gives all power unto me.
I choose to see my brother's sinlessness.
My sinlessness protects me from all harm.
Peace be to me, the holy Son of God. (163:I–IX)

Volume 3 is a "Manual for Teachers" of the *Course* which provides them with a sense of "divine destiny" for their spiritual "mission." The teachers of the *Course* are referred to as "teachers of God."

> Except for God's teachers there would be little hope of salvation, for the world of sin would seem forever real. The self-deceiving must deceive, for they must teach deception. And what else is hell? This is a manual for the teachers of God.
>
> A teacher of God is anyone who chooses to be one. . . .
>
> They come from all over the world. They come from all religions and from no religion. . . .
>
> There is a course for every teacher of God. The form of the course varies greatly. So do the particular teaching aids involved. But the content of the course never changes. Its central theme is always, "God's Son is guiltless, and in his innocence is his salvation." It does not matter who the teacher was before he heard the Call. He has become a savior by his answer. . . .
>
> Certain pupils have been assigned to each of God's teachers, and they will begin to look for him as soon as he has answered the Call. They were chosen for him because the form of the universal curriculum that he will teach is best for them in view of their level of understanding. His pupils have been waiting for him, for his coming is certain. Again, it is only a matter of time. Once he has chosen to fulfill his role, they are ready to fulfill theirs. . . .

> When pupil and teacher come together, a teaching-learning situation begins. . . . The relationship is holy because of that purpose, and God has promised to send His Spirit into any holy relationship. (166:2–5)

In addition to the three volumes described above, there is an additional manual suggested, *Psychotherapy: Purpose, Process and Practice*, integrating *Course* concepts with modern psychotherapy. This is for the professional therapist who wishes to use *Course* teachings in his counselling practice.

Finally, the encouragement toward psychic guidance is obvious. Brian Van der Horst, writing in *New Realities* observes:

> Above all, the *Course* instructs students in the discovery of their own inner guidance, the revelation of a spiritual voice that counsels one in all situations. The Voice or God or Holy Spirit, as it is called, that gives everything from direction for making decisions on business, career, and life purpose, to advice to the lovelorn. (159:50)

Biblical/Christian Evaluation

All in all the *Course* is a masterpiece of spiritual strategy. It claims to be a revelation from Christ Himself, is intelligently organized, and generally easy to read. It appeals to personal pride and can become almost "addicting" emotionally. It is carefully designed to radically restructure a person's perception against Christian faith and toward new age occultism.

In fact, we would say the text was designed not only for spiritually searching individuals of a secular or psychic persuasion, but especially for nominal Christians in the church who have recognized the bankruptcy of theological liberalism and desire more spiritual "reality" in their lives.

The course simultaneously indoctrinates its students in Eastern metaphysics and human potential psychicism while it specifically insulates them against Biblical revelation and true Christianity. Furthermore, in achieving this end, its manipulation of psychological and emotional states is impressive. It offers carefully thought out spiritual exercises (one for every day of the year).

Publisher Robert Skutch observes, "The concepts of the *Course* are such that anyone who studies the material seriously *must* find that his or her perceptions are changing." (165:78). (Skutch is also the author of *Messages from My Higher Self*, produced through a form of automatic writing.)

Eastern religion, particularly Hinduism (*advaita* Vedanta), plays an important part in the *Course*. Even Robert Skutch admits:

> What they now had in their possession was a spiritual document that was very closely related to the teachings of the non-dualistic Vedanta of the Hindu religion, and that the profundity of the Vedanta certainly paralleled the obvious profundity of the *Course*. He realized the basic spiritual teachings of both had many striking similarities to each other, and that the main difference between them was that the *Course* was stating the perennial philosophy of eternal truths in Christian terminology with a psychological application that seemed expressly aimed at a contemporary audience. (165:24)

Once assimilated by the philosophy of the *Course*, Biblical words undergo drastic changes of purpose. In fact, the new meanings are exactly the opposite of their Biblical meaning. For example, "atonement" no longer refers to the substitutionary death of Christ on the cross for human sin. In Biblical teaching, the atonement is based on the fact that man's sinfulness separates him from God. Before man can be reconciled to God, there must be a divine judgment of sin. Christ sacrificed His own life on the cross—He was judged in our place—to accomplish this. This is what Christians mean by the word "atonement" (John 3:16, 18; 1 John 2:2).

But in the *Course*, "atonement" involves the exact opposite realization—that one *is not* (and never has been) separate from God. It now refers to correcting the *false* belief that men are separate from God. Hence, because "the atonement" is not yet completed, *Course* students are told they have an important role to play in "the Atonement" (167:7, 10).

In *Course* teaching, "forgiveness" does not pardon sins before God because sins aren't real to begin with. Therefore, "forgiveness" merely involves the realization there never were any sins to pardon. "Sinners" do not exist because "sin" is an illusion. According to an interview with *Course* editor and teacher Kenneth Wapnick:

> In fact there's a line in the *Course* that says, God does not forgive because he has never condemned. Technically, God doesn't forgive, God simply loves. Forgiveness in the *Course* is the correction for the belief in sin, the belief in separation, the belief in guilt.
>
> SCP: Christ did not die for our sins?
>
> WAPNICK: No. Absolutely not. Because once you see his death in that way, then you make sin real. . . . The whole idea of the *Course* is that sin

> is an illusion, . . . The crux of the whole thing is that our relationship with God has never been impaired. It's only in our thinking that it was. In other words, for the *Course*, sin never really happened. . . . What Jesus did for us was show us that the separation never really happened. (156:13–14)

As a result of this distorted philosophy, the *Course* teaching on "salvation" lies in understanding that no one requires Biblical salvation because all men are already divine. "Salvation" is merely accepting one's "true" identity as being one in essence with God. Each individual *is* the Son of God; each is already perfect and therefore needs nothing "from" God because each person's true nature *is* God (167:chs. 13, 22–23).

Sin, guilt, death, judgment, propitiatory atonement, etc., are all viewed as "attack" philosophies by the *Course*—concepts which greatly hinder spiritual "progress" and severely damage our "true" divine nature. Men must become free of these false, enslaving, and evil ideas if they desire true spiritual freedom. Otherwise, they choose to "remain in hell" and to "kill" the God of love (167:chs. 5–6; pp. 374–378).

Thus, in the world view of the *Course*, it is orthodox Christian beliefs (Biblical teachings given by God) which are evil, insane, and anti-Christ.

It is possible to see how unbiblical the instructions of the *Course* are when we compare them to what the Bible teaches.

- The *Course* explains that men are not separated from God. But the Bible teaches, "But your iniquities have separated you from your God; your sins have hidden his face from you, so that he will not hear" (Isaiah 59:2, NIV).

- The *Course* explains that there was no atonement and that Jesus Christ did not die on the cross for our sins. But the Bible teaches, "He Himself bore our sins in His body on the cross . . ." (1 Peter 2:24 NAS) and ". . . Jesus Christ, the Righteous One . . . is the atoning sacrifice for our sins, and not only for ours but for the sins of the whole world" (1 John 2:1–2, NIV). Jesus Himself taught, ". . . the Son of man did not come to be served, but to serve, and to give his life a ransom for many" (Matthew 20:28, NIV).

- The *Course* explains that no one needs to believe on Christ for forgiveness of sins. The Bible teaches, "Salvation is found in no one else, for there is no other name under heaven given to men by which we must be saved" (Acts 4:12, NIV). Jesus Himself warned, ". . . if you do not believe that I am the one I claim to be, you will indeed die in your sins"

(John 8:24, NIV). He taught, "I am the way and the truth and the life. No one comes to the Father except through Me." (John 14:6, NIV)

In the following representative samplings of *Course* theology, remember that "Jesus" is supposedly speaking and that every individual is described as "the [or a] Son of God."

God	"The *Course* says that God is impersonal." (Kenneth Wapnick, in 156:11) "God Himself is incomplete without me." (324:182) "God [is] simply . . . a nonphysical love force that is neither vengeful, judgmental, nor punishing—only loving and forgiving." (324:43–44)
Man	God created you as part of Him. That is both where you are and what you are. It is completely unalterable. It is total inclusion. You cannot change it now or ever. It is forever true. It is not a belief, but a fact. (331:89) As God created you, you have all power. (330:67) "I am the holy Son of God Himself." Here is your declaration of release from bondage of the world. . . . You are the holy Son of God Himself. . . . Be glad today how very easily is hell undone. You need but tell yourself: "I am the holy Son of God Himself./ I cannot suffer, cannot be in pain;/ I cannot suffer loss, nor fail to do/ All that salvation asks." . . . The Son of God has come in glory to redeem the lost, to save the helpless, and to give the world the gift of his forgiveness. . . . You who perceive yourself as weak and frail, . . . hear this: All power is given unto you in earth and Heaven. There is nothing that you cannot do. . . . Then let the Son of God awaken from his sleep, and opening his holy eyes, return again to bless the world he made. Your glory is the light that saves the world. Do not withhold salvation longer. Look about the world, and see the suffering there. Is not your heart willing to bring your weary brothers rest? . . . They suffer pain until you have denied its hold on you. They die till you accept your own eternal life. You are the holy Son of God Himself. Remember this, and all the world is free. Remember this, and earth and Heaven are one. (163:353–54)
Sin	Sin is the grand illusion. (167:375) True perception . . . is the means by which the world is saved from sin, for sin does not exist. And it is this that true perception sees. (166:81) When you are tempted to believe that sin is real, remember this: If sin is real, both God and you are not. . . . Joyously [release] one another from the belief in sin. (167:377–78)
Guilt	The idea that the guiltless Son of God can attack himself and make himself guilty is insane. In any form, in anyone, believe this not. For sin and condemnation are the same, and the belief in one is faith in the other, calling for punishment instead of love. Nothing can justify insanity, and to call for punishment upon yourself must be insane. See no one, then, as guilty, and you will affirm the truth of guiltlessness unto yourself. . . . Guilt makes you blind, for while you see one spot of guilt within you, you will not see the light. Do not be afraid to look within. . . . Can you see guilt where God knows there is perfect innocence? (167:243–44)
Forgiveness	We are forgiven now. And we are saved from all the wrath we thought belonged to God, and found it was a dream. (163:475) *Forgiveness* is for God and toward God but not of Him. It is impossible to think of anything He created that could need forgiveness. Forgiveness, then, is an illusion. (166:79)

Jesus Christ	There is no need for [anyone's] help [in order to] enter Heaven for you have never left. . . . The name of Jesus is the name of one who was a man but saw the face of Christ in all his brothers and remembered God. So he became identified with *Christ*, a man no longer, but at one with God. The man was an illusion. . . . Yet who can save [anything] unless he sees illusions and then identifies them as what they are? Jesus remains a Savior because he saw the false without accepting it as true. And Christ needed his form that He might appear to men and save them from their own illusions. In his complete identification with the Christ . . . Jesus became what all of you must be. He led the way for you to follow him. . . . Is he the Christ? O yes, along with you. (166:83)
The Incarnation and Second Coming	The First Coming of Christ is merely another name for the creation, for Christ is the Son of God. The Second Coming of Christ means nothing more than the end of the ego's rule and the healing of the mind. (167:58)
Atonement	If the crucifixion is seen from an upside-down point 87 of view, it does appear as if God permitted and even encouraged one of His Sons to suffer because he was good. This particularly unfortunate interpretation, which arose out of projection, has led many people to be bitterly afraid of God. Such anti-religious concepts enter into many religions. Yet the real Christian should pause and ask, "How could this be?" Is it likely that God Himself would be capable of the kind of thinking which His Own words have clearly stated is unworthy of His Son? The best defense, as always, is not to attack another's position, but rather to protect the truth. It is unwise to accept any concept if you have to invert a whole frame of reference in order to justify it. . . . Persecution frequently results in an attempt to "justify" the terrible misperception that God Himself persecuted His Own Son on behalf of salvation. . . . *It is so essential that all such thinking be dispelled that we must be sure that nothing of this kind remains in your mind.* I was not "punished" because you were bad. The wholly benign lesson the Atonement teaches is lost if it is tainted with this kind of distortion in any form. . . . I have been correctly referred to as "the lamb of God who taketh away the sins of the world," but those who represent the lamb as blood-stained do not understand the meaning of the symbol. . . . The message of the crucifixion is perfectly clear: "*Teach only love, for that is what you are.*" If you interpret the crucifixion in any other way, you are using it as a weapon for assault rather than as the call for peace for which it was intended. The Apostles often misunderstood it, and for the same reason that anyone misunderstands it. Their own imperfect love made them vulnerable to projection, and out of their own fear they spoke of the "wrath of God" as his retaliatory weapon. Nor could they speak of the crucifixion entirely without anger, because their sense of guilt had made them angry. (167:32–33, 87, emphasis added)
Salvation	You are one with God. Again, how simple is salvation! It is merely a statement of your true identity. (163:125) A sense of separation from God is the only lack you really need to correct. . . . Salvation is nothing more than "right-mindedness" . . . . (167:11, 53) The journey to the cross should be the last "useless journey . . . ." Do not make the pathetic error of "clinging to the old rugged cross . . . ." This is not the Gospel I intended to offer you. We have another journey to undertake, and if you will read these lessons carefully they will help prepare you to undertake it. (167:47) The full awareness of the Atonement, then, is the recognition that *the separation [from God] never occurred.* (167:90)

Death	Death is the central dream from which all illusions stem. . . . And no one asks if a benign Creator could will this. . . . Death is the symbol of the fear of God. . . . The grimness of the symbol is enough to show it cannot coexist with God. . . . He did not make death because He did not make fear. Both are equally meaningless to Him. . . . Teacher of God, your one assignment could be stated thus: Accept no compromise in which death plays a part. . . . And what is the end of death? Nothing but this; the realization that the Son of God is guiltless now and forever. Nothing but this. (166:63–64)
Judgment	The Last Judgment is one of the most threatening ideas in your thinking. This is because you do not understand it. Judgment is not an attribute of God. . . . No one is punished for sins, and the Sons of God are not sinners. . . . Do not fear the Last Judgment, but welcome it. . . . The Second Coming is merely the return of sense. Can this possibly be fearful? (167:29, 88, 158)
Hell	As long as any mind remains possessed of evil dreams, the thought of hell is real. God's teachers have the goal of wakening the minds of those asleep. (166:66)
The Devil	The mind can make the belief in separation very real and very fearful, and this belief is the "devil." (167:45)
The Creation	The world you see is an illusion of a world. God did not create it. (166:81)
Time	The world of time is the world of illusion. (166:41)

The above teachings of the *Course* prove beyond any doubt that the Jesus of the New Testament could not be its author. The entity who dictated the *Course* to Helen Schucman lied when he claimed to be Jesus Christ. Thus, the most logical possibility for the true author of the *Course* is a demon, a spiritual underling of the one Jesus called a liar and "a murderer from the beginning" (John 8:44, NASB).

Occultic Potential

The spiritistic (demonic) nature of the *Course* should be obvious. We find several themes common to spiritistic revelations of which we mention only four: (1) dictation to a person uninterested and/or unlikely to write in the area of material being received; (2) forcing production of the revelations (cf. Edgar Cayce); (3) anti-biblical content; and (4) encouraging psychic guidance.

Even *Course* editor and promoter, psychologist Kenneth Wapnick "commented that if the Bible were considered literally true, then the *Course* would have to be viewed as demonically inspired" (157:23). The Bible itself literally warns, "Dear friends, do not believe every spirit, but test the spirits to see whether they are from God, because many false prophets have gone out into the world. . . . Every spirit that does not acknowledge Jesus is not from God. This is the spirit of the antichrist . . ." (1 John 4:1–3, NIV).

Because there really are false Christs and false prophets in the world—and lying spirits associated with them—Scripture warns that all who proclaim a false gospel are liable to eternal judgment: "But even if we or an angel from heaven should preach a gospel other than the one we preached to you, let him be eternally condemmed!" (Galatians 1:8) When the *Course* actively promotes another Jesus, a different spirit, and a false gospel, the Scripture itself claims its origin must be demonic (2 Corinthians 11:3–4, 13–15); (see also chapter 6).

That the eventual production of the *Course* was supernaturally arranged behind the scenes by demonic initiative should be obvious to those familiar with the methods of spiritual warfare revealed in Scripture and in the history of occultic revelations. The official version of the story is found in *Journey Without Distance: The Story Behind* A Course in Miracles (Celestial Arts, 1984) by publisher and psychic Robert Skutch. Apparently, complex human events and encounters were carefully (and miraculously) arranged via other worldly initiative and agency to ensure its production.

The extent of this occult collaboration and the power it represents on the part of the spirit world (to influence human affairs) is not small—but in light of Biblical revelation, it is neither unexpected nor unusual (2 Corinthians 4:4; 1 John 5:19). We find similar manipulation of events and people in the lives of innumerable psychics, occultists, mediums, etc. (168). As Dr. Helen Schucman, the "channel" for A *Course in Miracles*, confesses, "The birth of A *Course in Miracles* could not have occurred as it did without every single one of the cast being in the right place at the right time" (164:22).

Furthermore, the wholesale denial of God's word and God's Son is typical of spiritistic revelations in general (132).

Finally, the *Course* content promotes occultism and spiritistic guidance, another characteristic goal of demonic revelations. For example,

> There are, of course, no "unnatural" powers. . . . Certainly there are many "psychic" powers that are clearly in line with this course. Communication is not limited to the small range of channels the world recognizes. . . . The seemingly new abilities that may be gathered on the way can be very helpful. . . . They are valuable teaching aids. . . . Nothing that is genuine is

> used to deceive. The Holy Spirit is incapable of deception, and He can use only genuine abilities. . . .
>
> Any ability that anyone develops has the potentiality for good. To this there is no exception. And the more unusual and unexpected the power, the greater its potential usefulness. Salvation has need of all abilities, for what the world would destroy the Holy Spirit would restore. . . . The Holy Spirit needs these gifts, and those who offer them to Him and Him alone go with Christ's gratitude upon their hearts. (166:59–60) *

Not surprisingly, volume 2 of the *Course* ends with the promise of psychic guidance:

> Therefore obey your will, and follow Him Whom you accepted as your voice. . . .
>
> No more specific lessons are assigned, for there is no more need of them. Henceforth, hear but the Voice for God. . . . He will direct your efforts, telling you exactly what to do, how to direct your mind, and when to come to Him in silence, asking for His sure direction and His certain Word. His is the Word that God has given you. His is the Word you chose to be your own.
>
> And now I place you in His hands, to be His faithful followers, with Him as Guide through every difficulty and all pain that you may think is real. . . . He has earned your trust by speaking daily to you of your Father and your brother and your Self. He will continue. Now you walk with Him, as certain as is He of where you go; as sure as He [is] of how you should proceed; as confident as He is of the goal, and of your safe arrival in the end. The end is certain, and the means as well. To this we say "Amen." You will be told exactly what God wills for you each time there is a choice to make. . . . You do not walk alone. God's angels hover near and all about. His Love surrounds you, and of this be sure; that I will never leave you comfortless. (163:477–478)

As an example of the psychic guidance people have been led to accept through the *Course*, many people have received "Jesus" as their personal spirit guide—actually, a demon cleverly impersonating Jesus. In his *Good-Bye to Guilt*, Gerald Jampolsky confesses that "Jesus" became his spirit guide and even possesses him to act and speak through him:

> To my complete surprise, I began to develop what I would call a personal relationship with Jesus. . . . He demonstrated that death was not real, that

---

* For evidence that psychic powers are neither natural human abilities, nor gifts of the Holy Spirit, but demonically mediated (see 396).

> life is eternal, and that minds can communicate with each other forever, even after the body has been laid aside.
>
> I began to feel his presence in me, and at times I actually felt he was acting through me as an extension of his thoughts, his words, and his actions. I became absorbed by his message that the world could be transformed if all of us would practice forgiveness. At first, I was concerned about what other people might think of me, so I kept my relationship with Jesus a secret.
>
> As my relationship with Jesus has become more comfortable, I am now less concerned about what others might say, and today a prominent picture of Jesus hangs in my living room over the fireplace. . . . In a way which I cannot fully explain, I have chosen Jesus as my teacher. . . . (162:62–64)

Jampolsky even defines learning to listen to "the inner voice" as one of three key concepts of the *Course* (162:5). Thus:

> The voice of love goes by many names, such as the voice of God, Holy Spirit, voice of knowing, inner teacher, inner voice, inner guide, and intuition. . . . It comes from . . . the God-self, that is in the center of our being—always there to answer and give us directions in response to any questions that we may ask.
>
> In order to hear this inner guidance, we need to learn to still our minds, have the faith and a little willingness to ask for help—and expect to have our request answered. The voice, or guidance, can come to us as a thought; it can be experienced as inner dictation, or it can be a visualized form. . . . (162:52)

Dr. Jampolsky has had such amazing experiences by listening to his inner voice (such as an unexpected meeting with Mrs. Anwar Sadat, also reputedly psychic) that he now follows its guidance implicitly—"even when it seems irrational" (162:56). Even the dead themselves can be contacted, another practice the Bible explictly condemns:

> Let us know that "communication is never broken, even when the body is destroyed, provided that we do not believe that bodies are essential for communication." Isn't that what Jesus taught the world by the resurrection? (162:136)

No. What Jesus taught the world by His Resurrection was that "I am the way and the truth and the life. No one comes to the Father except through me" (John 14:6, NIV), and "I am the resurrection and the life. He who believes in me will live, even though he dies . . ." (John 11:25, NIV). Jesus would never accept contact with the dead when the Word of God specifically prohibited it. In the Bible God Himself warns that no person is to become one "who is a medium or spiritist or who consults the dead. Anyone who does these things is detestable to the Lord" (Deuteronomy 18:11–12, NIV).

❧ ❧ ❧

A *Course in Miracles* alleges to be the supernatural revelation of a personal, powerful, and controlling psychic "voice," a voice claiming to be Jesus, given through a skeptical and somewhat fearful atheistic research psychologist over a period of almost eight years. But the content of the *Course* forcefully supports the occult, adamantly denies Christ, and is intensely anti-Biblical.

The reader may decide for himself its probable origin.

CHANNELING

Definition: Channeling is a new age term for mediumism or spirit-possession, in this case, employing spirit guides in new age medicine. Channeling occurs when someone permits a spirit entity to possess him or her for new age healing purposes. The spirits may perform psychic diagnosis or healing through a healer, or they may speak through the person's vocal cords in order to give spiritual, medical, and other teaching. Automatic writing and inner voice dictation are other forms of spirit communication by channeling.

Founder: The first recorded incident of channeling per se is found in Genesis 3:1 (see also 2 Corinthians 11:3, 13–15; Revelation 12:9; 20:2).

How Does It Claim to Work? By meditation, visualization, hypnosis, altered states of consciousness, and other methods, the spirits are able to enter, possess, and control a person, much in the same manner a puppeteer controls a puppet. People claim that by permitting spirits to possess and speak through them, mankind can attain a wealth of spiritual and other wisdom directly from spirits who have "passed on" or are highly evolved. The spirits claim they can assist peoples' health concerns and direct them toward true individual and social enlightenment.

Scientific Evaluation: Certain aspects of the practice can be "scientifically" evaluated, as in parapsychological research, but science cannot evaluate the channelers' specific claims concerning the spirits' existence, nature, or purpose.

Occultic Potential: Channeling can be used for an endless number of occultic pursuits, including so-called higher (altered) states of consciousness, developing psychic powers, attaining new revelations. The new age movement as a whole is largely based upon channeled revelations and activities.

Major Problem(s): The spirits who claim to be "Ascended Masters" or wise and loving entities sent from God are really evil spirits the Bible identifies as demons (see below and chapter 6).

Biblical/Christian Evaluation: Channeling is part of what the Bible calls spiritual warfare (Ephesians 6:10–18) and is a practice specifically forbidden (Deuteronomy 18:9–12). The spirits' hidden purpose is to bring about people's eventual spiritual ruin by gaining their trust and exerting influence over them (2 Corinthians 4:4; 11:14).

Potential Dangers: Spiritual deception, occult bondage, demon possession, mental breakdown, physical harm, shortened life, and a host of other harmful consequences (refs. 396; 141; 123–127).

THIRTEEN

CHANNELING*

Channeling is a new age term for mediumship or spirit-possession. When men and women willingly give over their minds and bodies to spirit entities who enter and control people, who use them to heal or give occultic teachings and other information, this is "channeling." Recent books which promote channeling include Sanaya Roman and Duane Packer's *Opening to Channel: How to Connect with Your Guide* (288) and Kathryn Ridall's *Channeling: How to Reach Out to Your Spirit Guides* (290).

In America and throughout the world, channeling is a multi-billion-dollar business. Famous movie stars, corporate executives, scholars, artists, and businessmen are all turning to channeling. Various retreat centers and workshops are springing up around the country which teach people how to open themselves so that the spirits can possess them and they can become channels themselves (132:7–10).

Importance of Channeling in New Age Medicine

Channeling is important to new age medicine because many spirits who speak through channelers have given information on various new age heal-

* Some material is excerpted from the authors' *The Facts on Spirit Guides* (Harvest House, 1988) which provides specific documentation and is recommended as supplemental reading.

ing techniques. In addition, many new age health practitioners have spirit guides, and these beings instruct them in the use of new age health methods, psychic diagnosis, and related areas. As an example, new age healer Barbara Brennan explains the importance of channeling to her own healing work. Consider the following description of a typical healing session with a patient:

> I will usually both see and hear the guides. . . . I usually have about three teachers that guide me. . . . The guide also visually appears to fit over me like a glove. The guide begins to move my arms and hands. . . . My personality self seems to be floating off and above. . . . I feel merged with the guide. . . . (47:171–172)

Iona Teeguarden is a leading teacher of Jin Shin Do acupressure and co-founder of the Acupressure Workshop in Santa Monica, California. In the preface to her book, *Acupressure Way of Health: Jin Shin Do*, she has expressed her gratitude to her spirit guide, "Iajai," for its help in her new age medical practice (7:6).

Edgar Cayce is another example; his spirit guides produced thousands of pages of information on new age medicine over the years.

Another spirit entity, "Seth," has dictated various texts through medium Jane Roberts, on both attitudinal healing and another popular new age health technique, dreamwork. His book, *Seth: Dreams and Projection of Consciousness*, cites information showing how dreamwork can be used to secure a wide variety of new age goals. In particular, this spirit entity reveals how dreams can be used to develop altered states of consciousness and astral projection (33:6–13, 39–41, 63–64, 193–207, 350).

Another example of how channeling is also important is that spirits cooperate with many different doctors in diagnosis and treatment.

Consider the medical practice of neurosurgeon and former Harvard Professor C. Norman Shealy, M.D., Ph.D., founder of the seven-hundred member American Holistic Medicine Association. He is the author of *Occult Medicine Can Save Your Life* (50) and co-author with spiritist Carolyn Myss of *The Creation of Health: Merging Traditional Medicine with Intuitive Diagnosis* (51). Dr. Shealy has a working relationship with clairvoyant Myss (51:xx–xxiv), who is co-publisher of Stillpoint Publishing Company, which produces books received through channeling methods (329:1–15).

According to the Stillpoint catalog, Myss provides psychic diagnosis for Dr. Shealy's patients, apparently through the help of her spirit guide, "Genesis"—even when the patients are hundreds or thousands of miles away (329:5–6, 9). This, of course, is reminiscent of the psychic diagnosis channeled through medium Edgar Cayce. Scores of doctors, such as William McGarey, M.D., have spent several decades integrating the spiritistic revelations of Cayce into their modern medical professions.

Noted physician Bernard Segal, M.D., is another physician who uses a channeler in his medical practice: "One of my patients is a medium. She regularly gives me information about the living and messages from the dead . . ." (51:xviii). Robert Leichtman, M.D., also uses spirit guides for medical diagnosis (291) and has written almost forty books describing his contacts with the famous dead through the mediumship of D. Kendrick Johnson (263). W. Brugh Joy, M.D., has worked at Johns Hopkins Hospital and the Mayo Clinic in Rochester, Minnesota. In his *Joy's Way* (301) he details his conversion to occultism and its value to his medical practice. His experimentation in mysticism and mystical energies resulted one day in his being "commanded" by a voice to reform his medical practice:

> It was a Saturday morning. I had finished rounds at the hospital and was working on some patients' charts in my office when I felt an incredibly strong urge to enter into meditation. It was so strong that I did not understand what was happening to me. I completed the patients' charts and gave in to the impress. A vortex of energy, of a magnitude I had never before experienced, reverberated through my body and threw my awareness into a superheightened state. Then a loud voice—not that of the Inner Teacher—said, in essence: "Your experience and training as an orthodox physician is completed. It's over. The time has come for you to embark on a rededication of your Beingness to a deeper commitment and action. . . ."
>
> The voice didn't care about my many personal concerns and commitments. It next presented to my awareness that I would soon begin a journey into the world, going first to Findhorn [a spiritistic community] and to England, Egypt, India, Nepal near the Tibetan border and perhaps to Japan. . . . The voice explained clearly that my vision of being a physician had been distorted by boyhood ideals and by the current concepts of science and medicine, which overemphasized the body and external causes and ignored the journey of the soul. I was to begin the study of alternative healing practices and reach insights Western medicine had not yet dared to dream, insights that would unify exoteric and esoteric traditions and thus form the basis of an integrated approach to the art of healing. The last instruction the voice gave me was simply to detach from everything. (301:206–207)

Dr. Joy did indeed "detach" and today his commitment is given equally to new age medical care and the radical spiritual (occultic) transformation of his patient's world view (301:1–15).

Although exact figures are unknown, we expect that there are hundreds and perhaps thousands of qualified medical doctors around the country who are currently engaged in the practice of using channelers or spiritist mediums to help in patient diagnosis. Many are channelers themselves.

Physicians form a significant portion of the two-thousand member Academy of Parapsychology and Medicine, which devotes a good deal of time to research in psychic healing. Its president is Robert A. Bradley, M.D., a spiritistic medium and inventor of the Bradley method of natural childbirth. In his article, "The Need for the Academy of Parapsychology and Medicine," he states that this particular method of childbirth was given to him by his spirit guides either in dream states or by direct conscious communication:

> I'm a great believer in spirit guidance. I think it is the only logical explanation for some of the things that have happened to me. . . . I personally think spirit communication is going on constantly, that we are never alone. The talks I give, the ideas I have on natural childbirth came to me either in sleep or from direct spirit communication. (262:100–101)

In this article and elsewhere he underscores the importance of spiritism for modern medicine. He says that much important information "comes from altered states of consciousness which are spirit controlled" (262:100–101, 106).

In Great Britain, the World Federation of Healers has about ten thousand members, composed largely of professed channelers or mediums. With government approval, these mediums treat patients in some fifteen hundred hospitals in Great Britain. The organization has even been given corporate membership in the United Nations Association (48:50).

In America alone, thousands of physicians have been trained in "sophrology" and other new age methods utilizing Eastern and Western mind and body disciplines such as yoga, autogenics, Zen, Tibetan Buddhism, visualization, and various somatic therapies (441:1–3).

Because of facts such as these, numerous physicians are powerfully being persuaded to incorporate new age techniques into their medical practices. As it has in the past, spiritism is beginning to play a significant role in modern health-care.

Occultic Potential

Who or what are these spirits that are speaking through human mediums to influence healthcare? In our book, *The Facts on Channeling* (132), we supply documentation to prove that the spirits that speak through channelers are not the benign entities they claim to be. Rather, they are evil spirits, demons, whose leader is Satan.

In our book, we prove that these spirits are demons by citing their own teachings, proving they are liars, and citing the suspicions of channelers themselves who suspect these beings are not who they claim to be. We show that the consensus of history and religion, the testimony of active and former occultists, the phenomenon of spirit possession, the authority of the Bible, and the testimony of Jesus Christ, as well as the spirits' own teachings, coalesce to show that the spirits in modern channeling—and indeed all forms of spiritism—are really one and the same with the evil spirits the Bible calls "demons" (132:31–43; see also pp. 90–93).

Below we reproduce excerpts from *The Facts on Channeling* concerning some of the specific hazards of channeling.

❧ ❧ ❧

"As an introduction, consider the case of Bill Slater, head of BBC television drama. One evening, after attending an 'impromptu seance' with a Ouija board, he went home. In the early hours of the morning:

> I found myself half-awake, knowing there was some kind of presence massing itself on my chest; it was, to my certain knowledge, making every effort to take over my mind and body. It cost me considerable will-power to concentrate all my faculties to push the thing away, and for what seemed like twenty minutes this spiritual tussle went on between this awful presence and myself. Needless to say, although before going to bed I had felt perfectly happy and at ease with a very good friend, in a flat I knew well, I was now absolutely terrified—I have never known such fear since. I was finally able to call my friend's name; he woke up, put on the light, and was astonished to find me well-nigh a gibbering idiot. I have never since had any psychic experience. (442:451)

"Besides the above flirt with the demonic, there are many cases where occultic activity has directly resulted in the destruction of human life. It is not just that there are a few cases; the fact is there are thousands of them littered throughout the history of religion, occultism, spiritism, and parapsychology—mental illness, suicide, physical crippling, blindness, death (396). People who would never think of playing Russian roulette with a gun, even once, or who would never deliberately take a dangerous drug, have a very good reason for their decisions. The odds of disaster are too high. Yet the odds of harming oneself from occultic practices are apparently just as high or higher. What is amazing is that the evidence is there for all to see and yet it is ignored.

"In the Bible, demons are presented as inflicting numerous physical and psychological ailments upon their victims. Many of these parallel today's cases of channeling. While it must be stressed that most illness is not demonically wrought, the array of symptoms suggest the possibility of a virtual monopoly over the workings of the human mind and body; skin disease (Job 2:7), destructive and irrational acts (Matthew 8:28; Luke 8:27), deafness and inability to speak (Mark 9:25; Luke 11:14), epileptic-like seizures (Matthew 17:15; Mark 9:17, Luke 9:39), blindness (Matthew 12:22), tormenting pain (Revelation 9:1–11), insanity (Luke 8:26–35), severe physical deformity (Luke 13:11–17), and other symptoms. Demons can give a person supernatural strength (Luke 8:29) or attempt to murder them (Matthew 17:15,18).

"Not unexpectedly, there are numerous accounts of mediums, channelers and occultists or those who frequent them suffering physically in a variety of ways from their practice (ill health, alcoholism, spirit attacks, early deaths, etc.)

"Most people do not know the famous medium Arthur Ford became a morphine addict and alcoholic, which caused him no end of grief much of his life (378:16–17). Dr. Nandor Fodor observes: 'After prolonged exercise of mediumship intemperance often sets in. The reason is a craving for stimulants following the exhaustion and depletion felt after the seance. Many mediums have been known who succumbed to the craving and died of delirium tremens' (178:234). Bishop Pike died a tragic death from his involvement in spiritism (379). Medium Jane Roberts died at the age of 55. Others became addicted to drugs (380:142). Medium Edgar Cayce, a large man of 6'2", died in misery weighing a mere sixty pounds, apparently physiologically 'burned out' from giving too many psychic readings. The biography on Cayce by Joseph Millard reveals the extent of suffering Cayce's occultic involvement cost him—from psychic attacks to mysterious fires, the periodic loss of his voice, erratic personality changes and emotional torments, constant "bad luck" and personal set-back, and guilt induced by psychic readings that ruined others' lives (179:98–116, 198–201). Many channelers seem to succumb to various vices later in life, from sexual immorality (380:133,140;178:234) to numbing their conscience (Keene observes, 'cheating, lying, stealing, conning—these are sanctified in the ethics of mediumship as I knew it,' 380:141) to alcoholism and drug addiction (380:135, 142; 178:234) to crime and worse (381:17, 95, 116, 185 cf. ref. 177).

"M. Lamar Keene spent thirteen years among professional mediums as a famous (although fraudulent) medium. In his public confession, *The Psychic Mafia*, he observes,

> All the mediums I've known or known about have had tragic endings. The Fox sisters, who started it all, wound up as alcoholic derelicts. William Slade, famed for his slate-writing tricks, died insane in a Michigan sanitarium. Margery, the medium, lay on her deathbed a hopeless drunk. The celebrated Arthur Ford fought the battle of the bottle till the very end and lost. . . . Wherever I looked it was the same: mediums, at the end of a tawdry life, dying a tawdry death. . . . I was sick and tired of the whole business—the fraud bit, the drug bit, the drinking bit, the entire thing. . . . (380:147–148)

"Spiritist and guru Sri Chinmoy, a spiritual advisor at the United Nations, observes, 'Many, many black magicians and people who deal with spirits have been strangled or killed. I know because I've been near quite a few of these cases.' (354:62)

"Dr. Kurt Koch observed after forty-five years of counseling the occultly oppressed that from his own experience numerous cases of suicides, fatal accidents, strokes and insanity are to be observed among occult practitioners. And that 'anyone who has had to observe for forty-five years the effects of spiritism can only warn people with all the strength at his disposal' (300:238).

"In addition, over many years, the very act of channeling itself appears to have a destructive effect upon the human body. It is as if there is a type of, for lack of a better word, "psychic vampirism" at work which slowly eats away at a person's physical constitution (443:62; 178:235). Time and again in the lives of psychics, mediums, and spiritists, we have observed the power of the spirits in holding their captives to do their will (2 Timothy 2:24–26). When one attempts to suppress their channeling or mediumship, for example, the result will frequently be symptoms of disease or other serious problems, forcing a return to the practice. What is doubly tragic is that for all these people it started out so good, so promising" (132:38–40).

❧ ❧ ❧

This is why people should be concerned that so many in the field of new age medicine are receiving instructions, guidance, and diagnoses from the spirit world. The spirits are notorious for their deceptions, as many former occultists will testify. (See refs. 105–109; 123–126; 141.) Furthermore, as noted near the end of chapter 3, documentation exists that spiritistic healings are not true healings; rather, there is merely a transference of the illness from the physical level to a higher mental or spiritual level. The spirits may give a new age practitioner great insight into someone's medical problem or actually appear to heal the person. But this is only done to get people to accept occultic practices and philosophy that result in their spiritual deception, and often their eventual ruin (131).

Because the evidence indicates that these spirit entities are evil spirits bent on human destruction, no one who seeks out their guidance or healing will profit, least of all medical doctors and their patients. Perhaps an illustration of how one medical doctor became converted to spiritism would be instructive. The pattern for such contacts is fairly typical: It involves careful preparation of the spirits behind the scene, psychic development, contact with spirits, rejection of Christianity, and the spirits' assuming of influence or control in the doctor's life.

We select portions from psychiatrist Arthur Guirdham's autobiography (280) as an illustration. He recounts his conversion from orthodoxy as a child to the ancient heresy of the Cathar faith. Catharism, or Albegensianism, teaches that the creation, or the material world, is evil, a manifestation of the devil (who is Jehovah of the Old Testament). The true world is spirit and created by the true and good God. Man's purpose is to ascend to knowledge of the true world and the true God in the realm of spirit. Man's materially contaminated psyche is eventually purified through successive incarnations and by evolving to higher levels of consciousness. Catharism then, like many occult beliefs, provides a logical basis for spirit contact. The true realm of "the good" is the spiritual world, i.e., the spirit realm; the devil is found only in the material realm, which doesn't say much for the practice of conventional medicine. Regardless, once the spirit world is defined beforehand as the true realm of God, then all the phenomena of spiritual warfare are strategically camouflaged.

In essence, contacting the spirit world is encountering the truly divine realm, a form of contacting God. The spirits Dr. Guirdham contacts claim to be people who lived as Cathars in the thirteenth century who now wish him to revive the ancient heresy, and worse, prove it is "true" Christianity.

Dr. Guirdham's spiritism dramatically altered his medical practice, as the citations below reveal (cf. ref. 52). We conclude this chapter by citing the doctor's experiences in some depth. The citation below illustrates modern channeling phenomena, and will help the reader to understand its potential to influence medical doctors, as well as the consequences:

> I was positively intoxicated by the thought that at last I was wholly free from God. . . . To reject God may impart a feeling of freedom but what I then felt was exaltation. I did not know that this God I expelled like a weight from my shoulders was the Jehovah of the Old Testament. I did not know that the Cathar in me was already stirring. To the Cathars the God of the Old Testament was the Devil. . . . (280:66–67)

> I was not horrified by the fact of the Crucifixion. I detested and hated the attention given to it and loathed its visual representation. At that time it seemed to me I was indulging in a ferocious anti-Christian gesture. So I was, in terms of my orthodox Christian background. I was reliving the Cathar hatred of the Crucifix. They rejected the idea that Christ was truly incarnate. How could the Son of God be contaminated by matter? How could He die for our sins on the Cross? Seven hundred years later I repeated the Cathars' hatred of the Crucifix.
>
> Towards the end of this period when I was becoming more aware of the presences about me I had already begun to make contact with the people who were to guide me. . . .
>
> I was returning to my sources and being educated by psychic communication. . . . (280:68–70)

> Looking back I see how the process by which I was enlightened was beautifully accommodated to the idiosyncrasies and weaknesses of my nature. . . . (280:89)

> Our salvation lies in our freeing ourself from matter and in re-establishing contact with the spirit. . . . The more we move into the sphere of the psyche the more we are aware of discarnate entities and presences around us. . . . (280:98)

> During this time I moved in a circle of psychic communication. I constantly encountered cases of telepathy or precognition affecting myself or patients or people well known to me. People were constantly supplying me

with the answers to abstruse questions I had posed in their absence, a day or two previously. One patient would finish off a conversation begun by another. Some patients acted as catalysts to instigate improvement in others. The chronicle of this high peak of communication was revealed in my books *The Cathars and Reincarnation*, *Silent*, and *Obsession*. . . . (280:124)

The day was to come when I was to be urged by more than one discarnate entity from the thirteenth century to write a book and to write it quickly. I did not foresee that the day would come when I would be instructed, from the next world, as to its nature and contents. . . . (280:145)

I verify the evidence presented to me by different and often discarnate sources. I do this soberly and patiently. It is something which my daemon demands. I cannot deny what Braida [his spirit guide] asks of me because to do so would be a mutilation of my psyche. . . . As a compensation I am more at peace than I was. I am absolved from the necessity of hating God. . . . To me it is an inexpressible relief to find that what I had been brought up to worship was the Satanic God of the Old Testament. It is always a comfort to switch over to God from the Devil. . . . (280:202)

The Dualist attitude towards nature and the universe was certainly positive and a great help to me as a doctor. . . . Because I was a Dualist I was enabled to accept [astrological doctrines] easily that the stars and the moon influenced the patients' medical history, and how in those susceptible to the earth's vibrations the pattern of illness was related to the seasons. This was of special importance to me as a psychiatrist. . . . All I can say is that the more I became saturated with Dualism the greater was my usefulness as a doctor. (280:205)

Most important of all Dualism has given me a greater understanding of the nature of death. Because of what I have learnt of presences and spirits attendant on us I see it not as an abrupt cessation of sensation but as a subtle change of consciousness. . . . I know that, in the next life as in this, there are guides waiting to direct us. . . . It is over a year since Braida urged me to devote myself to Dualism at the expense of other activities. I have done my best to fulfill her wishes. I recognise that she is a surer guide in these matters. She lived seven centuries ago and has achieved the timeless condition. I am still locked in the prison of personality.

It is clear to me that I am the modest instrument of a cosmic design. I see now that the purpose of my life and its chief happiness is to be passively manipulated. . . . I know that the dead are not dead but are living in a state of altered consciousness. I know that they are around us, that they speak to us and guide us. I know, what I would never have imagined, that they guide us not only by vague exhortations but sometimes with a precision adapted to the unbelieving rationalism of our natures. In my case they have set me a specific task to perform. When my pen moves across the paper I am doing what is asked of me. . . .

What is required of me is that I write and talk as much about Dualism as possible. What it amounts to is that I devote myself to Catharism but the broader issue of Dualism is emphasized because it is necessary that we should know the spiritual antecedents of Catharism. The ground for my activity was carefully prepared. . . . (280:210–213)

It was also necessary for the purposes of the operation that I should be a doctor and above all a psychiatrist. It was even necessary that I should have also a degree in physiology and a B.Sc. for research. . . . (280:214)

For what purpose does Braida . . . wish to establish contact with me? Is it only to claim justice for the Cathars and to re-establish the good name of a dead heresy? The issue is bigger than that. . . . Braida also stimulated a flood of references which proved beyond doubt that Catharism originated in primitive Christianity. . . .

These days I accept that I am guided by her. I have ceased to marvel at my passive attitude even though for most of my life I was a person who wanted my own way. . . . The hands of many artists are directed by such guides as Braida. More often than not they are unaware that they are so inspired. (280:217–219)

Sadly, similar accounts could be cited from the lives of many other modern medical doctors.

Chiropractic

Definition: Physical adjustments to correct subluxations or "misalignments" of the spine.

Founder: D. D. Palmer

How Does It Claim to Work? Spinal misalignments allegedly impinge or cause pressure upon spinal nerves, interfering with the flow of nerve impulses to the rest of the body and producing susceptibility to disease. By correcting subluxations (spinal misalignments), proper performance of the nervous system is restored, thereby maintaining health.

Scientific Evaluation: Some physical manipulation employed by chiropractors may be both safe and beneficial. General massage for tension headaches and rational, conservative spinal manipulation therapy for some neuromusculoskeletal disorders is medically justifiable. However, the fundamental chiropractic theory of subluxations causing disease is false; subluxations have never been proven to exist or to function in the manner claimed.

Occultic Potential: May lead to occultic practices or beliefs or other new age health treatments in that these are often employed by chiropractors.

Major Problem: The basic theory underlying chiropractic treatment is false; the practice is employed far too extensively to be justified on the basis of its limited effectiveness. Furthermore, chiropractic theory and practice are easily integrated with many other new age therapies, thereby promoting new age medicine in general.

Biblical/Christian Evaluation: Avoid any irrational or potentially occultic aspects of chiropractic.

Potential Dangers: Misdiagnosis and/or delay of treatment of a serious illness; moderate to serious physical harm resulting from spinal adjustments; problems arising from overtreatment; treatment by occultic practices; overradiation from unnecessary full spine x-rays.

FOURTEEN

CHIROPRACTIC

The issue of chiropractic is an important one because in America today there are an estimated twenty-five thousand licensed practitioners. By 1969 chiropractors had treated over thirty million Americans and currently treat over five million people annually (270:138).

But is chiropractic based upon established principles of scientific medicine, or is it quackery? Is it possible to have a truly scientific practice of chiropractic? Can chiropractic properly be labeled new age medicine? Is there an occult history behind the founding of chiropractic? Can chiropractic be dangerous? These are some of the questions we will seek to answer in this chapter.

What we will discover is that although some chiropractors are, thankfully, seeking to reform their industry and to stay within the safeguards of scientific medicine, the majority of chiropractic practices today appear to fall into the realm either of marginal practices, occultic medicine, or quackery. That is, they are promoting a health system that does not work upon the basis of its stated principles and that rejects the findings of modern scientific medicine as these relate to its theory and practice. This is why "The scientific foundation of the practice has been generally disputed" (270:138). Medical encyclopedias often note that basic chiropractic theory is unproven:

> This theory has never been scientifically validated. (314:354)

> Physicians believe that no scientific basis for chiropractic theory has ever been established and that it is ineffective in the treatment of such common ailments as hypertension, heart disease, stroke, cancer, diabetes, and infectious diseases. (313:270)

One alternate health guide cited an editorial in the *British Medical Journal* which observed, "There is no evidence of a kind acceptable to medical science that chiropractic works" and that "what is wrong is the refusal . . . to accept the standards of proof that medical scientists have developed in the last hundred years." (325:94). The editorial also stated that when chiropractic claims to treat conditions other than bone and joint abnormalities it is the equivalent of "divining the future by examination of a bird's entrails" (325:94).

This is why William Jarvis, associate professor of Preventive Medicine at Loma Linda University School of Medicine, believes chiropractic is really a social problem, not a health asset. He asserts:

> Chiropractic is the most significant unscientific health-care delivery system in the United States. . . . It is so well entrenched that it must be viewed as a societal problem, not simply as a competitor of regular healthcare. (86:47; See ref. 428)

The main reason chiropractic is so widespread today appears to be simple ignorance; indeed, the number of people who uncritically accept chiropractic theory and practice is nothing short of amazing. In spite of its unscientific nature, in every state of the union, legislators have permitted chiropractors to be legally licensed as legitimate health-care practitioners.

The Nature of Chiropractic

Let us begin with an official definition of chiropractic. The Catalogue of the Palmer College of Chiropractic-West defines chiropractic in the following manner:

> Chiropractic is a natural health care system using the inherent healing properties within the body. It is based on the premise that displacement (subluxation) of the vertebrae can cause imperfect performance of the human nervous system by interfering with the flow of nerve impulses to and from the systems, organs and tissues of the body, thereby making the body susceptible to disease.
>
> By adjusting subluxations of the spinal column and its immediate articulations, chiropractic helps restore and maintain normal nerve function,

communications and body balance. . . . The human body thereby adapts to the environment and resists disease. Maximum physiologic potential is the objective. . . . Chiropractic is the science which concerns itself with the relationship between structure, primarily the spine, and function, primarily the nervous system of the human body, as that relationship may affect the restoration and preservation of health. (218:11–12)

In other words, chiropractic claims that spinal misalignment harms the flow of nerve impulses to and from the body's organs, tissues, and systems. This produces a general susceptibility to disease. Chiropractic "adjustment" supposedly restores proper nerve function, thereby maintaining health. As we will see below, this theory is false. However, this does not mean that all chiropractors can necessarily be labelled quacks. There is a legitimate, if very limited, application of chiropractic techniques.

Before we proceed, let us state our conviction that there are legitimate practices in chiropractic today. For example, physical manipulation of the spine and muscles are known to have limited benefit.

> Today, physiotherapists, athletic trainers, and several medical specialists sometimes employ manipulation for neuromusculoskeletal conditions. There is sufficient evidence of manipulation which can at least temporarily improve the range of motion of impaired joints and relieve pain—sometimes dramatically—to make it a worthwhile, albeit limited, medical procedure. Manipulation requires a great deal of individual skill, which many chiropractors apparently possess. (86:47–48)

In a highly critical report on chiropractic, Consumers Union nevertheless stated that:

> Government studies in the United States and Canada have judged manipulation to be a potentially useful technique for certain conditions, such as the loss of joint mobility. Research in manipulation is still meager, and controlled clinical studies are rare. . . . [Also] treatment of tension headaches by massage, for example, is well recognized. Those headaches can stem from tense muscles in the neck, and massage may relieve symptoms. (27:184–185)

To the extent chiropractors engage in such practices, the method is safe and may be effective for a limited number of ailments. Thus:

> There are . . . chiropractors who practice rational, conservative spinal manipulative therapy for neuromusculoskeletal disorders. They do not claim to be alternative practitioners but offer their skills as manipulation thera-

> pists when such treatment is medically justifiable. What proportion of chiropractors fits this description is unknown. The National Association of Chiropractic Medicine (NACM) was formed in 1984 as an attempt to organize reform-minded chiropractors. (86:52)

The problem in chiropractic is not with reformed-minded chiropractors who are attempting to use manipulation in a medically justified manner. These chiropractors are to be commended. The problem is with those chiropractors who either rely upon classical chiropractic theory, which is scientifically disproven, or who incorporate chiropractic with a wide variety of unsound and potentially harmful new age occultic practices.

In our view, there are three basic categories of modern chiropractic practice: First, traditional Palmerian chiropractic which continues to rely upon the occultic, quack, and unscientific theories developed by the founders of chiropractic, Daniel and B. J. Palmer; second, new age eclectic chiropractic which, in addition to chiropractic, uses a variety of other new age occultic techniques; and third, legitimate chiropractic which seeks to remain within the realm of modern medical scientific practice.

Unfortunately, it appears that the majority, perhaps the great majority, of practitioners fall into the first two categories.

Anyone concerned about his health should avoid chiropractors who fall into the first two categories. These categories are often labeled as the chiropractic "straights" and "mixers." Nevertheless, there is no hard and fast boundary between them. As one critic observes:

> Although straights may be labelled "cultists" for adhering to Palmer's dogma, the additional modalities mixers employ are apt to be just as nonscientific. Mixers utilize calonics, iridology, unproven devices, applied kinesiology (muscle testing), megavitamins, herbology, crystals, variations of acupuncture, glandular therapy, craniopathy, and a seemingly endless array of dubious diagnostic, prescription, and therapy procedures. (86:52)

Indeed, an influential new form of chiropractic called "network chiropractic" is actually a blend of the straight and mixer approaches (420; 421).

This widespread use of new age methods by chiropractors is why chiropractic belongs in a text on new age medicine. Perhaps many people would wonder at chiropractic being included in a text on new age medicine. They would consider such labelling out of place. Nevertheless, chiropractic has much in common with new age medicine, which is recognized by both new agers and chiropractors themselves. G. F. Reikeman is dean of Philosophy at the Sherman College of Chiropractic and co-founder of Renaissance Chiropractic Organization. In one of the standard compendiums on new age medical techniques, *The Holistic Health Handbook*, prepared by the Berkeley Holistic Health Center, Reikeman actually defines chiropractic as "A new age Philosophy, Science, and Art which focuses on correcting interference with the nervous system. . . ." (80:171).

Consider another example. Well-known chiropractor and developer of Touch for Health, John F. Thie, observes the connection between chiropractic and ancient Chinese philosophy based upon the meridian system, the flow of *chi*, and acupuncture points. He observes,

> There is a great similarity between the Chinese health philosophy and the philosophy of chiropractic. Palmer used magnetic healing techniques which he may have learned from the Chinese. Oriental acupuncturists are now coming to the Western chiropractic Colleges, and they, too, are finding great similarities between the two methods of healing. (20:16)

Thie also observes that modern chiropractic holds certain new age beliefs: The modern "Chiropractor believes that the innate intelligence that runs the body is connected to universal [cosmic] intelligence that runs the world [i.e., "God"], so each person is plugged into the universal intelligence through the nervous system" (20:6).

This is why new age psychics such as Joan Windsor can claim that, "The main advantage of seeking chiropractic healing is the aligning of bodily energies" (169:258). One text on the history of medicine observes:

> Chiropractic began from the assumption that a flow of energy from the brain was the essential life-giving force in the body, and that interference with this force produced disease. (312:159)

Furthermore, chiropractors themselves have often been involved in the development of many new age therapies:

- Bernard Jensen, the founder of iridology, is a chiropractor.
- George Goodheart, the inventor of applied kinesiology, is a chiropractor.
- John Thie, the inventor of Touch for Health, is a chiropractor.
- Ruth Drown and David Tansley, leaders in the field of radionics, are chiropractors.

- Oakley G. Smith, the inventor of Naprapathy, is a chiropractor. (Naprapathy is the belief that the main cause of disease is found in the derangement of the soft or connective tissues [73:133]).

And we have not begun to chronicle the list of chiropractors who have exerted influence in new age medicine. Chiropractic single-handedly began the quack practice of muscle testing in this country. Many chiropractors are also naturopaths. We have encountered people who have become teachers of new age therapies principally because their personal chiropractor used a particular new age treatment on them, sparking their interest. As examples, we could mention polarity therapy, reflexology, and homeopathy.

There is a logical reason for this association between chiropractic and new age medicine. First, historically chiropractic has occultic roots. Second, it is largely based on quackery. Therefore it bears more than its share in fostering the very essence of new age medicine: quackery and occultic practices masquerading as medicine. Because chiropractic is unscientific and potentially occultic, practitioners are naturally drawn to like-minded systems or to experimentation in questionable areas.

Origin

Chiropractic, like many new age therapies, began as the result of a simple misobservation. It began with the deaf janitor who worked in the office of Daniel David Palmer, the founder of chiropractic. Palmer had discovered that the janitor's deafness had allegedly occurred at the moment of a back injury, specifically a vertebra wrenched from its normal position. In his own words, Palmer himself explained how chiropractic was "discovered" in the following manner:

> Harvey Lillard, a janitor, in the Ryan Block, where I had my office, had been so deaf for seventeen years that he could not hear the racket of a wagon on the street or the ticking of a watch. I made inquiry as to the cause of his deafness and was informed that when he was exerting himself in a cramped, stooping position, he felt something give way in his back and immediately became deaf. An examination showed a vertebra racked from its normal position. I reasoned that if that vertebra was replaced, the man's hearing should be restored. With this object in view, a half-hour's talk persuaded Mr. Lillard to allow me to replace it. (26:18)

After restoring the vertebra, soon the janitor "could hear as before." Palmer was ecstatic:

> If no other discovery had been made, this, of itself, should have been hailed with delight. It was the key which has ultimately unlocked the secrets of functional metabolism. . . . (27:18)

Shortly thereafter, another alleged cure of a heart ailment convinced him that spinal misalignment was the key to health and disease:

> Shortly after this relief from deafness, I had a case of heart trouble which was not improving. I examined the spine and found a displaced vertebra pressing against the nerves which innervate the heart. I adjusted the vertebra and gave immediate relief—nothing "accidental" or "crude" about this.
>
> Then I began to reason that if two diseases, so dissimilar as deafness and heart trouble, came from [spinal] impingement, a pressure on nerves, were not other diseases due to a similar cause? Thus, the science (knowledge) and art (adjusting) of chiropractic were formed at that time. (26:18–19)

Palmer even claimed that "chiropractors correct abnormalities of the intellect as well as those of the body" (26:19).

Nevertheless, unaware that the nerves of hearing are entirely in the head and that the back vertebra do not affect the heart, Palmer wrongly concluded that spinal adjustment had solved hearing and heart problems and that misplacements of the vertebrae were the cause of all disease.

Thus, the essence of chiropractic theory as formulated by D. D. Palmer and his son, B. J. Palmer, is that all disease results from spinal misalignment, what was termed "vertebral subluxation." In the words of B. J. Palmer, who staunchly defended his father's theories:

> Chiropractic is ONE simple idea. Vertebral subluxation causes dis-ease, ALL dis-ease, EVERY dis-ease—not some, but all. Vertebral adjustment corrects THE cause of dis-ease, ALL dis-ease, EVERY dis-ease—not some, but all. That principal and practice is either right or wrong. If right, it is right all the way—one hundred percent. If wrong, it is wrong all the way—one hundred percent. (29:32)

As we will show, this idea "is wrong all the way—one hundred percent." But before we do so, we must first document the occultic background of chiropractic.

Chiropractors have argued that almost all medicine has some occult background, and therefore it is unfair to single out chiropractic for critisicm. But that is not the issue. Medicine may have an occult history, but modern medicine has repudiated it. The issue in chiropractic is whether or not its occult background continues to influence chiropractors today. This is why it is important to examine the occult background of chiropractic—because these beliefs continue to sway innumerable modern chiropractors.

Occultic Background

The occultic background of chiropractic can be seen in the life and activities of D. D. Palmer and B. J., his son. Connections to the occult may also be noted in ancient practices similar to chiropractic that were connected with occultic religion. Chiropractic or "Chiropraxy," for example, has been practiced among the ancient Egyptians, Greeks, Chinese, and Hindus (65:104–5). Palmer himself confessed that practices like chiropractic were not new and were associated with ancient pagan religion and cults and also in various contemporary occultic societies of his day (26:11–14, 21; 30:5–21).

But our principal concern here is not ancient chiropractic, but the occultic activities of the Palmers themselves. Both D. D. Palmer and his son were interested in the occult; one or both were interested or involved in radionics, masonry, phrenology, spiritism, and Eastern religious beliefs such as reincarnation (28:36; 30:21, 39–40; 24:29; 153:162–63, 220).

For over nine years, prior to discovering chiropractic, Daniel Palmer had been a psychic healer, a practice that during his day was associated with and/or part of magnetic healing. He was trained under one of the most famous magnetic healers in America at that time, Paul Castor (73:131). Palmer even confessed that chiropractic evolved from magnetic healing and was an outgrowth of it (26:17).

Palmer had also been a phrenologist (diagnosing by head bumps) and was interested in spiritism. (30:33).

Although the nineteenth-and twentieth-century practices of magnetic healing were sometimes explainable on psychosomatic principles, they were also indistinguishable from the practices of modern spiritistic psychic healing. This can be seen by comparing authorities such as Dr. Nandor Fodor in his *Encyclopedia of Psychic Science* under the heading "Healing, Psychic" (178) and Slater Brown's chapter, "The Magnetists" in his text *The Heyday of Spiritualism* (219).

Magnetic healing, also associated with animal magnetism or mesmerism, was often a spiritistic phenomenon. Indeed, magnetists routinely claimed that their powers derived from the spirit world (6:35–39).

This is why Palmer's confession that he was a magnetic healer is so significant:

> I was a magnetic healer for nine years previous to discovering the principles which comprise the method known as chiropractic. During this period much of that which was necessary to complete the science [of chiropractic] was worked out. (26:17)

In fact, as is common with most occultists, Palmer even transmitted his psychic powers to his son:

> Prior to becoming a magnetic healer in Davenport . . . he had been a fish dealer. . . . Those who knew him in his later career declare him to have possessed an unusually magnetic personality and qualities of a psychic order. These were strongly inherited by Dr. B. J. Palmer. . . . Both father and son are said to have been privately interested in spiritualism [spiritism] which seems in fact verified by the latter's possession of various works on this subject. (30:33)

That both D. D. Palmer and his son could properly be classified as occultists should be clear to anyone who examines their philosophy and activities. The texts by D. D. Palmer such as his *Textbook of the Science, Art, and Philosophy of Chiropractic for Students and Practitioners* (26) and B. J. Palmer's *Answers* (29) and *The Bigness of the Fellow Within* (28) are illustrative.

Consider the following statement which B. J. Palmer quotes approvingly:

> Occult power really exists and is the most forceful end result bringing things into the world. Everyone may absorb as much of it [occult power] as he will from divine energy. All nature shows that it is to be used for securing the needed things of life. One must learn to absorb and use it as surely as one must learn to draw if one would paint or to use one's legs if one would skate. (31:48–49)

This is why he strongly implies that one who uses chiropractic is engaging in the use of occult power and why in early chiropractic theory "God," "Divine Energy," and "Occult Power" become blurred (31:43).

The Palmers call this psychic energy that is used in the occult by a specific term, "Innate." Innate was a mysterious, divine life force within all men that flowed from the brain through the nerves to the organs of the body. But all manifestations of occult or psychic power fall within the domain of manifestations of the Innate:

> There are within the enclosure of this human shell certain active (dormant because unrecognized) spiritual energies.
>
> During the past decade, more so than before, there has been an active investigation of the "phenomena" produced among those commonly

> known as the occult. . . . Chiropractors have enlarged the field of man's mental processes by revealing the fact that below the threshold of man's consciousness lie many gradations. . . . The powers and activities of this Innate Intelligence . . . are now being adjusted scientifically. (31:14)

Innate was also a universal divine energy which manifested itself in the individual in the form of what they termed Innate Intelligence. Thus, B. J. described Innate Intelligence as "God in human beings" (28:53).

His father, D. D. Palmer, described "Innate" in the following terms:

> That which I named 'Innate' . . . is a segment of that Intelligence which fills the universe. (26:491, cf. p. 382)

> Innate is said to be part of the "All Wise, Almighty, Universal Intelligence, the Great Spirit, the Greek's *Theos*, the Christian's God, the Hebrew's Helohim [sic], the Mahometan's Allah, [homeopathy founder] Hahnemann's Vital Force, new thot's [sic] Divine Spark. . . ." (26:493, cf. p. 864)

> The New Theology enunciated by me more than ten years ago as the basis for chiropractic, is the identification of God with Life-Force . . . God—the Universal Intelligence—the Life-Force of Creation—has been struggling for countless ages to improve upon itself—to express itself intellectually and physically higher in the scale of evolution. (26:446)

But the Palmers sometimes describe the manifestations of Innate in the same manner as mediums describe the manifestations of their spirit guides. Thus, Innate can inspire one psychically and provide supernatural revelations on a wide variety of subjects (29:58–60, 67–73). Also, Innate is itself personal and acts in a personal manner toward the individual. "Innate is a personality. . . . Innate has lived for centuries, . . . Innate points the way. Innate opens one or more doors of unlimited wisdom. . . ." (29:72–73).

In fact, Innate was believed to be the true originator of chiropractic. Allegedly, because Innate was a personal, divine guide, B. J. referred to Innate as the "other fellow" or the "fellow within." He taught that this "other fellow" was the real inventor of chiropractic.

> The 'other fellow' [Innate], because of constant and consistent research throughout fifty-seven years, discovered and proved location of a specific cause of ALL dis-ease and developed and proved a specific adjustment technique for its correction, proving its results on thousands of sick by scientific processes which none dispute. . . . [sic] (29:424)

B. J. Palmer also taught that the chiropractor must uncover and utilize the power of Innate if he is to be successful in his practice (28:55). Thus, true power in chiropractic was believed to come from the divine within. In fact, this was the same energy Jesus supposedly discovered and utilized in working miracles. Now, because of the Palmers' discovery, this healing power became available to the chiropractor (28:x, 25, 33, 55).

Nevertheless, the following descriptions by B. J. Palmer are not reminiscent of the beliefs and methods of Jesus but of modern occultic psychic healers:

> The hand is adapted to work by an internal innate power. . . . (28:25)
>
> We chiropractors work with a subtle substance of the soul. . . . (28:33)
>
> Anything and everything the God of the universe knows is potential knowledge within us. (28:117)

Thus, for both the Palmers, true chiropractic could not be practiced apart from a personal working relationship with the Innate. B. J. emphasized:

> I can hardly conceive of any Chiropractic school being of service to its students or those graduates to their patients without a workable knowledge of Innate Intelligence. . . . Nobody can know the fundamentals of Chiropractic unless he knows [personally], understands, and has a workable knowledge of Innate Intelligence. (28:107)

As we have seen, Innate was really God or divine energy: "Many who read and study our writings re Innate [sic] frequently ask, 'HOW can WE contact Innate; HOW can WE get in tune with Innate; HOW can WE reach Innate?' This is equivalent to asking, 'HOW can WE contact God; HOW can WE get in tune with God; HOW can WE reach God?'" (28:67–68).

Innate is even described as a *personal being living within* an individual (28:84–85). As we noted earlier, B. J. Palmer referred to Innate as the "other fellow" or the "fellow within." Further, like many modern mediums, channelers, and spiritists, he claimed that this personality living within him not only inspired him but actually directed his life:

> The "Other Fellow" in this story [of chiropractic] is Innate. Innate was always crowding, pushing ME (little fellow) into doing things. It is fitting and proper that I (little fellow) give the "Other Fellow" (Innate) credit for doing all that the little fellow would like to take credit for but can't honestly do so. (29:422)

According to B. J. Palmer's text, *The Bigness of the Fellow Within*, Innate was contacted in the same manner that spirit guides may contact their human mediums: "How do you get into communion with your "Innate?" How do you get in tune with your "Infinite?" You don't! "Innate" communicates with you and when "Innate" is in contact, you are in tune with the infinite. "Innate" will seek you when convinced you are ready to receive and will then come unsolicited (28:55).

Indeed, during the Palmers' chiropractic treatments, such as nerve tracing, Innate would even assist them "in making a diagnosis" (26:384). In this process, the parallels to psychic diagnosis using a spirit guide become evident.

All of this is not unexpected. Given the Palmers' interest in spiritism, it is not surprising that they would find their lives directed by spiritistic powers (28:VII, XII, XXIX, 55, 57; 29:425; 24:33–36).

New age researcher Elliot Miller of the Christian Research Institute comments:

> that B. J. attributed his accomplishments to a living spiritual entity that worked through him. As can be adduced from B. J.'s comments above, he was controlled, directed, and governed by the "*Inner Fellow.*" He received his ideas by listening to the "inner fellow's" voice. Truly he could speak of himself as "we," for there was a spiritual person inside of him, empowering and directing his every move. As [Marcus] Bach wrote [in *The Chiropractic Story*, 1968, pp. 121, 162], "He spoke as the spirit moved him . . . spoke of his life's destiny, to be and to prove the power of Innate Intelligence working through the channel of man. That was his theme if THERE WAS ONE." B. J." I have achieved nothing. I do nothing. It is *Innate* that does the work." (5:215)

All of this is why chiropractic is logically related to new age medicine. Both Palmers claimed that chiropractic was based on the manipulation of energies. The problem is that it is impossible to distinguish this energy from the mystical energy that is commonly manipulated in many ancient and modern new age health techniques—such as *prana, mana, chi,* etc. (26:36; 31:14, 23, 43, 47, 57; 24:17–18, 31–33). For example, "The ancient [Polynesian] *kahunas* also used chiropractic techniques in order to stimulate the healing energy known as *mana*" (65:105).

Thus, the Innate was a divine life energy uniting us to cosmic energy or God. When this energy was not functioning properly, it caused disease. Chiropractic manipulation corrected the flow of energy and brought health. This is why the Palmers never separated practice (chiropractic) from theory (Innate).

That is, the "theology" of the Innate life force was *necessarily* bound together with chiropractic adjustments. This is the reason D. D. Palmer stressed that "Chiropractic links the spiritual with the material" (26:83).

Modern chiropractors are divided over the concept of "Innate":

> There is much controversy even among chiropractors over the principle of Innate. To some, this life force is nerve energy; to others, consciousness; to some, electrical impulse; to others, nature; to some, God in man. (65:104)

But there is no doubt whatever that thousands of modern chiropractors continue to accept Palmer's early theories of Innate or that such acceptance has become a strong link to new age medicine.

There is little doubt as to the occult involvements of the originators of modern chiropractic. B. J. Palmer went so far as to state:

> The Chiropractor says that man cannot get right with God until his subluxations have been adjusted, thus [Chiropractic permitted] educated man to get the proper currents [power from Innate Intelligence] with which to communicate and have fellowship with God. That fact is dominant and is a foundation from cover to cover of the Bible. A man cannot get physical help by prayer, but he can get physical help by adjustments. A man cannot get mental help or spiritual repentance until he can get the proper currents to think the proper thoughts. . . . (31:164)

Scientific Evaluation

For the most part, modern chiropractic is not a scientific practice. From its earliest days, chiropractic has been opposed to modern science (30:54–58). At the present time, this largely remains true. The highly respected text on health quackery by Consumers Union observes that, "Since 1895, in fact, chiropractic has largely rejected or ignored advances in medical science . . ." (27:157). Chiropractic's own history proves this beyond doubt.

Furthermore, one only need examine modern chiropractic advertisements and literature to see the situation is little improved. Those thousands of chiropractors who stand in the Palmer tradition continue to claim that chiropractic will cure virtually every ailment and disease, despite the fact that modern scientific medicine says this is impossible.

The following claims taken from a brochure on the "Atlas Orthogonal Chiropractic" method are typical of the claims made in chiropractic today:

> Since many of the nerves which travel through the vertebrae of the cervical spine serve all of the body's organs, it is obvious how any disruption of these vital impulses by subluxations may result in serious illness, disability and even early death. (25:4)
>
> If the spinal vertebrae are misaligned in such a way as to bring pressure and irritation to the nerves which travel through the openings . . . a condition exists which is referred to as "subluxations." (25:8)
>
> Since these nerves serve all the parts of the body, providing a vital pathway to and from the brain, any subluxation which hinders or disrupts their function endangers the well-being of the entire body. (25:8)
>
> Subluxations are often deceiving since the symptoms may appear at a point in the body far from the cause. (25:8)

This same brochure contains a chart where each segment of the spinal cord is related to specific regions or organs of the body, reminiscent of iridology and reflexology charts. This typical chiropractor's chart is found in most chiropractic offices. It states: "Every area of the body is controlled by nerves. The normal function of these nerves may be disturbed by the misalignments of the vertebrae which could cause the conditions shown below" (25:7). Some of the conditions listed are headaches, high blood pressure, nervous breakdowns, amnesia, sinus trouble, earache, blindness, deafness, acne, colds, whooping cough, functional heart conditions, asthma, pneumonia, influenza, liver conditions, poor circulation, stomach troubles, ulcers, kidney troubles, hardening of the arteries, allergies, rheumatism, hernias, varicose veins, miscarriages, bed wetting, backaches, and poor circulation of the legs (25:7).

But there is not a shred of scientific evidence to support these claims, or that chiropractic can cure them.

Since the cause of all, or almost all, physical problems was misaligned energy, regulated through the spine, the Palmers claimed their chiropractic treatments could cure at least ninety-five percent of all disease. Those who follow in their footsteps continue to have faith the Palmers were correct—in spite of literally massive evidence to the contrary.

Furthermore, note the parallel to other modern new age health quackery that assigns special functions to a key organ of the body, functions which could not possibly be true. Whether the key "organ" is the spine as in chiropractic or the eye in iridology, alleged zones in the feet as in reflexology, or muscles as in *behavioral* or *applied kinesiology*, the claim is that a particular physical area is necessary or crucial to diagnosing or curing endless health problems—even though it is already scientifically demonstrated that that particular area could not possibly influence those health problems.

Yet D. D. Palmer himself argued that chiropractic was a science of biology: "Chiropractic is the name of a systematized knowledge of the science of life—biology, and a methodological comprehension and application of adjusting anatomical displacements, the cause of biological abnormalities; . . . " (26:8). But even a chiropractic text published in 1931 admitted, "In fact, chiropractic rejects the entire medical theory of disease" (30:54).

Therefore, because all disease results from subluxations, all that the Palmer chiropractors really need do is to correct subluxations and let Innate do the rest. But consider how unscientific this is as revealed in the following citations. B. J. Palmer observed:

> CHIROPRACTORS are Innate scholars. (29:39)
>
> CHIROPRACTORS let Innate flow naturally. . . . (29:41)
>
> CHIROPRACTORS live in a constantly expanding Innate horizon. . . . (29:41)
>
> CHIROPRACTORS build a school on the incontrovertible and impregnable Innate basis and foundation. . . . They teach today's unpopular Innate principles and practices that will be educated's vogue one hundred years from now. They teach what they KNOW about Innate . . . that they might give others over the world what mankind has sought for centuries which is now revealed for the first time in history. (29:41–42)
>
> Innate CHIROPRACTORS are always PERMANENT successes . . . (29:45)

What's scientific about that?

Consider that "Innate" is personal and can perform miracles:

> Innate IS a personality, . . . capable of performing what educated mortals call miracles; . . . [you can] attain "inspiration" from Innate. (29:67)

In fact,

> God is in constant contact with man, via Innate. . . .(29:71)
>
> Chiropractors should be, and if he IS a Chiropractor will be, an Innate man and look to Innate to get [the] sick well after he adjusts [the] obstruction to Innate personification in [the] sick body. (29:71)

What's scientific about that?

Orthodox Palmerian chiropractors claim that as Innate flows from within, out into the patient, all disease can be cured:

> If all this were done, sickness, crime, perversities, monstrosities, mentally and physically sick [sic] would disappear exactly as night disappears when day appears. . . . (29:55)
>
> It takes a certain amount of intelligence, (1) to direct a certain amount of force or power, (2) in a certain amount of matter, (3) in a certain amount of time, (4) to keep man's functions running smoothly. . . . (29:93)
>
> Chiropractic KNOWS that Innate lives IN the body; it must flow from brain into and thru body. . . . (29:98)
>
> Men must utilize the BIGNESS OF THE FELLOW WITHIN; study Innate's ways, methods, and understandings, if chiropractors would let Innate do things, he would know his inner better self as he is. (29:100)
>
> The chiropractors must permit Innate to flow outward naturally and normally. THERE IS NO OTHER ROAD TO SUCCESS. (29:57)

What's scientific about that?

> Chiropractic is the first practical study of natural composite created forms to observe that which is all, does all in man is an INNATE INTELLIGENCE, a personality, a super reasoning greater than anything educated man accumulates within his three score and ten. . . . It is Innate within which grows trees, heals wounds, mends broken bones, directs salmon and homing pigeons, as well as creates human functions at all times, all ways. (29:102)

What's scientific about that?

Innate Intelligence, then, is a personal force, a power, that resides in man as a latent healing ability. The Palmer chiropractor who has successfully realized, awakened, and trained his own Innate can use that power to influence the Innate within another person. Ultimately, the chiropractor does not heal; he merely manipulates the spine. It is Innate who heals because Innate is part of an infinite power residing within all men. Chiropractic thus awakens this dormant inner power and directs it toward the goal of healing.

Again, this entire process is similar to the process that modern psychic healers claim to engage in. They themselves do not heal; they are only vehicles for a higher, divine power, dormant within man, which they arouse and consciously direct for healing.

Ideas such as the above are the reason why Palmerian chiropractic cannot be classified as a medical science: the theory of the Innate is occultic, not scientific.

Chiropractors who still believe Palmer's theories claim that vertebral misalignment is the principal or only cause of disease. But most other chiropractors have modified Palmer's theories to incorporate certain basic scientific realities: They recognize additional factors in illness such as bacteria and viruses. Although much modern chiropractic assigns these theories a back seat, it no longer ignores them.

Even though modern chiropractic has accepted *some* scientific facts, it continues to reject *other* scientific facts which discredit its basic approach to health. Consumers Union points out that while modern chiropractic now accepts that disease *may* be caused by bacteria or virus, it continues to teach the false idea that disease may also be caused or aggravated by subluxations and that mechanical disturbances in the nervous system may impair the body's immune system:

> Modern chiropractic, for example, agrees with medicine that germs are factors in disease and that the body has inherent defense mechanisms against them. However, chiropractic stresses that *mechanical* disturbances of the nervous system are what impair the body's defenses. According to this theory, minor "off-centerings" of the vertebrae or pelvis might disturb nerve function and lower the body's resistance to germs. Structural misalignments . . . may also disturb nerve impulses to the visceral organs, allegedly causing or aggravating such illnesses as heart disease, stomach ulcers, and diabetes. (27:160–161)

Thus, "While Palmer's theory of disease has been modified, the primary chiropractic treatment for all human illness remains the same as in 1895: spinal adjustment" (27:161).

The problem with chiropractic theory is that it is wrong. Not only has chiropractic never proven that a subluxation exists as defined, medical science *has* proven that the spine does not function in the manner chiropractic claims. Furthermore, the industry of chiropractic itself reveals a mass of contradictory theories and practices.

Contradictory Theory and Practice

When health therapies reject the findings of modern medical science and open the doors to speculation, any uniformity in treatment becomes impossible. Because no objective scientific standard exists by which to judge "wrong" theories and practices, everything can be permitted. This is precisely what happened in chiropractic. Today, confusion and disagreement rages over treatment methods, Palmers' theories, the nature of subluxations, and other issues (27:160–200).

There are over a dozen different notions on how the spine should be corrected. Some say that the sacral area is of prime importance; others say only the Atlas needs adjusting. Others adhere to specific vertebral levels for specific organs or diseases. Some attempt to measure the length of a person's legs or use applied kinesiology to test muscles. Some adhere to strict Palmerian doctrine; others have modified it to incorporate *some* facts of modern science. Many incorporate a variety of additional treatment methods into their practice.

This confusion in modern chiropractic was noted by the U.S. Department of Health and Human Services Office of Inspector General in 1986. Their report stated:

> Heated controversy regarding chiropractic theory and practice continues to exist. . . . On site and telephone discussions with chiropractors and their schools and associations, coupled with a review of backroom materials . . . result in a picture of a profession in transition and containing a number of contradictions. (86:51)

Even the fundamental chiropractic theory of subluxation is debated. First, "The current chiropractic definition of subluxation is so broad . . . that it takes in virtually any mechanical or functional derangement of the spine . . ." (27:162). In other words, there is no exact scientific definition of what a subluxation really is.

Second, chiropractic has never proven that subluxations even exist. William Jarvis, public professor of Health and Preventive Medicine at Loma Linda University School of Medicine in Loma Linda, CA, whose Ph.D. dissertation was on chiropractic theory, observes,

> Neither Palmer nor any other chiropractor has ever been able to reliably demonstrate the existence of "subluxations," much less validate their importance to health and disease.
>
> When Chiropractors are challenged to explain precisely what effect nerve impingement is supposed to have upon a nerve impulse (i.e., frequency of provocations, amplitude, etc.), they either fall back upon metaphysical notions of the Innate Life Force or evoke one of many common ploys: (1) make a virtue of their ignorance by retorting that they don't know how it works but that it does; (2) claim that studies to determine the mechanism are now under way or just completed but unpublished (the "Oh, haven't you heard? You're behind the times!" ploy); or (3) do as the

American Chiropractic Association has done—evade the issue by officially changing the rhetoric and adding uncertainties: "Disease *may* be caused by disturbances of the nervous system. . . . Disturbances of the nervous system *may* be caused by derangements of the musculo-skeletal structure. . . . Disturbances of the nervous system *may* cause or aggravate disease in various parts or functions of the body . . . (ACA 1984, pp. 8–9). They do this while continuing to practice as if subluxations were established reality. (86:48)

Discredited Claims

Chiropractors often claim that because of a supposed bias against chiropractic, modern scientific studies have never yet been undertaken to prove or disprove the validity of chiropractic. But this is false. In fact, sufficient scientific studies have *already* been done to disprove chiropractic theory. For example, one may consult the critique of the scientific validity of chiropractic theory published by the College of Physicians and Surgeons of the Providence of Quebec published in *The New Physician* for September 1966 (220).

In 1980, the respected Consumers Union published its text *Health Quackery*, containing a devastating critique of chiropractic. Their research was

> based on a six-month investigation that included an extensive review of chiropractic and medical literature, as well as the findings of pertinent national, state, and provincial government studies conducted in the United States and Canada during the last decade or so. CU visited three chiropractic colleges—Palmer, National, and Canadian Memorial—and also interviewed officials of the principal chiropractic associations, whose memberships at that time included virtually all of the fifteen thousand chiropractors in active practice in the United States and some fourteen hundred chiropractors in Canada. CU also conducted interviews with American Medical Association representatives and with medical practitioners in orthopedics, physical medicine, neurosurgery, radiology, and other specialties. In the interest of objectivity, the assistance of CU's medical consultants was sought only for clarifying medical terminology or practices. (27:158)

What did this significant and impartial investigation conclude? It concluded the following:

> According to [chiropractic], the nervous system is the overall master of all body functions, regulating everything from major organs to intricate cellular activities.

> However, not a single scientific study in the eighty-five-year existence of chiropractic or the entire history of medicine shows that manipulation can affect any of these basic life processes. But a vast amount of evidence suggests it cannot.
>
> Unless most medical research in the twentieth century is wrong, Palmer's disease theory belongs in the pages of nineteenth-century history, along with bleeding, purging, and other blind alleys of medicine.
>
> There isn't a shred of scientific evidence showing that those ailments [acne, appendicitis, stomach trouble, eye trouble, tonsillitis, etc.] respond to manipulation. (27:174, 176–177)

Finally, consider the scientific research of Dr. Edmund S. Crelin, an expert on the functional anatomy of the lumbosacral spine. Dr. Crelin is one of our country's leading scientists; he has two doctorates in science and is professor in the Section of Anatomy of the Department of Surgery and chairman of the Human Growth Development Study Unit at Yale University School of Medicine. His primary research has been involved with the muscular-skeletal system of birth defects, and he has published over one hundred and fifty research articles in scientific journals. In 1961, he received the F. G. Blake award for the most outstanding teacher at the Yale University School of Medicine. In 1973 and again in 1980, he received the Yale Physician Associate Program Award as the most outstanding teacher at Yale. In 1976, he received the Kappa Delta award from the American Academy of Orthopedic Surgeons for outstanding research. He is the author of such texts as *Anatomy of the Newborn*; *Functional Anatomy of the Newborn*; *The Human Vocal Tract: Anatomy, Function, Development and Evolution*; as well as five Ciba Clinical Symposia on human development (3:402).

Dr. Crelin became motivated to study chiropractic when he discovered that Bradley Straatsma, M.D., an ophthalmologist who had been his fellow student at Yale University School of Medicine, was prevented by a chiropractor from saving the life of an eight-year-old girl. On the chiropractor's advice, the mother removed her daughter from the hospital so she could be treated by the chiropractor. The little girl had a localized cancerous tumor of the eye:

> [The chiropractor] said that the doctors would treat her as a "guinea pig," cut her up and kill her. The mother took the child out of the hospital and the chiropractor began a daily manipulation of the little girl's spine . . . while providing a large supply of vitamins and minerals, food supplements, and laxatives. . . . She was taking one hundred twenty-four pills a day,

including such items as dessicated ox bile and extract of beef eyes. Although she got her daily adjustments and took her pills the tumor grew swiftly. Twenty-three days later it was the size of a tennis ball and pushed the eye out of the socket and down along the nose. Three months later . . . she died. (413:197–198)

The little girl's face was so hideous that the trial judge prohibited the showing of death pictures to the jury (413:197–198).

As a result of this experience, Dr. Crelin felt it was vital to investigate chiropractic. He states:

> For a number of years I have tried with little success or thanks to educate the public about the unscientific cult known incorrectly by an adjective, chiropractic.
>
> I had acquired over the years an extensive knowledge of the spine from both a basic science and a clinical aspect. Thus, I decided to take time out from a productive and successful research program to devote one last effort to expose chiropractic for what it always was, an unscientific cult.
>
> I designed an experiment to expose the basic tenet of chiropractic to be completely false, that is, vertebral subluxation—a condition that has been alleged to exist ever since chiropractic began.
>
> No one, living or dead, has ever seen a chiropractic subluxation. This includes the chiropractors.
>
> For many years my position as an anatomist at the Yale University School of Medicine has provided me with ample opportunity to study the dissection of the human spine in minute detail. . . . Therefore, I have long known that the chiropractic subluxation was an impossibility. However, I felt that a carefully conducted scientific experiment performed in such a manner that it could be easily repeated, would once and for all settle the question of whether or not there was such as thing as a chiropractic subluxation. (413:197,203–204)

In essence, Dr. Crelin removed the intact spines (with their attached ligaments) from six human bodies a few hours after the individuals had died: three infants and three adults. He then set up a foolproof method to test chiropractic theory and prove chiropractic theory a myth:

> The forces applied to the spine reached the level where the spine was about to break and not in one instance did the walls of the intervertebral formina impinge upon the spinal nerves passing through them. In order to have that happen, I had to break the spine. Here is definite scientific proof that the chiropractic subluxation causing impingement or pressure upon a spinal nerve is a myth! This experiment was published in 1973 [E. S. Crelin, "A Scientific

Test of the Chiropractic Theory" *American Scientist*, 61, 1973: (574–80)] and the chiropractic rebuttal came in 1974 [American Chiropractic Association *Journal of Chiropractic* 8 (1974): 54–64].

One should expect it [the rebuttal] in the form of a repetition of my experiment showing that I was wrong. However, an unscientific cult can only throw up a smoke screen of verbiage. As expected, the president of the American Chiropractic Association, Stephen Owens, after writing a tirade to discredit my research, could only conclude that my findings were irrelevant because they were done on dead bodies. . . . It probably never occurred to him that if a vertebra could be subluxed to impinge upon a spinal nerve, it would have occurred more readily in a dead body. . . . Thus, if the impingement on the nerves could not happen in a dead body, it definitely could not happen in a living one [cf. 27:174].

My tests were witnessed by faculty members of the Section of Orthopaedic Surgery at Yale University. It has been twelve years since I published that experiment, and to this day no one has repeated it and published contrary findings.

I participated in a similar experiment [with similar results] that was published in 1975 ["Clinical Orthopaedics," 3, (1975): 192–200]. (413:205)

Why has the chiropractic profession never responded appropriately to Dr. Crelin's research? Fifteen years now is certainly sufficient time to reply to such devastating information. Does this not suggest that many chiropractors will continue to practice chiropractic, whether or not their practices and beliefs are justified?

Dr. Crelin also testified at the trial of one particular chiropractor who was accused of false advertising. During the trial he described in scientific detail the inaccuracies of the standard chiropractic chart showing the alleged connections between spinal vertebrae and different body organs and diseases.

I described in detail the anatomical inaccuracies of the chart, and these were placed in the court records of the trial . . . the two lawyers took turns haranguing about everything but the anatomical inaccuracies of the spine chart . . . the defendant's attorneys were unable to show I was incorrect in any of my charges of inaccuracy. (413:212,216)

In addition, Dr. Crelin examined and investigated a number of chiropractic "devices" such as the ThermoScribe II, the Toftness Radiation Detector, and the Specific Adjusting Machine. All were found to be quack devices that are worthless (413:198–202).

Dr. Crelin concludes his chapter on chiropractic by noting,

> If any adult reads this chapter and is still willing to be treated by a chiropractor, he or she agrees to be cheated and to suffer the consequences. However, he or she should at least have the decency not to permit the chiropractors to treat their innocent children. (413:220)

We have not even begun to examine the scientific data against basic chiropractic theory. However, it should be evident that chiropractic does not work on the basis of its stated principles. Every chiropractor who claims to utilize chiropractic based upon those principles is not engaging in scientific medicine but quackery. Indeed, the problem of chiropractic is more serious: "The failure to require scientific validation of an entire health care delivery system sets a disturbing precedent for other non-scientific systems to lay claim to the public purse" (86:55).

Attempts at Reform

Some scientifically or Christian oriented chiropractors have told us that chiropractic has officially repudiated Palmer's Innate theories, and/or that the chiropractic concept of subluxation has been redefined in accordance with modern scientific data.

But after reviewing the literature sent in confirmation of these claims, we are not convinced. Granted that in 1975, finally, chiropractic officially repudiated the idea that subluxation was the only cause of disease, but more remains at issue than this particular item. We offer six points in response.

First, even the thousand-member Christian Chiropractic Association (CCA) admits that new age influence in modern chiropractic is substantial, bringing a variety of irrational and occultic practices into the profession (307).

Second, it appears that only most Christian and scientific chiropractors have questioned the occult aspects of Palmer's Innate. Many chiropractors continue to accept the concept of Innate, as the CCA admits:

> Never can we allow innate to assume a deification or personification. This is what B. J. Palmer did when he wrote *The Bigness of the Fellow Within* describing and attributing god-like qualities to innate. B. J. always spoke of "us" and said this mean[s] himself and his innate [sic]. In this sense, innate became B. J.'s spirit guide. B. J. always communed with his innate before making decisions and in seeking advice. This is exactly what modern new age activists do when they consult their "spirit guides". . . .

> Many of our present day lecturers on chiropractic circuits are doing the same thing. This is an occult practice and gives spiritual powers and god-like qualities to innate. (306:20–21)

Christian chiropractor I. Mark Brett, vice president of the CCA, noted:

> The first letter written by the new president of ICA to its membership includes the statement, "Let innate speak forth from your hearts and minds." (Letter dated 8/25/88.) There is chiropractic literature today that is promoting books, tapes and programs which are clearly unscriptural. (e.g. Inner Winners—"whose main function is to take the innate philosophy . . . to the masses of the world"). (327:8)

Third, even some who claim they are Christian or scientific chiropractors continue to accept Palmer's Innate theories.

Fourth, although neither deifying nor personifying Innate, the CCA maintains a belief in Innate as "a neuro-bioelectrical energy both measurable and recordable, giving life to the body" (306:20). Glen Hultgren, secretary-treasurer of the CCA, argues in the following manner:

> Innate intelligence is the measurable life energy, neuro-energy, bio-electrical energy which originates in the hypothalmus of the brain and is transmitted through the nervous system. This bio-electrical energy can be measured and recorded on an electro-encephalogram and controlled by a trans-epidural neuro-stimulator. It carries messages and instructions consciously and subconsciously from the brain to the various organs and tissues of the body, as well as sensations from the organs and tissues back to the brain. It is the intelligence transmitted by this energy that is controlling and regulating [the] function of the heart, lungs, stomach, kidneys and all other organs and tissues of the body without conscious control, which we call life, which is innate intelligence [sic]. (306:21)

He further maintains:

> When Einstein described his Law of Conservation of Energy, he gave important credence to the science of chiropractic. Until the time of Einstein's revelation, scientists had not been able to put the mechanical and material model together with the living model. Einstein described in far greater and explicit detail the working of energy in and through matter, e.g., innate intelligence, life, in a biochemical model, e.g., the body. (306:21–22)

But the Christian Chiropractic Association seems to have misstated matters in its attempt to demystify Innate and make the concept more acceptable. What chiropractic needs to do is abandon Innate altogether instead of vainly attempting to justify the theory. We asked Paul Reisser, M.D., a family physician whose objectivity toward chiropractic is unquestioned, to comment upon the above statements:

> The Christian Chiropractic Association in general, and Dr. Glenn Hultgren in particular, have made a laudable effort to repudiate an occult interpretation of the concept of "innate intelligence." Nevertheless, in his article, "The Christian Concept of Innate," Dr. Hultgren offers a confusing series of definitions. In various segments of the article he identifies innate intelligence as the overall governing function of the brain, the electrochemical messages which travel through the nervous system, and the energy of those messages. Furthermore, he states that Einstein's formulation of the relationship of energy and matter (presumably in the equation $e = mc^2$) applies to the interactions of biochemical energy (one form of the innate) and the physical body.
>
> How much of this is a matter of vague semantics and how much is a misunderstanding of neurology I cannot say, but the overall effect seems to be one of an attempt to accommodate in chiropractic some old and awkward conceptual baggage. Because of its unsavory links to the Palmers' mysticism, it would seem more prudent to abandon the concept of "Innate" altogether and communicate in more widely accepted scientific language. Furthermore, Einstein should be left out of the picture, since he was not a biologist, and his theory of relativity does not apply directly to biochemical events. It is, alas, the new agers who love to claim that Einstein proved that matter and energy are different forms of the same entity, and that by manipulating "energy" in the body (however they define it) one can cure various ailments. (388)

Fifth, the American Chiropractic Association offers the following official explanation and definition of the chiropractic subluxation. The explanation of the subluxation's relationship to disease was adopted in 1975; the definition of subluxation was adopted in 1987:

> Present day chiropractic does not hold that the subluxation is the only cause of disease. Whatever may have been said in chiropractic literature years ago, today's chiropractic education and practice recognizes multiple causes of, and multiple methods of treatment for, disease. . . . 'Subluxation is an aberrant relationship between two adjacent articular structures that *may* have functional or pathological sequelae, causing an alternation in the biomechanical and/or neuro-physiological reflections of these articular structures, their proximal structures, and/or other body systems that *may* be directly or indirectly affected by them.' (326; emphasis added)

The repudiation of the subluxation as the singular cause of disease is certainly welcome. The definition of the subluxation is less dogmatic, but still too generalized. It simply covers too much ground. It never tells us specifically what a subluxation is. Furthermore, to say that an indeterminant "something" *may* [or may not] have functional or pathological sequelae or *may* [or may not] directly or indirectly affect other organs and systems says nothing and appears merely to be an attempt to evade the real issue and, like Innate, hold on to the idea of subluxation for tradition's sake.

We asked two physicians, Daniel Bowden, M.D., and Paul Reisser, M.D., to comment on the definition given. Dr. Bowden says:

> This generalized description of subluxation gives a complicated definition to a simple term. This definition does not limit itself to the spinal column, but could be applied to any bone in the body. *Dorland's Medical Dictionary* defines SUBLUXATION as "an incomplete or partial dislocation" (of a bone).
>
> A true subluxation—as applied to the spinal column—is a *symptom* of serious damage to the spine, and *not* a diagnosis. When subluxation of the spine appears on X-ray, it implies that the ligaments on the front and back of the spine have been torn; the disc has been torn or ruptured; and the facet joints have been dislocated. Such injuries are quite serious, and usually require surgery to be corrected. Manipulation of the back in an office setting would be of little or no benefit. Further, the chiropractic view of subluxation is incorrectly cited as a possible cause of further complications that would be unrelated to a subluxation proper. (457)

Paul Reisser M.D., comments:

> This definition of subluxation at first glance sounds scientific but its scope is so broad as to allow for virtually any bodily process to come under its domain. The concept may be less assertive than it was in the good old days, but it also doesn't sound particularly restricted. Whether research and review by a new generation of chiropractors will lead to any needed refinements remains to be seen.
>
> It would appear that the original medical definition of subluxation and the current chiropractic definition are two distinct entities. (388)

In other words, any comparison between a true subluxation and the chiropractic definition, new or old, is irrelevant. Chiropractic has yet to demonstrate its view of subluxation.

In addition, the ACA holds as of June 1989:

> The relationship between structure and function in the human body is a significant health factor and that such relationships between the spinal column and the nervous system are highly significant because the normal transmission and expression of nerve energy are essential to the restoration and maintenance of health.
>
> Chiropractic is a branch of the healing arts which is concerned with human health and disease processes. (323)

Chiropractic continues to maintain that body structure and function are more important in health and disease than conventional physicians are willing to grant. It is simply not true that "the state of a person's health is determined by the condition of the musculoskeletal and nervous systems" as defined in a chiropractic context. (311:155)

Sixth, graduates of leading chiropractic schools continue to teach false ideas. Gersham Stein, D.C., a Life Chiropractic College-West graduate maintains that chiropractic is "the safest of all the healing sciences" and that proper nerve supply maintains health and corrects the cause of disease (321:26).

He also argues that chiropractors do locate subluxations which can affect the function of body muscles, glands, and organs. Dr. Stein teaches that the sudden heart attack is "in part, caused by a misplaced spinal vertebra which, years earlier, began shutting off power from the brain. When vertebral subluxations are not corrected, they set the stage for later health problems." (321:26)

Therefore, modern chiropractic continues to retain serious problems over its concept of Innate, the subluxation, and the claims practitioners make for the healing power of chiropractic. Marginal progress has been made, but even this has been too slow in coming. Until chiropractors abandon their concepts of Innate and subluxation, drastically revise their health claims, and limit their practice to areas where it is justified, they should not expect to find the respect from the medical community they complain of not having.

Potential Dangers

Chiropractic also presents potential dangers to a patient.

In addition to the material below, we suggest the reader refer to Ralph Lee Smith's *At Your Own Risk: The Case Against Chiropractic* (278).

We will cite six potential dangers of chiropractic: (1) the potential for occultic involvement; (2) the problem of diagnosis and referral; (3) the practice of overtreating patients; (4) the problem of deception; (5) the hazards of chiropractic X-rays and nutritional rip-offs; and (6) serious physical damage resulting from spinal adjustment and other chiropractic practices.

Occultic Involvement

Not surprisingly, many chiropractors become involved in additional occultic methods of treatment because of Palmer's theories concerning the Innate. The concept of the Innate is easily assimilated with various theories concerning occultic energies. Any practice which utilizes occultic or psychic energies can seem to be in harmony with Palmer's theories and of potential value to the chiropractor. This is why one who visits the chiropractor may also be visiting a psychic healer. In fact, many chiropractors *are* new age healers.

As one example, the healing philosophy of chiropractor D. V. Tansley is little more than the application of occultic principles and practices to medicine. He asserts:

> Any healer or physician who is actively and consciously seeking to work along new age lines, should have an extensive and intimate knowledge of the subtle [occult] anatomy of man. . . . Similarly, he should be able to determine the imbalances in energy flow relative to the pathology manifested in his patient. (221:42)

Consider the following illustration of how even a normal chiropractic adjustment may become the means to manipulate invisible energies. Some people have experiences under chiropractic care which they equate to other forms of psychic healing. In her book *In Search of the Healing Energy*, Mary Coddington explores many occultic energies, and yet her experience under chiropractic convinced her of its same potential:

> Usually, after having a competent adjustment, I feel a rush of energy surging up and down my back; it is rather like being recharged, and it seems to affect my mental as well as my physical health. For this reason, I have long been convinced that chiropractic must be closely associated with the [occultic] healing energy. Many of the chiropractors I spoke to about this, however, are very pragmatic about their work; and they attribute the feeling of energy to mere relief from nerve pressure.

> Nonetheless, I have always believed that there must be something more complex at work, and I finally found that something beautifully explained in a book called *The Chiropractic Story* by Marcus Bach. (65:102)

What Bach's book "explains" is the concept of the Innate, how chiropractic relates to magnetic healing and the aura, and the fact that Palmerian chiropractic has many similarities to occult healing (65:102–104).

Again, early chiropractic theories are the reason why many chiropractors today operate chiropractic in a psychic manner. An article in *Psychic* magazine reveals the potentially psychic nature of modern chiropractic. The article interviews several chiropractors and reveals their psychic orientation and also their belief that chiropractic may help to develop psychic abilities:

> "There is always an energy transfer from doctor [chiropractor] to patient," says Bill [Streiff], Jr. [the chiropractor]. "It's a nerve transference, I believe, which works with the nerve energy released by the [chiropractic] adjustment. In this way the patient receives energy from me and is also able to release more of his own. Touch is extremely important in healing; it gets you about as close to the patient as you can get."
>
> Another advantage that actual body contact with the patient seems to give the manually oriented healer is a heightening of his intuitive, or psychic abilities in the areas both of diagnosis and of correction of a problem. For example, many "magnetic" or "spiritual" healers claim that they can feel sensations of heat.
>
> Many chiropractors in palpating, or manually checking a patient's spine, can sense the heat released by nerve pressure with their fingertips, . . . [Bill Streiff, Jr. claims] . . . "I work this [psychic] way all the time."
>
> "Just to give you an example," adds Bill, Sr., "if a patient with flu walks into the room, I can usually 'feel' it as soon as I lay my hands on him."
>
> Rob Butts' method of arriving at a diagnosis follows the same intuitive pattern.
>
> "I just relax and ask within myself where I should work first, and in what way. I am frequently led to some part of the body and later I may wonder why in the world I went there. Academically, [scientifically, rationally] that shouldn't have been the point, and yet it worked. I don't usually try to explain my method of diagnosis to the patient. . . . It seems to me that a chiropractic physician, in general, *is more inclined to use intuitive, or psychic, factors in healing*. Whether this is because he works with his hand on the body, where the energy vibrations come through, or whether this type of [psychic] individual just has a tendency to go into chiropractic, I'm not sure."

> Dr. Butts feels that most chiropractors, if they don't start out with psychic ability, *tend to develop it* as they go along . . . they set up an energy flow which allows more intuitive feeling to come through.
>
> "For example, when I [Bill, Sr.] talk to a patient, I usually say that 'we' are treating him. He may not know what I am talking about, but that 'we' is me, the physical, and me, the innate intelligence. *Sometimes I am aware of the presence of the innate in the room. . . . This is when I get my best results.*" (154:11–12, emphasis added)

The occultic practices found in chiropractic today are not surprising when chiropractic schools and colleges pander to such activities. A friend of ours who visited a leading chiropractic school, for example, discovered that many students had become involved in the psychic and occult world. We have also been told of a Christian chiropractor who taught at another chiropractic college but eventually left in frustration over inability to change school policies that accepted or promoted psychic and other questionable practices.

Nevertheless, as an example of the problems one may encounter in seeking chiropractic care, we offer the following personal illustration verified by us:

> After a long period of illness in consulting several medical doctors, I went to a chiropractor for the first time. I was seventeen. She helped me a great deal and I was "well" after a two-year program of treatment. She talked about God a lot; however, she was not a Christian but a spiritist. I discovered that she was going to seances, crystal ball readers, and utilized spirit guides. Many of her friends were mediums, fortune tellers, and into other forms of the occult. I met many of these people while I was working for her. (I went to her for treatments for more than twenty years and worked with her for one year.)
>
> She talked a great deal about positive thinking, that we shape our future and can have anything that we put our minds to. She introduced me to Christian Science and Joseph Murphy and suggested that I go to his lectures. During my appointments, she constantly suggested that I would be well if only I had positive thoughts and rejected negative thoughts.
>
> For several years I was deep into Christian Science, positive thinking, and placing myself into a passive state to meditate, what I then thought was praying.
>
> Eventually I went to another chiropractor in Oregon who utilized applied kinesiology, ultrasound wave therapy, and heat therapy. A third chiropractor I visited in Oregon employed practices such as laying hands on certain areas of the body and breathing deeply while meditating. He said

> he was bringing healing energy into my body from his. He also practiced acupressure and applied kinesiology. (222)

Unfortunately, this woman's experience with occultic chiropractors, according to our research, is not unique. All of this indicates, at the very least, a need for caution when considering the use of chiropractic.

Unqualified Diagnosis and Referral

The issue of referral is also a serious one. From the perspective of scientific medicine, chiropractors have inferior medical training and education. Since chiropractors claim to treat virtually every disease and illness, and patients come to them with medical problems, how will the chiropractor know which problems are sufficiently serious that the patient's health and possibly life are at risk without proper medical treatment?

If their practice is not based on scientific medicine, how can they possibly recognize when to treat a patient and when to refer one to a qualified physician?

> There is considerable concern about the wisdom of permitting chiropractors to serve as entry-level health-care providers. Practitioners devoted to a pseudo scientific approach to disease are apt to miss serious diseases when hearing patient complaints. Reformist chiropractor, Peter Modde, states that malpractice is an inevitable result of chiropractic training and philosophy. (86:51)

Consumers Union pointed out, "There is virtually no denial that educational standards for chiropractors in the past were often a little short of appalling . . . glaring deficiencies were apparent until fairly recently" (27:167). But even into the 1970s chiropractic problems included poorly qualified teachers, inferior basic science courses, and notably low admission requirements: "The scope and quality of chiropractic education do not prepare the practitioner to make an adequate diagnosis and provide appropriate treatment" (27:168–169).

In the mid-1970s chiropractic schools began to raise their educational standards. Nevertheless:

> Despite improvement in other areas, education in diagnosis remains a stepchild—especially in comparison with training received by physicians. Part of the problem is historical. Traditionally, chiropractors believed it wasn't important to "name" a disease. The important thing was to find and correct the subluxation allegedly causing it. (27:171)

Furthermore, most chiropractors do not have access to many sophisticated diagnostic techniques available to the average physician. In addition,

> The scope, quality, and length of chiropractic education cannot provide the depth of diagnostic training a physician receives. Even more fundamental, however, is the validity of what the chiropractor learns. If it's unsound, more training may only compound the error. The crucial question, therefore, is whether chiropractic theory is true or false. (27:173)

Consider an illustration of the problem faced in chiropractic diagnosis: One committee against health fraud sent a healthy four-year-old girl to five different chiropractors for a physical checkup. One claimed the child's shoulder blades were "out of place" and that she had "pinched nerves to her stomach and gallbladder." Another said that the child's pelvis was "twisted." A third said that one hip was "elevated" above the other and that spinal misalignments might cause her headaches, digestive problems, nervousness, and other disorders in the future. Another predicted that if her "shorter left leg" were not treated she would have a problem in childbirth. The fifth found hip and neck problems and adjusted them without bothering to ask permission (3:219).

This same committee found one chiropractor who actually treated a boy with hydrocephaly (an enlarged head due to blockage of the cerebral spinal fluid circulation in the brain) for seven years by keeping the child's head wrapped in boiled cabbage leaves (3:219).

Actually, the problem of chiropractic diagnosis is serious enough to warrant avoidance of any chiropractor who does not treat his patients responsibly in accordance with the findings and practices of scientific medicine.

Overtreatment of Patients

Although chiropractic often claims to cure the root cause of disease (subluxations), in fact, chiropractic only treats and relieves effects—not causes (86:52).

> The fact that they mainly provide temporary somatic relief, rather than dealing with the causal factors of disorders, is evidenced by the large amount of repeat business they generate. Too frequent treating is a factor noted by nearly every commission that has evaluated chiropractic. (86:52)

Andrew Weil, M.D., observes:

> Chiropractors are quite successful in making patients dependent on them. I have never heard of a patient being told he or she has a normal spine on

a first visit to one of these practitioners. There are always subluxations. Most patients are told they must come in for regular manipulation to make the adjustment "hold." The tendency of chiropractors [is] to seduce patients into long and costly therapy. . . . (17:132–133)

Deception

When chiropractors are confronted publicly, they will often deny that they treat conditions such as allergies, infectious diseases, cancer, etc. But in reality, they will often treat virtually any and every disease. A six-month investigation conducted by Consumers Union revealed that the problem was fundamentally an economic one. Indeed,

> most chiropractic officials interviewed by CU frankly admitted the problem of over-claiming. . . . Neither in Canada nor in the United States, however, did CU find concrete evidence that abuses in the field were abating.
>
> For some chiropractors, economics probably plays a large part in the range of illnesses treated. A limited scope of practice can often mean fewer patients. And those who confine themselves to musculoskeletal problems—sprains, strains, and back or neck ailments—tend to cut their income potential. (27:178)

Another problem lies in how the powerful national chiropractic organizations sell their product. The U.S. Department of Health and Human Services Office of Inspector General reported in 1986 that despite the evidence for an increased emphasis on science and professionalism, "there also exists patterns of activity and practice which at best appear as overly aggressive marketing and, in some cases, seem deliberately aimed at misleading patients and the public regarding the efficacy of chiropractic care" (86:51–52).

To illustrate:

> Former ACA [American Chiropractic Association] public-relations consultant Eric Baizer says the ACA conducts an aggressive public-relations program aimed at selling chiropractors as family doctors and primary-care providers. Baizer (1983) describes how as a PR expert he defended chiropractic publicly by responding to negative press reports. He says he employed stock answers and reusable cliches—what one writer termed "factoids" (i.e. statements designed to *resemble* facts).

For example, Baizer wrote,

> If someone attacks the quality of chiropractic education, we would point out that chiropractors attended colleges accredited by an agency recog-

nized by the U. S. Office of Education—*implying* that the schools must be of high quality. [But] how good is the chiropractic curriculum? How qualified are the instructors? Are inspections of the colleges thorough? These are the kinds of the issues best left unexplored. (86:53–54)

Radiation and Nutritional Hazards

From many examples of misleading the public that could be cited, two concern chiropractic X-rays and nutritional scams. Chiropractors routinely use X-rays to "find" or verify subluxations or to "verify" that a subluxation has been corrected. But when pressed to verify the existence or correction of subluxations *from* X-rays, no chiropractor will be able to do so, nor will he claim that he can. This is in spite of the fact that "Congress included chiropractic under Medicare stating that payment would be made for treatment of 'subluxations demonstrated by X-rays to exist'" (414:204).

In addition, chiropractors use a potentially dangerous form of X-ray, the full spine X-ray, which exposes the sexual organs to radiation. The hazards this presents to the public are well illustrated by Dr. Crelin, the anatomy professor at the Yale University School of Medicine, whom we quoted earlier:

> It is pathetic that many people who publicly demonstrate against nuclear energy plants willingly submit to harmful irradiation by chiropractors. It is a sin that parents allow their innocent children to receive such irradiation. The physicists and radiologists of this nation are quite aware of the dangers inflicted by the full-spine X-ray. It is ten to one thousand times as much radiation as a routine chest X-ray. And yet, these morally-bound experts have done nothing significant to prevent chiropractors from harming their patients with irradiation, and the American Medical Association won't help the public either. (413:204)

Even Andrew Weil, M.D., one sympathetic to much new age medicine, observes:

> I agree that chiropractors are X-ray happy. They like to impress patients with gigantic films of the whole vertebral column, called "spinographs" that are totally unnecessary. Allopathic radiologists can get all the information they need about the spine with tiny, precise films that require insignificant amounts of radiation compared to a spinograph. Moreover, chiropractors often expose patients to frequent, large doses of X-rays, in order to check on changes in the spine as treatment progresses. (17:132)

But there are other areas of concern relating to chiropractic deception; for example, chiropractic misuse of nutrition principles.

Victor Herbert, M.D., J.D., is the chief of the Hematology and Nutrition Laboratory, Bronx V.A. Medical Center and professor of medicine at the State University of New York. He is board-certified in both internal medicine and nutrition, has taught fulltime at five major medical schools and has been a visiting professor at most other medical schools in both Canada and the U.S. He has published over five hundred papers, is the author of numerous books and awards, and has testified before Congress on health and nutrition issues. He is the past president of the American Society of Clinical Nutrition and the only person in the world listed in both *Who's Who in Science* and *Who's Who in American Law.* He is also listed in *Science Citation Index* as one of the scientists most cited around the world. He records that chiropractic also has a problem in the area of nutrition:

> Chiropractors generally tend to give credibility to the questionable claims of food faddists. . . . Nutrition articles and chiropractic journals almost always exaggerate what nutrients can do.
>
> Although some aspects of scientific nutrition are taught in chiropractic schools, most of the ideas which chiropractors absorb are as unscientific as their own basic theory of disease. (152:60)

He also discloses, after citing four full pages of illustrations, that "the number of chiropractors involved in nutrition schemes is not known to us, but it is probably several thousand" (152:64).

Physical Damage

Andrew Weil, M.D., warns that a number of problems may result from chiropractic practices. Paralysis is possible, although rare (55:132), but "strokes may be a greater risk, especially if the cervical spine is suddenly jerked rather than slowly moved after massage to relax the muscles" (17:132).

A personal friend of the authors had a stiff neck and went to see a chiropractor. During a procedure, the therapist suddenly twisted his neck causing what neurosurgeons later determined was a brain stem infraction. This innocent visit to a chiropractor resulted in partial paralysis, two hospitalizations, periods of invalidism, intransigent pain, constant headaches, vertigo, choking spells, and other problems that lasted an entire year (407:3). The authors have also been told of similar incidents.

In the area of abuses or hazards rising from chiropractic treatment, everything, of course, depends upon the training, skill, and orientation of the chiropractor. Is he sufficiently trained? What is his level of skill? Is his practice based upon theories that have been disproven scientifically? Does he limit himself to that small area of chiropractic practice which may be useful? Is the practitioner ethical, or does he use questionable or even fraudulent techniques or income building scams to bolster his income (27:179–180)?

Given the potential dangers and modern condition of chiropractic, and the fact that most ailments will cure themselves with time, the question of any chiropractic treatment becomes difficult. Are the risks worth the benefits?

Consider some of the dangers reported in the six-month investigation conducted by Consumers Union:

> The ACA states that spinal manipulation is "a painless and safe procedure." But a review of chiropractic and medical literature by CU indicates that manipulation is not without hazard. The adverse effects reported range from minor sprains and soreness to serious complications and death. Serious complications included fracture, spinal disk rupture, paraplegia, and stroke. Chiropractors say that such catastrophic consequences of manipulation as stroke are relatively rare; and, indeed, CU investigation uncovered only twelve documented cases of severe stroke from chiropractic manipulation from 1947 to 1976.
>
> The exact incidents of injury is virtually impossible to determine, however. Unlike medical reports, none of the many chiropractic surveys and journals CU reviewed gave any statistics on complications. The only data are from isolated medical studies by a few physicians. (27:186–187)

But research published in 1971 in *Clinical Orthopaedics and Related Research* concluded that "injury associated with spinal manipulation appears more frequent than the present North American medical literature suggests" (27:187).

Another problem pointed out by Consumers Union is that many chiropractors are uneducated in pharmacology and drug therapy even though they prescribe drugs. This involves what "CU views as a dangerous approach to drugs by many chiropractors" (27:188).

Consumers Union also lists several illustrations of what happens when chiropractors advise their patients to *stop* their medication:

- An elderly woman with high blood pressure suffered a stroke.
- A diabetic patient died.

- Parents of a six-year-old epileptic girl stopped anti-convulsive therapy on the advice of their chiropractor. She had been doing well until then. After the medication was stopped, a prolonged seizure resulted in brain damage and subsequent mental retardation (27:189).

In addition, CU provided illustrations of how chiropractors had misdiagnosed or misprescribed treatment.

For example, one reason chiropractic is successful is because many physicians do not want to treat back problems; and most who visit a chiropractor seem to go initially because of back troubles.

However, back pain can arise from many different causes ranging from a sprain to heart disease. Back pain can even be a symptom of ulcers, cancer, or disorders of the uterus or ovaries; it may be caused by diseases of the bladder, intestines, kidneys, liver, lungs, or other organs (27:190–191). If chiropractors suspect a disorder of the internal organs, they should refer the patient to a physician, but how can they know? And those chiropractors who are convinced that subluxations alone will cure disease won't refer a patient to anyone.

Unfortunately, no data exists concerning serious problems that have developed as a result of a delay in diagnosis from lack of referral or late referral. According to AMA officials, physicians are reluctant to report these instances due to fear of lawsuits. Nevertheless, court cases have shown that "delays in proper treatment have resulted in mental retardation, paralysis, and deaths from tuberculosis, spinal meningitis, and cancer" (27:191). Unfortunately, in most of these cases the victims were young children. Perhaps this explains why the "most bitter criticism of chiropractic" CU encountered came from pediatric hospitals (27:191).

CU also found that even today there is still reason to be concerned about chiropractic treatment of children, as well as claims that chiropractic can treat a wide variety of illnesses and diseases (27:191–194). It, too, noted the problem with chiropractic X-rays, observing that their "X-ray diagnosis is twice removed from reality"—that it depends upon an unscientific appraisal (chiropractic) of a nonexistent disease (subluxations). "In CU's opinion all such radiation is unwarranted" (27:195).

In essence, CU's report did an excellent job of explaining why chiropractic can be classified as one of the largest forms of modern medical quackery. Despite the dangers of unscientific treatment and diagnosis, however, "Chiropractors today enjoy wider latitude in their scope of practice than any other health practitioner except the physician" (27:196). As CU observes, a dentist does not treat heart conditions; a psychologist doesn't treat kidney disease; an optometrist does not treat cancer or epilepsy. But chiropractors may treat all of these and more:

> And they are permitted to offer treatment in specialties ranging from pediatrics to psychiatry—without having scientific training in any of them. Chiropractors have won that freedom without engaging in research or demonstrating professional capability in those fields. They have won it by one method alone: political action. (27:197)

❧ ❧ ❧

Chiropractic is successful today not only because of vigorious political action but because far too few are willing to stand against it. Further, it commands a loyal following of clients who have experienced temporary somatic relief through physical manipulation. Chiropractors will often validate patients' problems, which some conventional doctors may tend to minimize; they will offer simple explanations about health and disease and may work hard at being friendly (86:53). Unfortunately, the effectiveness of chiropractic is often due to psychological or other factors, not to chiropractic theory (86:52–54; 27:163–164, 181–183, 197–198; 3:219).

Chiropractors who care about their patients' health need to be actively involved in the reform of chiropractic practice.

In addition, patients who continue to support chiropractors that reject scientific data and potentially endanger the health and lives of others need to recognize their own responsibility in supporting such a profession.

We are not saying that no one should ever visit a chiropractor. We are saying that a person should exercise common sense and visit only those chiropractors who they know are practicing based on scientific medicine and restricting their chiropractic therapy to proven treatments.

The conclusion of CU's major six-month investigation into chiropractic was that, "overall, Consumers Union believes that chiropractic is a significant hazard to many patients" (27:198).

We agree.

Crystal Healing/Crystal Work

Definition: The use of a supposed "power" inherent within crystals for healing, developing psychic abilities, spirit contact, and other new age goals.

Founder: Unknown; but similar practices (e.g., the use of amulets and other magical stones or gems) have been employed for millennia.

How Does It Claim to Work? Crystals supposedly contain the ability to focus and direct psychic energies for healing and other practices.

Scientific Evaluation: Discredited.

Occultic Potential: Psychic development; spiritism.

Major Problem(s): Crystals per se have no magical powers and easily become an implement behind which spirits can work.

Biblical/Christian Evaluation: Forbidden on the basis of occultic usage.

Potential Dangers: Misdiagnosis, occultic influences.

FIFTEEN

CRYSTAL HEALING/ CRYSTAL WORK

A recent issue of *Time* magazine observed that "crystal power" and "crystal healing" are among the most favored of new age techniques for curing what ails you. One method of using crystals to heal is given as follows:

> According to the nature of the illness, the crystal will become hot or cold as it is passed over the person's aura. The crystal is absorbing the bad energy out of the body, according to these teachings. It is important to remember that "the crystals are your teachers. Hold one in your hand. Be open to its power. It will teach you." (414:67)

New age superstar Shirley MacLaine's books and lectures, which have reached millions of people, actively endorse the use of crystals. For example, MacLaine tells us of her commitment to using crystal power as part of her bath routine:

> I checked the positions of my four quartz crystals sitting on each corner of the tub. I had been learning to work with the power of crystals and that discipline had become part of my daily life.
>
> As I chanted my Hindu mantras I visualized white light flowing through my bloodstream. It made me feel centered and balanced. I had learned to draw in white light that I visualized coming from some source above me, and with the sound vibrating through my body, the light traveled through me causing a sensation of calm alignment. (170:8–9)

A leading contemporary authority in crystal work is DaEl Walker, a spiritist who founded The Crystal Awareness Institute. This organization is even recognized by the state of California to offer continuing education credit for registered nurses who take crystal classes (83:cover). The Institute stresses "research," development, and training in crystal work, psychic healing, and the expanding of human consciousness along new age lines. Nationwide, over ten thousand people have attended Walker's lectures, workshops, and seminars—yet he is only one of dozens of popular teachers in the field (83:265). Indeed, it appears that hundreds of thousands of people are seeking the alleged power within crystals.

As in much new age medicine, crystal work is fundamentally an energy therapy:

> Crystal Healing is *only* concerned with energy. We believe the physical body is the end result of energy. If the energies of the body can be stimulated and balanced, the physical body *must* repair itself. Crystal Healing is non-intrusive and non-invasive. It only adjusts energy fields. (83:24)

This is why crystal work is employed in various of occultic practices, including manipulating the body's alleged life energy, (*prana*) for healing; awakening the *chakras*, alleged psychic centers in the body; and for arousing *kundalini* energy. Crystals are employed in such practices as astral projection, dream work, visualization, divination, spirit channeling, muscle testing, dowsing, astrology, the use of mind-expanding drugs, and even psychic surgery (82:28, 34, 53, 73, 84, 94, 101, 168, 180, 183).

The Historical Antecedents of Modern Crystal Work

New age crystal healing is a minor variation upon an ancient occultic theme: that of working with objects called talismans and amulets having supposed supernatural powers. Throughout history, these items have been associated with the spirit world, and because of this, are believed to possess magical abilities. This is why metaphysical traditions of every stripe, East and West, use these magical stones in their occult work:

- Crystal work is a component of both ancient and modern shamanism. In native American healing, the shaman will utilize the crystal as a method of both diagnosis and treatment; the crystal is believed to be a vehicle through which the healing spirits work (58:138–143).

- The medieval occultist Paracelsus, in many ways the father of modern new age medicine, was the owner of a talismanic jewel which he believed to be the dwelling place of a powerful spirit named Azoth (85:6).
- In many Eastern religions, actual living spirits are believed to dwell within particular stones. For example, concerning the star sapphire, the cat's eye, and the moonstone, "It is supposed in the East that a living spirit dwells within these stones" (85:8).
- In a variety of ancient and modern religious traditions, gems and stones intended for use as amulets are fashioned as beautifully as possible "that they might become fitting abodes for the benevolent spirits believed to animate them and render them efficacious [powerful]" (85:23).
- The talismanic nature of precious stones is associated historically with astrology: "The influence over human fortunes ascribed by astrology to the heavenly bodies is conceived to be strengthened by wearing the gem appropriate to certain planets or signs, for a subtle emanation has passed into the stone and radiates from it" (85:339).

Because spirits were believed to indwell and to work through these stones, healing properties were naturally assigned to them: "It was believed that certain spiritual or planetary influences had aided in their production and were latent in them" (85:369–70). The color and appearance of the stone was also magically associated with particular spirits or "angels":

> The color and appearance of the stone was not merely emblematic of the angel, but, by its sympathetic quality [magical power] it was supposed to attract his [the spirit's] influence and to provide a medium for the transmission of his benevolent force [power] to the wearer. (85:339)

Occultic Potential

What then is the real source of power behind modern new age crystal healing and crystal work? As was true in the past, the true source of power today is the spirit world. Although most crystal healers believe that the crystals themselves contain magical powers, the truth is that the crystals have no power and are merely vehicles through which spirits may choose to work. In essence, modern crystal healing is simply a variation upon this ancient theme: gems and minerals may contain great spiritual power which can be psychically directed for various of uses, such as diagnosis, healing, developing psychic abilities, astral projection, and spirit contact. But because modern crystal work actively seeks occult power, the practice is replete with spiritistic influence. Below we will cite several examples in documentation.

The medium Edgar Cayce encouraged the use of gems as amulets (containers of occult power) in *Scientific Properties and Occult Aspects of 22 Gems, Stones and Metals.* Texts such as Crow's *Precious Stones: Their Occult Power and Hidden Significance* (264), Fernie's *Occult and Curative Power of Stones* or Julia Lorusso's *Healing Stones: The Therapeutic Use of Gems and Minerals* (84), all underscore the spiritistic reality of crystal use. In the latter book, "[Medium] Julia Lorusso, like Edgar Cayce, found herself constantly channeling references to gemstones in the due process of her current and past-life [reincarnation] readings. Her application of mineral crystals serve many purposes in healing" (84:V).

No matter where we look in modern new age crystal healing, we discover that the real power in crystals comes from the spirit world, not the crystal itself. Every crystal worker we have talked with, and every book on crystal healing we have read, underscores this fact. Let us give you two examples of popular texts on crystal healing.

Uma Silbey's *The Complete Crystal Guidebook*, reveals that through crystal work,

> You can meet [spirit] guides and beings from different dimensions and uncover ESP abilities. . . . A curious thing starts to happen as you work with crystals. You start becoming aware of an energy or force or a "potential" higher than yourself. You start becoming aware of and can begin to interact with something very powerful and wonderful. (82:1)

She observes that those who work with crystals become "channels" for this energy and she specifically identifies it with the dangerous occultic *kundalini* energy:

> Kundalini energy is often awakened when you start working with crystals. You will need to know how to channel this in yourself, to utilize the unleashed energies and powers and learn how to create this in others. There are chakra systems or energy matrixes in the body that become activated as you work, and these can be activated in those you work with. Because the work you will be doing is on the subtle planes, you will need to know about the astral and mental planes, and how to work with them. . . . Because you begin drawing tremendous forces of energy through your body as you work . . . you will need to expand your consciousness beyond your physical body, beyond the environment and into other [spirit] realms.

> To work effectively [as a crystal healer] you must be in a state of surrender, becoming a channel through which the creative force or spirit can do its work. You are merely the vehicle. You become like a hollow tube through which this spirit can flow without impediments. . . . To become this channel, you need to learn to become centered, to learn what this state [of altered consciousness] is. (82:2–3)

Silbey also explains that those who work with crystals typically develop psychic powers. Thus,

> both obvious and subtle changes will happen as you continue work with the exercises and practice with your crystals. . . . You may experience a separation of the physical and psychic selves and the abilities to use one or the other. . . . Psychic energy will become deeply integrated and used in your everyday life . . . an unlimited flow of creative energy will open up for you that you can direct in any way. (82:4)

And,

> Various states of higher (and different) . . . consciousness begin to be perceived, experienced and intertwined with "normal" consciousness. Sometimes when this happens you may feel as if you are "going crazy."
>
> As the kundalini rises, different powers tend to develop. These can help you in your crystal work. . . . These powers tend to be those of clairvoyance, clairaudience, psychic healing abilities, astral projection . . . (82:74)

Another aspect of crystal work is the dramatic change in world view it can bring to the practitioner:

> You might be able to sense into the past or the future, see subtle colors and auras, hear subtle sound, astral travel and experience various forms of extra-sensory perception. . . . After experiencing these exercises and doing your crystal work [you discover] that the crystal and other metaphysical work is not an end in itself. Something else is happening with you that is much more important. You seem to be developing a new consciousness and way of being. . . . You seem to experience a state of infinite expansion. (82:225)

But again, that the real power comes from the spirit world and not the crystal itself is proven by the fact that after spirit contact is made, the crystals are no longer needed. Several crystal healers have told us that crystals are merely devices for attracting the spirits who supply the real power. Even when the crystals are dispensed with, the occult power remains.

These crystal workers have also told us that whether the crystals are used or not, they are always treated with the respect and devotion given to a holy power or a living god; to do otherwise may invite personal disaster.

Silbey herself confesses that "after some time of working with the crystals, you may find that you can do without them just as effectively. Don't be afraid to let go" (82:5). She further describes the process by which the crystal practitioner can become a channel or medium and receive information from the spirit world. This method is similar to that described for learning Therapeutic Touch and other new age therapies (see chapter 20). "What does it feel like to channel? . . . The feeling you have when channeling is as if the information or impressions flow through you" (82:116). She observes that "some people feel as if they must be 'taken over' by another being who proceeds to use their body" and that this "is one possible technique, but it is unnecessary"; channeled information can be received from a spirit source outside the body as well (82:115).

DaEl Walker is another illustration of the spiritistic nature of crystal work. His main book on crystal work is dedicated to the spirit "Michael" and other spirits in the spirit world whom he calls "The Masters of the Crystal Brotherhood" (83:V). The book and most of his information on crystals is, in fact, channeled material (83:2,22). Walker himself is a spirit medium.

How did Walker become involved in crystal channeling? It began with a new age seminar called Silva Mind Control. This course seeks to develop psychic abilities and help participants establish contact with psychic guides. Walker confesses that after taking the course, "Later explorations introduced me to my spiritual guides who began my internal training" (83:19). During a seance,

> The voice offered, in the name of a group called the Hierarchy, to channel this information to us. We were told to come together each week and sit in the same formation with crystals. We sat and channeled once a week for over two years. We recorded and transcribed all the material. (83:20)

Walker comments that it was his spirit channeling which "was the real beginning of my crystal training" (83:20). Thus,

> The amount and degree of knowledge channeling through me deepens and widens. It is a veritable flood which flows unabated. . . . My internal Master Teacher and Guide is [the spirit entity calling itself] Lord Michael. . . . I am a messenger for the Crystal Brotherhood, whose purpose is to open

the powers of the mind for all who will be part of the coming Aquarian Age (83:22).

Walker freely admits that in crystal work, "We can receive assistance from the healing masters from the nonphysical world. They can help understand problems of the client, even in past lives, and add their energy in making corrections" (83:251).

In his practice, Walker uses the Chinese acupuncture points and meridians as well as the Hindu yogic *chakras* (83:7–9, 31). Like other crystal users, he observes that working with crystals tends to develop psychic abilities (83:18–19). He points out that crystal work can be used in conjunction with any number of other methods and that practitioners of those other methods will discover benefits from using crystals. Some of these other methods include dowsing (83:25), applied kinesiology or muscle testing (83:28), visualization (83:34), balancing *chakras* (83:87), using amulets (83:39), auric scans (83:108), acupuncture and chiropractic (83:113), absent healing (83:168–170), color therapy (83:225), and meditation (83:39).

For example, "Our favorite tool is the dowsing rod [460]. By measuring the [psychic] energy field before and after any change, we can get an idea of the principles and properties of those changes." (83:39)

❧ ❧ ❧

Despite the fact that hundred of thousands of people currently use crystals, crystals themselves possess no power, spiritual or otherwise. As has been true for thousands of years, they are only a clever disguise behind which the spirit world seeks to operate and influence human beings.

Herbal Medicine

Definition: The use of herbs and other plant products to cure a wide variety of physical ailments; the use of "spiritually potentized" herbs and plants for psychic healing and/or other occultic pursuits.

Founder: Unknown; the practice is ancient and cross-cultural.

How Does It Claim to Work? Particular herbs, plants, or flowers are believed to possess particular healing properties, physical or spiritual. Roots, leaves, stems, plants, seeds, etc., are prepared in various ways, sometimes through psychic methods, and then either consumed orally as medicine or used on the skin as ointment.

Scientific Evaluation: Some herbs and plants do contain medicinal properties and in extracted or synthetic forms are used in modern health care and medical treatment. Unfortunately, new age herbalism largely ignores scientific facts or concerns and pursues its own methods and interests.

Occultic Potential: Developing altered states of consciousness and spirit contact by hallucinogenic plants; practicing psychic healing through a supposed occult power in herbs.

Major Problem(s): New age herbal medicine is largely, if not exclusively, a combination of questionable commercialism and wishful thinking based on ignorance.

Biblical/Christian Evaluation: Prior to the Fall, human and animal life was vegetarian; seed-bearing plants and fruits were the intended diet of both man and animals (Genesis 1:29–30; cf. 9:3; Isaiah 11:7; 65:25). This might suggest that plants were not only nutritious but also medicinal (see Isaiah 38:21). Nevertheless modern popular herbalism presents both physical and spiritual risk; quack or occultic applications should be avoided.

Potential Dangers: Many commonly sold herbs are potentially harmful by themselves or through synergism; using ineffective or dangerous treatments which delay or otherwise ascerbate serious illness; spiritistic influences through occultic herbalism.

SIXTEEN

HERBAL MEDICINE

Herbal medicine exists almost everywhere new age medicine exists. Even when it is not a primary treatment method, it is used as a supplemental regime by an endless number of holistic health practitioners.

As part of its basic philosophy, new age medicine stresses the importance of nature and "natural" healing methods. What could be more "natural" than using what nature has already given us? What could possibly be wrong with herbal medicine?

Plenty.

In this chapter we will discuss three concerns. First, we will prove that popular new age herbalism has nothing to do with the scientific study of the health properties of herbs. Second, we will document the physical dangers which can result from popular herbalism largely because it ignores or rejects scientific findings. Third, we will reveal the possible spiritual dangers of new age herbalism and show how it functions in harmony with the goals of spiritism and occultism.

Scientific Evaluation

Scientific research into the potential medicinal value of herbs is a legitimate field of investigation and has produced great benefits over the years. The extracts of various plants and herbs have proven their usefulness in numerous treatments. For example, the alkaloids vincristin and vinblastin are extracted from a Madagascan evergreen plant; in past eras, salicylic acid, related to aspirin, was derived from willow or poplar bark; morphine is a poppy derivative; the Indian poison *curare* is used in anesthesia to relax the muscles, and the substance digoxin, derived from an extract of foxglove, has saved the lives of many with cardiovascular diseases. Everything from hypertension and glaucoma to asthma have been treated with medicines derived from plants or herbs (2:112–113).

However, new age herbal medicine has little to do with the scientific study of herbs for their medicinal properties. Pharmacognosy involves the scientific study of plant drugs; but popular herbal medicine is often little more than quackery (see 405). Dr. Varro Tyler, dean of the Schools of Pharmacy, Nursing, and Health Sciences at Purdue University and the first president of the Society of Pharmacognosy, is the author of *Pharmacognosy*, *Experimental Pharmacognosy*, *Progress in Chemical Toxicology*, and almost two hundred technical and educational articles. As a leading expert in the field, he observes the wide gap between the scientific and new age approach to herbal medicine:

> A very wide chasm now exists between the scientific study of plant drugs—a part of the discipline known as pharmacognosy—and the field of popular herbal medicine. The former is an exact science, requiring considerable knowledge of biology, chemistry, and pharmacology for the mastery of its subject matter. The latter is, at best, a commercial enterprise and, at worst, a fraud, composed of varying parts of outdated information, folklore, superstition, wishful thinking, hokum, and even hoax. (422:323)

Dr. Tyler documents some of the quackery found in herbal remedies; for example, that diabetes can be cured by pumpkin seeds or black walnuts; that poke root can cure ulcers and chronic rheumatism; that burdock root will treat snake bites; that celandine applied externally will cure kidney trouble and is effective in treating insomnia, atherosclerosis, and angina (422:326).

In his article, "Hazards of Herbal Medicine," he observes that the writings on popular herbal medicine outnumber those in scientific pharmacognosy in the range of several *thousand* to one (422:323)!

Potential Physical Dangers

There exists today a widespread use of various plants and herbs that may produce mild to severe toxic reactions. We present below some of the potential physical hazards found in popular herbalism.

Ignorance Concerning Plant's True Properties

Most herbal medicine is conducted by laymen who are characteristically ignorant not only of the properties of a given plant or herb, but also of its effect upon people. Only such ignorance can explain why potentially dangerous plants and herbs continue to be prescribed and sold in health food stores.

Victor Herbert, M.D., J.D., is chief of the Hematology and Nutrition Laboratory, Bronx V. A. Medical Center, and professor of Medicine at the State University of New York, Downstate Medical Center. He is board certified in both internal medicine and nutrition, has taught full-time at five major medical schools, and has been a visiting professor at most other medical schools in the U.S. and Canada. He has also published over five hundred papers, received numerous awards, was past president of the American Society of Clinical Nutrition, and is the only person in the world who is listed both in *Who's Who in American Science* and *Who's Who in American Law*. He is also listed in *Science Citation Index* as one of the scientists most cited by other scientists throughout the world. In his "Toxic Reactions to Plant Products Sold in Health Food Stores," he describes some of the potential hazards of herbal medicine:

> Some of the plant materials sold in health food stores, particularly in herbal teas, may be harmful. Such teas may have only a single ingredient or may be blends of as many as twenty different kinds of leaves, seeds and flowers. . . . [For example] *shave grass* or *horsetail* plants contain nicotine and thaminase; in horses and other grazing animals, these plants have caused excitement, loss of appetite and muscular control, diarrhea, labored breathing, convulsions, coma and death.
>
> Ingestion of a half cup of *burdock root* tea purchased in a health food store has resulted in typical anticholinergic symptoms of blurred vision with enlarged pupils, dry mouth, inability to urinate and bizarre behavior and speech, including hallucinations.
>
> A number of other herbs that are smoked or used in tea contain anticholinergics and other substances that may have euphoric, stimulant or halluninogenic effects. These include such common plants as *catnip, juniper, hydrangea, lobelia, jimson weed* and *wormwood. Nutmeg* can cause hallucinations, and very high doses can cause liver damage and death.
>
> Camomile tea . . . may cause skin reactions, anaphylactic shock, and other severe hypersensitivity reactions in people allergic to ragweed, asters, chrysanthemums, or other members of the Compositae family.
>
> *Licorice* root in large amounts can cause low blood potassium, high blood pressure, heart failure. . . . The entire poke plant . . . is toxic. Eating

> the uncooked plant can cause . . . death. Children have died from eating the berries.
>
> Seeds or pits, bark and leaves of *apricot*, *bitter almond*, *certain beans*, *cherry*, *choke cherry*, *peach*, *pear*, *apple* and *plum* contain compounds, which, after being eaten, liberate hydrogen cyanide, sometimes in sufficient quantities to cause cyanide poisoning. Children have been poisoned and some have died after eating such seeds. Adults have also been poisoned by drinking milkshakes that included apricot kernels. (152:167–169)

The above is only a partial listing of toxic reactions supplied by Dr. Herbert, who also points out that some teas are incorrectly labeled, and some are wrongly identified by suppliers. Severe liver damage has been documented because of such errors (152:169).

Contamination

Many herbal products appear to be contaminated. For example, one study observed that almost all packages of devil's claw examined "were heavily contaminated with coliform bacteria, especially *E. coli*. As such, they were definitely hazardous to health and should not have entered into commerce" (422:326).

In addition, spirulina was frequently found to be infested with insects. One examination of cargos from Mexico to the United States revealed high levels of ephedra fly fragments in many shipments. "Since this insect is often associated with the alga [spirulina], extreme care in production and processing is required if this problem is to be eliminated" (422:326).

Dr. Tyler also noted that packages are sometimes mislabeled and cites the case of a woman drinking what she thought was burdock root tea. She was subsequently admitted to the hospital suffering from atropine poisoning. "Since burdock root does not contain atropine, it must be concluded that belladonna root, or some similar product, was erroneously substituted in its place" (422:327).

Delayed Treatment

Because an endless variety of health claims are made for ineffective herbal remedies, a person using them could possibly delay or even prevent someone from seeking appropriate medical treatment, thereby allowing a serious illness to progress to life-threatening proportions.

Even when a herbal remedy is properly supplied (i.e., actually contains a medicinal property for the treated illness), this is no guarantee it will work effectively. Time-honored methods are not necessarily better methods, which is why synthetic derivatives are often superior to "natural" herbal remedies:

> Nevertheless, it is reasonable to suppose that in most cases the valuable practices of old will need substantial modifications to bring them in line with current theories and up to current standards. Herbal remedies provide a case in point. The American Indians and country folk of past eras were on the right track when they treated fevers with a concoction made from the bark of the willow tree, for willow bark contains salicyclic acid, which is related to acetylsalicylic acid, better known as aspirin. Modern physicians, however, prescribe aspirin, not willow bark, since the purity and dosage are better controlled in the synthetic product, and it is much less irritating. (409:152)

Other Specific Hazards

A major problem in herbal medicine is the lack of uniformity concerning treatment. For any particular ailment, a given herbalist may prescribe almost anything. Medical writer Dr. Brian Inglis and parapsychologist Ruth West are authors of a sympathetic text on new age medicine, *The Alternate Health Guide* (325). They observe the following:

> And although there is a mass of information available about herbs from folklore and from the experience of individual herbalists, the range of agreement over what remedies to use for particular disorders is surprisingly small. (325:45)

We have already noted there is widespread ignorance concerning a plant's true properties. Now, there is no agreement concerning the "proper" remedy for a particular illness. This combination of double ignorance can be particularly hazardous for those who seek out new age herbalists or employ self-treatment based on popular books and opinion.

Dr. Tyler emphasizes that "the specific hazards associated with herbal medications are quite numerous," and he cites them according to category and physical risk involved (422:327). He cites scientific evidence that particular herbs can produce everything from bowel catharsis and respiratory problems, to cancer and fetal malformations, to abortions and other serious effects. Thus, at least four basic types of carcinogens exist among herbs (pyrrolizidine alkaloids, phenylpropanoid compounds, aristolochic acid, tannins, 422:327); others herbs are photosensitizers, allergens, those which produce potentially dangerous hormone-like effects, cellular respiratory inhibitors, cathartics, abortifacients, and irritants, etc. (422:327–334).

For example,

> Ingestion of pokeweed produces severe stomach cramps, persistent vomiting, followed by slowed, difficult breathing, weakness, convulsions and even death. One cup of tea prepared from about 2 g. of pokeroot caused a forty-three-year-old woman to be hospitalized and to require twenty-four hours of intensive medical treatment before her condition stabilized. (422:336)

Dr. Tyler concludes his article by noting that herbs should be treated with the respect due conventional drugs because they carry the same kinds of disadvantages that prescription drugs do: "Some are inherently toxic, many have associated, unpleasant, even serious, side effects, and all must be used with intelligence and understanding if they are to be at all effective" (422:337). Unfortunately, pharmacognosy is still in its infancy. Because there are thousands of herbs and plants and only a paucity of careful scientific and clinical studies in the field, using herbal medicine with intelligence and understanding is difficult even for the professional; "For the layman with access only to advocacy literature, it is almost impossible." (422:337)

Anyone using or considering the use of herbal medicine should do so only on the basis of personal confidence concerning both the properties and effects of a given plant or herb. One should be confident that:

- the one supplying herbal treatments is qualified;
- package labeling is correct;
- no contamination exists;
- scientific testing has established effectiveness; and
- one is knowledgeable concerning potential side effects, including allergic reactions.

If one is not confident of the above, one should probably not risk one's health. Certainly, at the least, one should be aware of the potential problems and hazards before one endorses herbal medicine (422:323–340; 4:167–169; 2:110–126; two other recommended texts include *Toxicants Occurring Naturally in Foods*, National Academy of Sciences, 1973; and V. E. Tyler, *The Honest Herbal*, 1982.

Occult Influence

Another major concern with herbalism is its traditional tie to occultic practices and philosophy. For example, historically, herbalism is often associated with astrological practices. Herbs and plants may be used in the world of the occult in a variety of ways.

First, those plants with psychedelic properties are often used in witchcraft, by other occultists such as satanists, and in shamanistic cultures to produce altered states of consciousness and contact with the spirit world.

The immensely popular writings of modern "white shamans," such as anthropologists Carlos Castaneda and Michael Harner, reveal how crucial these plants with mind-altering properties are for the initiation, development, and training of the shaman. By breaking down the barriers of normal consciousness, these substances open the doors to contacting the spirit world. The books of Carlos Castaneda alone have sold some eight million copies and sparked the interest of perhaps millions in using plant drugs for spirit contact, or other occult pursuits (265). Dr. Michael Harner, author of *The Way of the Shaman* (58), has edited an entire book on the codependency of plant drugs and shamanism, *Hallucinogens and Shamanism* (266). Their use in witchcraft is documented in Harold Hansen's *The Witches Garden* (267) and by former leading witch, Doreen Irvine (105). Former Satanist high priest Mike Warnke and others reveal their importance to satanic practices (refs. 322; 382).

There are other direct associations between plants, herbalism, and the spirit world. *The Perelandra Garden Workbook: A Complete Guide to Gardening with Nature Intelligences* (147) explains how the spirit world can be contacted and used in gardening, herbalism, and related practices. In the Findhorn community in Scotland, various alleged "nature spirits" of particular vegetables and plants are routinely contacted and their advice is recorded and published. The philosophy revealed by these nature spirits is characteristically occultic and new age (226:1–40).

The animistic use of plants either for psychic communication or in medical diagnosis is discussed in the best-selling book by Peter Tompkins and Christopher Bird, *The Secret Life of Plants* (268), and in John Whitman's *The Psychic Power of Plants*.

Third, there is the practice of aromatherapy and related methods. In such cases the supposed internal "etheric spiritual essences" of the flowers or plants are used for occult purposes—or flowers are said to be externally "spiritually potentized" by the sun or other means, as in many of the "flower remedies."

Fourth, many occult societies produce herbal remedies or related products on the basis of their own metaphysical philosophies. Rudolf Steiner's *Anthroposophy* utilizes what it calls "biodynamic" farming and gardening. This method claims to be "working with [occult] energies which create and maintain life" (228:15; cf. ref. 227).

Thus, normal agriculture is seen as a "science of dead nature;" but allegedly, nature is metaphysically related to the spiritual world, and underlying it is the etheric substructure which produced the physical plants in the first place. Only by acknowledging and utilizing the spirit forces behind plants can man use them "properly" (227:10–17).

A standard text on anthroposophy discloses some of the ideas underlying biodynamic agriculture:

> In Anthroposophical agriculture and horticulture . . . nature is theurgically [magically] "dynamized" in the making of manures, compost harmonizers and so forth. Similar magical practices govern the mode and timing of application. . . . [this] ritual and natural magic . . . is intended to produce good quality. . . . [Further] Plants reflect what is taking place in the planets. Gnomes, below the earths surface, help plant roots to grow; the astral aura of cows nourishes the gnomes. (334:57–58)

Nevertheless "because, on conventional scientific analysis, the efficacy of many of its medicines (which are branded under the name of 'Weleda') is difficult to establish, there has been trouble in some countries" (334:59).

Fifth, we should observe that a very large number of herbal practitioners use occultic radionic methods such as the rod and pendulum in diagnosis and treatment. These instruments provide a connection between herbalism and the mystical life energies of new age medicine. Dr. Pfeifer explains how many herbalists use the pendulum in this fashion and end up with a form of psychic diagnosis based on *radionic* principles:

> Let me concentrate here only on the use of the pendulum in the diagnosis and treatment of herbal practitioners. The pendulum is supposed to pick up the slightest change in a patient's energy balance. Thus history taking and lab testing become unnecessary. Occult herbalists find out the diagnosis simply by consulting their pendulum or using other psychic means. . . .
>
> The pendulum is supposed to indicate the substance most likely to counteract the energy deficit of the patient.

> While the healer touches the patient or an object belonging to the patient he literally asks the pendulum some questions. One dowsing herbalist writes: "I ask my pendulum, 'Is the appropriate remedy Ammonium phosphoricum? If it responds with 'No,' I try the next product until I have found the right one, and the pendulum answers with 'Yes'."
>
> This question-answer ritual makes nonsense of some herbologists' assertions that they measure radiation. (2:124–125)

Let us briefly examine two common "schools" of herbal medicine—aromatherapy and flower remedies—to further illustrate the occult use of plants.

Aromatherapy is one term to describe the process of using so-called occult energies latent within flowers, plants, and herbs. It employs a treatment in which a plant's essential oils or aromatic essences are blended with, for example, vegetable oil and rubbed into the skin, used as bath oil, inhaled, or injested. In *The Art of Aromatherapy: The Healing and Beautifying Properties of the Essential Oils of Flowers and Herbs* by Robert Tisserand, we find a discussion of plant use based on astrology, a categorization of plant oils undergirded by the Chinese Taoist philosophy of *yin* and *yang*, and the idea of extracting psychic energy from the plants for various occult purposes. For example, "the knowledge of astrology has great bearing on [the] kind of [herbal] knowledge we are rediscovering . . ." (101:37).

Tisserand begins by explaining how the occult properties of plants work upon the mind and emotions:

> Plant and herb essences are like the personality, or spirit, of the plant. The essence is the most ethereal and subtle part of the plant, and its therapeutic action takes place on a higher, more subtle level than that of the whole, organic plant, or its extract, having in general a more pronounced effect on the mind and emotions than [physically oriented] herbal medicine. . . . What we are really talking about here is qualities, or vibrations. . . . The more we develop our intuition the more we will be able to see the order and perfection of the universe. . . . (101:10–11)

Tisserand proceeds to discuss a theme common to much new age medicine, the supposed universal, cosmic life-force, how we must work with it, and how it can be extracted from plants to produce health:

> Aromatherapy belongs to the realm of natural therapeutics. As such it is based on certain principles which are shared by acupuncture, herbal medicine, homeopathy, etc.

> The main principles of our therapy are: life force, *yin/yang*, organic foods.
>
> The Chinese call it [the life force] *ch'i*, the Indians call it *prana*, we call it energy, but everybody is referring to the same thing, the same life force that is keeping everyone of us alive. . . . There can only be one life force, one Truth. . . . [It is] the essence of everything. . . . The power that gives us consciousness. It is this same life force which manifests itself . . . in every plant. . . . Just as we each have our own individual personality, so does each species of plant have its own personality or set of properties.
>
> Extracting the [life force] essence of a plant is one of the ways of isolating this personality. . . . The life force is an extremely sensitive thing, and if we tamper with it too much we will lose much of its power. By careful extraction and storage the life force of an essence can be preserved.
>
> If we recognized the existence of this life force, and that is the only power which can produce health within us, we will realise that we must work with it and not against it. (101:45–47)

Various "flower remedies" are also typically involved in the world of the occult. Flower remedies such as the *Vita Florum* and *Bach Flower Remedies* typically claim to operate on the basis of cosmic forces which permit psychic diagnosis, prognosis, and other forms of guidance. The psychic "Mrs. Bellhouse . . . the founder of *Vita Florum*, believes that she is led to the proper flowers by 'Divine guidance.' She then holds the flowers 'in water, in sunlight until their power passes into it'" (2:122).

What is the purpose of the flower remedies? Among other things, they are intended to alter one's state of consciousness and develop psychic abilities (2:122).

Occultist Douglas Baker discusses the supposed theory underlying the *Bach Flower Remedies* in his magnum opus *Esoteric Healing*:

> Dr. Bach had discovered that dew which accumulated on the petals of wild flowers before sunrise, was changed dramatically by the presence of sunlight so that it now had an energy potential within it. . . . Each plant's dew had a quality of its own, a type of energy absorbed into the dew that could be used as a specific remedy. We should not be surprised, after our careful examination of the occult forces at play . . . that these could be applied to correct imbalances in the astral and mental auras of Man. (54:114)

Karen Schultz observes in her article, "Bach Flower Remedies" in the *New Age Journal*, that originator Edward Bach was a "metaphysical herbalist" who had psychic abilities (171:63). She even refers to him as a twentieth-century Paracelsus. She notes, "This system tends to attract what Bach called 'the trueborn [naturally mediumistic] healers who exist in every generation'" (171:64). She observes that the Bach flower healer, through "careful study and meditation" should be able to diagnose and prescribe proper flower remedies based on flashes of clairvoyant knowledge and guidance (171:64). Another commentator on the Bach remedies asserts,

> Though the theory of action is obscure, presumably relying on some as yet undiscovered 'subtle energy' present in plants and humans, the anecdotal reports of success seem to justify further investigation and controlled studies. (77:268)

But, in almost all these systems which claim to utilize herbs, plants, and their etheric energies for diagnosis, healing, psychic development, altered states of consciousness, etc., the herbs and plants themselves possess no mystical power. As in crystal healing and similar methods, they are merely implements behind which spirit powers can work. They are no different than dowsing rods, crystals, radionics devices, Tarot cards, *I Ching* sticks, rune dice, or the Ouija board. No power resides in any of these implements themselves; they merely become a focal point behind which the spirits secure their goals.

That the occult and spirit world has utilized herbs and plants for millennia to their own purposes can be seen in such texts as W. B. Crow's *The Occult Properties of Herbs*, (100; Crow is also the author of *A History of Magic, Witchcraft and Occultism*); leading theosophist and spiritist C. W. Leadbeater's, *Vegetarianism and Occultism*, asserts, "How does occultism regard vegetarianism? It regards it very favorably, and that for many reasons" (99:4); and in Ralph W. Kerr's *Herbalism Through the Ages* (102), published as part of the Rosecrucian Library, by the leading American Rosecrucian Society, AMORC, Inc.

❧ ❧ ❧

New age herbal medicine should be avoided. It is easily distinguished from the scientific discipline of pharmacognosy, by a use of plants and herbs which is often unscientific, folklorish, fraudulent, and/or occultic.

Ignorantly using new age herbal remedies is potentially dangerous and may inadvertently ruin the physical health of people or introduce them to the world of the occult.

Homeopathy

Definition: Homeopathy is a system of diagnosis and treatment based on the principle of "like cures like"—that the same substance causing symptoms in a healthy person will cure those symptoms in a sick person.

Founder: Samuel Hahnemann

How Does It Claim to Work? Homeopathy claims to work by correcting an imbalance or problem in the body's "vital force" or life energy that is currently or will later be manifesting as disease. By an almost ritual process of diluting and shaking, substances supposedly become powerful energy medicines which, in turn, either stimulate the immune system or correct problems in the supposed vital force of the body, thereby curing the illness.

Scientific Evaluation: Discredited.

Occultic Potential: Psychic healing, spiritism, astrology, and other occult philosophies; use of pendulums, radionic instruments, and other occult devices.

Major Problem(s): Homeopathic diagnosis is ineffective; homeopathic medicines are so diluted they cannot possibly exert a physical effect.

Biblical/Christian Evaluation: Any system of medicine that is quackery or occultic should be avoided.

Potential Dangers: Incorrect and/or harmful diagnosis and treatment; occultic influences.

SEVENTEEN

HOMEOPATHY*

In many ways homeopathy is the modern medical father of new age healing, predating it by almost two hundred years. The founder, Samuel Hahnemann observed,

> My system of medicine has nothing in common with the ordinary art, but is in every respect its exact opposite. (386:176)

Homeopathy is the epitome of new age medicine in both its adherence to occultic principles and practices and also its desire for scientific recognition. Psychic researcher William Tiller, chairman of the Materials Science and Engineering Department at Stanford University, reflected new age hopes when he observed, "It is clear that we are going out of the age of chemical and mechanical medicine and into the age of energetic and homeopathic medicine" (36:back cover).

But in its January 1987 issue, the popular magazine *Consumer Reports* issued a warning to the public concerning homeopathy. After twelve months' research it concluded:

> CU's [Consumers Union's] medical consultants believe that any system of medicine embracing the use of such [homeopathic] remedies involves a potential danger to patients, whether the prescribers are M.D.'s, other li-

* Please note that in section two we observe three different categories of practicing homeopaths.

> censed practitioners, or outright quacks. Ineffective drugs are dangerous drugs when used to treat serious or life-threatening disease.
>
> Moreover, even though homeopathic drugs are essentially non-toxic, self-medication can still be hazardous. Using them for a serious illness or undiagnosed pain instead of obtaining proper medical attention could prove harmful or even fatal. (114:62)

We agree. In cases of non-serious illness, homeopathic medicines are probably non-toxic and harmless (assuming responsible preparation and sufficient dilution) because they are so diluted that the patient is simply taking a sugar pill or placebo. But in cases of serious illness there is a problem with this approach, particularly since homeopathic treatments are so often self-administered. And homeopathy *itself*, because of possible occultic associations, may be spiritually dangerous.

In essence, homeopathy is potentially dangerous because it is new age medicine. It is new age medicine because it often opposes modern medical science and supports occultic or quack medicine.

Nevertheless, in the U.S. at the turn of the century, homeopathy could boast twenty-two homeopathic medical schools, over one thousand homeopathic pharmacies, and over one hundred homeopathic hospitals (246:54)! But a half century later the influence of modern scientific medicine upon homeopathy was evident. By 1960 every single medical school, pharmacy, and hospital had disappeared. Even the fourteen thousand homeopathic physicians had dwindled to about five hundred. Homeopathy had all but died out.

In the last two decades, however, with the revival of Eastern religion, the new age movement, and the occult, homeopathy is making a comeback. Dana Ullman is director of Homeopathic Educational Services in Berkeley, CA, and has greatly assisted the modern resurgence of interest in homeopathy. Stephen Cummings is a former editor of the *Journal of Homeopathic Medicine* and has taught homeopathy as a member of the faculty of Pacific College of Naturopathic Medicine. Ullman and Cummings are authors of *Everybody's Guide to Homeopathic Medicines*. They assert that conservatively, by 1984, there were "about a thousand medical doctors and osteopathic physicians actively involved in homeopathic practices in the United States" (112:50). In addition, another thousand licensed health care professionals, such as nurses, dentists, chiropractors, naturopaths, and psychologists, "are also practicing homeopathy independently or with a physician. And there are an undetermined number of lay practitioners" (112:50). Naturopaths in particular are often found to practice homeopathy (see 325:69).

The influence of homeopathy is greatest in countries outside the U.S., although the U.S. appears to be catching up. In France, approximately ten-to-fifteen percent of the population (up to eight million people) regularly use homeopathy; twenty percent of French doctors prescribe it; three to four thousand M.D.'s specialize in it and incredibly only fifteen percent oppose it (246:52; 273:81; 117:140; 247:6; 112:50). Of France's twenty thousand pharmacies, an amazing ninety percent sell homeopathic remedies. Even the French government sanctions homeopathic practice, which is covered by social security (246:53).

In Britain, an estimated forty percent of doctors refer patients to homeopaths (273:81). According to the Queen's physician, England's royal family has been under homeopathic care for over one hundred and fifty years. The Queen herself is the patron of the Royal London Homeopathic Hospital and the British Homeopathic Association (117:139; 112:50).

Samuel Pfeifer, M.D., a critic of homeopathy who practices medicine in Switzerland, asserts that Germany has over a thousand medical doctors and thirty-five hundred "officially accredited health practitioners" who employ homeopathy (2:70).

Another European physician testifies:

> Like other ancillary paramedical practices, homeopathy is assuming an increasingly respected position in society, even inside the medical profession. . . .
>
> From the orthodox side, there is a growing number of doctors, and especially chemists, who are attempting to treat their patients by homeopathic means. In France, homeopathy is being taught in faculties of pharmacy. In this country, Switzerland, the number of enrolled homeopathic practitioners stands at fifteen-hundred. Doctors in France, Germany and Switzerland have the opportunity regularly to attend courses on this method. In French-speaking areas there is seldom to be found a chemist shop which does not have the word "homeopathy" displayed in large writing on the window. (37:1)

Ullman and Cummings, quoted above, claim there are homeopaths practicing in almost every country in the world and observe that "homeopathy is particularly popular in India, England, France, the U.S.S.R., Mexico, Brazil, and Argentina." They assert that there are seventy thousand registered homeopathic practitioners in India and that it is almost as widely practiced in Pakistan (112:50). They further report that in Brazil "the government requires schools of pharmacy to teach homeopathy, and at least four medical schools offer classes as part of their regular curriculum" (112:50).

Perhaps homeopathy is more accepted in places like Europe, Brazil, and India because they are more paganized and farther along the path of occultism than the U.S. One critic observes that the widespread acceptance of homeopathy in Germany is the "result of habitual modes of thinking in Germany [where] science is as much pestered with spirits as poetry is" (78:215).

But the U.S. is catching up with other pagan countries. Although the figures vary, there is little doubt that in the U.S. there are many hundreds of licensed homeopaths and many thousands of unlicensed homeopaths. In fact, the trend appears to be toward a growing number of unlicensed and untrained people who are calling themselves homeopaths and setting up practice. Home remedy kits are available from a dozen companies and over-the-counter sales of homeopathic products have risen significantly.

All this is why the American homeopathic marketplace has dramatically expanded its operations in the last decade. New firms have sold all kinds of products directly to consumers through health food stores and other outlets. Even Jay Borneman, whose family has been marketing homeopathic remedies since 1910, is concerned because

> there is a lot of insanity operating under the name of homeopathy in today's marketplace. Companies not committed to homeopathy's principles have been marketing products that are unproven, untested, not included in the *Homeopathic Pharmacopeia*, and combination products that have no rational or legal basis. Some are simply quack products called homeopathic for marketing purposes. (87:59)

Even the FDA is concerned and getting more concerned as time passes (114:61). According to *Consumer Reports*,

> In a survey conducted in 1982, the FDA found some over-the-counter products being marketed for serious illnesses, including heart disease, kidney disorders, and cancer. An extract of tarantula was being purveyed for multiple sclerosis; an extract of cobra venom for cancer. (114:61)

Because many homeopaths think they can cure anything from high blood pressure and heart disease to diabetes and cancer, these products are not unexpected.

Dr. Richard Grossinger is a research associate in anthropology at U. C. Berkeley, an authority on ancient medicine and its relation to contemporary fringe medicine and author of *Planet Medicine: From Stone Age Shamanism to Post-Industrial Healing*. After ten years of research into homeopathy he observes, "In a certain sense, homoeopathy is the only branch of hermetic [occult] science that has succeeded, if temporarily and incompletely, in gaining quasi-professional standing as a secular institution" (78:169).

Our own research has brought us to the following conclusions: First, homeopathy is unique in its ability to successfully blend scientific medicine with occult philosophy and practice; Second, no other new age medical practice is, at its core, so radically and ultimately opposed to scientific medicine.

How then can we account for so many thousands of scientific practitioners, among them a sizable number of qualified M.D.'s, nurses, dentists, etc? And why do millions of people around the world use homeopathic remedies, including a large number of Christian believers? The answer is simple: They think homeopathy works (see chapter 4). Even if the occasional homeopathic remedy works, is this sufficient reason to conclude that homeopathic theories are true? We don't think so.

Definition of Homeopathy

Homeopathy is a system of diagnosis and treatment begun in the early nineteenth century by medical rebel and mystic, Samuel Hahnemann (386:167). It claims to be the only positive medical science known to man. In order to understand homeopathy, we need to briefly examine some of its major assumptions.

Four fundamental "laws" or premises of early and much modern homeopathy are the following: (1) the law of similars, (2) the law of minimum dose, (3) the law of single remedy, and (4) the law of spiritual cause. We will briefly examine these four laws in turn.*

The Law of Similars—"Like Cures Like"

The first homeopathic law is the law of similars:

---

* The authors own summary evaluation of these "laws" are set off for stylistic purposes; they are not unreferenced citations.

> This "law" teaches that the very substance which causes symptoms in a healthy person will, in microscopic doses, cure a sick person having those symptoms. For example, in a healthy person large doses of coffee or caffeine will cause insomnia. But homeopathy believes that a microscopic dose of coffee or caffeine (often so small it cannot be physically detected) will cure a person suffering from insomnia. Thus, bee venom, in an infinitesimal dose, will supposedly cure and even insulate against allergic reactions to bee stings.

This theory of "like curing like" means that, in principle, any substance producing symptoms in healthy people is a potential homeopathic medication for sick people having those symptoms. This could include literally thousands and thousands of different items in the animal, plant, insect, and mineral kingdoms. This is why homeopathic researchers are busy testing, or "proving" as they call it, any number of substances for their alleged medical use. Substances are given to healthy subjects to see what symptoms they cause, in the mistaken belief that this reveals what symptoms these substances will cure in a sick person.

Therefore, "remedies" can be made from almost any material: asparagus and other plant life, herbs, minerals, animals, bee venom, snake (e.g., cobra) or spider venom, sand, gun powder, lobster, gold, arsenic, deadly nightshade, wildflowers, hemlock, TNT (glonoine), cockroach, etc. In homeopathic isotherapy, a subspecialty, the base substance is taken from a sick person: ". . . extract from someone with a sore throat is prepared and sold as treatment for sore throats" (246:92). In auto-isotherapy the substance is taken from your own body, diluted, packaged and sold back to you as medicine.

Boiron Laboratories in France keeps track of some fifteen hundred different plants plus an additional thirteen hundred minerals, chemicals, and toxic creatures which it uses as medicines (246:92). Whatever the substance, it is rarely dangerous, at least on *known* physical principles (see section at the end of this chapter on potential dangers) because it is given in such infinitesimal dilution.

The Law of Minimum Dose

The second homeopathic law, the law of minimum dose,

> teaches that any homeopathic medicine is made more powerful the more one shakes and dilutes it. In fact, the medicine has no power at all apart from the ritual of shaking-diluting. After the first dilution, its power in-

creases proportionately. When a product has been repeatedly diluted and shaken, it has been subjected to what is called successed high dilutions. One part substance is diluted with nine parts neutral solution, such as water and alcohol. The mixture is shaken, and then one part of this product is mixed with nine parts neutral solution, etc. The process is repeated until the "proper" dosage is achieved. Beyond a certain level of dilution, not a single molecule remains of the medicine and yet these are considered by many homeopaths the most powerful of all medicines.

The second law of homeopathy is perhaps its most notorious and controversial element. Homeopaths themselves are sharply divided on the issue (not on the principle of dilution, but its extent), and conventional scientific medicine thinks the entire approach daffy.

The Law of Single Remedy—Prescribing Only One Remedy at a Time

The third homeopathic law is the law of single remedy. It

> teaches that the homeopathic doctor must prescribe only one remedy at a time if he is to "properly" treat his patient.

Medical historian Harris L. Coulter, author of *Homeopathic Medicine* (1972), observes:

> Homeopathy holds that when the patient receives the one remedy whose symptomatology most perfectly matches his or her own symptoms, the whole disease is removed, root and branch. . . .
>
> The homeopath must isolate one single remedy from the thousand-odd remedies in the homeopathic materia medica. This demands a very precise matching of the patient's symptoms with those in the books. Many remedies, after all, have approximately similar symptomatologies, but only the one "most similar" remedy will act curatively in the given case. . . .
>
> Treating the whole person means being guided by the unique aspects of his or her physical and mental life, and, in homeopathy, by the peculiar symptoms that he or she manifests. (81:48)

In fact, prescribing a second remedy may annul the curative power of the first remedy or can even make it harmful to the patient: "Every medicinal substance must be administered in a state of the most perfect purity, and uncombined with any other. The union of several remedies in a single prescription destroys its utility, and, according to the *Organon*, the "Bible" of classical homeopathy, written by Samuel Hahnemann, frequently adds a new disease" (347:223).

The Law of Spiritual Cause

The fourth and final law of homeopathy we will examine is the law of spiritual cause.

> Hahnemann believed that true disease was *not* a physical entity. Rather, illness began at the spiritual level as an aberration or imbalance of the spirit-like power, or the vital principle that animates the human body. Only *later* does this aberration manifest as physical illness or disease. This means that any medical doctor who treats the outer illness per se is only treating a physical symptom, not the true illness. Thus the practice of conventional medicine is ultimately useless for true healing. Because the true cause of disease is "spiritual," it must be treated with a "spiritual" medicine or remedy. A physical drug or remedy will only compound the problem and actually drive the illness deeper (38:17–18). But a substance that has been homeopathically potentized has become a medicine that can operate on an energy level to counteract the imbalance in the vital force. (38:67, 101)

Because of this assumption (not to mention the others), the warfare that has existed between homeopathy and scientific medicine was, in fact, predestined. Medicine, operating on a material basis, was a fraud; a genuine danger to patients' health. Only homeopathy treats the true cause of disease; therefore, only homeopathy is effective. Hahnemann was convinced of this and so also are most modern homeopaths. Hahnemann emphasized there was "no other mode of employing medicines in diseases" that was useful (38:109) and that "only homeopathic medicine" can properly treat the affected vital force (39:14).

Nevertheless, modern homeopaths disagree among themselves concerning the last two of these laws, (the laws of single remedy and spiritual cause), and, as we shall see, over much else.

The Basic Errors of Homeopathy

Discovering how homeopathy began is crucial to understanding why it is a false method of diagnosis and treatment. Homeopathy was developed by Samuel Hahnemann (1755–1843). In 1810 Hahnemann published his *Or-*

ganon of the Rational Art of Healing (38), the "Bible" of classical homeopathy.* Editions today are frequently titled *Organon of Medicine*.

Hahnemann was a physician who had wisely rejected many of the somewhat barbaric medical practices of his day, but this left him without a profession. In order to support his family, he resorted to translating books into German and practicing other vocations. Nevertheless, he always retained his interest in medicine; for example, he experimented with drugs and conducted other research.

One day he was translating a book which had described the effects of quinine or Peruvian bark on malaria. Out of curiosity, Hahnemann took the drug himself and discovered that it appeared to cause symptoms similar to malaria: general malaise, chills, fever, etc. Hahnemann was struck with a revolutionary thought: The possibility that a substance which causes symptoms in a healthy person might cure those symptoms in a sick person. He therefore continued testing this idea on other substances using himself, his friends, and his family as subjects. Believing the results confirmed his theory, he developed the basic theory of homeopathy: "like cures like." In other words, any substance producing symptoms in a healthy person similar to those symptoms in a sick person will cure the sick person.

The word "homeopathy" comes from two Greek words which reflect this basic idea: *Homoios*, meaning like or similar and *pathos* meaning pain or suffering. Homeopathic medicine, then, is that substance which produces *similar pain or suffering* in a healthy person to that experienced by a sick person. In Hahnemann's own words:

> By observation, reflection and experience, I discovered that, contrary to the old allopathic method, the true, the proper, the best mode of treatment is contained in the maxim: *To cure mildly, rapidly, certainly, and permanently, choose, in every case of disease, a medicine which can itself produce an affection similar to that sought to be cured!*
>
> Hitherto no one has ever *taught* this homeopathic mode of cure, no one has *carried it out in practice*. (38:80)

Hahnemann proceeded to conduct experiments on other people by examining and recording their "reactions" to a wide variety of different substances. These were termed homeopathic "provings." Once a particular item

* Hahnemann published his first work on homeopathy in 1805, although in 1796 he had published his first paper containing similar ideas (347:221).

was given to a person, everything that happened to that person for a number of days or weeks (physically or mentally) was carefully observed and recorded as a supposed "effect" of that particular substance. Hahnemann also culled the literature of his day to see if similar effects had been noted by anyone else.

Over time, Hahnemann and his followers conducted an endless number of "provings," administering minerals, herbs, and other substances to healthy persons, including themselves, and recording the alleged "actions" of these items. Each substance, of course, produced a large number of symptoms; according to Hahnemann's research, the *lowest* was ninety-seven different symptoms, the highest being over fourteen hundred symptoms! With each new edition of his *Materia Medica Pura* the symptoms increased. As one biographer observed:

> The number of medicinal manifestations he noted and recorded increased daily. While the first edition of his *Materia Medica Pura* contains information about six hundred and fifty proved reactions to belladonna, the number rises to 1422 in the second edition. In the same way, the figures for nux vomica mount from 961 to 1267, and the first edition's 1073 citations for pulsatilla become 1163 in the second.
>
> This method of homoeopathic practice remains a unique psychic phenomenon. It goes far beyond the frontiers of what may be learned, and demands an almost oriental capacity for absorption and concentration. (386:166)

Eventually these records were compiled into a reference book, the homeopathic *Materia Medica* (Latin for "materials of medicine"), which lists the substances or "medicines," giving a detailed account of the physical and mental symptoms they supposedly cause and will therefore supposedly cure.

But Hahnemann's "discovery" of homeopathy was flawed from the start in at least eight major ways.

Misinterpretation

First, Hahnemann had apparently *misinterpreted* the symptoms he experienced after taking quinine. He thought they were symptoms of malaria, but they weren't. "Hahnemann had taken quinine earlier in his life, and it is quite probable that his experiment had caused an *allergic reaction*, which can typically occur with the symptoms Hahnemann described. However, he interpreted them as malaria symptoms" (2:65).

Thus, not surprisingly, the particular symptoms described have been unique to Hahnemann and a few other homeopaths. Those researchers outside of homeopathic ranks who tested quinine for similar symptoms have never been able to produce the effects that Hahnemann claimed. In other words, experiments using healthy test persons have never produced the symptoms Hahnemann claimed should be produced.

Lack of Independent Verification

The second problem was that the "provings" conducted by Hahnemann and other homeopaths and recorded in the *Materia Medica* have also never been capable of replication by non-homeopaths. In fact, only homeopaths appear to be able to produce the symptoms cited in their *Materia Medicas*. For example, as long ago as 1842, one hundred and fifty years ago, homeopathic "provings" were tested and failed to produce the symptoms homeopathy attributes to them. In a critical lecture series delivered in 1842, "Homeopathy and Its Kindred Delusions," the famous Oliver Wendell Holmes, M.D., for thirty-five years an eminent anatomy professor at the Harvard Medical School, observed:

> Now there are many individuals, long and well known to the scientific world, who have tried these experiments upon healthy subjects, and utterly deny that their effects have at all corresponded to Hahnemann's assertions.
>
> [The] distinguished physician [Andral] is Professor of Medicine in the School of Paris, and one of the most widely known and valued authors upon practical and theoretical subjects the profession can claim in any country. . . . Assisted by a number of other persons in good health, he experimented on the effects of Cinchona [Peruvian bark], aconite, sulpher, arnica, and the other most highly extolled remedies. His experiments lasted a year, and he stated publicly to the Academy of Medicine that they never produced the slightest appearance of the symptoms attributed to them. . . .
>
> M. Double, a well-known medical writer and a physician of high ranking in Paris, had occasion so long ago as 1801, before he had heard of Homeopathy, to make experiments upon Cinchona, or Peruvian bark. He and several others took the drug in every kind of dose for four months, and the fever it is pretended by Hahnemann to excite never was produced.
>
> M. Bonnet, president of the Royal Society of Medicine of Bordeaux, had occasion to observe many soldiers during the Peninsular War, who made use of Cinchona as a preservative against different diseases—but he never found it to produce the pretended paroxysms.

> If any objection were made to evidence of this kind, I would refer to the express experiments on many of the Homeopathic substances, which were given to healthy persons with every precaution as to diet and regimen, by M. Louis Fleury, without being followed by the slightest of the pretended consequences. (347:230)

Lack of Sufficient Controls

A third major flaw was Hahnemann's basic method. He wrongly assumed that his own experimental safeguards proved that the particular substances actually had the observed effects. But his safeguards were ineffective, and he proved nothing. All that Hahnemann and earlier homeopaths observed was the normal variety of "symptoms" that any people would experience over a period of days or weeks, which were then falsely attributed to the substance itself.

In essence, the basic error of the *Materia Medica* is that the physical and mental symptoms that people would have normally experienced, even without the substance, were attributed to the effects of the substance itself. Remember, the substances themselves were often given in minuscule or non-existent doses, so how could they produce any symptoms at all? Further, these "provings" were carried out over days and weeks and the subjects themselves were told to *expect* symptoms:

> Hahnemann seems to have somehow overlooked the fact that people regularly experience "symptoms," unusual physical and emotional sensations, whether taking drugs or other stimulants, or not—especially if they have been forewarned that the experimental pills that they have been given might, nay probably will, cause symptoms and that the symptoms might be mild and take several days or weeks to manifest themselves. Thus prepared by suggestion, Hahnemann's provers were inclined to regard the morning backache formerly charged to poor sleeping posture as a consequence of drugs. . . . (350:31–32)

Consider the alleged "symptoms" of chamomilla as given by Hahnemann in his *Materia Medica Pura* (1846, Vol. 2, pp. 7–20): "Vertigo. . . . Dull . . . aching pain in the head. . . . Violent desire for coffee. . . . Grumbling and creeping in the upper teeth. . . . Great aversion to the wind. . . . Burning pain in the hand. . . . Quarrelsome, vexatious dreams. . . . heat and redness of the right cheek. . . ." (3:32; cf. 79:295–297).

In fact, Hahnemann listed some *thirteen pages* of "symptoms" of chamomilla. Can it seriously be maintained that this substance will produce some thirteen pages of symptoms in healthy people? Or that it will cure these symptoms in the sick?

As medical historian Harris L. Coulter observes:

> The allopathic physician takes a contrary view, feeling that the measurement of physiological and pathological parameters are more reliable guides to treatment precisely because they are "objective," while the "subjective" symptoms [of homeopathy] are too ephemeral and unstable to be reliable. (79:297)

Irrelevant Additions to Diagnosis

A fourth major flaw in Hahnemann's method was his assumption that a host of unrelated issues were important to the diagnosis and treatment of a particular illness. What most people would consider irrelevant information was for Hahnemann crucial. He discusses how the homeopathic physician must be concerned with a nearly endless number of issues which a modern doctor would simply ignore. For example, Hahnemann explains that,

> the physician sees, hears, and remarks by his other senses what there is of an altered or unusual character about him [the patient]. He writes down accurately all that the patient and his friends have told him in the very expressions used by them. . . . (38:173)
>
> He begins a fresh line [of questioning] with every new circumstance mentioned by the patient or his friends, so that the symptoms shall all be ranged separately one below the other. (78:180)

The questions asked are often unrelated to any physical problem. For example, the homeopath may ask, "In what position do you like to sleep?" Or, "When do you become dizzy?" He will want to know how the person feels before a storm—or how they feel when their collar is unbuttoned. He thinks it important to know if they walk in their bare feet or whether they like or dislike having a belt around their waist. Questions will be asked concerning susceptibility to heat and cold, about times of sadness, frustration, or anger.

The homeopath will want to hear about the person's fantasies and aspirations, their dreams and fears. Homeopath Dr. Jacques Michaud comments, "Dreams are a mysterious but important aspect of the personality. . . . The information we draw from them is sometimes precise enough to indicate a remedy" (148:143).

The homeopath will also want to know the exact location or pattern of pimples and itches. He will observe the physical appearance of the patient, including the complexion and manner of dress. The homeopath observes patient idiosyncrasies and wants to know what the patient thinks concerning how others think of him. He wants to know how he behaves during sleep; whether he snores at in-breathing or exhaling. Does he lie only on his back or on his side? Which side? Does he sleep covered up; what does he wear to bed? (see 79:196).

What any of this has to do with medicine has never been demonstrated by the homeopathic community. That homeopaths might be good counselors who ask picturesque questions may explain their popularity, but it does little for their medical standing.

Experience Determines Truth

A fifth major problem in the birth of homeopathy was that Hahnemann's experiences alone convinced him of the truth of his theories. Nor was he concerned with a proper explanation of what he experienced; the fact that it "happened" was sufficient proof. Hahnemann emphasized, " . . . pure experience [is] the sole and infallible oracle of the healing art" (38:110). Concerning his results, " . . . it matters little what may be the scientific explanation of how it takes place; and I do not attach much importance to the attempts made to explain it" (38:112).

This basic approach of Hahnemann has been the model of homeopaths since the beginning. It illustrates the inherent flaw of homeopathic practice: To rely wholly upon experience can be misleading. By relying on one's experience—that homeopathic medicines *seem* to cure, and never asking the reason why—homeopaths have done nothing more than perpetuate Hahnemann's own error. They have never proven that the homeopathic substance itself is the reason behind the cure. As we have repeatedly emphasized throughout this text, it is not good enough that something seems to work; it must be proven to work.

Susceptibility to Magical Thinking

The sixth major error undergirding the birth of homeopathy was Hahnemann's susceptibility to magical thinking. Hahnemann discovered that certain substances produced severe and unwanted reactions in some patients. He therefore sought to reduce the dosages given. In attempting to find the smallest effective dose for his substances, he thought he encountered a curious phenomenon. The more he diluted a given substance, the more powerful it seemed to become. In fact, he believed the medicines were *immensely* powerful when not even a single molecule of the original substance remained (39:19; 350:33).

Thus, homeopathic medicines were and are prepared according to what are called "successed high dilutions." As noted earlier, homeopathic substances or "medicines" are diluted according to a standard scale of measurement. One part of the original substance is mixed with nine parts of water or other inert solution. This may be termed potency one or 1X. To get a potency two or 2X, one part of this diluted mixture is added to nine parts of the neutral substance and again shaken. In other words, at potency 2X, the original substance has been diluted one hundred times. At 3X the substance has been diluted one thousand times; at potency 4X it has been diluted ten thousand times and at potency 6X one million times, etc. Sooner or later, a limit must be reached where there is not even a single molecule of the original substance left. This occurs at approximately 24X and is known in chemistry as Avogadro's number.

Remember, with each dilution the mixture is shaken, which allegedly "potentizes" it, making it effective. As Dr. James Michaud, a modern homeopath, observes, "Dilution means diminishing the quantity of the substance, according to a geometric progression, to the point to where there are no more detectible molecules, and even beyond. But although there's less and less matter as dilution increases, there is more and more energy" (148:142). In homeopathic medicines, dilutions where not even one molecule of the original substance remains are common (409:154).

These dilutions are identified in homeopathy according to a *decimal* scale or a *centesimal* scale.

In the *decimal* scale the scale is 1:10. The starting point is one drop of the original substance mixed with nine drops of water, identified as D1. Mixing one drop of this solution with nine drops of water is identified as D2, etc.

In the *centesimal* scale the scale is 1:100. This involves the mixture of one drop of substance with ninety-nine drops of water, and is identified as CH1. Then, one drop of this liquid mixed with ninety-nine drops of water produces CH2, etc. Thus, the centesimal scale involves much higher dilutions. For example, a D3 solution would represent one part per thousand of the original substance; a CH3 solution would represent one part per *million* of the original substance.

What is certain is that by dilution CH12 (or D24) there is simply nothing left of the original substance.

But as noted, homeopathy often uses medicines that go far, far beyond these figures, even to the point of greater absurdity:

> This process continues, usually to the thirtieth decimal, but often as far as the one-millionth centesimal, and there is no reason to assume it should stop there. This amount of dilution is beyond comprehension. There is nothing left at the twelfth centesimal, and yet that substance continues to be diluted, one to a hundred, one to a hundred, one to a hundred, almost a million times more to produce the millionth centesimal. Furthermore, there is another scale, called the millesimal, in which substances are serially diluted one part to fifty thousand of neutral medium up into the hundreds of thousands of times. It is worse than putting a sugar cube in the ocean. A bewildered Abraham Lincoln called it the "medicine of a shadow of a pigeon's wing." Yet we are in the "other" [hermetic or occult] science and a different law holds. . . .
>
> It is no wonder that homeopathy finds little acceptance in mainstream medicine. (78:195)

But Hahnemann was actually convined that diluting medicine was the key to its power. In his own words: "Modern wiseacres have even sneered at the thirtieth potency . . . [but] we obtain, even in the fiftieth potency, medicines of the most penetrating efficacy . . ." (39:19). Hahnemann's experience with allegedly making substances more powerful by diluting them into oblivion leads us to his seventh major error.

Rejection of Physical Medicine and Acceptance of Energy Model

No wonder Hahnemann did not want to try and scientifically explain how homeopathy works! What could possibly be discussed scientifically when you are dealing with medicines that don't even exist? But he did offer a suggested explanation. This was his seventh major error. He reasoned we must be dealing with energy, not matter. If one can really produce dramatic healings with virtually no physical medicine, then we must be dealing in the realm of a vital force, or some spiritual power that resides within matter itself (38:112–113; 49:104). He concluded that homeopathy must produce spiritual medicines, not physical ones.

But if so, how could spiritual medicines affect and cure *physical* diseases? Apparently, they could not; the only way a spiritual medicine could work on a physical illness was if a physical disease was only a symptom of a much deeper *spiritual* disease. Hahnemann thus concluded that disease was not ultimately physical in nature but "spiritual." Therefore, because disease represents an improper function or imbalance of vital force or energy, it must be cured by a like healing or realignment of energy. This, he believed, was accomplished by medicines prepared homeopathically.

Therefore, homeopathic medicines are spiritual, energetic medicines, not physical medicines, and the homeopath works ultimately with *energies*, not physical disease. In his *Organon of Medicine*, Hahnemann declares the following:

> The diseases of man are not caused by any [material] substance, . . . any disease-matter, but . . . they are solely spirit-like (dynamic) derangements of the spirit-like power (the vital principle) that animates the human body. Homeopathy knows that a cure can only take place by the reaction of the vital force against the rightly chosen remedy that has been ingested. (38:18)
>
> Thus, *the true healing art is . . . to effect an alteration in . . . energetic automatic vital force . . . whereby the vital force is liberated and enabled to return to the normal standard of health and to its proper function. . . . Homeopathy teaches us how to effect this*. (38:67)

But once Hahnemann believed he had discovered that the true cause of illness and disease was based in energy not matter, his hostility toward the medical profession re-doubled.

> *They only fancied* that they could discover the cause of disease; they did not discover it, however, as it is not perceptible and not discoverable. For as far the greatest number of diseases are of dynamic (spiritual) origin and dynamic (spiritual) nature, their cause is therefore not perceptible to the senses; so they [doctors] exerted themselves to imagine one. . . . (38:32)

Unfortunately, once Hahnemann entered the realm of "spirit," all bets were off; he could never really know the true cause of disease. He could never again practice medicine based on the physical body in the way the average physician does. He even confessed,

> It is the morbidly affected vital energy alone that produces diseases. . . . *How* the vital force causes the organism to display morbid phenomena [symptoms], that is, how it produces disease, *it would be of no practical utility*

> *to the physician to know*, and will forever remain concealed from him. . . . (38:99, 102, final emphasis added)

Thus, for Hahnemann, "There was nothing he would ignore except the immaterial, metaphysical sources of illness" for nothing could be ever known about how disease originates (386:137).

Here we see the fundamental problem between classical homeopathy and modern medicine. Physicians are trained to painstakingly uncover the root cause of disease. But Hahnemann maintains the entire procedure is worthless. Hahnemann again confessed,

> It is unnecessary for the cure to know how the vital force produces the symptoms. To regard those diseases that are not surgical as [physical] . . . is an absurdity which has rendered allopathy so pernicious. . . . It is only by the spiritual influences . . . that our spirit-like vital force can become ill; and in like manner, only by the spirit-like . . . operation of medicines that it can be again restored to health. (38:21, cf. p. 112)

The spirit-like operation of medicines is how homeopathy claims to cure. Hahnemann taught that:

> Homeopathic Dynamizations are processes by which the medicinal properties, which are latent in natural substances while in their crude state, become aroused, and then become enabled to act in an almost spiritual manner on our life;. . . . (39:17)

In speaking of the "healing energy" of his medicines, he freely admitted such energy did *not* reside in the "corporeal atoms" of the substances themselves:

> That smallest dose can therefore contain almost entirely only the pure, freely-developed, conceptual medicinal energy, and bring about only dynamically such great effects as can never be reached by the crude medicinal substance itself taken in large doses.
>
> It is not in the corporeal atoms of these highly dynamized medicines, . . . that the medicinal energy is found. (38:101)

Finally, he confessed that homeopathy alone could restore the vital force to its proper functioning, increase its energetic powers for healing, and that such powers had divine origin:

> Only homeopathic medicine can give this superior power to the invalidated vital force. . . .

> We gradually cause and compel this instinctive vital force to increase its energies by degrees, and to increase them more and more, and at last to such a degree that it becomes far more powerful than the original disease. . . .
>
> The fundamental essence of this spiritual vital principle, imparted to us men by the infinitely merciful Creator, is incredibly great. . . . (39:14–15)

In essence, Hahnemann taught that diseases are simply too profound and spiritual for any physician to ever locate them by scientific instruments or specific tests; furthermore, classical homeopaths would claim that any modern "scientifically oriented" homeopathic physician who does so is only deceiving himself. Diseases are the result of energy imbalance, and it is the energy imbalance that must be corrected.

One Disease, One Remedy

The eighth flaw of Hahnemann was to assume that regardless of the symptoms a person has, there is only one underlying illness having only one proper cure. Classical homeopathy teaches that any and all symptoms are only reflections of a single underlying "energy" disease. Because they are reflections of only one particular disease, they require only one particular medicine. It is the homeopath's job to determine this one, and only one, medicine which most closely corresponds to the one disease with its given set of symptoms. "The use of a single medicine at a time is a basic principle of classic homeopathy. Thus, . . . although a person may have numerous physical and psychological symptoms, he or she has only one disease. . . ." (112:19).

Traditional homeopaths believe that only one medicine should be given at a time; to violate this principle is to bring damage to the patient. But many modern homeopaths ignore this principle and prescribe whatever they think is needed. Regardless,

> the homeopathic physician is trained to spot the one medicine, or the group of complementary medicines, out of the two thousand-odd substances in the homeopathic pharmacopoeia, which the patient before him needs. He will make regular use of perhaps eight hundred different medicines in his day-to-day practice. (79:303–304)

In essence, the above eight flaws of Hahnmann explain our distrust of homeopathy. They also underscore the problems faced by modern homeopaths. How can they justify a procedure based upon a flawed approach to medical practice?

But to conclude this section, let us cite just one illustration of the difficulty Hahnemann's theories present to the modern homeopath, and the consequences of such difficulty.

Homeopathy believes that because the true disease is spiritual and not physical, the entire organism is affected, physical and mental. Therefore mental symptoms or problems may be as significant or even *more* significant than physical symptoms in diagnosing the true disease: "Homeopathic physicians since Hahnemann's time have made further study of the different grades of symptoms and of their relative importance. They have found that mental symptoms when well defined, are usually the most useful [in diagnosis]" (79:301–302).

Further, the homeopathic diagnosis is contrary to that of the physician practicing scientific medicine. The homeopath does not look for symptoms which are common to all men that would assist the diagnostic process. For example, he does not look for symptoms such as coughing, temperature, runny nose, and sneezing that could indicate a cold or flu.

The homeopath takes an opposite approach and looks for absolutely unique symptoms that are not found in any other person. This is why he must examine and question the client so thoroughly. It is only in this manner he thinks he can make an effective diagnosis.

The homeopath examines (1) the mental symptoms, (2) the general symptoms, and (3) the particular physiological symptoms. "In all three of these categories the symptoms which are absolutely dominant are the 'strange, rare, and peculiar' symptoms which qualify the given patient and distinguish him from all others with similar mental, general, or particular symptoms" (79:302). Thus, the homeopath does not look for symptoms the patient has that are common to known illness but "those which *distinguish and differentiate*" the patient "from any other patient in the world with a similar complaint" (423:48)!

This is why the homeopathic exam can be extremely time consuming. Because illness and disease are not primarily physical, to treat them in such a manner is wrong, misleading, and harmful. The true "spirit" illness is what produces the outward symptoms of disease, whether physical or mental in nature. Thus, only by exhaustive analysis of the physical, mental, and emotional *symptoms* can the root disease be determined so it may then be properly treated. Thus, "most [root] disorders or diseases . . . produce symptoms which are emotional, mental, and/or physical in nature . . ." (423:49).

Because both emotional and physical "symptoms" of an illness are diagnosed, the homeopath must determine the emotional and physical "condition" of a patient. As we saw, questions must be asked on the basis of patient likes and dislikes in various areas, such as food, his relationship to the weather and environment, and many other things a normal physician would never consider as having any relationship to an illness or disease.

But Hahnemann was adamant about this approach and so are modern homeopaths. Without detailed questioning, the totality of the symptoms and a whole picture of the disease cannot be accomplished (38:172–186). Dr. Harris Coulter states:

> The alterations in the vital force are to be perceived only by a most careful and exhaustive analysis of symptoms. . . . Thus the homeopath must record a long list of symptoms, including many which would be ignored by the orthodox physician. He must pay special attention to the "modalities": is the particular symptom aggravated or relieved by heat, cold, motion, rest, noise, quiet, wetness, dryness, and changes in the weather? . . . These changes in the symptoms produced by different environmental conditions are often the key to the correct medicine. (79:295–296)

And what are the consequences to such an exhaustive procedure of symptomatology? As we will see, this draining and subjective approach to examination leads many homeopaths into psychic means of diagnosis in order to save time. Furthermore, it also proves that homeopathic diagnosis is a myth.

Contradictory Theory and Practice

It goes without saying that any false system of medicine that has existed as long as homeopathy will have generated its share of confusion and contradiction. Thus, as a whole, homeopathy operates on contrary principles and offers contradictory treatments.

Homeopathic Categories

We have divided practitioners of homeopathy into three basic categories: (1) the traditional homeopathist who largely follows the unscientific and potentially occultic theories of the founder of homeopathy, Samuel Hahnemann; (2) the scientifically and/or parapsychologically oriented homeopath who attempts to bring homeopathy into the twentieth century, including, however, the suspect practice of "infinitely" diluting its medications; and (3) the "demythologized" homeopathist who thinks homeopathic medicines may work by unknown principles but questions that homeopathic medicines can be effective in dilutions so high that none of the original medicine remains. The first category, the traditionalist, stands in contrast to the second and third categories which reflect more of a modern approach to homeopathy. However, both categories one and two stand in contrast to category three in their more occultic approach.*

The traditional homeopath generally follows the teachings and philosophy of Samuel Hahnemann, offering the least amount of revision, if any, in light of modern scientific knowledge. This group almost blindly accepts all or most of Hahnemann's ideas and is the most overtly reactionary, anachronistic, and perhaps occultic among the three. They readily prescribe homeopathic medicines in such high dilutions that not a single molecule of the original substance remains. They believe that the homeopathic practice of repetitive shaking and diluting the substance somehow energizes it to become an effective medicine. They may employ astrology, radionics devices, pendulums, or spiritistic revelations in their work.

The second category is comprised of both scientifically oriented homeopaths and parapsychologically oriented practitioners. The scientific homeopath usually operates in conjunction with scientific medicine and believes that homeopathy works on the basis of physical principles that have not yet been discovered. This group thinks science will one day prove the truth and efficacy of homeopathy.

In France, there are some three thousand M.D.'s who use homeopathy; many of them think its "effectiveness" is caused by some material reaction in the body not yet scientifically understood. They do not necessarily accept the idea of immaterial, mystical forces or spiritual energies. Boiron Laboratories, the major homeopathic pharmaceutical in France, allocates four to five percent of its profits (of $150 million in global sales yearly) to research for discovering the supposed scientific mechanism behind homeopathy (247:2; 246:53).

This group is embarrassed by the many false theories of Hahnemann that continue to be accepted by homeopaths. These practitioners are at-

---

* These categories are for purposes of general contrast; the descriptions given do not necessarily apply to every practitioner.

tempting to bring new support to homeopathy based on scientific medicine and modern scientific theories such as those in quantum physics.

But the approach based on supposed parallels to the phenomena of quantum mechanics is suspect at best, and plain wrong in many formulations (cf. 319:107–125). For example, neither the actions of sub-atomic particles nor their observed paradoxes are applicable to the homeopathic claim that infinite dilutions of a substance somehow produce extremely powerful medicines.

The scientific approach of this practitioner is sometimes legitimate, but it is also sometimes compromised by the other "scientific" homeopath, the parapsychological practitioner. The parapsychological homeopath combines scientific research with occultic practices or principles. This group often employs such things as divinatory pendulums and occultic radionic devices in their attempt to lend "scientific" credibility to homeopathy. They, too, may accept astrology or spiritistic revelations. They are little different from the modern parapsychologist in general who attempts to use scientific methods and experiments in order to investigate clearly occultic phenomena.

But even in the category of scientific homeopath, problems remain in the classification of their practices. Many of them maintain that homeopathy is only effective in such high dilutions that not a single molecule of the homeopathic medicine remains. This raises the issue of how scientific such practitioners really are.

Dr. Desmichelle, an M.D. and honorary president of the Centre Homeopathique de France, states his conviction that "The homeopathic remedy, to be efficient, has to be given in extremely low dosage. The more diluted the active principle, the more powerful the remedy" (248:2). But what is the "active principle" when not a molecule remains? Homeopaths can't say.

Further, even when homeopathic M.D.'s use *both* homeopathy and scientific medicine, the two categories of practice remain distinct and separate. No truly scientific homeopath ever maintains that homeopathy is the practice of scientific medicine; he only maintains a faith that someday, somehow, science will finally discover its alleged workings and then homeopathy will become an accepted part of scientific medicine. But whether such faith is ever justified is clearly open to question.

The third category, the modern "demythologized" homeopath, usually does *not* prescribe the "infinitely" diluted homeopathic medications nor do they attempt to "cosmically energize" them. These homeopaths are fundamentally pragmatists; they are less concerned about philosophical backgrounds or scientific proof and are attracted to homeopathy because of its "natural" approach to medicine. They believe that homeopathic treatments in the lower potencies (6X–12X) have a legitimate physical, curative effect, probably on the immune system, even though no such effect has ever been scientifically demonstrated. They employ homeopathy primarily because it works and they are not necessarily concerned why.

Despite their differences, the above three categories of homeopathist share two common themes. Neither of the three is, strictly, operating under the principles of scientific medicine, and all of them may potentially be dangerous to one's health and/or involve one in the occult.

The Nature of the Disagreement

These categories reveal why the homeopathic community is so divided: they cannot agree on either the theoretical basis of homeopathy or its practical application.

To understand how serious this is, imagine the modern medical community vociferously arguing over the nature of a disease, its cause, its symptoms, and the proper remedy. No one outside the profession could possibly know what to believe or the proper method of treatment when the profession itself remained in the dark.

Traditional homeopaths feel that "modern" revisionists have betrayed their tradition and have offered sharp criticism, maintaining they are "pseudo-homeopaths" and "charlatans." (We tend to agree; because of its premises, homeopathy cannot be so radically compromised without destroying its nature.) In essence, a true homeopath is a Hahnemannian purist; modernists are only engaging in speculations and largely futile research endeavors by attempting to force homeopathy to become what it can never be: scientific medicine. They are muddying the waters and producing confusion over what real medicine is and is not.

To these pure Hahnemannian homeopaths, the scientifically oriented and/or "low dose" homeopaths are essentially heretics performing a travesty upon true homeopathy; they cannot be *true* homeopaths (36:81, 87). Further, by their low doses and/or multiple remedies, they are aggravating an illness, not curing it. This is why "Hahnemann viewed these hybrids as 'worse than allopaths . . . amphibians . . . still creeping in the mud of the allopathic marsh . . . who only rarely venture to raise their heads in freedom toward the ethereal truth" (78:231).

Perhaps an illustration will help us understand the issue involved here. A true Christian is a Biblical purist; he accepts the Bible's claim to be the literal word of God and therefore authoritative over his life. Because basic Bible doctrines can objectively be established through accepted hermeneutical principles, modern, liberal, and cultic revisions of Biblical teaching simply do not have the right to the name Christian. Their mere claim to be Christian cannot alter the fact that they deny and reject fundamental Biblical doctrines.

But right or wrong, the true principles of homeopathy are Hahnemannian; to violate those principles is to violate homeopathy. This is why even Dr. Grossinger concludes, "These events prove that Hahnemann was right when he denied the possibility of half-homeopathy. Half-homeopathy is nonhomeopathy" (78:238, cf. p. 234).

Nevertheless, all this reveals why homeopathy will never agree on even fundamental issues; the divisions in theory and practice are far too deep and unmanageable.

If classical practitioners reject modern heretics, modern "homeopaths" think the traditionalists are ignorant and deceived.

The traditional homeopath is perfectly comfortable with the following statement made by the leading homeopathist at the turn of the century, James Tyler Kent, M.D., a statement which makes the more modern homeopath cringe: "There is no disease that exists of which the cause is known to man by the eye or by the microscope. Causes are infinitely too fine to be observed by any instrument of precision" (36:ii).

Significantly, Hahnemann was his own worst enemy. It was the extremely bizarre nature of his theories which caused the divisions and confusions among his own followers. For example, Hahnemann claimed that it took him twelve long and arduous years of diligent research and study to discover the major cause of almost all human disease. He claimed that seven-eighths of all disease including things like cancer, asthma, paralysis, deafness, madness, and epilepsy was directly attributed to *psora*, in less refined terms, *itch*..

According to Hahnemann's *Organon*, this "psora, [is] the only real *fundamental cause* and producer of all the other . . . innumerable forms of disease" (38:167).

But "a large majority" of Hahnemann's own followers refused to accept the idea and, according to Wolff, a leading homeopath and contemporary of Hahnemann, it "has met with the greatest opposition from Homeopathic physicians themselves" (3:242 cf. p. 225). (In his 1842 critical lectures on homeopathy, Oliver Wendell Holmes referred to it as "an almost insane conception, which I am glad to get rid of") (347:241).

But homeopaths have always been at each other's throats, so to speak. For example, in 1900 in James Tyler Kent's *Lectures on Homeopathic Philosophy*, a commentary on Hahnemann's *Organon*, he observes that even though homeopathy was extensively distributed throughout the world, its own doctrines were perverted and polluted primarily by homeopaths themselves.

As a whole, little has changed. Homeopathy is everywhere a contrary practice. Hahnemann himself was aware of contradictory methods and results among his followers (e.g., 39:18), and this problem has been the plague of homeopathy ever since. Some homeopaths are purists when it comes to Hahnemann's theories; some pick and choose what seems suitable to them, and some reject most of his ideas entirely. Some are thus adamant about one aspect of homeopathy that others reject entirely; some prescribe homeopathic medicines in low dilutions, others in incredibly high dilutions, and both claim that only their method is proper. Some homeopaths are vitalists; others allegedly materialists. Some are modern and ecletic, prescribing a variety of additional remedies or therapies along with homeopathy; some stick to homeopathy alone.

In addition, the drugs and their symptoms vary considerably: "Thousands of homeopathic drugs are listed in the cults' *Materia Medicas*—handbooks that vary widely from time to time and from country to country" (117:133).

Furthermore, homeopathic *Materia Medicas* are not exactly reliable. As Oliver Wendell Holmes commented over a century ago in his critical lectures on homeopathy:

> What are we to think of a standard *practical* author on Materia Medica, who at one time omits to designate the proper doses of his remedies, and at another to let us have any means of knowing whether a remedy has even been tried or not, while he is recommending its employment in the most critical and threatening diseases? (347:230)

Some homeopaths think their medicines must be administered in a state of absolute purity, unmixed with other substances, otherwise you will destroy its effectiveness. But other homeopaths mix substances freely and claim it is too cumbersome to try and find the one "correct" remedy according to classical homeopathy (347:223; 148:143).

With homeopaths employing anti-scientific methods, subjective evaluations, and occultic practices and with wide disagreements about theory and practice, it is hardly surprising that the world of homeopathy lives in such disarray (347:225, 242; 36:81).

As noted, Dr. Richard Grossinger spent ten years researching homeopathy. He concludes that in recent years around the world, "Standards have deteriorated; far worse, there is controversy from country to country, and even from doctor to doctor, as to what constitutes acceptable homeopathic treatment" (78:240). He ends his discussion by noting:

> Different levels and types of homoeopathy are inevitable as long as basic contradictions within the system and the practice are unresolved. A person today seeking homeopathic treatment truly enters a great metaphysical riddle, further compounded by historical and ideological variations. We are finally left without an absolutely clear sense of what homeopathy is, without a sense that will allow us to judge practitioners and give clear advice to people seeking doctors. (78:244)

Perhaps James Taylor Kent was correct when he commented, "We cannot rid ourselves of confusion until we learn what confusion is" (36:55).

Evaluation of Evidence

Homeopathic practitioners offer two basic lines of evidence for their art, one theoretical and the other practical.

Theoretical Argument

Homeopaths observe alleged similarities to scientifically demonstrated realities and suggest that these indications supply theoretical evidence for homeopathy. Here the practitioner appeals to such things as vaccination, allergies, and the body's hormones and biochemical reactions. How do these relate to homeopathy?

Vaccinations allegedly demonstrate the "like cures like" principle because an individual is immunized against a disease by giving him a small part of that which causes the disease. Allergies allegedly demonstrate that substances which are often in a very weak concentration can produce very powerful and even violent reactions in the human body. Hormones and biocatalysts also demonstrate that minute amounts of a substance can powerfully affect the physical organism.

Homeopaths will cite illustrations. One milligram of acetylcholine dissolved in 500,000 gallons of blood will lower a cat's blood pressure. Pure penicillin will inhibit the development of some microorganisms even when it is diluted at one part to fifty million; the thyroid hormone is effective at one part per ten trillion of blood plasma, etc.

The problem with these illustrations is that even if they were legitimate applications, they could still not prove homeopathy. They could only suggest it might be true in theory; but, in fact, they are usually not even legitimate applications.

Vaccinations and homeopathic remedies work on entirely different principles and have different effects. Vaccinations deal with physical substances designed to stimulate the production of specific antibodies to act against specific microbes. It is scientifically demonstrated that they are effective in this.

How does this have anything to do with homeopathy? Homeopathic treatments are not *intended* to stimulate antibodies, do not produce them, and, in fact, often do not contain even a single molecule of the alleged medicine. Vaccinations work on a physical, material level; homeopathic treatments work on an entirely non-physical level, allegedly altering the "vital force" of the body. Or, they claimed to work in a scientifically undemonstrated manner supposedly acting on the immune system in some unknown way. But such supposed action is not much different from magic; magic is also scientifically undemonstrated and works in an unknown manner.

In the cases of allergies, hormones, and biocatalysts, we are again dealing with the *demonstrated* effect of known material substances on the body. They are proven to work as claimed. But homeopathic medicines or effects do not work as claimed; they are not material, not demonstrated, and probably never can be demonstrated.

In addition, although hormones, biocatalysts, and the entities producing allergies are much smaller than tiny grains of sand, they are gigantic suns in comparison with homeopathic medicines. Homeopathic remedies are infinitely more minute or even non-existent, yet such "medicines" of homeopathy are said to work even when *none* of the original medicine remains.

Another approach is to cite the mysteries of modern theoretical physics as a defense for homeopathic practice. The new age movement as a whole, including new age medicine, appeals to the mysteries of theoretical physics as a justification for its practices, but largely upon a fraudulent basis (445:24–35; 252:108–110). There are indeed mysteries in quantum physics—wonderful mysteries. But the argument is invalid as a defense of homeopathy or any other new age medicine. Physicists and other scientists around the world are indeed studying the mysteries of particle physics. Why aren't they studying the mysteries of homeopathy? If what homeopathy claims is true, then the implications are far more important to men than those of theoretical physics. They would virtually demand attention. If homeopathy had even demonstrated genuine *mysteries*, it would literally command the attention of the scientific world.*

Why then does the scientific world ignore homeopathy? In fact, because homeopathy has not yet demonstrated a real mystery exists.

Where is the theoretical evidence for homeopathy? The alleged parallels to classical medicine which attempt to provide a "scientific" explanation or justification for homeopathy are largely irrelevant. The proposed arguments from quantum mechanics are inapplicable. Nevertheless, homeopaths still claim their practices work.

Practical Argument

The other major evidence cited by homeopathic practitioners is that homeopathy works. This is the one claim we find repeated again and again. Believers in homeopathy offer endless testimonies to its curative powers (e.g., 347:236–237). Homeopaths themselves claim, "The best reason to use homeopathic medicines in self-care is that they work" (112:17), and ". . . homeopathy must be judged by its results . . ." (446:91).

As Coulter remarks,

> When asked how he can be sure that his theory is valid, the homeopathic physician will respond that it has served for one hundred and fifty years as the basis for the successful homeopathic treatment of disease and the preservation of health. And if the homeopathic physician *can* cure his patients

---

* For example, consider the furor over the French research reported in Nature for June 30, 1988; (117).

> consistently and methodically on the basis of this theory, this set of assumptions, who is to say that it is wrong. Practice is the only test. (79:293)

Iridologists and believers in endless other new age techniques say the same thing. *Claims* to healing are cheap; proof is another matter. So then how do we really know it was *homeopathy* that cured any practitioner's patients when there is no proof? Often the anecdotal evidence is the weakest of all because it is wholly uncontrolled and subject to the errors of observation or logic of both patient and practitioner. Astrologic medicine has made similar claims for much longer than one hundred and fifty years. Astrologers also think their practices have served as the basis for successful astrological treatment of disease. But, like homeopaths, they are wrong and have been proven wrong.

Another claim is that homeopathic medicines have been demonstrated to work on infants and animals. This allegedly proves homeopathy is effective, because placebos would not work on babies or dogs. But if such an effect had really been proven, we think everyone would know it. It would have spurred a multi-billion-dollar research program, and homeopathy would have been accepted long ago. For Americans, the discovery of a dramatic new healing power for their infants and pets would hardly go unnoticed. Furthermore, corporate interest would have been secured by the promise of vast profits in the neo-natal industry and veterinarian care. Such a discovery would have caused a public sensation from the implications alone. This is why we do not think homeopathic cures have ever been proven in such cases.

Regardless, homeopaths often say they don't care how it works or why it works, only that it does work. They are content to wait for "further research" for the explanation. For most homeopaths explanations are irrelevant, and that is the danger (112:21).

Consider that even the scientifically oriented homeopaths are willing to discard homeopathic theory. They use it merely because it works. "In fact, many doctors who use homeopathic remedies dismiss the [homeopathic] interpretation of disease and human history as nonsense and claim that even the medicines are impossible and unbelievable. They go on practicing *only* because it works" (78:191–192).

Of course, the same could be said of psychic healing and a variety of other occultic methods of curing. They may indeed work. But knowing why something works is just as important to knowing that it works. Many things work and yet are still dangerous (see chapter 4).

None of the claimed evidences offered in support of homeopathy, theoretical or practical, proves that homeopathy is an effective medical procedure. The parallels to medicine are inapplicable; quantum theory is no help; and the supposed cures of homeopathy, including among infants and animals, are undemonstrated. This means that people who trust homeopathy to cure their diseases are being deluded. Let us give one key illustration showing why homeopathy cannot be considered a legitimate medical practice. Some of this material is redundant, but we think it important.

The Difficulty of Diagnosis and Treatment

If the practicing homeopath cannot guarantee an objective basis for medical diagnosis and treatment, his practice cannot be considered legitimate. Supposedly only homeopathy is effective and only homeopathy can truly cure disease (38:14, 34, 109; 80:89; 78:171). But disease must first be diagnosed properly before it can be treated properly. For the homeopath, a plethora of psychological and historical questions allegedly revealing the patient's unique illness is necessary to determine the proper medicine. Without knowing the patient's unique illness, the homeopath cannot prescribe the correct remedy. But when homeopaths seek a totally unique disease that they cannot demonstrate exists, how can we trust them to prescribe the proper medicine? And when they do prescribe, they encounter more problems. The proper dilution must somehow be decided and they must then choose between contradictory theories of application, such as single or multiple doses (one or more medications per dose) and single or multiple remedies (one or more remedies per illness). Further:

> The conscientious homeopath selects his or her curative from 2,500 base substances: plants, minerals, chemicals, animals and insects. He or she then chooses among at least 30 degrees of dilution and finally among 20 different pill forms—over one million possible combinations. (246:92)

And this doesn't even scratch the surface of potential problems in diagnosis and treatment as a promoter of homeopathy confesses:

> Conventional thinking has insurmountable problems comprehending how trained homeopaths can ferret out some remote "cause" dating back gener-

> ations, the symptoms or traces of which defy analytical methods. [How can a homeopath claim to identify] . . . the residual energy frequency or pattern recorded in a human organism long after a disease, such as measles or smallpox has been cured.[?] Further, this same energy may also be identified as the underlying, primary cause of such a condition as multiple sclerosis, or allergies. (245:83)

Indeed, how *does* one objectively diagnose the condition of the "vital energy" or the astral body?

How do an endless number of questions concerning a patient's habits, background, mental and emotional states, etc., help diagnose a disease which can't even be verified? How do homeopaths correctly pick out that one single medicine out of the thousands available that cures the "true" disease of the patient, assuming that true disease has actually been revealed?

How does a homeopathic physician accurately diagnose when there is no uniform agreement among homeopaths concerning the means of diagnosis and the proper treatment? "There is no consistent pharmaceutical code linking diseases and remedies" (78:182). How then do homeopaths know that the information in their *Materia Medica* is really accurate?

Further, classical homeopaths believe, "Every medicinal substance must be administered in a state of the most perfect purity, and uncombined with any other. The union of several remedies in a single prescription destroys its utility, and, according to the *Organon*, frequently adds a new disease" (347:223).

Yet many modern homeopathic practitioners do, in fact, prescribe several different remedies in a single prescription. According to classical homeopathy, these homeopaths are actually making their patients sicker.

Then who is right? When so many homeopathic practitioners contradict one another on important principles relating to diagnosis and treatment, who is to be trusted? How does Gauss, for example, know there are twenty-four different forms of fear, each requiring a different medication? (2:71)

How does Kent know that a person who will be cured by *nux vomica* (vomit nut) will exhibit the symptoms of having a stuffed up nose, being chilly, irritable, wanting to kill someone, wanting to throw one's child into the fire, wanting to kill one's mate, and having constipation? (36:211)

If homeopaths have no rational basis for assigning a variety of mental, emotional, and other conditions to precise physical illnesses and then prescribing on that basis, why do they think their practice is legitimate?

Because they have no objective basis upon which to work, if they are frank, most homeopaths will admit that their diagnosis and treatment of a patient is largely subjective. Homeopathy itself is their real problem. Ideally, there is one *proper* remedy per illness; but one homeopath who discusses the prescribing of remedies confesses this method is "long, tedious, uncertain and disappointing":

> The ideal would be to prescribe only one [remedy]. There's a school of homeopathic doctors who do that. . . . [However] I no longer try to find a single remedy. That's true of most homeopaths, because the search for a single remedy is long, tedious, uncertain, and disappointing. And even if you think you've found one, how can you be sure? (148:143)

But a search for multiple remedies is no better. The simple truth is that both homeopathic diagnosis and treatment are impossible on any objective basis; the homeopathic practitioner is either using useless homeopathic guidelines or is guessing (78:180–186; 65:93–97).

This uncertainty and the tediousness of homeopathic diagnosis and treatment leads many homeopathic practitioners into the realm of the "intuitive"; the psychic and the occult. Homeopaths find that psychic methods of diagnosis save a great deal of time and are also more accurate. The very reason why homeopaths use psychic methods so frequently is that they believe these offer a more reliable basis for diagnosis and treatment than they can otherwise give through standard homeopathic methods and teachings (see pages 322–323).

Science and Homeopathy

Modern homeopaths often claim that homeopathy can be used effectively with scientific medicine. Dr. Desmichelle, M.D., honorary president of the Centre Homeopathique de France, answered the question, "Are allopathy and homeopathy irreconcilable?" by maintaining that "they are two complementary medicines that can be alternatively used" and that if allopathic physicians were better informed "allopathy and homeopathy would each have their own place" in modern medicine (247:2).

Wyrth Baker, M.D., claims that homeopathy "is compatible with most areas of medicine (including obstetrics and surgery), immunotherapy, nutritional therapy (including vitamin supplementation), endocrine therapy (including hormones), psychotherapy, physical therapy, osteopathy, chiropractic, and naturopathy" (81:49).

Homeopathy and medicine can indeed be combined by the scientifically oriented homeopath, but this is not the issue. Oil and water can also be combined, but to what end? Astrology and medicine can also be combined; this does not prove astrology is true or that it assists medicine. The real issue is whether homeopathy contributes anything legitimate to medical practice.

Homeopathic Premises and Scientific Response

What is ironic about the attempted synergism is that in the entire history of medicine, perhaps no other alternate therapy has ever been more distinct from or opposed to scientific medicine than homeopathy. In fact, the acceptance of medical science is directly related to the decline of homeopathy *and vice versa.* Consider the following ten comparisons and contrasts between homeopathy (classical and/or modern) and modern medicine:

Homeopathic Premise 1: Disease results from an energy imbalance or dysfunction at the deepest non-physical level of the human organism. Physical conditions themselves (cancer, heart disease, AIDS, etc.) are *not* the disease; they are *only* the symptoms or manifestation of the deeper energy imbalance, which is the real problem, the real disease. To heal effectively, medicine must operate on the principle of vital force, or energy, not matter.

Scientific Response: Disease *is* primarily physical; medicine must operate on the principle of physical science, not energy. To accept this homeopathic premise that disease is energy based and not physical would destroy modern medicine.

Homeopathic Premise 2: An effective medicine is that which produces a sick person's symptoms in a healthy person, the principle of "like cures like."

Scientific Response: An effective medicine is that which has been clinically proven to cure physical disease. In rare cases there is a resemblance between the effects of a remedy and the symptoms of diseases in which it is beneficial, but this is true of only a very small number of useful medicines. The vast majority of medicines operate in a manner contrary to homeopathic principles.

Homeopathic Premise 3: Homeopathic substances release their vital force, power, or cosmic energy and become increasingly powerful as they are diluted and shaken. They are most powerful when the original substance (the medicine) has completely disappeared. As noted earlier, Hahnemann remarked, "Modern wiseacres have even sneered at the thirtieth potency . . . [but] we obtain, even in the fiftieth potency, medicines of the most penetrating efficacy" (39:19).

How powerful are homeopathic medicines that do not have even a single molecule of the remedy in them? Incredibily, Hahnemann referred to the "infallibility" of homeopathy "laid before the eyes of the world through facts . . . [e.g.,] typhous contagious epidemics must now allow themselves to be speedily turned into health by a few small doses of rightly-selected homeopathic medicine" (39:26).

Scientific Response: Unfortunately, typhous and other contagious epidemics are still with us. All diseases that have been eradicated were not defeated by homeopathy, but by scientific medicine. Hahnemann's prediction failed to materialize because homeopathic substances are not medicines and they have no curing powers. Outside of homeopathic circles, no evidence exists that substances become more powerful by dilution and shaking. The sciences of chemistry and pharmacology teach the exact opposite—that the more diluted a substance, the weaker it becomes. This is why homeopathic medicines cannot be effective at any level of potency, low or high; homeopathic solutions are so diluted it is impossible they could have any physical impact. At potencies above 24D (12CH), homeopathic treatment is no different from drinking a glass of water and considerably more expensive. Homeopathy remains imprisoned by Avogadro.

Thus, homeopaths ask us to believe in magic: that the equivalent mixture of one drop of water in a million billion trillion oceans the size of our solar system has great medicinal powers: "It is like taking a grain of a substance and dissolving it in billions of spheres of water, each with the diameter of the solar system" (117:133) and then claiming that the resulting mixture is powerful medicine. That is nonsense, not medicine.

Homeopathic Premise 4: Because illness has both mental and physical symptoms, treating disease requires an evaluation of emotional and mental conditions as well.

Scientific Response: Physical illness per se does *not* result in the *kinds* of mental symptoms homeopathy assigns to them. Using mental and emotional factors in the evaluation of physical disease *may* be relevant but it is not always relevant. Physical disease is primarily a physical problem. Even in those areas where the mental and physical realms may be considered related, emotional factors are not accorded the interpretation nor the importance homeopathy assigns to them.

***Homeopathic Premise* 5:** Once administered, the homeopathic treatment will remove the entire disease, from its root cause—the vital force dysfunction in the "spiritual" body—to the physical symptoms in the outer or material body. Merely treating outer symptoms—physical disease—is futile and dangerous. This will only drive the disease deeper and cause additional, more severe mental and physical symptoms.

Scientific Response: Where is the evidence that homeopathic medicine will cure the entire disease from its "root" cause to its outer symptoms? Homeopaths who claim to be practicing scientific medicine and yet operate on the premises of vitalistic or occultic principles are engaging in deception. Further, the entire history of modern medicine proves that its treatment of disease and illness is effective and beneficial. No evidence anywhere suggests its methods cause the harmful consequences homeopathy claims for them.

***Homeopathic Premise* 6:** Diagnosis and treatment must be totally individualized. The homeopath does *not* seek to ascertain the symptoms a patient has in *common* with other men, as a means to diagnosis—e.g., headache, fever, and stuffy nose usually indicate a cold. Rather, he seeks those symptoms that are unique and which the patient does *not* have in common with other men. Hence, the need for extremely detailed questioning of the patient's personal history, emotional state, habits, etc.

Scientific Response: Homeopathic diagnosis and treatment is wasteful and ineffective to the extent that it fails to utilize diagnosis based on common symptoms revealing common illness or disease capable of common treatment.

***Homeopathic Premise* 7:** The treatment methods of modern medical pharmacology, such as prescription drugs, should be opposed because homeopathic remedies are rendered ineffective when such drugs are used. If a person wants to be treated homeopathically, he should avoid the services of a physician, at least during his period of homeopathic treatment. Thus, homeopathy is "most effective in treating infants, children, and individuals who have received little or no physiological (allopathic) medication" (81:49).

Scientific Response: Homeopathic medicines were ineffective in the first place. Perhaps the reason homeopathy is more effective with people who have had no medication (if that is true) is that these people are more healthy to begin with. Furthermore, the vastly superior effectiveness of modern drugs and treatments put homeopathy out of business in the early twentieth century. In fact, modern drugs and medicine became so effective that not a single homeopathic hospital, school, or pharmacy remained, and of fourteen thousand practioners, only a few hundred survived. Finally the homeopath thinks his medicines are effective because over a long period of symptom classification and treatment he sees his patient improve. But the patient would have improved anyway. And if homeopathy has never established the effectiveness of its treatments, how can anyone know it was modern drugs that supposedly made them ineffective?

***Homeopathic Premise* 8:** What is important is that homeopathy works. How or why it works is irrelevant.

Scientific Response: Establishing how and why something works is crucial; it is the essence of modern scientific medicine. This is the only possible means to determine if a treatment is truly effective. To willfully remain in the dark about whether or not a treatment works on the basis of its stated principles and is truly effective is irrational and dangerous (see chapter 4).

***Homeopathic Premise* 9:** Homeopathy itself is the absolute authority; it is a "perfect science" with almost infinite power to cure almost anything (35:18; 36:28, 55, 242; 39:21, 26; 76:26; 148:142).

Scientific Response: Scientific testing has proven that homeopathic principles and methods are false and ineffective; if and when homeopathy works, it is working on other principles besides those it holds true. The burden of proof rests with the homeopathic community to prove its claims. Merely asserting that homeopathic medicine somehow magically influences the immune system and that it will be scientifically proven to do so in the future is an inappropriate response to critics. *Anyone* could claim that *anything* magically influences the immune system and will be proven in the future, like, for example, watching butterflies. That is hardly a reason to believe those who make such claims.

***Homeopathic Premise* 10:** Only homeopathy is true medicine, because it alone treats the true inner cause of illness. Modern scientific medicine is ineffective. At best, it only has the power to treat symptoms, not root causes. At worst, modern scientific medicine is an unmitigated evil employed by deceived malpractitioners who are portrayers of death and destruction (78:170–180, see below).

Scientific Response: Modern scientific medicine has demonstrated its benefits; homeopathy remains unproven; therefore, the real danger lies in homeopathic practice.

These above ten comparisons between homeopathy and modern medicine reveal that the two methods are fundamentally incompatible. Doctors who mix the two practices are certainly free to do so; nevertheless, one can only wonder at the attempt.

Antagonist Attitude Toward Science

The previous comparison of the premises of homeopathy and modern medical practice reveal why it has so consistently opposed scientific medicine from its inception. By their very natures, homeopathy, especially classical homeopathy, and scientific medicine must remain antagonists because their view of the cause of disease and the cure for disease are so radically different and opposite from one another.

The founder of homeopathy itself, Samuel Hahnemann, felt that nonhomeopathic medicine was "pernicious" because it considers disease as residing in the physical frame, thereby preventing real cure (38:21). Medical doctors are simply deluded, indeed they are fools, if they think they can discover the cause of disease; when they claim such a discovery, it is only their vain imaginings (38:32; 386:98, 110).

This is why James Tyler Kent, M.D., perhaps the greatest leader in homeopathy at the turn of the century, believed that modern physicians cannot properly treat the ill—because they cannot even determine what real sickness is to begin with (36:18–20).

For Dr. Kent and many other classical and modern homeopaths, physicians who think of curing physical disease are confused at best: "To think of remedies for cancer is confusion, but to think of remedies for the patient who appears to have cancer is orderly. . . . Cancer is a result of disorder [in the vital force], which disorder must be turned into order and must be healed" (36:82). He emphasized "no [physical] organ can make the body sick" and "neither can any disease cause be found with the microscope" (36:42, 55). He further emphasized: "All diseases known to man are . . . an invisible something that cannot be detected by the chemist or the microscopist, and will never be detected in the natural world. Disease . . . is not capable of investigation by the natural senses. . . . Disease causes are invisible" (36:90). Thus, he taught that non-homeopathic beliefs and treatments had accomplished nothing more than "the establishment of confusion" in medicine; that its procedures were a "farce" and that it was full of folly and even insanity (36:22, 44, 53). Dr. Kent concluded,

> He who considers disease results to be the disease itself, and expects to do away with these as disease, is insane. It is an insanity in medicine. . . . The bacteria are results of disease. In the course of time we will be able to show perfectly that the microscopical little fellows are not the disease cause, but that they come after . . . that they are perfectly harmless in every respect. (36:22)

But bacteria and viruses are not "perfectly harmless in every respect"; they continue to destroy many thousands of lives each year. Is the AIDS virus "harmless in every respect?" Anyone who thinks so is deluded. But Hahnemann, Tyler, and other homeopaths rejected and continue to reject the very prescription drugs that may kill deadly bacteria and viruses and save patient lives. For example, Kent believed that whenever a prescription drug was given "let it be clearly understood that a cure of this patient is abandoned" (36:244). Traditional homeopaths think the prescriptions given are harmful and evil because people who use them will only become sicker and sicker at the mental or spiritual level, even if they are cured at the physical level (78:170–190). Statements like these indicate why classical homeopathy and medicine must remain forever hostile (cf. 78:170–190; 36:18, 28, 57, 76, 79, 85).

But matters deteriorate even further. Classical homeopathy believes that not only are scientifically oriented physicians ultimately purveyors of illness and death; not only do they destroy their patients' health; but, as we will shortly see, their malpractice contributes significantly to the social problems of the entire planet!

Nevertheless, because they claim to be healers and yet are destroyers, they are frauds. As Dr. Grossinger comments,

> The conflict with allopathy is head-on here. If the visible disease is not the disease and if its alleviation is countertherapeutic, then the whole of medicine is involved in a system of superficial palliation leading to more serious disease. Doctors do not cure; they merely displace symptoms to

> ever less optimum channels of disease expression, each of which they consider to be a separate event because of its location in a new organ or region of the body. The disease meanwhile is driven deeper and deeper into the constitution because its mode of expression is cut off each time. (78:170–171)

In other words, homeopathy teaches that, in treating only visible disease, normal medicine must always drive disease deeper and deeper into the person; even to the point where it is incapable of cure, and *insanity* is the end result:

> As disease becomes more serious . . . pathology moves from the physical level to the emotional level to the mental level, its ultimate expression being insanity and loss of reason. (78:170–171)

According to homeopathy then, almost everything the modern physician does is *wrong*, and this, of course, can never truly help his patients (78:172–173).

> It is certainly clear from the above why a rapprochement between standard medicine and homeopathy is impossible. Just on the principles [of homeopathy] alone, without even including the exotic and spiritual pharmacy, homeopathy condemns orthodox medical science to a wild goose chase of symptom classification when the dynamics of symptoms in no way reflect the dynamics of the disease. In treating imaginary categories, physicians were doomed to make their patients worse.
>
> Modern homeopathy has developed new language to explain how conventional medical treatment must always make the patient sicker, even if it gives him the delicate illusion of health. (78:173–174)

In fact, according to classical homeopathy, modern medicine is so destructive that it not only makes the patient sicker; it not only ends up producing mental derangement and life threatening illness; but it even causes massive social disruption and disintegration!

In homeopathy, disease itself can ultimately be seen as a curative process, but one that must be managed in a very specific homeopathic manner to be effective. Properly managed, the disease process itself can result in great personal and social benefit. Why? In theory, when disease is treated homeopathically, the organism increasingly becomes resistant to physical and mental illnesses. If homeopathic methods were universal, the physical and mental condition of humanity would progress toward utopian levels. But when disease is mismanaged, its recuperative powers are lost. By preventing the proper treatment of disease, modern medicine drives it inward on both an individual and social level. As individuals become sicker and more mentally unstable, society itself disintegrates inwardly. Because the practices of modern medicine are universally producing severe physical and mental disease, they are, then, to a significant degree responsible for the grave social and political conditions in the modern world. Dr. Grossinger explains:

> From a homeopathic point of view, the allopathic medical care provided in civilized countries has driven disease inward to such a degree that we see an exponential increase in the most serious pathological expressions—cancer, heart disease, and mental illness.
>
> Seventy years ago Kent said that if we continue to treat skin disease palliatively, the human race will cease to exist.
>
> The cumulative charge of poor medical treatment against the doctors of the West is so serious as to be mind-boggling, and, as we have suggested, it places conventional malpractice in a totally new light. It [scientific medicine] is, finally, *all* malpractice.
>
> The implications, to the homeopath, pyramid from here. If the disease is invisible, then all the [medical] research is for naught . . . then the entire medical profession becomes an extortionist gang. The "sting" would outdo any "con game" on record. The older, sicker people, their diseases assured by earlier [medical] treatment, require extraordinarily expensive hospital treatment.
>
> Ultimately the patient dies, and the sting is complete, with perfect above-ground legal disposal of the body. What makes the whole thing a mockery . . . is that the *real* disease cause is invisible anyway. Any quest for an impossible object will become exponentially more expensive at each level of refinement, for, as long as there is no limit to the variety and subtlety of equipment that can be developed to aid in this grand delusion, there is also no limit to the cost. (78:175–176)

In this sense, homeopathy is the world's savior. It alone knows the true problem of man, it alone can cure man, and it alone has the potential to produce a social utopia. To the extent homeopathy is rejected, to that extent man will suffer with disease, insanity, war, crime, hunger, apathy, and a host of other evils which only homeopathy can cure:

> From a homeopathic standpoint, social and economic problems are the collective result of the disease driven inward. . . . Slaughter in Uganda or Cambodia or Guatemala is the work of disease driven inward to the mental plane on an epidemic level. Pornography, sexual violence, mayhem in

the United States, and terrorism in Western Europe . . . are diseases. (78:185, 190; cf. pp. 170–190)

But such a bizarre theory also provides a convenient rationale for homeopathic inefficacy. Thus, classical homeopathy teaches that even its own failures are not really due to homeopathy which, in theory, can be infallible; they are due to the fact that disease has been driven so far inward that even homeopathy itself has become powerless (78:217).

Thus, homeopathy is the intractable adversary of modern medicine. Here we find a paradox. Contemporary physicians seem to have ignored homeopathy largely because its medicines are relatively inert, like sugar water. They seem to think homeopathy is relatively harmless. By now it should be obvious that there is a problem with this assumption. The philosophy underlying homeopathy is anything but harmless to modern medicine; the one who believes in the principles of classical homeopathy cannot accept scientific medicine; indeed, he must oppose it. Nor is homeopathy harmless when it treats serious conditions with sugar pills and permits such conditions to go untreated by conventional medicine.

Perhaps modern medicine should take another look.

Scientific Evaluation

Like many other new age medical techniques, homeopathy claims to be a "science" or to be "scientific." Science deals in the observable world of demonstrated cause and effect. It is based on the discovery of natural laws and seeks to determine how things work in the physical world. This is all contrary to homeopathic practice. Homeopathy teaches that true causes are "invisible to the natural eye but visible to the spiritual eye or understanding. The materialist cannot grasp this idea, he cannot think in this way" (36:86). Therefore, "you will never find a material entity as in any way causing anything" (36:85). This kind of thinking is the very antithesis of modern science. Thus, when homeopaths claim that they are practicing "science," what they often mean is *metaphysical* science.

Many people think that homeopathy is scientific because many homeopathic practitioners work so hard to make it *appear* scientific. For example, the chief coroner in Germany's capital of Bonn, Dr. Prokop, acknowledges the "brilliant ability" of some homeopaths "to identify scientific data with homeopathic foundations—[based on] reasoning that is irrational" (2:76).

Practitioners also often deny their practice is unscientific in any way. One commentator observes, the "vital force" "in no way implies a 'mystical,' 'eighteenth-century,' or 'unscientific' approach to medicine" (78:292).

Below we will continue to document why homeopathic practice is not scientific and why scientific research into homeopathy disproves it.

Nonscientific Approach

The philosophy and premises of homeopathy aren't scientific. Homeopathy teaches that true causes are found only in the invisible world. To the extent this premise pervades the whole of homeopathy, it demands the rejection of material science at every level.

The very premise of homeopathic treatment, that "like cures like," has already been discredited. We saw earlier that the alleged "symptoms" produced by a given homeopathic substance through homeopathic "provings" were not caused by that substance and were explainable on other principles.

The methods of diagnosis in homeopathy are subjective, contradictory, and often intuitive or psychic. Consider the assessment of a major alternate health guide endorsing new age medicine:

> Diagnosis is made not so much on the basis of objective tests of the kind that allopathic physicians use to decide what illness a patient has, as on the [subjective] evaluation of what the homeopath sees, feels, and hears. The course the homeopath will take in deciding upon treatment is little changed from Hahnemann's time. (325:70)

Indeed, ". . . the modern homeopathist still rejects and views with the greatest mistrust, the valuable diagnostic methods" of modern medicine (386:137). Further, because microorganisms are not seen as the true cause of disease, diagnosis is carried out on a wholly different level. "Since homeopathic medicines do not kill germs directly, the agent associated with the illness, be it bacteria, virus, fungus, or other microbe, makes little difference" (112:23).

But in medical diagnosis, the agent associated with the illness is crucial. Scientific laboratory work is used in conjunction with hospitals and physicians' offices because determining the true cause of a given illness or disease is vital. Again, determining the physical cause of the illness is the only way to prescribe proper treatment.

Let us illustrate. Lyme disease, for example, is caused by a corkscrew shaped bacteria named *Borrelia burgdorferi*, something homeopaths apparently aren't interested in. But Lyme disease may be asymptomatic, which means it is only detectable by laboratory testing. A person can be infected and never know it. Even when symptoms occur, they can be relatively minor. Regardless, they soon disappear.

The disease then enters a dormant stage that may last for months or years. At this point it is incurable. When it finally resurfaces, the patient will be afflicted with one or more debilitating or permanently crippling conditions, including seizures, arthritis, severe heart damage, meningitis, encephalitis and fetal damage in pregnant women (383). One can only wonder how many people with early stage Lyme disease may have sought homeopathic treatment and been unnecessarily doomed to a life-long illness?

But hundreds and even thousands of serious or even fatal illnesses are caused by fungi, bacteria, viruses, etc. What about AIDS? We ask again: How many hundreds or thousands of people continue to suffer from viral based illnesses which remain undiagnosed because of homeopathic or other ineffective new age health "treatment"?

The "medicines" of homeopathy aren't scientifically validated; they are scientifically discredited. Homeopathic medicines are not even medicines; they are diluted to such high levels that hardly anything remains of the homeopathic "substance" and often literally nothing remains, not even a molecule. As the 1977 report of an Australian Parliament Committee of Inquiry summarized, "There is not one example in the whole of pharmacology in which simple dilution of a drug enhances the responses it produces any more than diluting a dye can produce a deeper hue, or adding less sugar can make food sweeter" (87:57). Laboratory research has proven time and again that chemical analysis of homeopathic remedies shows only the presence of the base substance. Thus, "The *least* probable factor in a homeopathic cure is a homeopathic remedy itself. Organically there is no effect from a remedy in homeopathic potencies over 6X" (2:78). In fact, "If the FDA required homeopathic remedies to be proved effective in order to remain on the market, homeopathy would face extinction in the United States" (87:62). (But the FDA apparently thinks homeopathic remedies are harmless and that there are more important priorities.)

All of this is why *Consumer Reports* observed in its January 1987 issue,

> Unless the laws of chemistry have gone awry, most homeopathic remedies are too diluted to have any physiological effect. For that reason, medical scientists consider them to be innocuous but absurd drugs. Last year, for example, faculty members from forty-nine U.S. pharmacy schools responded to a questionnaire we sent inquiring about homeopathy. Virtually all said the remedies were neither potent nor effective, except possibly as placebos for mild, temporary ailments that commonly resolve on their own. (114:62)

Many homeopaths admit that scientific research into homeopathy is fruitless. This should be obvious and yet not all homeopaths will frankly admit it. True causes are invisible. How does science research the world of the "invisible?" How does it deal with the "vital force?" Remember, it is not ultimately the homeopathic medicine that brings the cure; it is the vital force released by the medicine. How does science investigate this? "Since the disease cause is unknowable, the cure cannot come from knowledge. The worst damage an ailment causes tells no more than [does] a minor symptom, for both are expressions of the unknown" (78:178).

All of this is why "many homeopaths still maintain that homeopathic effects cannot be investigated by scientific methods" (2:74). Indeed, a number of texts have been written proving this, such as Prokop and Prokop, *Homoeopathie and Wissenschaft* (*Homeopathy and Science*) (Stuttgart, 1957) (2:74).

Research into homeopathy is often parapsychological. Those homeopaths who say that homeopathy *can* be investigated scientifically are often not doing scientific research. Rather they are engaging in parapsychological investigations using occultic premises. They may employ *radionic* instruments and pendulums in their research. One might suspect they are really less concerned with scientific results, because they know homeopathy works metaphysically. Their "science" is really occult science.

Invalid Testing

In discussing homeopathy and scientific testing, we make four observations: 1) homeopathic research is rarely subjected to independent critical review; 2) homeopathic premises conveniently serve to rationalize their own failures; 3) scientific testing does not validate but invalidates homeopathy; 4) the scientific research discrediting homeopathy is sufficient to cause even devoted followers to forsake it.

1. Homeopathic research is rarely subjected to independent critical review. Promoters of homeopathy often claim that research has established the effectiveness of their methods. But one must distinguish homeopathic research and that which has been subject to independent analysis.

Homeopathic research is rarely subjected to critical review by independent researchers. But when it is, it fails the test. The research reported in June 1988 in *Nature* is a good example. What was initially hailed as proof of homeopathy in the homeopathic community was later discredited (117:133–145; 404:90–95).

The basis upon which this initial research was published in such a prestigious journal as *Nature* (*seemingly* valid scientific results) is reminiscent of the days of earlier falsehoods such as "N-rays," "phlogiston," and "polywater." (117:133–145). Repeated scientific testing disproved the existence of N-rays or polywater, but not before a great deal of faith in the substances had been generated. In the case of the principal homeopathic researcher who published in *Nature*,

> He rushes into print with a claim so staggering that if true it would revolutionize physics and medicine, and guarantee him a Nobel Prize. Yet he did this without troubling to learn the most elementary techniques for conducting truly double-blind tests or for supervising self-deceiving observers. (117:140)

Unfortunately, disproven scientific research may take years and even decades to die among true believers. Homeopaths could be citing the above research as "proof" of homeopathy for years to come.

The problem raised by homeopathic research is also illustrated by the response to a 1986 research report in *Lancet* which was criticized as "the first randomized, double-blind trial of one placebo against another" (273:82). Since homeopathic medicines contain no medicine, much homeopathic research is simply testing one placebo against another. How can scientific results be produced from such research?

2. Homeopathic premises conveniently serve to rationalize their own failures. As is true in many forms of new age medicine, homeopathy presents a problem to scientific testing because of the manner in which it claims to work:

> A drawback to most homeopathic research is that it has not been published in respected scientific journals and, therefore, has not been sub-

> jected to strict review by scientists. Yet scientific experiments testing homeopathy on humans are impeded by a major catch-22. To give the same medication to many patients at one time, the obvious and only starting point for clinical research, is homeopathic heresy. Homeopaths insist on individualizing treatments. (246:93)

Let us give an example. Even homeopaths disdained a study with initially positive results, reported in 1980 in the *British Journal of Clinical Pharmacology*. But three years later, the research was repeated and homeopathy failed, as reported in another British journal, *The Lancet*. But in both cases, homeopaths say they expected poor results because "using the same remedy for everyone was an assurance of failure" (248:1).

So how does one ever finally disprove homeopathy by clinical trial when only individualized treatment is acceptable? Likewise, how can homeopaths ever prove it really works? Since it is the homeopaths who make the claims for efficacy, the burden of proof clearly rests with the homeopathic community, and not its critics. And as we will now see, they have never supplied it and the scientific testing which has been conducted provides no basis for confidence in the practice. To the contrary.

3. *Scientific testing does not validate but invalidates homeopathy.* Stephen Barrett, M.D., is the author of over twenty books on health topics. The argument against homeopathy is made especially evident when he observes that homeopathy has yet to *demonstrate* positive results:

> Homeopathic leaders insist that their remedies are effective and that studies do support this viewpoint. They also suggest that homeopathy's popularity and long survival are evidence that it works. But the only way for homeopathy to gain acceptance by the scientific community would be to demonstrate positive results through repeated experiments designed with the help of critics and carried out with strict safeguards against experimenter bias and fraud. (87:62)

This is exactly what homeopathy has not done. True Hahnemannian homeopathic practitioners must, by definition, have abandoned the research principles of scientific medicine. Furthermore, neither have scientifically oriented homeopaths proved the effectiveness of their procedures. Although homeopaths often allege that scientific medicine has never thoroughly investigated its claims (79:307), this is not true. In different ways homeopathy has been investigated and disproven from its inception.

The real problem is the homeopathic claims themselves. They are so radical they evoke characteristically proportionate responses: "Homeopathy couldn't possibly be true, so why waste valuable time and money to prove what you already know?" Or, "the only way homeopathy could ever be accepted is on the basis of the most stringent testing; heroic claims demand heroic proofs."

Oliver Wendell Holmes, M.D., was for thirty-five years the Parkman professor of Anatomy and Physiology at the Harvard Medical School (1847–1882); he also served as dean of the Harvard Medical School. In a devastating critique of homeopathy, given in his 1842 lectures and published in volume 9 of his *Works* (1892), he observed that the claims of homeopathy were so astounding and bizarre that

> nothing but the strictest agreement of the most cautious experimenters, secured by every guaranty that they were honest and faithful, appealing to repeated experiments in public, with every precaution to guard against error, and with the most plain and peremptory results, should induce us to lend any credence to such pretensions. (347:228)

He believed that the theories of Hahnemann himself were so absurd that, "unless the facts in their favor are overwhelming and unanimous, the question naturally arises, is not this man deceiving himself, or trying to deceive others?" (3:228). He cited a number of experiments which had completely disproven homeopathy, some of which we earlier noted. This esteemed medical man concluded that homeopathy was absolutely and totally false (347:221–243). He also gave illustrations as to why Hahnemann's own character was not always to be trusted; for example, Hahnemann even misrepresented and misquoted other writers to defend his false theories. "Professor Joerg, of Leipsic, has proved many of Hahnemann's quotations from old authors to be adultered and false" (347:232).

Neither have modern researchers been able to demonstrate homeopathic effectiveness. "No study of homeopathy to date would appear to be significant. No experimentation authenticates the theory" (37:8). To begin with, scientific research conducted by homeopathic practitioners is generally poor. For example, A. M. Scofield, Ph.D., a professor of biochemistry in Britain, thoroughly reviewed homeopathic research and reported his findings in a two-part article in the *British Homeopathic Journal* (Vol. 73, 1984). He concluded, "It is hardly surprising, in view of the quality of much of the experimental work as well as its philosophical frame work that this system of medicine is not accepted by the medical and scientific community at large" (87:61).

Dr. William Jarvis, professor of Public Health and Preventive Medicine, Loma Linda University Medical School and president of the National Council Against Health Fraud, discusses the sectarian nature of homeopathy, its scientific failings, and why, even if a specific homeopathic remedy works, we are not justified in concluding that homeopathy is true.

> Homeopathy is a form of sectarian medicine; *sect*: "A group adhering to a distinctive doctrine or to a leader" (*Webster's New Collegiate Dictionary*). Sectarian systems do not adhere to objectivity or the pursuit of disconfirmation as do scientists. Rather, they attempt to selectively affirm the tenets of their dogma. Homeopathic advocates allude to twenty-two studies that they allege confirm the value of homeopathy while ignoring innumerable dose-response studies which disprove the homeopathic Law of Infinitesimals; and, the absence of verification by basic scientists of the Law of Similars, Potentizing or Provings.
>
> Further, the fact that a remedy labeled as "homeopathic" proves to be safe and effective for an intended purpose only serves to validate that specific remedy—not the entire sectarian system of homeopathic philosophy, metaphysics, pharmacology, assumptions, and practices. Every major erroneous theory of health and disease of the past can cite practices which appeared to work according to its theory. Medical scientists have learned to accept each procedure on the basis of its demonstrated safety and effectiveness, not its imagined theoretical basis. . . .
>
> [Furthermore] Remedies labeled as "homeopathic" may be effective due to adulteration. Morice reports that a homeopathic remedy which appeared to be effective in treating asthma was found to be adulterated with prednisolone and betamethasone. Neither was listed on the label.* (*The Lancet*, April 12, 1986, pp. 862–863) (458)

All this is why Dr. Grossinger observes:

> Homeopathy, in fact, was doomed to failure from the beginning. It was an uncompromising, rigorous system, demanding a kind of commitment and purism few could maintain, especially in light of the very same demonstra-

---

* With literally thousands of homeopathic substances being widely marketed and consumed, it is at least possible, at low dilutions, a few might have medicinal value (cf. pharmacognosy). But each substance would require stringent testing to prove efficacy. Further, this would not prove homeopathy true. It would only prove that the actual preexisting medicinal properties of certain substances (not their "vital force") were being employed and that these were having a physical effect, not a "spiritual" one.

> tions that the whole thing was impossible and unscientific. Clinical homeopathy cannot be verified in the laboratory, which means, pessimistically, that standard scientific testing has already disproved *all* homeopathic claims. Many homeopaths would deny this, and they have cited various experiments in the chemistry of enzymes, colloids, trace elements, hormones, and drugs. These experiments with microdilutions are interesting and provocative, but they are isolated events, without controlled retesting and general orientation to the rest of science, nor do they test the exact claims of homeopathy. (78:230–231, 164)

Scientific testing does not validate homeopathic claims. Homeopaths may respond by saying that scientific testing has not been carried out on a sufficiently large scale to conclusively prove this. But after one hundred and fifty years, homeopathy has been granted more than ample time to prove its assertions. The failure of homeopathy to justify itself brings us to our final point.

4. Scientific research discrediting homeopathy is sufficient to cause even devoted followers to forsake it. Some homeopaths have used genuine scientific methods to investigate their discipline and have followed their results to their logical conclusion: They have abandoned and repudiated homeopathy. Dr. Samual Pfeifer, M.D., discusses the research of Dr. Fritz Donner, M.D., a homeopath who made his goal the scientific proof of homeopathy.

This was perhaps the first serious attempt by a homeopathic M.D. to scientifically examine homeopathic claims. But it ended with Dr. Donner completely turning away from his own practice (2:74).

Dr. Donner's initial doubts were sparked by a lecture given at a homeopathic hospital in Stuttgart, Germany. The lecturer was well-known homeopath Robert Bosch. Bosch explained that the homeopathic remedy "apis mellifica" (bee venom) was most effective with patients who had diseases on the right side, plus the symptoms of the "lack of thirst" and "a swelling under the right eye." His curiosity piqued, Dr. Donner began reading old homeopathic reports on the effects of bee venom. He discovered that not only had it been used for twice as many diseases on the *left* side, but the symptom of "swelling under the eye" had actually been caused by the bee venom itself (2:74–75).

As a result, Dr. Donner began more serious investigations into homeopathy. Over the years he conducted experiments with some two hundred doctors, testing potencies of 4X to 12X, comparing homeopathic medicines with entirely neutral substances or placebos. But in the end, the results showed only the power of faith in homeopathy, not of homeopathy itself.

The first tests with the ineffective placebos, for example, "caused numerous symptoms in those test subjects who believed in homeopathy, in some cases so fiercely that the test had to be discontinued" (2:75). But those subjects who did not believe in homeopathy didn't register any symptoms either with the placebos or with the homeopathic remedies.

An experiment with vomit nut revealed why homeopathic "provings" are not to be trusted. In this case, the homeopathic doctor, a member of the board of supervisors for the test, had forgotten that placebos had been given first. He mistakenly thought "nux vomica" had been given. Thus, when he examined the test reports he began to select those symptoms that he expected "nux vomica" would produce. But, of course, "nux vomica" wasn't "producing" anything; he was reporting "symptoms" caused by the placebo. The good doctor's bias was uncovered; symptoms that did not fit the homeopathic listing of the symptoms of "nux vomica" were simply omitted.

This reveals that homeopathic researchers can selectively bias the results of their scientific testing in favor of homeopathy. "This incident showed another weak point in the long lists of 'proving symptoms' that were compiled in the history of homeopathy: When the test supervisor knows what remedy is given, he only takes those symptoms he regards as significant and drops the rest" (2:75).

Other tests have also revealed that homeopathic practitioners may be so deeply conditioned by homeopathic philosophy and reasoning that they are often incapable of critically evaluating the facts.

Additional experiments conducted by Donner had similar results. Professor H. Rabe, president of the German Homeopathic Society, believed that he had proven the effectiveness of silicea-produced symptoms in several experimentees. But he later found that he was working with the *wrong* group. Again, "All those displaying symptoms had received placebos not silicea" (37:6–7).

Dr. Donner published the results of his years of research in 1966, in which he confessed all the failures and errors of homeopathic practice. Although the publication of his results caused a debate within the homeopathic community, few if any homeopaths abandoned their practices. It appears that modern homeopaths prefer to ignore scientific testing and are content with the "successes" of their individual practices (37:7).

In conclusion:

> It must not be forgotten that this brand of medicine has a long way to go before its curative powers are proven. With this in mind, it is possible that

> these heydays might be homeopathy's last, a final sputter before a long-postponed natural death. Even among homeopaths, there is a clear sense that the burden of proof is here and now upon them. (246:93)

The Nature of Its Appeal

The ability of homeopathy to fascinate scientists and physicians alike can be seen in the recent furor over the research conducted by the French laboratory INSERM-U 200 in Clamart, France. This research was initially reported in the prestigious British science journal *Nature* (June 30, 1988) and widely publicized in the popular media (*Newsweek*, July 25, 1988; *Time*, August 8, 1988, etc.) as having possibly validated aspects of homeopathic practice. Reports also appeared in *Science*, *Chemical and Engineering News*, *New Scientist*, *The Wall Street Journal*, *New York Times*, *Washington Post*, *The Scientist*, and others. In the end, homeopathic practices were not scientifically validated, but the entire debacle was a powerful illustration of how scientific research into homeopathy can fool even scientists (117:132–146).* Scientists also number among the gullible.

Still, scientifically oriented professionals who become homeopaths do so on a largely fraudulent basis. That basis is the premise of empirical medi-

---

* "The more evidence there is for a hypothesis, the greater its degree of confirmation; and the better confirmed it is, the more it demands acceptance. The criteria for assessing the degree of confirmation of a hypothesis include the following: (1) The number of confirming instances (in general, a large number is better than a small number); (2) The variety of confirming instances (a small number observed under a variety of conditions is better than a large number observed under identical conditions); (3) Disconfirmation of competing hypotheses (the evidence yields a higher degree of confirmation for the hypothesis if it also at the same time disconfirms a competing hypothesis); and (4) Successful prediction (confirming instances observed after the hypothesis has been proposed offer better support than those observed before).

"These criteria tell us how much weight to assign to a whole set or collection of instances. . . .

"If most or all of the instances are questionable, then no matter how large their number or how great the variety of conditions, they will not confirm the hypothesis. Unless unreliable data are constantly guarded against and weeded out, the hypothesis may come to be accepted on the basis of support that it really does not have.

"It is a mark of pseudoscience to think that sheer quantity of evidence makes up for any deficiency in the quality of individual pieces of evidence. Yet this is precisely the sort of reasoning exhibited by Louise Oftedal Wensel, M.D., in her account of a three-year study conducted by the Washington Acupuncture Center. Dr. Wensel writes: 'Although the methods for collecting this information were not entirely objective and scientific, this is the largest study of acupuncture treatment results that has ever been made in the United States.' She then goes on to present the data 'to give an indication of the effectiveness of acupuncture for treating the conditions listed.' " (447; 156)

cine—the idea that personal testimonies of cure prove the validity of a theory. Thus, the only reason that some respected professionals are converted to homeopathy is because it *seems* to work. But so do scores of other false therapies. Because homeopathy seems to work, it is assumed to be true and operating on the basis of some unknown principle.

These individuals may attempt to make homeopathy appear as scientific as possible, but they are operating upon fundamentally unjustified premises. Despite good intentions, they only further the cause of unscientific or quack medicine: positive personal testimonies are exchanged in place of careful scientific evaluation. The result is always the same: Falsehood is proclaimed as a truth.

Occultic Potential

Hahnemann himself was not unfamiliar with the world of the mystical and the occult. Therefore, it is not surprising he would develop a system of healing with occultic potential.

Hahnemann's Background

First, Hahnemann was a follower of the powerful spiritist and medium Emanuel Swedenborg. Those familiar with the occultic philosophy and theology of Emanuel Swedenborg, such as his blending of the world of nature and the occult, can recognize the parallels in Hahnemann's thinking. Andrew Weil received his M.D. from Harvard Medical School, is a research associate in Ethnopharmacology at Harvard, and is somewhat sympathetic with aspects of new age medicine. He observes that Hahnemann was "steeped in the mysticism of Emanuel Swedenborg" (17:14).

Not surprisingly, homeopathy and Swedenborgianism developed an affinity. In *The Formation of the American Medical Profession: The Role of Institutions*, 1780–1860, Joseph F. Kett observes:

> Homeopaths who were usually susceptible to the lure of Mesmerism were attracted in considerable numbers to Swendenborgianism. . . . Homeopathy was so popular among New York and Philadelphia Swedenborgians that a question arose whether one could follow Swedenborg and still reject the way of Hahnemann. (427:149–151)

Today, it is no coincidence that Swedenborg conferences, such as the Science and Spirituality symposium held August 24–27, 1988, in Tarrytown, NY, have workshops on homeopathy. This particular conference had a workshop by Jacquelyn Wilson, M.D., titled "Homeopathy, The Energy Medicine of Past, Present and Future."

Hahnemann was also a Freemason, and, as the authors have demonstrated elsewhere, the study of Freemasonry presents an excellent opportunity for delving into mysticism and the occult (249:215–253). Dr. Bopp, M.D., observes, "We know that he was a member of a Lodge of Free Masons" (37:3). Dr. Pfeifer, M.D., observes, "As a young man Hahnemann had become a member of the Free Masons. . . . It is no surprise that Hahnemann, as a member of the lodge, disparagingly *called Jesus an 'arch-enthusiast.'*" One of his biographers writes:

> He took offense at the arch-enthusiast Jesus of Nazareth, who did not lead the enlightened on the straight way to wisdom but who wanted to struggle with publicans and sinners on a difficult path toward the establishment of the kingdom of God. . . . The man of sorrows who took the darkness of the world on Himself was an offense to the lover of etheric wisdom [Hahnemann]. (2:67)

Hahnemann even placed the motto of Freemasonry, "Aude Sapere" (dare to be wise) on the title page of his *Organon* (38:1).

Hahnemann was also an admirer of the occultists Paracelsus and Mesmer (386:25 cf. 340:189–198). Thus, he was a firm believer in the practice of animal magnetism (or mesmerism, an early term for hypnotism), which was often indistinguishable from modern forms of psychic healing. In his *Organon* he confessed similarities between the practice of homeopathy and mesmerism:

> I find it yet necessary to allude here to *animal magnetism*, as it is termed, or rather *Mesmerism*. . . . It is a marvelous, priceless gift of God . . . by means of which the strong will of a well intentioned person upon a sick one by contact and even without this and even at some distance, can bring the vital energy of the healthy mesmerizer endowed with this power into another person dynamically. . . .
>
> The above mentioned methods of practicing mesmerism depend upon an influx of more or less vital force into the patient. . . . (38:309, 311)

What Hahnemann has just described is no different from many descriptions given of modern psychic healing. In both instances we find distant healing, healing by magnetic passes, and a transference of psychic power from healer to client. In fact, early mesmerism shared many similarities to blatant spiritism (6:34–39; 2:79).

Hahnemann had also been influenced by animism (386:20) and Eastern religion. In discussing the writings of Hahnemann and leading homeopaths, Dr. Bopp comments:

> As a matter of fact the vocabulary is esoteric and the ideas are impregnated with oriental philosophies like Hinduism. The predominant strain of pantheism would place God everywhere, in each man, each animal, plant, flower, cell, even in homeopathic medicine. (37:9)

Dr. Pfeifer also mentions the influence of Eastern thinking upon Hahnemann by quoting a biographer who reveals that "he is *strongly attracted to the East. Confucius is his ideal*" (2:68). Dr. Pfeifer comments:

> On Confucius, Hahnemann himself writes in a letter: "This is where you can read divine wisdom, without [e.g., Christian] miracle-myths and superstition. I regard it as an important sign of our times that Confucius is now available for us to read. Soon I will embrace him in the kingdom of blissful spirits, the benefactor of humanity, who has shown us the straight path to wisdom and to God, already 650 years before the arch-enthusiast. . . ."
>
> The reverence for Eastern thought was not just Hahnemann's personal hobby, but rather the fundamental philosophy behind the preparation of homeopathic remedies. (2:68)

Perhaps this explains why many modern homeopaths are so influenced by Eastern metaphysics. Dr. Pfeifer also refers to a leading Swiss homeopath Adolf Voegeli:

> When I asked him about the cosmic energy which was supposedly working through homeopathy, he explained: "You know, I believe in the power of the zodiac."
>
> Dr. Voegeli has written an article on the mechanisms of homeopathy which was published in the *Zeitschrift fuer Klassiche Homoeopathie* (Journal for Classical Homeopathy). The bibliography resembles a collection of occult, hinduistic, and anthroposophical literature.
>
> Voegeli underscores that the effect of high potencies in homeopathy is of a "*spiritual nature.*" His best explanation is supplied by the *hinduistic Sankhya philosophy*. According to it man not only has his physical body but also an ethereal body with a special system of energetic channels. It is this *ethereal body* that co-ordinates the immunological functions and enhances the wound-healing process. And it is here that homeopathy is active.

> Another energy system, he continues, is the *astral body* controlling the emotional responses of man. But the highest energy plane is the human spirit. Its purpose is to develop into an ever more perfect instrument for divine cosmic impulses. "The goal of man is a continuous evolution; his spiritualization." As one life is never enough, he logically brings in *reincarnation*, which would finally lead to perfection.
>
> Eastern philosophy seeps through the writings of many other authors. (2:68–69)

Finally, Hahnemann himself claimed to be "inspired" in his homeopathic writings. In a letter to the town clerk of Kothen in 1828, he said he had been "guided by the invisible powers of the Almighty, listening, observing, tuning in to his instructions, paying most earnest heed and religious attention to this inspiration" (37:3). Of course, Swedenborg, Hahnemann's mentor, also claimed to have been inspired by God and yet was really only inspired by the demonic spirit world (328:339; cf. ref. 387). At least for us, there is little doubt that Hahnemann too was ultimately inspired by the spirit world. Hahnemann's "inspiration" is recognized by homeopaths and non-homeopaths alike. Dr. Kent confesses to Hahnemann's "being directed by Divine Providence" (36:87). In the *Swiss Homeopathic Journal*, #4, 1960, the president of the International League on Homeopathy, Dr. Gagliardi stated at the Montreux Congress in 1960: "It's futile to reject this or that principle announciated in the 'Organ' [Organon]. There remains more than enough to recognize the unfathomable intuition and divinitory spirit of its author" (37:3).

Dr. Richard Grossinger, who classifies homeopathy as a vitalist (e.g., occultic) medicine, also notes the strange suddenness with which it sprung from Hahnemann's mind:

> Homeopathy is neither the first nor the last attempt to develop a scientific Vitalist [occult] medicine. Alchemists, gnostics, animists, and other naturalist-magicians worked for millennia toward a cure based on the life force in the primal energy of nature. Goethe, Steiner, Jung, and Reich followed. . . . It [homeopathy] persists [today] as a clinical occult discipline. . . .
>
> Although aspects of homeopathic thought were in existence before Hahnemann, the system itself arises as suddenly from his mind as Mormonism did from the golden tablets of Joseph Smith. Before Hahnemann, there was no homeopathy. Since Hahnemann, homeopathy has changed only to a minor degree. . . . To his supporters, Hahnemann is the single genius in the history of recorded medicine. . . . (78:162–163)

Hahnemann's system carries certain hallmarks of occultic inspiration, such as the promotion of occultic philosophy and occultic healing. It is unlikely that Hahnemann himself, without inspiration, could have developed homeopathy. Even Grossinger remarks, "It is not clear how he came to know all he did" (78:205, cf. pp. 169–205). In addition, the *Organon* itself is believed by many homeopaths to be an almost mystical book (36:87; 37:32; 39:6). Indeed, "whoever knows the *Organon* knows also the spirit of homeopathy" (386:146).

Another area that may reflect Hahnemann's occult involvement is the personality alteration and personal tragedies which so often accompany those involved in occult practices. His children lived in terrible poverty; his medical practice in Leipzig was a failure; both he and his family had a tragic history. One son died shortly after birth; another who was mentally ill left one day and never returned. Three of his daughters' marriages ended in divorce; two daughters were murdered in a mysterious way. Another daughter died at birth. Another died when she was thirty. His only remaining son deserted his wife and child. Over the years Hahnemann's character and personality had changed in strange ways (2:65; 386:173; 37:2). A. Fritsche, one of his biographers, observes: "Hahnemann had to empty the cup of demonism with which his father had endowed him" (2:65).

Even homeopathic treatments may cause the same kind of problems found in other forms of occult healing. At least one physician relates his own clinical experience: "The occult influence in homeopathy is transmitted to the individual, bringing him consciously or unconsciously under demonic influence. . . . It is significant frequently to find nervous depression in families using homeopathic treatments" (37:10).

Occultic Tradition

If the founder of homeopathy was involved in the occult, it is not unexpected that he would develop a health practice supportive of the occult.

Homeopathy exists within that tradition of occult medicine known as hermetic vitalism, (although a mixture of this and biological vitalism is also found in homeopathic practice):

> Vitalism is, at once, a science, a religious philosophy, and a doctrine which radically alters all other theories of matter and being. . . . There is perhaps no more succinct way to define vitalism than to say it is everything which

> modern science is not. . . . There are two types of vitalism: biological and hermetic. . . . Hermetic and biological vitalism overlap in a number of ways. . . . Whereas the biological vitalist believes in the single life force and seeks it as an unknown energy within science, the hermetic vitalist understands an enormous variety of occult associations which he derives by intuition and meditation. (78:116, 122–23)

Homeopathy is linked to occult medicine by any number of commentators. For example,

> Psychic healing, homeopathy, acupuncture, orgone therapy, and various shamanisms and voodoo all suggest that there must be an energy outside of contemporary definition. . . .
>
> Dozens of books in the last fifteen years alone have explored the similarity of these various systems—vitalist, Eastern and Western occult, homeopathic, Reichian, parasychological, etc. (78:128–129)

Hahnemann's homeopathy is also noted in connection with perhaps the foremost occult scientist of the Middle Ages, Paracelsus. Paracelsus used alchemy, spiritistism, astrology, and other occult arts in his research into disease and health (253:45–46; 38:6; 76:22; 37:2). According to the *Encyclopedia Britannica* he "was the first to declare that, if given in small doses, 'what makes a man ill also cures him' and he experimented by giving plague struck patients a pill made of bread mixed with a minute amount of their excreta" (274:984).

We noted earlier the problem of the extensive time required for homeopathic diagnosis and treatment. We said this was often resolved by recourse to psychic methods. Wallace F. MacNaughton, M.D., is a good illustration of how many homeopathic practitioners have turned to psychic methods of diagnosis as a means to save both time and energy. In his practice, Dr. MacNaughton combines homeopathy, color therapy, and radionics (64:XI–XII).

In *Vibrations: Healing Through Color, Homeopathy and Radionics*, two friends of Dr. MacNaughton describe this problem of homeopathic practice and its solution:

> This time-consuming process of diagnosis and remedy selection has proved a serious hindrance to the expansion of homeopathy. . . . Dr. MacNaughton's methods are not as time consuming . . . in that his radionic instrument has offered him an effective shortcut to diagnosis. . . . Over the years he has therefore been able to dispense with the standard physical examination and a prolonged period of questioning the patient, greatly

> saving time and energy usually expended by the good homeopath in the diagnostic process. His [radionic] instrument also enables him to determine accurately the best remedy for a given patient with a given condition, including the selection of [specific treatments]. . . . (64:43–44)

Many homeopaths with a scientific or Christian orientation have denied that Hahnemann or homeopathy have ever intended an occultic application of his vital force, or that it is equivalent to the mystical/cosmic energy of new age medicine. It is true that many mystical energy concepts such as *prana, chi, orgone, od, mana,* etc., have unique aspects due to their historical context and background. Nevertheless, in some fashion they are invariably associated with the occult. The issue is not whether Hahnemann's energy concept is a strict equivalent to others in new age medicine, but whether it is occultic or potentially occultic. The vital force may not be an equivalent to *prana,* but potentially it is occultic. Hahnemann himself related his vital force to Mesmer's animal magnetism, stating that "vital force" was an energy that could be *transferred* into another person.

It is also possible that the influence of the powerful occultist Swedenborg on Hahnemann may have swayed his particular concept of energy (vital force) and its relation to the divine. Swedenborg, like Rudolf Steiner who founded the occult system of *Anthroposophical Medicine,* also attempted to blend Christianity, paganism, and the occult. If Hahnemann was so influenced by Swedenborg, one could expect an occultic application of the vital force. Regardless, similarities to new age energy concepts remain. If nothing else, they provide the logical basis for an extension into full-blown new age energy teachings.

Concerning this, we think that the statements of Hahnemann cited under the basic errors of homeopathy are clear enough. What Hahnemann taught was that mystical energies were at the base of both human nature and the medicines themselves, thus at the very base of creation itself. This is why many commentators, both sympathetic and critical, teach that Hahnemann *was* referring to new age spiritual or cosmic energy when talking of his vital force.

Dr. Michael Radner is associate professor in the Department of Philosophy at McMaster University, author of *Science and Unreason,* and co-editor of *Theories and Methods of Physics and Psychology.* In "Holistic Methodology and Pseudoscience" he discusses the new age tendency for arguing in spurious similarities, and he identifies the homeopathic teachings on energy as a fundamentally new age energy belief:

> Like Chinese medicine, homeopathy posits an energy field or "vital force." Disease is a disorder of the body's energy field, and the way to cure it is to manipulate that field. The energy field of the medicine stimulates that body's own fluid to induce healing. As with Chinese medicine, it is maintained that the energy fields are similar to those of modern physics. Again the principle cited is the interchangeability of matter and energy. (409:154)

Dr. Samuel Pfeifer observes the orientation of many homeopaths when he discusses their healing method. "The healing power, say the homeopaths, is coming from cosmic power transferred to the remedy through the ritual of potentiation" (2:72).

Also, the descriptions that many homeopaths give of the energies released in treatment is almost indistinguishable from descriptions given by occult practitioners who claim to manipulate new age energies by radionics devices and pendulums (e.g., 113:24). In his commentary upon Hahnemann's *Organon of Medicine*, James Tyler Kent spoke in terms which closely parallel new age energy concepts and beliefs (36:68–84). Not only did the vital force underlie and pervade the creation, it actually held it together (36:68–70); it had intelligence (36:69); and was related to or part of "the Supreme Power Himself [God]" (36:71); it was connected to the soul and/or human "aura" (36:71–75).

Leading homeopath Herbert Robert clearly related homeopathy's vital force to a pantheistic deity in his *Art of Cure by Homeopathy*. It was spoken of as part of "the moving Energy, the activating Power of the universe," as being "passed on in all forms and degrees of living creatures," and as permeating the universe:

> If therefore this force, this energy, actuates or permeates all forms and degrees of life from the most humble and inconspicuous to the very planets, we may reasonably assume that vital force is the most fundamental of all conditions of the universe, and that the laws governing the vital force in the individual are correlated with the laws which govern all vital force, all forms of energy, wherever or however expressed. . . .
>
> This energy . . . is responsible for all growth and all development in all spheres of existence. (35:50)

This is why so many modern homeopaths have claimed that homeopathy is really a practice that is linked to the universal movement and flow of cosmic or divine "energy" (e.g., 148:141).

Disease is caused by energy; it is cured by energy; the physical manifestations of disease are only the result or symptom of the energy imbalance (38:101–104, 112–113). Homeopathy can thus fit squarely with the "energy model" of new age medicine in general. This is why Dr. Richard Grossinger observes, "Homeopathic medicines are 'spiritual' medicines. . . . The medicines cannot be considered drugs: They are parallels, vibrations, spiritual entities, intelligences, messages—they are any of these images we use to understand their action" (78:194, 197).

Thus, when the homeopathic physician uses modern medical procedures, he is not seeking to determine the cause of a disease at the physical level, but only to determine in what manner the physical symptoms reflect the imbalance in the body's energy. A homeopathic physician may appear scientific and yet may be operating on fundamentally spiritual or occultic priciples: " . . . chemical, microscopic, and other tests of the patient's tissues . . . yield knowledge of the *consequences* of pathological alterations in the vital force" (79:295). This is why James Tyler Kent, M.D. emphasized:

> There is no disease that exists which the cause is known to man by the eye or by the microscope. Causes are infinitely too fine to be observed by any instrument of precision. They are so immaterial that they correspond to and operate upon the interior nature of man, and they are ultimated in the body in form of tissue changes that are recognized by the eye. Such tissue changes must be understood as the results of disease only or the physician will never perceive what disease cause is, what disease is, what potentization is, or what the nature of life is. (36:ii)

This is why homeopathic physician Herbert Roberts, M.D. states:

> One of the first and foremost elements with which the homeopathic physician must be conversant is the different forms of energy, *for it is on this basis only that we can prescribe homeopathically*. . . . Disease [is a] dynamic disturbance of the harmony and rhythm of the vital energy. . . .
>
> In treating disease we are drawing also upon another store house of dynamic force. . . . This is the reason why the remedies are potentized so that they *may reach more surely* the vital energy of the individual. (35:34–38, emphasis added)

This is also why so many homeopathic practitioners emphasize the importance of the underlying *philosophy* of homeopathy for successful treatment: "The necessity of constant study of the philosophy that underlies homeopathy becomes more and more apparent if we would be masters of our work" (35:46).

Even some leading homeopaths have confessed that the energy they claim to manipulate in curing people is indistinguishable from that occult energy in general which has gone by a wide variety of names throughout history. Others do not make specific equations, but the connection is plain. George Vithoulkas who is described as "the most internationally renowned homeopath" (78:242) argues,

> there is a fundamental recognition that all living beings are animated by a Vital Force which when disturbed leads to sickness and when activated leads to health. This force has yet to be scientifically isolated, observed or measured. . . . (4:149)

Dr. Jane Gumprecht, M.D., comments that "Vithoulkas openly reveals that the real purpose of homeopathy is to help open 'the higher centers [of the brain] for spiritual and celestial influx'" (4:150). Homeopathic authority James Kent states that there are two worlds, the physical world and the invisible world. He says that the whole of homeopathy is bound up in the invisible world, which is indistinguishable from the spiritual world of the occult realm (36:75–76).

At the John Ankerberg Show, we received the following letter from a Christian supporter and user of homeopathy who disagreed that the "vital energy" of homeopathy was anything occultic. She set forth the following arguments:

> The expressions "dynamism", or "vital energy" are used by homeopaths, but it is a distortion to give them any spiritual meaning. These remedies have an energy, force, etc. . . . just like antibiotics have an energy or power to ward off germs. In the case of homeopathy, the remedy triggers a reaction from the body, or according to the *Family Guide to Homeopathy* [by Alain Horvilleur]:
>
> *p.* 86, "*Dynamism*" By their energy they probably furnish a kind of coded signal that tells the body to react in a certain way . . . "vital energy corresponds to reality . . . even if it has yet to be proven" and
>
> *p. 189* "symptoms are the expression of a person's reactional mode. By reacting, the body tries to ward off disease; reactional mode is a part of vital dynamism . . . if you swallow a poison, you vomit. This is the body's

way of reacting and eliminating the danger . . . The defense mechanism can be found throughout nature: a pearl is no more than an oyster's reactional symptom to a foreign body inside the shell . . . "

p. 128, "How Homeopathy works": "The precise mechanism of action of Homeopathy is not known. It can be stated however that homeopathic remedies stimulate the body's natural defense systems. It is not the quantity of homeopathic medicine that counts, but rather its presence that determines its activity. Immunology (see this entry) will one day help us to discover exactly how homeopathic remedies act."

p. 133 "Immunology": "The scientific connection between Homeopathy and classical medicine lies in immunology: the body's own natural systems of immunity and how they can be safely called into action." [463]

That the material process has not been discovered yet does not allow to discount its efficacy, or its value, but should promote more research. (247:3–4)

The only problem with the above arguments are that first, as we have seen, it is not so easy to distinguish Hahnemann's "vital energy" from occult energy. To argue that he never used the term in an occultic sense is an unlikely assertion given his acceptance of Swedenborgian philosophy, animal magnetism, and Eastern religion.

Second, no one argues that scientific homeopaths may reinterpret or ignore possible occultic associations to Hahnemann's "vital energy." But that is not the issue. Many other homeopaths do employ an occultic interpretation as demonstrated by their writings and practices.

Third, "vital energy" may indeed "correspond to reality" and it may just as easily be an occult reality, not a scientific one.

Fourth, how can it logically be stated that "homeopathic remedies stimulate the body's natural defense systems" when it is admitted that "The precise mechanism of action of homeopathy is not known?" To claim homeopathy stimulates the immune system is an assumption or guess, not a fact.

Fifth, it is claimed that it isn't the quantity, but rather the "presence" of the homeopathic medicine that determines its activity. But how is this reconciled with the fact that often absolutely no "presence" of medicine exists in the higher dilutions? What "presence" remains to "determine its activity?"

We readily grant that lack of explanation does not demand a practice be false or worthless. But after two hundred years, homeopathy should be much, much further along the path to verification. And the longer the time span and the more the problems with verification increase, the greater the odds that the problem lies with homeopathy, not its critics. Again, the burden of proof lies with the homeopathist, who has yet to make a reasonable case.

The astral body. Hahnemann's "Vital Force" which "rules" the physical body, is similar to the soul or the astral or etheric bodies of many occult disciplines (38:97–99; 36:69–75). Because homeopathists operate in the realm of the "invisible" and not in the realm of the visible and material, many admit that homeopathic medicines really work upon the etheric or astral bodies. This is where disease begins and spreads outward into the physical body as symptoms (36:18–22, 75).

This is why a number of occultic religions such as Hinduism and anthroposophy employ homeopathy. Its philosophy fits well with their occultic views of man and health.

Radionics. Radionics is the practice of using a mechanical device to supposedly detect occult energies or vibrations. As we noted above, many homeopaths employ radionics instruments in their diagnosis and treatment. In fact, two new age health commentators observe that radionics "is a logical development of eighteenth century homeopathy" (113:25). A major alternate health guide correctly points out, "Its links are particularly strong with radionics" (325:69). However, radionics devices are merely instruments through which spirits can work; they have no power or ability on their own (396).

Nevertheless, the use of radionics in homeopathy reveals some interesting facts about the practice of homeopathy itself. Those who use radionics instruments discover they don't really need to use the standard approach for deciding which homeopathic medicines to employ. In fact, they don't even need the standard medicines. Remember, the medicine allegedly works on an energy level anyway. So why not use a machine that can supposedly detect and influence energies to do the same job, and save a good deal of time and money? This is why the *Visual Encyclopedia of Unconventional Medicine* asserts that the use of radionics in homoeopathy is "perhaps the most radical advance" since the time of Hahnemann himself (76:28).

Thus, rather than using specific homeopathic preparations, radionics claims it can use various radiations or forces to stimulate the body's "vital force" to cure disease and bring health:

> [Radionic devices] enable the preparation of homeopathic remedies without recourse to the biological materials—plant, animal or inorganic—from which these remedies are normally prepared. . . . It was found that the

remedies so produced were as effective in treating illness as were traditionally prepared remedies. (76:28)

So who is surprised? The "biological materials" don't operate at the physical level anyway; they operate at the "energy level." This proves that when a homeopath uses standard organic or inorganic homeopathic treatments they are not unique. Radionics devices which ultimately rely on spirit guides will also work in the same manner. Both work in the psychic realm, with psychic effects that influence the "vital force." So why are orthodox homeopathic remedies even needed? Why spend tremendous research costs involved in "proving" the alleged "symptoms" of endless substances, when in the end they are really unnecessary? This is why in the future we may expect even more homeopaths to switch to psychic methods.

Psychic healing. Psychic healers claim to transmit energy into their clients for healing. Whatever the claimed source of this power, none can deny pervasive spiritistic associations in all forms of psychic healing (6:87–113). Just as the psychic healer cannot know that the energy he or she transmits is not demonic, so the homeopathic practitioner has no guarantee that the supposed energy transmitted in the homeopathic treatment is never demonic as well: "The power that is transmitted directly in psychic healing through the laying on of the healer's hand, is now thought to be carried by the homeopathic medicine and conveyed indirectly" (2:64). If demonic spirits work directly in transferring psychic energies in psychic healing, how can we be sure they may not also operate behind the concept of homeopathic medicines? Does not the history of animism prove that spirits often seek to work behind material objects such as idols, Tarot cards, dowsing rods, and many other items? Then could they not also work behind homeopathic medicines?

The above discussion of homeopathy and radionics also reveals that in many cases homeopathy is little more than psychic healing. Homeopathic practitioners claim that a cosmic "vital force" is transferred from the homeopathic "medicine" into the patient. But the same effect is supposedly accomplished by radionics devices which employ spiritistic power (6:53–65). Furthermore, how is this different from any number of psychic healers who claim they transfer cosmic or psychic energy into the patient directly through their spirit guides?

The text, *In Search of the Healing Energy*, links homeopathy to a long standing tradition of ancient and contemporary occult energies and observes that "the homeopathic doctor analyzes his patients psychically as well as physically and chooses his remedies accordingly" (65:93).

No one can deny that many homeopaths engage in both psychic diagnosis and psychic healing.

Astrology. Many homeopaths diagnose on the basis of astrological signs or otherwise employ astrology in their practice (37:5; 2:69). For example, one homeopath confesses, "In homeopathy we have to put more stress on individual differences, and that leads us to an interest in such things as astrology and acupuncture" (148:142).

Rod and pendulum. The rod and pendulum is one of the most popular occultic devices used among homeopaths. Dr. Bopp, M. D., observes,

> To find the cure, that's to say, the herb for the original tincture of the preparation, the researchers often have recourse to occult practices such as the pendulum. Dr. A. Voegeli, a famous homeopathic doctor, has confirmed that a very high percentage of homeopaths work with the pendulum. (37:8)

Dr. Pfeifer, M.D., also notes the use of pendulums by homeopaths because "it is easier to take a short cut with the radionic pendulum" (2:73). For example,

> This is how the former Lutheran pastor, Bolte, got his "gift" of soothsaying—by means of a radionic pendulum. Like many other homeopaths, he chooses the appropriate remedy for a patient by using the pendulum. In his booklet *From Pendulum Research to Miraculous Healing* he writes: "I would sit at the desk, take the pendulum out, let it circle over Schwabe's list of homeopathic remedies and then order the remedy at their pharmacy in Leipzig." (2:79–80)

Bolte also claims to "magnetically charge" entire bottles of substances for homeopathic remedies—but by spiritistic power (2:80).

Seance spiritism. We have always suspected that Hahnemann picked up a spirit guide from his occultic practices and that many homeopaths do the same today (cf. 132). Direct spiritistic activity among homeopaths is not rare:

> There are groups whose [homeopathic] research is carried out during seances, through mediums who seek information from spirits.
>
> The testimony of a person who worked in an important homeopathic laboratory of high standing in France is very interesting. She told me

> about the interview she had with the former director and founder of the establishment with a view to her recruitment. After a short introduction, this director asked her which astrological sign she was born under. He then wished to know whether she was a medium. As this was so, he confided to her the secret of the practices of the place. New treatments were researched there during seances, through the agency of persons having occult powers—mediums—by which to question spirits. (37:8)

Another homeopathic connection to spiritism is historical. It is explained by Dr. Grossinger who discusses a possible reason for Hahnemann's discovery of homeopathic potentization:

> Then he tried shaking the vials very hard at each dilution. It is uncertain what caused him to try this, and there is no one explanation in Hahnemann's known studies, although many different hermeticisms, including alchemy, urged creative interaction with substances. Later ethnographic literature shows that primitive peoples prepare medicines by pounding, grinding, . . . scraping . . . punching [etc.] . . . —all to wake the spirits in the medicine or bring spirits to attach themselves to it. African [witch] doctors have claimed that medicines contain no power in themselves but gain it from [this] dynamic contact. The well-read Hahnemann may have been aware of some of this lore. (78:214; cf. 112:22)

In other words, the very reason for the ritualized interaction with substances was to attract the spirits' attention and to derive their assistance and power. That this could occur in pagan, animistic cultures is not surprising. But most people would never suspect such a phenomenon in the modern homeopathic office or laboratory. But if we are dealing with occult medicine, can the possibility logically be ruled out? Can it never happen? Furthermore, the one-hundred-year history of parapsychology proves that the spirits are not reluctant to enter the domains and laboratories of parapsychologists (396; 6:341–390). The fact is that spirits can be found to support anything that helps achieve their purposes. Perhaps all of this is why the spirits themselves actually prescribe homeopathic treatments in their writings when speaking through human mediums. The famous medium Edgar Cayce sometimes prescribed homeopathic remedies when in trance; he would then refer his patients to various homeopaths, naturopaths, and chiropractors for treatment.

The occultic religion known as anthroposophy was founded on the basis of spiritistic revelations given to occultist Rudolf Steiner. The spirits told Steiner that he was to contribute to the art of healing, and they prescribed specific homeopathic remedies. Today there are several thousand anthroposophical practitioners including approximately one thousand M. D.'s who use Steiner's homeopathic treatments (113:25).

If the spirit world is interested in promoting homeopathy, one would think the practice should be questioned before it is uncritically adopted. Why would spirits want to promote homeopathy? What do *they* know that we don't?

Even more interesting, homeopaths have found that their medicines simply do not work unless both dilution and shaking occur.

Leading homeopaths Dana Ullman and Stephen Cummings (112:50) note this odd phenomenon:

> Homeopaths have found that the medicines do not work if they are simply diluted repeatedly without vigorous shaking or if they are just diluted in vast amounts of liquid. Nor do the medicines work if they are only vigorously shaken. It is the *combined* process of dilution and vigorous shaking that makes the medicine effective. . . . (112:20)

In light of the spiritistic connection to homeopathy, this could mean that when homeopaths have spirit guides, the spirits will not work to confirm the homeopathic treatment until the necessary "religious" ritual is properly observed (78:214). Why would spirits want to act in such a manner? It would seem obvious: to confirm the spiritual (occult) medicine of homeopathy and all it implies in terms of supporting occultic philosophy and practice.

This raises the issue of Christians who are practicing homeopaths or use homeopathic remedies. Spiritism is clearly forbidden in Scripture (Deuteronomy 18:9–12). Since homeopathy was founded by a disciple of Swedenborg (a spiritist), is scientifically disproven, and potentially opens many doors to the occult, why would Christians want to practice it? It should be evident that Christians who use homeopathy and also claim the practice can never be occultic are wrong. Do Christians who go to a homeopath have any guarantee of the kind of "treatment" they will receive? Are Christian homeopaths who are trying to avoid the occult in their practices guaranteed success? On what basis?

Additional occultic practices. Dr. Pfeifer warns, "I see spiritual danger in homeopathic remedies coming from psychic healers and doctors who use the pendulum, practise palmistry, rely on 'spiritual energies' or claim to heal at a distance" (2:81–82).

A former new age healer and psychic observes that "it is a fact that many homeopathic practitioners try to make sure their remedies are working by putting a magic spell on them" (2:81).

In addition, in either philosophy or practice, homeopathy is related to the following: auras and aura healing (37:9; 36:75); naturopathy, which often employs occult methods (4:148; 64:44–45); Eastern religious philosophy and practices such as yoga, meditation, and *kundalini* arousal (2:66–69; 64:28); Jungian psychology (disease and medicine as archetype, 78:200); shamanism (78:98, 197); acupuncture (114:61); iridology and hypnosis (37:9); and other occultic or potentially occultic practices.

In conclusion, we must assert that many homeopaths are involved in the occult in one way or another. Whether this involves a majority of homeopaths is unknown. What is suspected is that it is possible for homeopaths to be involved in the occult and/or have spirit guides and yet not even know it.

Potential Dangers

If homeopathy is false, how can it work? Hahnemann himself confessed that homeopathy was often ineffective (39:18, 27–29). But when it is effective, it is not effective because of anything having to do with homeopathic theory and practice. We offer the following as explanations for those cures which homeopaths think are produced by homeopathy. When homeopathy "heals" a patient, it does so by placebo or faith, the body's own recuperative ability, or spiritistic power.

Its "Healing" Nature

First, some cures are produced in homeopathy because of the faith of the patient in the homeopath and the faith of the homeopath in the patient. As homeopath James Tyler Kent noted, "The confidence of the patient helps the physician to find the right remedy" (36:242). Dr. Pfeifer observes that, "The *placebo effect* is probably the most important factor in the success of homeopathic remedies" (2:77). He explains that studies have proven the importance of a patient's faith in both the medicine and the physician. Sometimes, a medical doctor who prescribes relatively ineffective medicine with great confidence can produce good results. On the other hand, an usually effective medicine may fail if it is prescribed by a doctor who is pessimistic and critical. He also observes that one of the most important factors in curing is the physician himself. "When there is no confidential relationship between doctor and patient, the use of placebos and homeopathic remedies is of little avail" (2:77).

The healing atmosphere of the homeopathic office or clinics is also important because it serves to encourage the faith of the patient. The "medical" atmosphere gives the patient the feeling that he really is being treated medically, even though he isn't. Homeopaths may also recommend common sense prescriptions such as daily walks, rest and relaxation, health spas, etc. All of this may help cure a particular ailment.

Second, some healings are produced by the body's own recuperative power. The time required for homeopathic treatments is sufficiently lengthy that a large number of ailments would naturally be healed even if no treatment were given. Homeopathic treatments can last days, weeks, months, and even years (112:19–20).

Homeopaths admit that their medicines can't possibly have a physical effect, yet they allegedly stimulate the disease. Homeopaths also confess that people treated with homeopathy often get worse before they get better. The fact that the disease is "stimulated" indicates that it is probably following its natural course, and the body is healing itself. Nothing at all is happening homeopathically. That homeopaths freely admit their treatments cause the disease to worsen can easily be proven. In fact, they even admit that considerable suffering is produced by homeopathic remedies:

> Experience with homeopathic treatment has shown that, following the administration of the correct medicine, symptoms on the deeper [energy] levels improve while those on the more external levels often temporarily worsen. . . . It is common for individual symptoms to become worse than they had been before treatment. These aggravations are welcomed by the knowledgeable homeopath. . . . (112:21–22)
>
> [Homeopathy] often requires suffering. . . . A promising sequence [of treatments] may have the most painful eruptions. . . . Superficially, things get worse. However, if the flare-ups did not occur, the entire disease would not be removed. . . .
>
> If the person has been under suppressive allopathic treatment which has been halted for the substitution of homeopathy, the aggravation [of the

remedy] may be more painful and symptomatically severe than the disease. . . . The initial effect of a homeopathic remedy is to aggravate the disease. . . . (78:184–185)

It is characteristic of homeopathic remedies that they often produce a temporary aggravation of symptoms: the pain increases, diarrhea is set off or made worse or the skin breaks out even more severely. This indicates that the vital force has been aroused and strengthened to the degree that it is able to produce a reaction—in effect a crisis leading to cure. (64:42)

But what homeopath can prove that any of their medicines are really curing the "vital force?" How can they be certain their "treatment" is not wholly ineffective and that the illness or disease is simply taking its normal course? But when a patient actually gets worse than he should according to his condition, isn't this an indication he needs genuine medical treatment? And isn't it true that the homeopath who does not recognize this may be placing the patient's health and possibly life in danger?

Third, homeopaths who are occultists and have spirit guides can produce genuine physical healings by spiritistic power. The physical illness may be cured, but as the forty-five-year research of Dr. Kurt Koch has shown, occult healings are not true healings; in exchange for a cure at a physical level they bring about the illness on a higher level, mental, emotional, and/or spiritual (126:121–125, 184–195, cf. refs. 123–125).

Thus, homeopathy can work for many reasons unrelated to homeopathy itself.

Physical Dangers

That homeopathy may be dangerous to one's health should be evident. Both the obscurity of homeopathic diagnosis and treatment, plus the time required to effect a "cure," can permit serious disease to progress unabated (78:177–184, 187, 202–203, 217–219; 36:242; 3:240). One physician observes,

> This form of treatment becomes dangerous in the case of infectious disease. Thus the same [homeopathic] Guide proposes Pyrogenium 7CH, high dilution of a fever-producing substance for Septicaemia. The condition of Septicaemia is a serious one and may terminate in death should immediate, appropriate, antibiotic treatment not be administered. (37:7)

Furthermore, on what basis is a homeopath who is not an M.D. qualified to practice medicine? We noted even leading homeopaths have admitted "there is a lot of insanity" operating under the name of homeopathy

(114:61). Unfortunately, it isn't always so easy to distinguish the insanity from normal homeopathic treatments. Below we present five illustrations.

First, Hahnemann and other homeopaths recommend "dilutions of metallic gold as the antidote for suicidal tendencies" (79:306). But how many suicidal persons will this treatment really help? And if it doesn't help them, how many will be successful in their attempts to commit suicide because they never got proper treatment?

Second, some homeopathic companies offer "remedies" for cancer, stroke, and a dozen other serious conditions or diseases. Because these remedies are wholly ineffective, they are dangerous (87:59–60). This is why some people die as a result of being treated homeopathically and why one respected French physician commented that homeopathy has "many deaths on its conscience" (246:52). Four-year-old Jerold Winston, for example, died of leukemia after being treated for sixteen months with a homeopathic remedy (117:138). In our research for this volume, we encountered many such incidents.

Third, when homeopaths are trained to believe that recurrence of symptoms or worse symptoms are an indication of *cure*, the problems for those with serious illnesses are only compounded (78:173).

Fourth, when a homeopath can believe that a person's craving for *broccoli*, or his manner of talking, are actually more important indicators of heart disease than an actual heart attack, something is seriously wrong:

> A patient having recently suffered a heart attack may find the homeopathic doctor more interested in hand gestures while speaking or a minor ailment that was treated and cured several years back. . . .
>
> The doctor . . . encourages the patient to talk because the talk, in its intensity and rhythm, must be a manifestation of the disease too. He asks about taste in food in order to see what the person is seeking or avoiding, or even what he thinks he is seeking, thinks he is avoiding. It takes a *brilliant diagnostician* to work through such a puzzle, but the good homeopath must be this. The symptoms are the clues of the mystery, the only visible remnants of an invisible and unperceived attacker. . . .
>
> Hahnemann knew that a heart attack was more serious and worse than a wart or a craving for a particular food like broccoli, but as an expression of the constitution *they are comparable*. In fact, the craving for broccoli may be *far more significant* if its specificity suggests a medicine that the heart attack does not. The treatment by diagnosis from the broccoli will then improve the heart condition in a way that emphasis on the immedi-

ate mechanical causes of the heart attack could not. (78:179, 181, emphasis added)

Fifth, another potential danger is that once an occultic system of medicine is adopted, no one has a guarantee that occult forces will not enter the picture, even when a practitioner is attempting to remain scientific. Remember, there is no actual substance in most homeopathic remedies. And yet they can sometimes apparently have dramatic effects. Some of these effects may be explained by occult powers. Grossinger observes,

> These potencies are really quite dangerous. . . . Substances that have absolutely no effect in low potencies suddenly have a very high one in the high potencies. And they usually are far more marked mentally than any other way. . . . *Silicea* . . . has a profound mental effect. . . . (78:198)

He proceeds to cite a 1974 publication of the American Institute of Homeopathy, which emphasizes:

> The homeo-discipline denies that the drug possess any power or virtue, but postulates that contact between the drug and the living organism sets in motion an influence. The drug is not injected, digested, assimilated, or transported physically. In and of itself it can do nothing. . . . (78:198)

However, it does "set in motion an influence." But what exactly is this influence? Consider another illustration provided by Grossinger:

> A strong remedy can have suicidal consequences if the patient cannot integrate the new implications. It is also possible that a remedy can be driven back onto the physical plane in a debilitating or life-threatening way. One homeopath mentioned a patient who was chronically ill until she joined a very expressive religious sect. She was both fanatic and miserable and sought homeopathic treatment through her new belief in spiritual medicine. Soon after taking the remedy, she lost interest in religion entirely and developed multiple sclerosis. (78:191)

It is always more than possible there may be normal explanations for such things, but as noted there may also be occult influences at work. How does a client tell when such influences are at work and when they are not? This is why one Christian physician warns,

> There are to be sure some honourable and conscientious ones seeking to utilise a homeopathy detached from its obscure practices. Yet, the occult influence, by nature hidden, disguised, often dissimulated behind a parascientific theory, does not disappear and does not happen to be ren-

> dered harmless by the mere fact of a superficial approach contenting itself simply with denying its existence. *Homeopathy is dangerous*. It is quite contrary to the teaching of the Word of God. *It willingly favors healing through substances made dynamic, that is to say, charged with occult forces*. Homeopathic treatment is the fruit of a philosophy and religion that are at the same time Hinduistic, pantheistic and esoteric. (37:9)

❧ ❧ ❧

For all these reasons and more, we believe homeopathy is potentially hazardous to one's health and should be avoided. If a person accepts homeopathic premises in general, he must reject conventional scientific medicine as naive and ineffective; rely upon a system which is unscientific and may be dangerous on medical grounds; and accept a method which is conducive to the influences of occultic and spiritistic powers.

Christians, of all people, should be the last to be practicing homeopaths or using such persons for medical treatment. Grossinger observes that "It was Hahnemann's stubborn blindness that led him to keep calling this system medicine and science" and yet at the end of his life "he returned to the pagan forces whose system it was" (78:222–223). Christians should not think that adopting an occultic, pagan system of healing can never have an influence on their spiritual life. Those whose "stubborn blindness" persists may find themselves as aligned with pagan forces as Hahnemann was.

In spite of the many glowing testimonials for its effectiveness, in spite of the many famous people who can be cited as believers, in spite of its acceptance by many Christians, homeopathy does not work on the basis of its stated principles and is not a scientifically established medical practice. If it works, it "works" either on the basis of the body's own healing ability, psychological factors, or spiritistic powers. Because classical homeopathy never has been scientific, and never can be scientific, when it cures, it cannot cure on the basis of scientific principles; in addition, its occultic premises and often practices only help to open doors to spiritistic influence and "healing."

The procedure cannot be recommended.

Iridology

Definition: Iridology is the study of the iris of the human eye to diagnose present and even future illness and disease.

Founder: Ignatz von Peczely is considered the modern founder; however, similar practices can be seen in ancient Chinese practices related to astrology. Bernard Jensen is considered the leading U.S. authority.

How Does It Claim to Work? Iridologists claim that the eyes can "mirror" the health condition of the body because the iris displays in detail the status of every organ system. The iris's connection with the central nervous system allegedly permits detailed information to be sent from the rest of the body back to the iris. Furthermore, each iris reveals what is happening on its own side of the body.

Scientific Evaluation: Discredited in numerous scientific tests.

Occultic Potential: Possible psychic diagnosis and healing.

Major Problem: The diagnostic ability of iridology for both present and future illness is a myth.

Biblical/Christian Evaluation: Quack and potentially occultic practices should be avoided.

Potential Dangers: The progression of a serious illness that iridology fails to uncover; personal anxiety and loss of finances from misdiagnosis that a serious illness exists; occult influences.

EIGHTEEN

IRIDOLOGY

Iridology, or diagnosis by the iris of the eye, is a common practice in Europe and commands a growing audience in the U.S. Also known as iris science, iriscopy, irisology and iris diagnosis, proponents make repeated claims about its "astonishing" accuracy.

Even the dictionary supplement of the *World Book Encyclopedia Yearbook* gives credibility to iridology by the definition it supplies:

> A method of examining the iris of the eye as an aid in medical diagnosis: iridology can identify an organ that has degenerated enough to become cancerous. The basis for iridology is the neuro-optic reflex, an intimate marriage of the estimated half million nerve filaments of the iris with the cervical ganglia of the sympathetic nervous system (Esquire). (271:412)

Until recently iridology has been practiced primarily by chiropractors, naturopaths, and homeopaths. But in recent years, many other new age therapists have begun to use iridology and even some physicians and optometrists have become converts. One alternate medical guide observes, "Many therapists, including osteopaths, acupuncturists, herbalists and homeopaths, use iridology as an aid to diagnosis alongside their other physical tests" (325:279). According to International Iridologists in Escondido, California, there are an estimated ten thousand practitioners of iridology in Europe and over one thousand in the U.S.

One example of a medical convert to iridology is optometrist Dr. James Carter. He became a believer by reading leading iridologist Bernard Jensen's text on iridology and testing the practice for himself. He has proceeded to teach iridology to numerous doctors in the San Francisco area and is conducting studies at San Francisco General Hospital. His research there involves "several double blind studies on the accuracy and reproducibility of the schematic or homunculus (miniature body) relationship of the iris fibers and the body, and also some study into the possible pathways involved in iris changes as a result of systemic disease" (173:52).

The Nature of Iridology

The iridologist claims he is able to diagnose the physical condition of the body through examining the iris, the colored part of the eye. He also claims that he can diagnose the probability of future illnesses and diseases by the same method.

Iridology is based upon the idea that each organ of the body is represented by a corresponding area within the iris. The left iris represents and is a picture of the left side of the body; the right iris represents and is a picture of the right side of the body. Thus, the head is at the top of the iris, the feet are at the bottom; the areas in between the head and the feet are arranged top to bottom in rough parallel sequence to their arrangement in the human body. Organs that are paired or symmetric, such as the kidneys and nose, are found in both irises.

Iridologists characteristically give scientific sounding descriptions of how iridology allegedly operates. Jessica Maxwell in *The Eye-Body Connection*, a self-help book on iridology, claims that "The basis for iridology is the neuro-optic reflex, an intimate marriage of the estimated half million filaments of the iris with the cervical ganglia of the sympathetic nervous system. The neuro-optic reflex turns the iris into an organic etch-a-sketch that monitors impressions from all over the body as they come in" (175:56).

Optometrist Dr. James Carter and chiropractor Dr. Bernard Jensen also supply scientific sounding explanations of how iridology works. (40:9–21; cf. 5:175–176; 3:170–173) But the claimed scientific foundations are not justified as many doctors of optometry and opthamologists have pointed out (e.g., 344:172–178). Detailed neuroanatomical study of the eye and central nervous systems prove there is no evidence for the alleged neurological pathways required for such a powerful relay of information. Russell S. Worrall is assistant clinical professor in the School of Optometry at the

University of California, Berkeley. Citing *Adlers Physiology of the Eye* (1975, pp. 367–405) he comments:

> The visual system (including the optic nerve) is probably the most intensively studied and best understood neural system in the body. The Nobel Prize recently awarded to Hubel and Wiesel was the result of many years of work on this intriguing system. All of the accumulated research unequivocally demonstrates that the mammalian optic nerve is primarily an afferent pathway, that is, one in which the signals travel from the eye to the brain. There is no evidence suggesting that any fibers from the optic nerve make connections with the iris. This, combined with the fact that only half of the fibers in the optic nerve cross, makes the proposition that the optic nerve is the final link to the iris untenable. (344:173)

Paul Reisser, M.D., points out that:

> Iridologists have generally sidestepped the neurological details of their practice in favor of a simpler observation that the iris is indeed connected with the autonomic nervous system. But merely being connected to the system does not prove that all of the body can be monitored. My telephone is connected to a massive communications network, but it does not send me messages about the equipment or conversations of everyone in America. (1:143)

Nevertheless, the scientific sounding descriptions impress many people and convince them that iridology is a legitimate diagnostic technique.

The idea that a particular organ of the body, in this case the eye, constitutes a miniature version of the entire body is not new. Throughout its in glorious history, quack medicine has held that many different body organs constitute a miniature representation of the human body. The human body has been "compressed" and inserted into the outer ear, the nose, face, head, and even the anus and other parts or organs of the body (115:26, 39, 59, 65, 84, 108). Reflexology does the same with the hand or foot, and homuncular or auricular acupuncture does the same with the outer ear. In its own manner, chiropractic does the same with the human spine (see the chapter 14).

Background

Iridology can be traced to ancient Chinese astrological practices, however, according to Dr. Carter, the first precursor published on iridology was Philippus Meyens' *Chiromatica Medica*, (Germany, 1670).

Nevertheless, the credit for developing and promoting modern iridology usually goes to Dr. Ignatz von Peczely of Hungary (*Discoveries in the Field of Natural Science in Medicine*, Hungary, 1880) and Nils Liljequist, a Swedish homeopath and minister (*Diagnosis from the Eye*, Sweden, 1893; cf. 42:13).

When Ignatz was eleven years old, he made what he thought was an amazing discovery. Being attacked by a mother owl in the woods one day, he was forced to break the bird's leg to escape. At that very moment he noted a black line running down the iris. He concluded that the break in the owl's leg had registered in the iris, perhaps an understandable conclusion for a frightened young boy. Nevertheless, this event became the basis for von Peczely's later development of iridology. Research, however, has proven that breaking an owl's leg leaves no such mark in the iris and that the lad had probably misinterpreted the visual effect produced by the black inner lining of the upper lid when the owl opens the eye (2:89).

Iridology was introduced into the U. S. in 1904 with the publication of Henry Lahn's *Iridology: The Diagnosis from the Eye* (1904). More recent American texts include *Iris Diagnosis* by a student of Dr. Lahn, Henry Lindlahr; Theodore Kriege's, *Fundamental Basis of Iris Diagnosis*, London, 1975 (42); and Bernard Jensen's *The Science and Practice of Iridology*, U.S., 1952 (40), and its sequel *Iridology: Science and Practice in the Healing Arts*, U.S., 1982 (172).

In the U.S., the "father" of American iridology may be considered chiropractor and naturopath Bernard Jensen. By far, he has been the most influential proponent of the practice. Surprisingly, it is often claimed by iridologists that Jensen has supplied the most scientific defense of iridology.

However, this claim cannot be substantiated. In a nutshell, the scientific quality of his books leaves much to be desired. Russell S. Worrall, O.D., Assistant Clinical Professor in the School of Optometry at the University of California, Berkeley, has published works on optical topics in journals such as *Review of Optometry*, *Optometric Monthly*, and *Journal of the American Optometric Association*. In his article, "Iridology: Diagnosis or Delusion," Worrall observes of Jensen's most recent text, *Iridology: Science and Practice in the Healing Arts* (vol. 2, 1982), "This volume contains countless misinterpretations of established anatomical and physiological knowledge and includes references to many pseudosciences, such as Kirlian photography and personology" (344:173). Jensen's earlier volume contains similar problems, as a perusal will reveal (e.g., 40:1–126).

Despite the claims of over-zealous followers, Jensen is not a scientist, but a popular new age healer, a fact revealed in his various works, such as *Iridology: Science and Practice in the Healing Arts* (172). In this text, he discusses his belief in reincarnation, astral travel, psychic development, and other occultic practices and philosophies (172:3–12, 458). He also confesses his great indebtedness to occultist Manly P. Hall, gurus Sai Baba and Jiddhu Krishnamurti, homeopath V. G. Rocine, occultist and polarity therapy founder Randolph Stone, and those of similar persuasion (172:568).

In fact, his new age faith in various energy forces, psychic vibrations, and radionics apparently supplied the theoretical basis for his ideas on how iridology allegedly works: "It seemed to me that finer [occult] forces, that functioned as if by direction of some innate intelligence, were operating through the autonomic nervous system." (172:566, cf. pp. 457–467, 567 and also the chapter on chiropractic).

Iridology is shown to be compatible with new age medicine in general. One chart in particular reveals how iridology can be correlated to the practices of Chinese acupuncture and philosophy (as well as Hindu yogic principles and Ayurvedic medicine (172:34).

Jensen's new age philosophy is also evident in the section titled "A Deeper Look," giving an extensive bibliography replete with new age texts, several of which originate from the spirit world. Books listed as those "which have helped me" include the standard spirit-inspired theosophical text by medium H. P. Blavatsky, *Isis Unveiled* (345); new age bible *The Aquarian Conspiracy* (149) by Marilyn Ferguson; parapsychologist Jeffrey Mishlove's *The Roots of Consciousness* (253); as well as the spiritistically inspired text *A Course in Miracles* (167).

Jensen also lists many books which stress the typical new age mystical energy themes such as psychic Jack Schwartz' *Human Energy Systems* (63); parapsychologist Shafica Karagulla's study of psychic abilities *Breakthrough to Creativity* (315); and chiropractor and occultist David V. Tansley's *Radionics and the Subtle Anatomy of Man* (56) (172:568).

The influence of Jensen upon so many modern American iridologists perhaps explains why much of contemporary U.S. iridology is associated with various occultic arts and practices.

Claims

Like everything else in new age medicine, iridology claims to be a logical, scientific, and natural system of diagnosis. Bernard Jensen thinks that the only reason critics of iridology exist is because they have never studied it, and furthermore, that no medical doctor who has used it has ever rejected it:

> Whenever anyone, whether doctor or layman, tells me he thinks there is nothing to it, I make it a practice to ask first if he has studied Iridology and whether he has spent more than three months with it. Invariably I find that those who have condemned it never have spent more than ten minutes or so reading about the subject. . . . *Every medical doctor who has ever used it gave up many of his medical remedies* and turned to nature cure methods for healing. (40:13 emphasis added)

As we will show later, Jensen is clearly wrong. Nevertheless, iridologists persist in calling iridology "a true, definite, accurate science" (41:cover jacket).

Jensen even claims iridology is one of the most essential of diagnostic methods. Consider his assessment of its powers:

> Iridology can be used in conjunction with any other form of analysis and diagnosis.
>
> The iridologist can determine the inherent structure and the working capacity of an organ, can detect environmental strain, and can tell whether a person is anemic and in what stage the anemia exists. . . . He can determine the constructive ability of the blood, . . . He can determine the nerve force, the responsive healing power of tissue, and the inherent ability to circulate the blood.
>
> The iris of the eye can show acute, subacute, chronic, and destructive stages in the body. Many other factors are also revealed such as organic and functional changes. . . . It foretells the development of many conditions long before they have manifested into disease symptoms.
>
> No other science tells so accurately the progress from acute to chronic states.
>
> Only iridology is capable of directing attention to impending conditions; only iridology reveals and evaluates inherent weaknesses.
>
> In using iridology you need ask no questions yet you can tell where pain is, what stage it is in, how it got there, and when it is gone. (40:xv, 10, 21, 26)

But this is nonsense.

Because the iris of the eye has no such diagnostic powers, to conventionally trained physicians such claims smack of magic. In his article "An Eye for the Future" in *Iridologist International Manual for Research and Development*, 2–11/12, Jensen further argues for the powers of iridology: "We must realize that iridology represents a law of nature that cannot be changed. I believe that it is just as immutable and unchangeable as any of the laws that govern the universe" (in 344:170).

Practitioners and proponents of iridology repeatedly assert that the practice is a legitimate and valid clinical procedure, but surprisingly, they may also claim that they do not actually engage in the diagnosis of illness or disease. This is incredible because iridology is fundamentally a diagnostic procedure. No one argues that iridologists do not diagnose in the same manner that normal physicians do, but they do diagnose. Iridologists who claim otherwise may simply be protecting their assets by guarding against expensive lawsuits.

Articles in Jensen's own publications prove that iridologists engage in diagnosis. For example, *Iridologists International Manual for Research and Development*, 2–11/12, contains an article by Fernandiz titled "Hemicrania (Migraine) and Its Diagnosis by Means of the Iris" (3:174). Iridologists even claim that their iris diagnosis can divine *future* illness or disease, even though not a shred of evidence exists for such a conclusion—other than what iridologists think they see in the eye. But we cited Jensen above as teaching that iridology "foretells the development of many conditions long before they have manifested into disease symptoms" (40:26).

Consider a second example. Armand Ian Brint is a charter member of Iridologists International and has taught iridology and other new age practices throughout California. He is the founder of the Berkeley Holistic Health Center and currently works with chiropractors. He argues that through iridology, "It is possible to detect signs of an impending heart attack or a cerebral stroke" (80:161).

What is even more incredible is that iridologists may claim that they can determine unknown past or future events—whether a patient will commit suicide and even whether or not the suicide will be bloodless; or whether or not a family member such as a grandfather or great aunt died from a stroke! (155:38–39). Iridologists who diagnose in such a manner are just as likely to be engaging in diagnosis by psychic means, using the iris as a contact point for divination.

Scientific Evaluation

Before we proceed to examine the basic theory of iridology and why it is scientifically incorrect, we should note that there are certain medical conditions that can be recognized by a medical examination of the eye. For example, jaundice usually shows up first in the white of the eye. Also, the transparent cornea of the eye can be affected by viruses, usually the herpes virus. The lens of the eye itself can be involved in general disease. Physicians routinely examine the inner lining of the eye called the fundus. Here the arteries may give an indication of general diseases such as high blood pressure and diabetes (2:88).

But none of this is iridology. No iridologist's exam is in any way comparable to a physician's exam, either in theory or practice. Iridologists claim to read endless physical conditions from the iris alone. The renowned ophthalmologist Professor Schreck, M.D., observes:

> The iris interpreters employ a completely different and in no way comparable examination technique. They claim to "see" diseases of the human body from normal tissue by simply looking at its surface.
>
> We have here a grotesque, absurd paradox, unique in all medical history, that these people want to read diseases out of completely normal tissue. Worse still, they do not even refer to disorders of this tissue itself, but to diseases of organs that are far from it, and in no way related in any way to the iris. . . . What the iris-interpreters refer to and where they claim to "see" bodily diseases is nothing else than simple variations of the normal structure and coloring of the iris that carry no pathological significance and therefore have no value for diagnosis. (2:88–89)

The Problem of Diagnosis

Scientific medicine is based upon consistent and proven methods of medical diagnosis. But a major problem of new age medicine is that, having rejected science, practitioners as a whole rarely agree when it comes to methods of diagnosis. This is illustrated in iridology.

For example, there are some twenty *different* iridology charts that a practitioner may choose from in his practice. As Dr. Worrall observes, "Confusion is the first order of business in the clinical application of iridology" (3:174). The iridologist has the same problem as the astrologer. Which chart among many conflicting charts does the iridologist choose? On what logical basis is one's chart proven to be better than another that contradicts it? Even though most charts are in general agreement in major divisions (such as the leg area being positioned at the six o'clock P.M. segment) this does not help the case of the iridologist. Considering iridology as a whole, there are a great number of differences in both interpretation and location of iris signs.

Iridologist Theodore Kriege confesses that "Nearly every iris researcher has tried to evolve something special for himself, with the result that varying perceptions and interpretations are current. . . . In comparing the available literature in this respect we find considerable differences" (42:14–15).

Incredibily, Bernard Jensen freely admits that the charts do not agree and yet says, "Let us look at all charts with an open mind. We do not wish to criticize or break down anyone else's ideas." (40:88). One can only wonder how the problems of diagnosis revealed in contradictory iridology charts can be remedied by an "open mind." In fact, only *his* chart "can be used for certain of our purposes" (40:88). Why, one wonders, if iridology is really a "science" as he claims?

But to see how unscientific iridology is, one only need compare iridology charts with standard medical anatomy charts, such as the kind you see posted on the walls of doctors' examining rooms. The iridology charts are not uniform. This means that when an iridologist trusts one particular chart, another chart will contradict it. This makes deriving useful information from such charts impossible. But it is an entirely different situation with standard anatomical charts. Do these scientific charts conflict and disagree? Not at all. One may compare the charts published by a dozen different companies. They will each agree down to the smallest anatomical details. Can we imagine the confusion in medical schools, not to mention operating rooms, if all of the charts contradicted one another and doctors could not agree on basic human anatomy? Why then do iridologists claim their practice is scientific when their most fundamental premises are in conflict?

Dr. Samuel Pfeifer illustrates the problems faced by the iridologist in diagnosis:

> Although every iris-interpreter tells the patient that there was only one diagnostic key, one author has counted no less than 19 different Iridology charts. According to the various charts, the same small area between 230 and 240 degrees—an area the width of a pin—can indicate disorders of the following organs: the liver, the little finger, the arm, the diaphragm, the hand, the ribs, the axillary lymphnodes, and the gall bladder.
>
> It is estimated that there are about 10,000 diseases. It is not clear how they would all find their reflection in the tiny space of the iris. (2:89)

For this chapter, we examined the iridology charts of Bernard Jensen, LaDean Griffin, Theodore Kriege, Korvin-Swiecki, and others. Anyone who does this will prove to himself that iridologists do *not* agree on what parts of the iris relate to what parts of the body (42:92–107; 41:205, 208; 40:85–96, 3223; 3:168–170).

How then can iridologists possibly claim that they can give accurate diagnoses based on their conflicting charts?

Another characteristic of new age medicine is its expertise at rationalizing failures. It is particularly adept at finding reasons to ignore or reinterpret scientific testing disproving its claims.

Scientific tests of iridologists reveal a high degree of what are called false positives—iridologists diagnosing diseases that are not even present. How do iridologists respond?

They seek to explain this by telling us that iris diagnosis has the magical ability to predict diseases that will happen even years in the future—so, of course, they will not show up through a physical examination in the present! In other words, even though not a shred of evidence exists to confirm the iridologists diagnosis, it must still be true, because iridology cannot fail.

Bernard Jensen argues, "Many times the conditions revealed in the iris today will not be apparent in the body for years to come, but time will *inevitably* show the analysis to be correct" (40:13, emphasis added).

In other words, we are to have faith that iridology is always correct. This is true even though the underlying theory of iridology is anatomically false and iridologists routinely fail scientific testing of their diagnostic abilities.

Faith in iridology is what is important, not anatomy or clinical trials. This means the iridologist is willing to risk the health of his patient on the flimsiest of rationalizations. It is equivalent to arguing in the following manner: faith in gambling is what is important; the odds against winning are irrelevant.

Iridologists have no excuses for other aspects of their practice; for example, diagnosing illnesses that are not even known to exist. "Many of the conditions detected by practitioners of iridology are 'diseases' whose existence has been disputed or discredited by scientific investigation. A common finding is a toxic bowel settlement. . . . The toxic settlement theory of disease was soundly discredited in the early part of this century" (344:175).

In another text, Paul Reisser, M.D., observed:

> Another fundamental theory problem for iridology is its insistence that each iris reveals what is happening on its particular side of the body. (That

is, the right iris shows right-sided problems, and similarly for the left.) This contradicts a fundamental observation that incoming nerve impulses from one side of the body nearly always cross to the opposite side on their way to the brain. Dr. Jensen has proposed, in response to this problem, that the optic nerve serves as the final messenger between the nervous system and the iris. This explanation would allow for a second crossing of information back to the eye on the same side of the body, but creates two new problems. First, the optic nerve has been shown without question to be only a "one way" messenger, carrying information from the retina to the brain and not in reverse. (Indeed, the optic nerve is not known to connect directly to the iris at all.) Second, only half of the fibers of the optic nerve cross to the opposite side of the brain.

Since the precise way in which the iris tells us about distant organs is at best poorly defined, Iridology characterizes itself as an "empiric" science. That is, it is based upon the experience of its practitioners rather than controlled studies. Presumably, over the years iridologists have noted the appearance of the irises in many patients and then correlated these observations with the patients' health problems. Unfortunately, however, iridologists use disease classifications which are not generally accepted outside of the subculture in which they practice. Terms such as "toxic accumulations" or "lymphatic congestion" abound in Iridology literature, but they are at best vaguely defined and at worst meaningless to the health care community at large (1:144–45).

The Results of Testing

In *New Age Medicine*, Reisser, Reisser, and Weldon briefly discussed the issue of iridology and science.

> If the iris is indeed blessed with such enormous diagnostic potential, why is iridology not taken seriously in the scientific community?
>
> In fact, iridology is taught neither in medical school nor in high school biology classes, nor is it practiced . . . by optometrists or ophthalmologists. As with many alternative therapies there are two fundamental reasons for this wholesale lack of acceptance: iridology's basic premise is highly suspect, and its performance has not earned a passing grade using ordinary methods of scientific investigation.
>
> One major theory problem is the assumption that the iris' connections with the central nervous system allow detailed messages to be sent to it from the rest of the body. . . . Unfortunately, the elaborate neurologic pathways necessary for such a powerful capability have yet to be demonstrated, or even deemed plausible, in spite of years of neuroanatomical studies of the eye and central nervous system. (1:142–143)

But Dr. Jensen boldly challenges, "I am willing to put iridology to the most severe tests. During the eighteen years in which I have been studying and applying this science, I have not been trying to fool myself" (40:10). The reader may judge for himself.

Scientific studies have proven that iridology is worthless. In fact, iridology has failed every carefully controlled scientific test given it; at least, we could find no exceptions. Consider the following illustrations. (In the tests cited below, photographs of patient's iris were used, for obvious reasons. Iridologists routinely claim they can effectively diagnose by photograph, thus all parties agreed on the procedure at the start of these tests.)

As reported in the *Journal of the American Medical Association*, scientfic researchers at University of California San Diego tested three iridologists (including Dr. Jensen himself), and three opthalmologists by having them study the iris photographs of 143 subjects, 48 of whom had overt kidney failure (174). The researchers gave iridology its best shot. Two of the three iridologists had been "using the technique as their primary method of analysis of patients for more than forty years." But the iridologists failed miserably. The number of false positives (healthy people diagnosed as having disease) and false negatives (diseased people diagnosed as healthy) was frightening. In fact, the iridologists' accuracy was found to be *worse* than what one would expect with chance guessing. In other words, the iridologists would have been more accurate by picking their answers out of a hat than by deriving them from an examination of the iris. Thus,

> the 2.5 percent level of renal disease diagnostic accuracy with iridology—only 11 of 20 patients with disease are correctly identified, while 421 normal people are identified as having disease—does not warrant reliance on this technique in the detection of renal disease. . . . There is a serious potential psychological harm to the subject of carrying the burden of detected "disease." Of greater interest to physicians is the false-negative analysis. One of the observers (an iridologist), who employs the technique and draws conclusions based on it, correctly identified only 26 percent of the patients undergoing dialysis as having kidney disease. Physicians are well aware of the harm that can be done to these patients if they were to rely on iridology and thereby go without proper treatment. (174:1388–89)

Dr. Jensen afterwards criticized the study, allegedly for other reasons than the fact he miserably failed it. He argued that the study's use of serum creatinine level to indicate kidney disease was not valid (448:176). Serum creatinine, however, is accepted and used around the world as a significant indicator of kidney function.

Iridologists have also claimed that the 421 people in perfect health identified as having kidney disease would certainly have kidney disease in the future because, as noted earlier, iridology can allegedly discern "subclinical" disease, that is, disease that will appear in the future. But, of course, at this point the iridologists prove nothing. If the patient never develops the problem, they claim that their treatment prevented it. If the patient does develop it, then they were right all along (1:145).

Consider another study. In this case a physician examined 762 patients with very severe disease. Among them were 60 Army veterans, many of whom had amputated limbs. Iridology was again proven false and harmful:

> Among the 762 patients only 18 (that is 2.7 percent) had a sign in the area that the iridology chart assigned to the affected organ. More than 50 percent, however, had pathological signs in areas of organs that had never been involved. The same investigator made a test with one of the most prominent iris-interpreters of his time which was witnessed by several doctors and laymen. Iridologist Klaeser was asked to diagnose patients with severe ailments and mutilations that were obvious even to medical laymen. (2:89–90)

But after eight successive attempts, the experiment was discontinued because the iridologist had given nothing but wrong diagnoses. One patient with an amputated leg, for example, was discovered to have only "marked congestion of the spinal cord" (2:90).

A different scientific study was done at the University of Melbourne in Australia and reported in the *Australian Journal of Optometry* for July 1982. This controlled clinical study compared iridology evaluations with patients' known medical histories. One phase of the study had iridologists diagnose "before" and "after" iris photographs of subjects who had developed a serious disease. Iridologists were then asked to determine whether or not a change in the iris had occurred and to tell which organ had been affected.

Significantly, the *only* set of photographs "determined to have changes was a set taken as a control on the same subject two minutes apart!" The conclusion of the study was that "there were no detectable iris changes of the type depicted in the commonly used iris diagnosis charts" (448:175).

Another study was conducted at the University of Lindbergh in the Netherlands and reported in the *British Medical Journal* for December 17, 1988. It also revealed that iridology does not work.

All of this is why Dr. Russell Worrall concluded in the October 1984 *Journal of the American Optometric Association*,

> After 104 years, the facts of iridology have yet to be established. . . . To my knowledge there are no well conceived, documented and published studies which support the validity of the clinical information presented on the iris charts or which demonstrate the underlying anatomical and physiological processes. (Scientific Studies in English and Extensive Critical German Citations) *demonstrate that there is no statistical correlation between a diagnosis based on iris signs and actual medical conditions.* (449:737, emphasis added)

Unfortunately, scientific studies discrediting iridology are rarely reported in the popular press; experiments which seem to validate it appear more desirable. This is why claims in the popular press must be evaluated critically. For example, Jensen cites the work of two researchers in Russia reported in *The National Enquirer* for May 23, 1978, that reported a 95 percent accuracy in 1,273 subjects with diagnosed disease. Jensen also reported another study with an alleged 92 percent efficiency through iridology in the detection of kidney disease. However,

> Jensen does not describe the details of these investigations, the nature of the controls or the standards used for diagnosis. These are important, because one iridologist in the San Diego study could also boast of having correctly identified 88 percent of those with kidney disease. Unfortunately, he reported that 88 percent of the normal subjects included in the study as a control were also suffering from kidney disease. . . . Therefore, without specific details of the design, the use of these studies is of no value when offered in support of iridology. (344:176)

Supposedly Correct Diagnosis

How do we explain the many claims of correct or "astonishing" diagnoses that occur in iridology? Such correct diagnoses can be impressive; for example, Dr. James Carter's interest in iridology was sparked by a Canadian artist "whose astoundingly accurate iris reading" dissolved his skepticism (80:157).

Such "accuracy" can occur in a number of ways that have nothing to do with the validity of iridology. Below we briefly show why iridology can *seem* to be effective when it really isn't. We will also indicate that when genuinely accurate diagnoses are made, it may occur through spiritistic power, but not the power of iridology.

Why can iridology appear to be an effective method of diagnosis? First, consider that most patients will tell an iridologist their medical history, including the symptoms they are having, well before he examines their iris. This may supply the iridologist with sufficient clues to make an accurate diagnosis at least some of the time.

Second, iridology diagnosis characteristically involves speaking in vague and general terminology. The patient is left to fill in the details, but the initial diagnosis sounded right and the treatments seem to be helping, so the patient concludes that the diagnosis must have been correct.

For example, what does it mean that a liver or pancreas is "weak"?

> The bulk of the diseases reported are vaguely stated conditions in organs, such as an "underactive" pancreas or "chronic weakness" in the lungs. Such vagueness permits clinicians to capitalize on any improvement in the way a patient "feels" as proof that the treatments are doing some good. Under those conditions, the cure rate and patient satisfaction in a clinical practice can be very high. (448:177–178)

Third, iridologists, like many other new age healers, are adept at self-justification. Because practitioners assume iridology is never wrong, some novel explanation is always available to explain errors, no matter how implausible. For the true believer, no conditions exist which could ever disprove iridology.

Consider a typical "safe" diagnosis, which although proven false, was nevertheless rationalized. An investigative reporter was told by the iridologist that the whitish color coming from the iris of her eyes indicated acidity and mucus throughout the body and could result from eating too much meat, bread, and milk products. When the iridologists was informed the reporter was a *vegetarian*, she was told the acidity "could be a reverse effect from eating too much fruit and vegetables" (450)!

Fourth, iridologists do not usually provide one single diagnosis but offer the patient an entire list of actual or potential problems. The more problems listed, the greater chance of being right at least once.

Some clients are amazed when their iris might "indicate" that a family relative has a particular problem or illness. But if the illness is common enough and if the word "relative" is defined generally enough (parents, children, spouse, aunts, uncles, third removed cousins, etc.), the iridologist may be proven true. Then there is always the entirely "safe" prediction of "future" disease which has absolutely no symptoms or indications in the present—except, of course, in the iris.

All the above factors—and more—can provide iridologists with a clientele of converts who are ready to broadcast the "amazing discoveries" of iridology far and wide.

But there is a further explanation for the possible success of iridology and this brings us to our next category.

Occultic Potential

Like much new age medicine, iridology makes use of the concept of mystical energy. In fact, the pupil of the eye is held to be a repository of sorts for the body's "energy," according to many iridologists. "Most iridologists agree that the integrity of the body's energy is reflected by the quality of energy in this [pupil] hub, or core" (80:159).

But how does one possibly diagnose the "energy" condition of the body based on the "energy" condition of the pupil? Clearly one way is through psychic or "intuitive" methods. Thus, one does not study iridology long before one uncovers iridologists who claim to diagnose the iris on the basis of psychic powers or even on the basis of spirit guides.

Iridologist Brint observes, "Some of the skills involved [in learning iridology] are mechanical, but others are definitely intuitive" (80:161).

When asked whether or not a psychic ability was involved in iris diagnosis Dr. Carter responded:

> Intuitive skills do come into play here, and whether we want to call this "psychic ability" or not . . . remains to be defined. What do we mean by "psychic?" Is that just a paranormal state? It is very easy to label it as such. We may find that these skills are just a further progression of the conscious ability of the individual . . . a kind of hyperconscious or ultra-conscious state. (173:51–52)

In other words, for Carter, psychic powers are merely normal human "intuition." Nevertheless, presumably because of the energy connections, Carter has incorporated the principles of Oriental medicine and philosophy with iridology practice (173).

One of the leading authorities in the area of the occult, Dr. Kurt Koch observes:

> Many of our healers and occult practitioners use eye-diagnosis mediumistically. . . . That means that they are only interested in the iris as an mediumistic contact. In this way the human eye serves a psychometric purpose in much the same way as hand lines do when a fortune-teller uses them as contact material or as an "intuition stimulant." When this is the case, eye-diagnosis becomes a form of fortune-telling. Because of this, these eye-diagnosticians are often very successful. Indeed, some of them with little or no medical training can diagnose illness with 100 percent accuracy. (155:40–41)

The occult and spiritistic potential of iridology can also be illustrated by noting its historic ties to the occult, in particular astrology. Iridology can ultimately be traced to Chinese astrology practiced four thousand years ago (2:84–85).

The occult concept of "as above, so below" is an ancient hermetic formula expressing a magical occult principle. The very term "hermetic" is derived from Hermes Trismegistus, the Greek name for the Egyptian god Thoth, the alleged inventor of the occult sciences. It refers to a universal principle of correspondences said to exist between the heavens and the earth.

Just as ancient and modern astrologers believe that the destiny of the individual below on earth is dependent on the heavens above, so the ancient Chinese astrologers taught that the organs of the big world (macrocosm) of man were reflected in the small world of the eye (microcosm).

The famous occultist, astrologer, and medieval father of modern new age medicine, Paracelsus, also regarded the eye as the microcosm and man as the macrocosm (253:46; 2:85). A modern astrologer observes, "The eye reflects the cosmos of the human body from the point of its birth and it registers all changes that have happened since" (2:85).

The supposed interrelatedness of the macrocosm and the microcosm forms not only the basis of astrology but a great deal of additional occultism and significant portions of new age medicine, including general magic, palmistry, acupuncture, anthroposophical medicine, Ayurvedic medicine, and other practices.

Iridologist Brint notes this hermetic application of iridology and how it can allegedly become a means to detect levels of individual consciousness in a new age sense:

> From an Eastern point of view, the eye may be viewed as a *mandala*. . . . The mandala links the microcosm and the macrocosm. . . . Through the mandala man may be projected into the universe and the universe into

> man. . . . In iridology, the macrocosm and the microcosm are linked in our eyes. . . . Iridology may be summed up as the observation of the change that arises from the interplay of various levels of consciousness and results in one's unique evolution into greater [occult] truth and light. (80:155, 162)

This connection between iridology and astrology supplies one avenue for spiritistic influences in iris diagnosis. Why? Because astrology is often a spiritistic practice, as the authors have documented in detail elsewhere (44:201–256). Since many iridologists employ astrology, spiritistic contacts are therefore possible.

How do we know many iridologists employ astrology? For one reason, Dr. Jensen himself does, and we have already noted his influence in American iridology. He has even named the spiritistic, astrologically oriented sect of the Rosicrucians as his "spiritual abode" (136:226). In an interview conducted in the Rosicrucian magazine *Rays from the Rose Cross*, he explains how astrology and iridology may be blended:

> Because astrology has its effect on the body, and the condition of the body is revealed in the iris of the eye, we find that various organs work in harmony with the [astrological] influences existing at birth—the influences with which we came into this world. For instance, people who are waterlogged or who have lymphatic gland congestions tend to hold water in their bodies. By looking at their [astrological] charts, we see that they are greatly influenced by the water signs. (136:227)

Perhaps the potentially occultic nature of iridology is one reason why even Jensen occasionally confesses that iridology is, after all, not really a true science. He calls it a science that cannot be proven through scientific testing—in other words, an occult science:

> Iridology is based on scientific observation. [However] It is the kind of science that cannot be related through scientific tests, for *it does not provide clinical information*. . . . Iridology can only be judged by those who use it properly. Iridology has not been used properly by those who have criticized and say it fails the test. (in 333:176–177 emphasis added)

This is quite a confession: Iridology only works for true believers and can be properly evaluated by them only. In essence, to practice iridology "effectively" requires faith on the part of the iridologist, who must not only know and believe iridology but have intuitive or psychic abilities as well, and perhaps knowledge of other occult sciences such as astrology. The iridologist who is properly trusting and "sensitive" will have favorable results.

The critic and unbeliever will not, and are excluded from commenting on the practice by definition.

❧ ❧ ❧

Thus, we find the peculiar hallmark of new age medicine—a failure to justify one's practices:

> Even though proponents may have used iridology "properly" since von Peczely published his theories in 1866, they have failed to publish even one well-documented study to support the validity of any of the information presented on their iris charts. Since efficacy has not been established, the ultimate questions faced by practitioners of iridology is one of ethics in their relationship with patients.
>
> It is clear from a logical, theoretical, and clinical perspective that iridology is a pseudoscience of no clinical value. Unfortunately, the use of iridology by unorthodox practitioners is all too common today. (344:177)

Therefore, iridology is worthless as a diagnostic technique, and it may involve a person in the occult. Whether considered from the perspective of logic, scientific tests, or iridology theory itself, iridology is a pseudoscience of no value. The practice has deceived both practitioner and patient alike.

Meditation

Definition: New age (Eastern/occultic) meditation involves the control and regulation of the mind for various physical and spiritual purposes or goals.

Founder: Unknown; the practice is ancient and cross-cultural.

How Does It Claim to Work? Meditation claims to work by "stilling" or otherwise influencing the mind; the meditator is allegedly able to perceive "true" reality and his own "true" nature, and achieve spiritual "enlightenment." Meditation promoters also claim the practice has numerous health benefits.

Scientific Evaluation: Apart from a "relaxation response," scientific studies have also confirmed psychophysiological influences of meditation, but their meaning and value is variously interpreted; science cannot comment on its spiritual claims.

Occultic Potential: The development of psychic powers, altered states of consciousness, astral projection, spiritism, *kundalini* arousal.

Major Problems: New age meditation uses the mind in an abnormal manner to radically restructure a person's perceptions to support new age philosophy and goals; regressive states of consciousness are wrongly interpreted as "higher" or "divine" states of consciousness; meditation-developed psychic powers are falsely interpreted as evidence of a latent divine nature; meditators often do not realize the possible long-term results or consequences of these practices, such as *kundalini* arousal, nor would many have been likely to begin the practice had they known them.

Biblical/Christian Evaluation: The nature, context, purpose, and type of meditation determines its validity and outcome. Biblical meditation (Psalm 19:14; 77:12; 119:97, 99) is a spiritually healthy practice; new age meditation is an occult practice with harmful spiritual consequences.

Potential Dangers: Occult influences; demon possession; physical, spiritual, and psychological damage.

NINETEEN

MEDITATION*

One of the most popular of all new age health practices is meditation. Meditation techniques have assumed a prominent place in many physical, spiritual, and health therapies where relaxation is a primary goal. One recent article titled "Unwind and Destress" in *Prevention*, American's leading health magazine, endorsed Maharishi Mahesh Yogi's transcendental meditation (224) and a form of Buddhist "mindfulness" meditation (339:85–86). Herbert Benson, M.D., is the author of a popular text, *The Relaxation Response*, which also emphasizes the stress-reducing benefits of meditation (395).

Because meditation is widely viewed as a positive health practice, almost any technique in this book may employ meditation as an adjunct therapy. This is why Eastern, occultic, and other new age forms of meditation are increasingly practiced in our society among both lay people and professionals.

New age meditation is typically combined with an Eastern/occultic religion or world view. This world view sees the very purpose of meditation as inducing a form of religious "enlightenment," one that agrees with the occultic goals and beliefs of the particular religion. Spiritual goals aside, these methods are recommended enthusiastically, if ironically, for their alleged mental and physical health benefits. But as we will see, such meditation is far from "healthful."

---

* Meditation typically induces altered states and is often a form of yoga or used in conjunction with a yoga program (cf. 224).

The Influence of New Age Meditation

The number of people practicing meditation today has made this a significant social problem. In 1975, William Johnston warned in his *Silent Music: The Science of Meditation*:

> Anyone with the slightest experience of meditation knows about the uprising of the unconscious and the possible resultant turmoil, to say nothing of the increased psychic power that meditation brings. All this could have the greatest social consequences if meditation becomes widespread. (451:26)

Today meditation has become widespread. Meditation is practiced by literally ten to twenty million people in this country (cf. 400:135). Almost three million people have been initiated into Maharishi Mahesh Yogi's occult system of transcendental meditation alone (224).

- Dozens of Hindu and Buddhist gurus or groups all require meditation practice in conjunction with their religious programs: Nichiren Shoshu Buddhism, Swami Kriyananda, Bhagwan Shree Rajneesh, SYDA Foundation (Muktananda), Sai Baba, Yogi Bhajan, Swami Rama, Maharaj Ji, Kirpal Singh, Self Realization Fellowship (Paramahansa Yogananda), Chogyam Trungpa, Sri Chinmoy, ISKCON, Da Free John, and many others all stress the importance of meditation. Rajneesh's "chaotic meditation" is particularly potent—and particularly dangerous (111; 426).
- Hundreds of new and old religions and cults also have meditation agendas: the Association for Research and Enlightenment (Edgar Cayce), the Church Universal and Triumphant (Elizabeth Claire Prophet), Eckankar, the Gurdjieff Foundation, the Rosicrucians, Theosophy, Anthroposophy, Astara, and many more.
- Mystical, occult religions in America, such as Sufism, Sikhism, Taoism, Tantrism, and others all stress the importance of their meditation procedures.
- Scores of new age therapies, such as those found in the growing field of transpersonal psychology, require or recommend some form of meditation in conjunction with their therapy (397; 384).
- Endless occult practices offer their own brand of meditation, such as witchcraft, druidism, kabbalism, and mediumism.

Meditation is also offered in many new contexts: at the local YMCA, churches, sports clinics, and some hospitals. Even the United Nations has an official meditation advisor, guru Sri Chinmoy, who is a practiced meditator and spiritist (43:53–68; 355:9–20, 26–29). Chinmoy also conducts meditation for government officials in the U.S. Congress and the British Parliament (281:311).

Meditation and the Church

Unfortunately, questionable or Eastern forms of meditation are practiced by many church members. The modern interest in Christian mysticism (whether Catholic, Protestant, or Eastern Orthodox forms) has sparked a renewed appreciation of meditation among Christians. But the practices recommended often involve more than simple Biblical meditation—i.e., meditation on the content and application of Scripture. One discovers forms of meditation which draw upon or are similar to Eastern varieties.

Given the fact that many Christians are insufficiently instructed in these areas, we think this presents a potential problem. Below we cite illustrations.

Richard Foster is the evangelical author of *Celebration of Discipline*, a book on the Christian bestseller lists for many months. His chapter on mediation stresses discovering "the inner reality of the spiritual world [which] is available to all who are willing to search for it" (193:18). Foster is careful to distinguish between Eastern meditation and Christian forms, noting they are "worlds apart" (193:15). His commitment to Christian faith also modifies his basic approach. Unfortunately however, his methods offer a number of similarities to new age or Eastern techniques employed in meditation, such as use of the imagination and dreamwork. For example:

> The inner world of meditation is most easily entered through the door of the imagination. We fail today to appreciate its tremendous power. The imagination is stronger than conceptual thought and stronger than the will. . . .
>
> Some rare individuals may be able to contemplate in an imageless voice, but most of us need to be more deeply rooted in the senses. Jesus taught this way, making constant appeal to the imagination and the senses. (193:22)

And,

> In learning to meditate, one good place to begin is with our dreams, since it involves little more than paying attention to something we are already doing. For fifteen centuries Christians overwhelmingly considered dreams as a natural way in which the spiritual world broke into our lives. Kelsey, who has authored the book *Dreams: The Dark Speech of the Spirit*, notes, ". . . every major Father of the early Church, from Justin Martyr to Irenaeus, from Clement and Tertullian to Origen and Cyprian, believed that dreams were a means of revelation. . . ."
>
> Dreams can help us find increased maturity and health.
>
> If we are convinced that dreams can be a key to unlocking the door to the inner world, we can do three practical things. First, we can specifically pray, inviting God to inform us through our dreams. We should tell Him of our willingness to allow Him to speak to us in this way. At the same time, it is wise to pray a prayer of protection, since to open ourselves to spiritual influence can be dangerous as well as profitable. We simply ask God to surround us with the light of His protection as He ministers to our spirit.
>
> Second, we should begin to record our dreams. . . .
>
> That leads to the third consideration—how to interpret dreams. The best way to discover the meaning of dreams is to ask. "You do not have, because you do not ask" (James 4:2). We can trust God to bring discernment if and when it is needed. Sometimes it is helpful to seek out those who are especially skilled in these matters [e.g., dream interpreters]. (193:23–24)

Foster also encourages "centering" exercises and concentrating on one's breath, also a common Eastern technique:

> Another meditation aimed at centering oneself begins by concentrating on breathing. Having seated yourself comfortably, slowly become conscious of your breathing. This will help you to get in touch with your body and indicate to you the level of tension within. Inhale deeply, slowly tilting your head back as far as it will go. Then exhale, allowing your head slowly to come forward until your chin nearly rests on your chest. Do this for several moments, praying inwardly something like this: "Lord, I exhale my fear over my geometry exam, I inhale Your peace. I exhale my spiritual apathy, I inhale Your light and life." Then, as before, become silent outwardly and inwardly. Be attentive to the inward living Christ. (193:25)

Dr. Foster is convinced these methods, such as use of the imagination, visualization, dreamwork, centering, and breathing, may be effectively employed by Christians within the context of a Christian form of meditation, especially as part of a program of spiritual growth. He cites their use in church history (including Christian mystical traditions) as one illustration of how believers have used them in the past. "Nor should we forget the great body of literature by men and women from many disciplines. Many of these thinkers have unusual perception into the human predicament. [For example,] Eastern writers like Lao-Tse of China and Zarathustra of Persia." (193:62).

But we don't think Dr. Foster's approach answers all the questions that may be raised over such practices. Thankfully, he does warn practicers are engaging in a "serious and even dangerous business" (193:16).

But the reason for our concern is twofold: (1) Because Christians are insufficiently instructed in these areas, they may slip into more potent forms of meditation practices as a result of their introduction to these techniques found in Eastern occultic varieties and (2) our conviction that these methods are questionable to begin with.

We should emphasize that we have no doubt as to Dr. Foster's evangelical commitment or sincerity. We also appreciate his desire that Christians be more committed to Christ. We simply disagree with his basic approach to meditation and sanctification.

Fringe psychotherapy in the church has also encouraged the use of "novel" spiritual practices. Clinical psychologist E. S. Gallegos, for example, works at the Lutheran Family Service in Klamath Falls, Oregon, and is co-author of *Inner Journeys: Visualization in Growth and Therapy* (402). In "Animal Imagery, the Chakra System and Psychotherapy," he offers the church a psychotherapeutic approach using occult theory and technique plus imagery or visualization for attaining an "assessment" of the *chakras* (according to Hindu theory, alleged psychic centers in the body).

By a common technique of occult meditation, each chakra is "contacted" and then permitted to "represent itself" in animal form within the counselee's imagination. The function of the animal is to guide and counsel the person. In essence, this is quite similar to the shaman's "power" animal—a spirit guide who assumes the form of an animal and becomes the animal familiar to help, guide, protect, and instruct the shaman in his occult quest. Thus,

> This therapeutic process was initially developed when the author observed similarities between the chakra system and the totem poles of the Northwest Coast American Indians. This therapeutic process also acknowledges a relationship between those tribal [Shamanistic] Indian transformation rituals and modern psychological transformation. (393:136)

So, here we have a licensed psychologist, working in a Lutheran Family Service Center, who has combined elements of occult yoga/meditation theory and shamanism in his counseling practice. But if the therapist is also an occultist with occult power who transfers such power into his patients (like a true shaman) or if he brings his spirit guide into the therapy session (knowingly or not) or if the person seeking help pursues shamanism on his own as a result, then the therapy has become a vehicle for introducing people to the occult. If the client is encouraged to use meditation, yoga, visualization, chakra energizing, etc., spirit-guides could certainly take advantage of these areas.

While such "therapy" is not common in the church, neither is it rare. We have no precise idea of how widespread such practices are in the nominal church, but we are convinced hundreds of illustrations could be cited and that the evangelical church itself is being impacted. The combination of several factors: (1) occultism (in modified forms) entering the field of psychotherapy which itself has infused Christianity, (2) a pragmatic orientation in evangelicalism, (3) the current state of occult revival and naivete, (4) the church's adopting elements of its surrounding pagan culture, and (5) the rejection of Biblical authority in some portions of evangelicalism means that such things are likely to occur.

To cite an illustration: The occult-oriented *Yoga Journal* ran an article by two evangelicals titled "Christians Meditate Too!" Their words speak for themselves. First, they are teaching courses on meditation at their evangelical church and offer seminars on "Christian" meditation at other evangelical churches:

> Last year the two of us taught an eight-week seminar on meditation—a fairly bold offering at our conservative evangelical church. The course was an enthusiastic success, and we'd like to share its highlights with *Yoga Journal* readers. . . . Our own background includes practicing yoga, t'ai chi and aikido, and studying the *Bhagavad Gita*, the *Upanishads*, Lao Tzu, and the teachings of Buddha and Confucius. (393:27)

They observe, correctly, that "In both East and West, meditation is introspective: we learn to look within to discover spiritual realities" (393:27). Thus, not surprisingly,

> We of the West stand to gain by learning discipline and spiritual awareness from the East. . . . The new age movement in this country is already moving toward a personalizing of Eastern disciplines. (393:28)

There is no critique of the new age, no mention of the dangers or occultic nature of most meditation. There is no questioning of yoga; there is no awareness of the anti-Christian philosophy underlying Eastern systems or the fact of spiritual warfare. There is merely a presentation of the "benefits" of Eastern spirituality, an endorsement of "Christian" meditation involving among other things questionable exegesis, and an uncritical acceptance of Christian mysticism, such as the mindless repetition of certain phrases found in many Christian mystical traditions. They tell the reader of the *Yoga Journal*, "Christians meditate, too. When they do, they are falling behind Isaac and David, Ignatius and Francis and Christ Himself" (393:45).

Still, we can't remember Jesus sitting in yoga positions or encouraging his followers to practice "yoga, t'ai, chi, and aikido" or to study the pagan *Bhagavad Gita*, the *Upanishads*, Lao Tzu, or the teachings of Confucius and Buddha. These evangelicals were probably trying to "reach" readers of the *Yoga Journal* with some kind of Christian influence; while the motive is noble, we question the efficacy.

The authors of the above article recommend three books. The first is Thomas Merton's *New Seeds of Contemplation*. Merton was an influential ascetic Catholic monk who had incorporated Eastern beliefs and practices into his Catholicism and who has led many Catholics into contemplative Eastern traditions. He believed he had found genuine spiritual truth in many Eastern scriptures and practices—including Hindu, Buddhist, Sufi, and Zen traditions. The second text recommended is mystic Evelyn Underhill's *Mysticism*, which is anything but Biblical. Significantly, the third text is Richard Foster's *Celebration of Discipline*, described as being "prominent in the revival of interest in Christian meditation" (393:45).

All this reveals that questionable forms of meditation are influencing the church; but they are influencing much more than the church.

Meditation and Professionals

Many professional people, in science, business, and academics, practice meditation. Roger Walsh has both the M.D. and Ph.D. degrees and works in the Department of Psychiatry and Human Behavior in the College of Medicine at the University of California Irvine campus. He is a committed student of both Buddhist Vipassana ("mindfulness") meditation, as well as the spiritistically-inspired *Course in Miracles* (198:69, 81–82, see chapter 12).

Deane Shapiro also has impressive academic credentials and practices a different form of meditation. He is recipient of a Kellogg National Fellowship to study meditation, has served on the faculty of the University of California and the Stanford University Medical School, and is president of the Institute for the Advancement of Human Behavior. He is the author of *Precision Nirvana: An Owners Manual for the Care and Maintenance of the Mind* (1978) and an editor of *Meditation: Self-Regulation Strategy and Altered States of Consciousness* (1979) (198:69, 81–82).

Walsh and Shapiro have edited *Meditation: Classic and Contemporary Perspectives* (282). This text has over seven hundred pages in sixty chapters by thirty authors and includes almost all Eastern Asian systems now practiced in the West, involving dozens of methods and techniques. Their bibliography is extensive, over six hundred items including many articles relating to empirical studies and interacting meditation with psychology, psychiatry, biochemistry, psychophysiology, the neurosciences, and more.

Elsewhere Shapiro states his belief that "the most promising future meditation research may lie in the model of a personal scientist, using ourselves as subjects—and combining the precision of Western phenomenological science with the vision of Eastern thought and practice " (199:128–129).

The field of transpersonal psychology is the so-called "fourth" school of modern psychology, behind psychoanalysis, behaviorism, and humanistic psychology. According to Walsh in "A Model for Viewing Meditation Research," the "large majority" of transpersonal psychologists are involved in meditation:

> The number of Westerners who have learned to meditate now number several million, and surveys of transpersonal psychologists suggest that the large majority are involved in some form of this practice. . . . One of the long-held goals of transpersonal psychology has been an integration of Western science and Eastern practice. (198:69)

To illustrate further the impact that meditation is having in our culture, we only need cite the research bibliography on meditation compiled by Steven Donovan and Michael Murphy. Murphy is a former psychologist and well-known co-founder of the Esalen Institute. The bibliography concerned research data on meditation from 1931 to 1983 and contained 776 English language entries. This was *not* a bibliography of the religious, philosophical, or metaphysical literature on meditation; it dealt with scientific research only (194:181–229).

Most people's view of meditation as simply a form of relaxation has not only masked its true nature, but has also sparked the interest of many researchers who would ordinarily avoid the occult. Clinical psychologist Gordon Boals, who has taught at Princeton and Rutgers universities, observes:

> Viewing meditation as a relaxation technique has had a number of consequences. One result has been to make meditation seem more familiar and acceptable to the Western public so that subjects are willing to learn and practice it and researchers and psychotherapists are interested in experimenting with it. Another outcome is that therapists have been able to find a variety of ways of using it as a therapeutic technique. If meditation is relaxation, it should serve as an antidote to anxiety. (391:146)

Nevertheless, meditation is often much more than a relaxation technique, and its goals encompass far more than anxiety reduction.

The Claims and Goals of Meditation

The goals of Eastern and occultic meditation are to change a person's view of his or her self and his or her world view. In the end, as far as the meditator is concerned, "It lastingly changes his consciousness, transforming his experience of himself and his universe" (201:118). Dr. Roger Walsh, M.D., Ph.D., is author of several books on meditation and is with the faculty of the California College of Medicine at the University of California. He is also an editor for the *Journal of Transpersonal Psychology*. Frances Vaughan is a past president of the Association for Transpersonal Psychology and psychology professor at the California Institute of Transpersonal Psychology. These authors describe the impact of meditative practice:

> The rewards of meditative practice tend to be subtle at first. . . . Old assumptions about oneself and the world are gradually surrendered and more finely tuned, comprehensive perspectives begin to emerge.
>
> Such immediate benefits, however, are only tastes of what is potentially a profoundly transformative process, for when practiced intensely, meditation disciplines almost invariably lead into the transpersonal realm of experience. . . . A progressive sequence of altered states of consciousness can occur, which may ultimately result in the permanent, radical shift in consciousness known as enlightenment or liberation. (400:136–137)

Meditation teachings claim that in our normal state of mind we misperceive and misunderstand ourselves (our true nature) and our world (its true nature). Meditation claims it can correct these false perceptions and replace them with true perception brought by meditation practice.

Almost all forms of meditation involve the deliberate cultivation of altered states of consciousness and the subsequent development of psychic powers. These altered states of consciousness are wrongly interpreted, however. First, they are viewed as allegedly "higher" states of consciousness, presumably divine states. Second, the psychic powers developed by meditation are often seen as alleged indications of the awakening and developing "god-nature" of the individual.*

Yoga meditation, which is typically Hindu, and "mindfulness" meditation, which is typically Buddhist, are two powerful forms of meditation designed to radically alter the meditator's state of consciousness. By practicing them, one tends to "confirm" or "validate" his or her religious teachings by the occultic mental experiences one has. Meditators may become convinced they are one with God or ultimate reality, with all this implies. This change can occur not only through cultivating altered states of consciousness but also by the acceptance of meditation-developed psychic abilities, by meditation-induced spirit contact, and by internal (mental) experiences that support the religious teachings. Unfortunately, such experiences lead to conclusions that are implicitly hostile to Biblical faith.

Occultic Influences

We have seen throughout this text that one of the principal characteristics of new age medicine is the factor of an alleged universal or cosmic energy circulating throughout the body (*prana*, *chi*, *orgone*, etc.). This energy can be manipulated for various purposes and is even palpable. But energy manifestations are also the principal characteristic of the meditative experience as well. Although in the East psychic powers are accepted as a natural by-product of meditation, the vehicle through which these psychic abilities are produced is often viewed as a form of "cosmic" energy.

A major study on meditation asked respondents to check characteristics of their meditative experience. One descriptive item was stated as follows, "I felt a great surge of energy within me or around me" (197:121), and

* The frequent warnings concerning the "distraction" of these powers or their misuse are just as frequently ignored.

meditators whose experience could be described in this manner were to check this item. Significantly, this item received the highest "loading score" of all sixteen items in the category of "Intensification and Change of Consciousness" (197:127).*

This indicates that the experience of a "great surge of energy" (which the authors relate to the spiritistic *mana* of Polynesian Shamanism and the *prana* or *kundalini* of Hinduism [197:132–133]) was the dominant characteristic of the meditative experience (cf. refs. 425, 426). Furthermore, the experience of this surge of energy or power was directly related to the cultivation of an altered state of consciousness (197:132–33). For us, the key issue is determining the nature of this energy. If meditation brings a person into contact with this energy and this force infuses a person and dramatically alters their consciousness, don't you think it is important to determine what we are dealing with?

Energy Manifestations

Transpersonal psychotherapist Dr. Frances V. Clark, who wrote her Ph.D. dissertation on "Approaching Transpersonal Consciousness Through Affective Imagery in Higher Education," refers to our culture's modern fascination with occult energies: "In recent years we have learned much about releasing energy, raising energy, transforming energy, directing energy, and controlling energy flow. Yet the energy we are talking about remains undefined" (207:163).

In the preface to "Kundalini Casualties," an article discussing the dangers of yogic *kundalini* arousal from meditative and other new age therapies, *The New Age Journal* points out that,

> Traditionally, spiritual teachers have warned their students of the dangers and possible side effects of meditative techniques and helped practitioners deal with these difficulties as they arose. Now that meditation is being marketed as a mass commodity, the information concerning the dangers and the necessary help is often not part of the package. Moreover, certain body therapies and human potential techniques appear to be triggering off the Kundalini syndrome completely outside the context of spiritual training, and often the therapists themselves have no idea what this energy is, let alone how to deal with it. (390:47)

---

* The method used was the Verimax Orthogonal Factor Analysis; the loading score was .66.

There is little doubt that the energy experienced in new age meditation and especially yogic *kundalini* arousal is the result of spiritistic influence or even possession. That meditation produces energy manifestations clearly associated with primitive shamanism, the occult, and Eastern and Western spiritism is undeniable. In fact, the particular meditation-induced energy manifestations found are so often associated with spiritism, that the certainty is that this energy is not human energy, and certainly not divine energy, but rather spiritistic, or demonic energy (cf. refs. 425–426; 111; see chapters 5, 6).

Whether the phenomena is described in terms of the Eastern guru's *shaktipat diksha*, classical shamanism, *kundalini* arousal, or similar phenomena in other traditions, we are dealing with one and the same occultic energy.

Many primitive traditions directly attribute this energy to the working of the spirit world; others view it as an internal manifestation of divine power residing potentially within all men. Regardless, whether or not it is directly attributed to the spirit world, the spiritistic associations and manifestations are so blatant and pervasive one would be hard-pressed to conclude that we are dealing with anything other than a form of spirit influence and/or possession.

Great surges of energy are typically felt by Eastern and Western gurus who freely confess they are possessed by spirits, demons, or gods (111), by endless numbers of occultists who freely confess the same condition (e.g., 104:129–132) and by many practitioners of yoga (232). Swami Rudrananda writes in *Spiritual Cannibalism* that while in meditation his master touched him and "I immediately felt within me a surge of great spiritual force . . . movements similar to those of an epileptic controlled my body for about an hour. Many strange visions appeared and I felt things opening within me that had never been opened before" (284:85). In another experience, "Slowly [the spirit of my guru] Swami Nityananda came toward me and entered into my physical body. For three hours, I felt nothing of myself but that the saint had possessed me" (208:13).

The leading popularizer of Tibetan Buddhism in this country, Chogyam Trungpa observes, "I will say that for beginners, it is extremely dangerous to play with [this] energy, but for advanced students such work becomes relevant naturally" (209:74). And the danger is one can experience temporary (or permanent) insanity by contact with it. (See pp. 376-377, 380-83, 386-390)

Consider a few illustrations of its power from practitioners of meditation who follow guru Da (Bubba) Free John:

> Bubba's eyes rolled up, and his lips pulled into a sneer. His hands formed mudras [yogic movements] as he slumped against Sal, who also fell back against other devotees sitting behind him. Almost immediately, many of those present began to feel the effects of intensified Shakti [power], through the spontaneous internal movement of the life-force. Their bodies jerked or shook, their faces contorted, some began to cry, scream, and moan. The whole bathhouse seems to have slipped into another world. . . .
>
> I saw Bubba just enter into Sal, just go right into Sal. From there he went out over everybody else, and then everybody else started going crazy. (229:47)

> My hands were glowing and vibrating. It felt like electricity, like they were on radar or something, and they were just being directed to all of the people around me. I felt like I was conducting the Force through me to the others there. People were screaming and howling, crying and yelling out. . . . (229:60)

> As soon as I went into the room, I felt the Force. My head started jerking, and I sat down next to Billy Tsiknas and Joe Hamp. The Force went through and through my body, at first warm, then hot. It started to hurt. I was in a sitting position. My hand was raised, and I couldn't move it because of the Force moving through it. My head was bent down. I was so full of intensity, I started to cry. (229:61)

> I was so insane I didn't know what was happening at all. . . . Everybody sitting here started to have incredible Shakti [power] manifestations, and other things. It was absolutely intense. . . . When I was sitting here with everybody, I was shaking, and it felt sort of like I was possessed, . . . the "terror of being destroyed, totally destroyed." (229:66)

> Suddenly his body exploded with movement, his arms and legs flying outward, his head rolling around and snapping. Force seemed to be flung from his body into the others present. (229:72)

In essence, what is called "intensification" or possession by energy is described as a core experience in the historical literature of meditation and many occultic practices. This "energizing" is experienced as a dramatic and even overwhelming influx of spiritual power. It can be wild, uncontrollable—and deadly. But irrespective of the interpretation placed on it, it shares many characteristics with spirit-possession phenomena long-noted among those in contact with the spirit world, such as mediums, spiritists, channelers, gurus, etc.

Abundant relevant literature could be cited such as Bhagwan Shree Rajneesh's *The Book of the Secrets* (283); Swami Muktananda's *Play of Consciousness* (223); Swami Rudrananda's *Spiritual Cannibalism* (208); and Da Free John's *Garbage and the Goddess* (229).

What is troubling, however, is the pervasive denial in many quarters that what is operating here is, in fact, a form of spiritistic or demonic influence and/or possession. The following cartoon illustration underscores our concerns:

> There is a cartoon by Feiffer that illustrates some of these component aspects of meditation, and it proceeds something like this: Harry is sitting meditating; Madge walks in and asks, "Harry, what are you doing?" "I am concentrating on my mantra." "A mantra? What's a mantra?" "It's a secret. I cannot tell." "Harry, what is a mantra?" "I cannot tell." "Harry, I must know what a mantra is. Tell me what is a mantra? It's either me or the mantra." Harry doesn't tell and she packs up her bags and leaves, and Harry says, "See it works; no stress." Meditation may be working for a variety of reasons other than the ones that the literature cites, and I think we need to research these reasons. (210:128)

The fact is that no one really knows how meditation "works," and the theory of spiritistic influence is as valid as any other. Consider the Merv Griffin Show of July 25, 1986. Griffin interviewed new age channeler Jach Pursel and actor Michael York and his wife. They, along with Griffin and many other top Hollywood stars, were described as disciples of "Lazaris," the spirit entity who possessed Pursel and spoke through him while on television.

On the show, Pursel described how he met his spirit guide simply by engaging in his normal practice of meditation. In October of 1974, he recalled, he was meditating as usual; there was nothing abnormal in his experience. But all of a sudden—totally unexpectedly—he became possessed. The entity proceeded to take him over entirely, to completely control him and to use his vocal chords to speak through him. His wife recorded the statements of the entity and thus Pursel's career as a spiritistic medium was launched.

The significant fact here is not the birth of another spiritistic medium, but how easily Pursel became possessed from a simple and widely practiced form of meditation, one used by literally millions of people.

What millions of people today do not realize is that most meditation is occultic in nature. The practices (some form of daily meditative discipline), results (altered states of consciousness, psychic powers, *kundalini* arousal, spirit contact), and goals (some form of "cosmic" consciousness or development of the "higher self") may all be classified within the sphere of the practices, results, and goals of the occult world in general.

Most forms of meditation involve three related occultic phenomena: the cultivation of particular altered states of consciousness, the eventual development of psychic powers, and the possibility of spirit possession.

Most forms of meditation involve similar goals: They produce similar experiences leading meditators to similar conclusions about the nature of man and reality.

Cultivation of Altered States of Consciousness

The research of parapsychologist Dr. Karlis Osis and others reveals that the most central factor in meditation is an altered state of consciousness. Similarly, parapsychologist Dr. Gertrude Schmeidler, former president of the Parapsychological Association, observes that a state of "Trance shows many similarities to meditation." (202:30).

Cultivation of altered states of consciousness and trance states have been traditionally associated with the world of the occult, demonism, and other forms of spirit contact (shamanism, witchcraft, neo-paganism, magic ritual, Satanism, mediumism, yogic disciplines, etc.).

Whether one is a short or long-term practitioner, meditation is designed to change one's view of things by altering one's consciousness. Noted parapsychologist Karlis Osis and others in their "Dimensions of the Meditative Experience" reveal that "the most central and complex factor" of the meditative experience is an "intensification and change of consciousness," that is, an altered state of consciousness (197:121).

They further observe:

> In spite of the almost universal claim that the meditation experience is ineffable [indescribable], clear dimensionalities [characteristics] emerge. Even more, these dimensions seem not to express everyday states of consciousness: The way of experiencing [reality] definitely changed. . . . The subject's free comments support the view that successful Meditation leads to altered states of consciousness. (197:130).

Thus, they conclude, "Effective meditation induces radical changes in a meditator's way of experiencing [reality]" (197:109).

Any number of additional studies prove that meditation induces altered states of consciousness [ASCs]:

> Ludwig (1966) pointed out that ASCs have both maladaptive expressions (for example, acute psychotic reactions and manifestations of organic lesions) and adaptive expressions (for example, the shamanic trance for healing purposes and new experiences of knowledge and growth in mystical states). . . . Meditation of any denomination or persuasion has been the religiously sanctioned method for the induction of the highest state of consciousness or Meditative ASC. A review of the psychological and philosophical analyses provided by many authors (James, 1902; Susuki, 1952; Stace, 1961; Deikman, 1966; Prince and Savage, 1972) revealed a commonality of features. . . .
>
> These experiential characteristics permitted the categorization of meditative experiences as ASCs. (214:78)

Despite the authors' erroneous claim that the shamanistic ASC is an "adaptive expression," it is important to note their "categorization of meditative experiences *as* ASCs" or altered states of consciousness. In other words, meditation experiences themselves constitute an altered state.

The altered states of consciousness that meditation typically develops tend to finally result in a radically restructured and false view of one's self and society. Characteristically, one ends up thinking the material universe is a dream or an illusion and that one's true nature is one essence with God. Haridas Chaudhuri observes in his *Philosophy of Meditation*:

> On attaining cosmic consciousness a person's world view undergoes a radical transformation. The consensus of all mystics and sages . . . is that the world of normal experience is now revealed as unreal, as phenomenal, as a mere appearance, as a bad dream from which one wakes up with a sigh of relief. (195:59).

Further:

> Decisive behavior changes follow from this state of consciousness, and the full realization of nirvana actuates a permanent alteration of the meditator's consciousness per se. With the meditator's realization of nirvana, aspects of his ego and of his normal consciousness are abandoned, never to arise again. (400:148)

The individual *person* is radically affected, and aspects of his being are destroyed, "never to rise again."

Dr. Jack Kornfield was trained for six years in Southeast Asia and teaches Buddhist *Vipassana* meditation. As a *result* of his experiences he eventually became a Theravadin Buddhist monk. He also has a doctorate in psychology and is the author of *Living Buddhist Masters*. He observes, "One articulation of the purpose of spiritual practice and a viewpoint that is a product of it as well is to come to understand *that we don't exist*" (400:15 emphasis added). Our body and personality are illusions, and the goal of meditation is to escape from, or "transcend" them in order to discover our "true" inner nature.

There are personal and social consequences to such as a view. In the words of Maharishi Mahesh Yogi, the guru of transcendental meditation, the true self of the enlightened meditator "is uninvolved with activity . . . and it is uninvolved with the selves of individual beings" (225:212). For the meditator, the entire world and all its activities is "like a world of dolls and toys" whom he long ago discarded as an adult (225:157).

Furthermore, gurus and meditators often think they are one nature with God as a result of what they experience in their meditation practices: Muktananda says, "The Guru is God Himself . . ." (235:98; cf. pp. 99–106); Sai Baba tells his followers, "You are the God of this universe" (236:112) and "You *are* God in reality" (237:68); Rajneesh says, "As you are, you are God" (238:362).

Because the very purpose of meditation is to reinterpret what we think of as reality as "illusion" and what we normally think of as "illusion" as greater or "higher" reality, most meditation systems view the perceptions of normal consciousness as *maya* or illusion, as a "trap" that one must escape from if one is to find true liberation and spiritual enlightenment. As Dr. Walsh observes,

> To date, I have seen no explanations other than the almost universal ones among the meditative—yogic traditions that normal man is an automaton, more asleep than awake, etc.

And,

> A remarkably wide range of meditation and yogic disciplines . . . assert that whether we know it or not, untrained individuals are prisoners of their own minds, totally and unwittingly trapped by a continuous inner fantasy-dialog which creates an all-consuming illusion or *maya*. . . . "Nor-

mal" man is thus seen as asleep or dreaming. . . . When the individual permanently disidentifies from or eradicates this dream he is said to have awakened and can now recognize the true nature of his former state and that of the population. This awakening or enlightenment is the aim of the meditative-yogic disciplines. (200: 156–157)

Development of Psychic Powers

Almost all forms of meditation lead to the eventual development of psychic abilities. This is acknowledged by researchers and practitioners alike. *Psychology Today* associate editor and psychologist Daniel Goleman has a Ph.D. in clinical psychology from Harvard and is an authority on Buddhist *Vipassana* [mindfulness] meditation. In his article, "The Buddha on Meditation and States of Consciousness," Goleman observes that " . . . every school of meditation acknowledges them [psychic powers] as by-products of advanced stages of mastery." (194:218).

A popular teacher of meditation, Anthony Norvell, teaches:

> Psychic power expresses itself in many forms. It is known as intuition, clairvoyance, clairaudience, precognition, mental telepathy, telekinesis, cosmic perception and spiritism. The techniques for developing all these various forms of psychism are the same. Mystic meditation is the means by which you may reach into the higher psychic centers of consciousness and channel the tremendous forces that await your joyous discovery. (206:91)

Leading consciousness researcher John White acknowledges that "psychic development is likely in the course of one's [meditative] practice" (203:48). A three-year study by Karlis Osis and Edwin Bokert also revealed a correlation between meditation and psychic ability (394).

Television personality and parapsychologist Patricia Mischell testifies that "one of the unforeseen bonuses of meditation is that many people experience an increasing or unfolding of their mental-telepathy abilities, clairaudience, and clairvoyance through meditation" (204:126).

The conclusion of several experimental studies is that "Meditation is an effective means of producing controlled psi [psychic] interactions" (205:339).

Another writer discusses the ability of meditation to induce astral projection and spirit contact:

> Transcendental meditation is used as the means for releasing the soul from the physical body and projecting it into the astral realms. While you are

out on the astral [plane], your soul may acquire knowledge from [dead] ancient masters. You may become instructed in the arts, music, languages, history or the mystical secrets back of the cosmos. When you enter that mysterious fourth dimensional world of spirit, you can tap unlimited powers and soar to mystic realms where the immortals dwell. (206:153)

Psychic powers, however they are mediated in men, are typically spiritistic powers, not the result of some allegedly divine human potential. We know this is true because whenever spiritism is found, psychic powers are also found (396). Thus, the individual who develops these powers through meditation invariably involves himself in the world of spiritism, whether knowingly or unknowingly. Because new age meditation develops psychic powers, a common goal of occultism, such meditation is properly classified as a form of occult practice.

The Possibility of Spirit Possession

One problem with altered states of consciousness and psychic abilities is not only the false ideas they characteristically produce, but that they can easily lead to direct spiritistic influence or possession. Even advanced practitioners of meditation freely confess this.

Rolling Thunder, a Shaman leader in the Shoshonee and Cherokee tribes confesses, "If it is not done correctly, evil spirits can get into people while they are meditating" (196:110). The problem is that even when it is done *correctly*, altered states of consciousness produced by meditation tend to foster spiritistic influence or possession (see chapter 10).

Despite the modern reluctance to deal forthrightly and responsibly with the category of the demonic, the fact remains that meditation is one of the major methods available for becoming possessed by spirits who are really demons (see chapter 6).

The personal testimony of endless numbers of gurus, psychics, mediums, other occultists, and scholarly authorities testify to this. Dr. Weldon's Ph.D. dissertation, for example, researched over twenty different Hindu and Buddhist gurus; every one had been spirit-influenced or possessed, the apparent result of their meditative practices (294; cf. ref. 111). In other words, it was *during their meditation* that these gurus became spirit-influenced or possessed.

Do we really believe that spirits will not make use of meditative practices which alter states of consciousness and facilitate their ability to possess individuals when this is what serves their purposes of influencing men? Indeed, the very nature and goals of meditation suggest the probability of spiritistic involvement. In her book *Spirit Communication for the Millions*, Doris H. Buckley observes that through meditation, "greater power [becomes available] so that the [mediumistic] channel develops more quickly" (211:156).

Furthermore, the spirits themselves actually endorse new age meditation. In the books dictated through their human mediums, the spirits enthusiastically recommend meditative practices as a means to contact them. Ruth Montgomery was a former hard-nosed, skeptical newspaper reporter, but she was eventually converted to the world of spiritism, became a medium herself, and has published over a dozen books inspired and/or dictated by her spirit guides. Singlehandedly, she has interested millions of people in the spirit world. In one of her books, *A World Beyond*, the alleged spirit of the famous dead trance medium, Arthur Ford, communicates through her. The spirit actively endorses new age meditation: "Now let's speak of the value of meditation. . . . Remember in meditation to breathe deeply at first. . . . use the mantra . . . and feel yourself melding with the universal whole. . . . spend at least fifteen or twenty minutes each day in this stillness" (212:141).

India-born Douglas Shaw, the grandson of Yogi Ishwar Dayal, observes, "I have watched Hindu worshippers by the scores chanting for hours before idols during a special *Puja* (worship) Season, and I have literally felt the supernatural presence of the gods they were invoking" (239:98). He comments that "being taken over by an evil spirit . . . is a very real possibility" in meditation (239:102).

British scholar Os Guinness observes: "Many . . . who practice yoga or Zen meditation have found they have opened their minds to blackness and spiritism, seeing themselves as mediums and describing themselves as possessed" (240:298).

Consider the following experience of Swami Muktananda who describes the results of his meditation in his spiritual autobiography. He observes that "when I sat for meditation" his own body acted as if he "were possessed by a god or a bad spirit" (223:122). Muktananda details an entire chapter of such experiences, including more bizarre encounters than we list below. We quote at length to give the reader an accurate feel for the potential consequences of meditation:

I was assailed by all sorts of perverse and defiling emotions. My body started to move, and went on like this in a confused sort of way. . . . After a time, my breathing changed, becoming disturbed. Sometimes my abdomen would swell with air, after which I would exhale it with great force. Often the breath that I took in would be held inside me. I became more and more frightened.

My mind was sick with fear. I called Babu Rao and said to him, "Babu, go home now. The rhythm of my heart and the state of my mind are not good. I feel sure that I am going to die tonight of heart failure. . . . I don't think I shall live through this night, and if I do, it will be to go mad. I am losing my mind. . . . "

My thoughts became confused, meaningless. My limbs and body got hotter and hotter. My head felt heavy, and every pore in me began to ache. When I breathed out, my breath stopped outside. When I breathed in, it stopped inside. This was terribly painful, and I lost my courage. Something told me that I would die at any moment.

By now it was after 9:00. Someone had seated himself in my eyes and was making me see things. It seemed that I was being controlled by some power which made me do all these things. I no longer had a will of my own. My madness was growing all the time. My intellect was completely unstable.

My fear increased every second. I heard hordes of people screaming frightfully, as if it were the end of the world. I looked out of the small window of my hut and saw strange creatures from six to fifty feet tall, neither demons nor demigods, but human in form, dancing naked, their mouths gaping open. The screeching was horrible and apocalyptic. I was completely conscious, but was watching my madness, which appeared to be real.

Then, from over the water, a moonlike sphere about four feet in diameter came floating in. It stopped in front of me. This radiant, white ball struck against my eyes and then passed inside me. I am writing this just as I saw it. It is not a dream or an allegory, but a scene which actually happened—that sphere came down from the sky and entered me. A second later the bright light penetrated into my *nadis* [psychic channels]. My tongue curled up against my palate, and my eyes closed. I saw a dazzling light in my forehead and I was terrified. I was still locked up in the lotus posture, and then my head was forced down and glued to the ground. . . . Afterward I sat down in the lotus posture and once again started to meditate on the Guru. As soon as I sat down, my mind became completely indrawn. My body, fixed in lotus posture, began to sway. . . . This Meditation went on for an hour and a half, and then a new process began.

> I started to make a sound like a camel, which alternated with the roaring of a tiger. I must have roared very loudly, for the people around actually thought that a tiger had gotten into the sugarcane field.
>
> I am in a terrible state. I have gone completely insane. . . . My body began to twist. Now, it was not I who meditated; Meditation forced itself on me. It came spontaneously; it was in all the joints of my body. All the blood cells in my body were spinning, and *prana* flowed through the *nadis* at an astounding speed. Then, suddenly, a red light came before me with such force that it seemed to have been living inside me. It was two feet tall and shone brightly. I clearly saw myself burning, but I did not feel the heart of the fire on the outside. Every part of my body was emitting loud crackling and popping sounds. (223:75–79)

After it was all over, Muktananda concluded that he had been spiritually enlightened. Like endless gurus with similar experiences, he teaches his students that while following the meditative path, they too will experience what he did. But, he tells them they should not worry, for it is all part of the normal results of meditation leading to "enlightenment." He also observes how easily their meditation will lead them to spirit contact: "They talk to and receive instruction from gods and goddesses" (223:xxii).

Muktananda's experience and teachings are not unique; they are the norm among gurus and their followers. Consider the following examples:

Swami Rudrananda.

> Slowly Swami Nityananda [in spirit form] came toward me and entered into my physical body. For three hours I felt nothing of myself but that the saint had possessed me. It was a terrifying experience and it required all my faith not to fight it. (208:13)

Swami Satchidananda.

> I felt myself fall into a sort of trance. . . . I was overjoyed with the feeling that my Master [Sivananda] had entered into my own system [body]. (230:119–120)

Da (Bubba) Free John.

Da (Bubba) Free John (Franklin Jones) illustrates the state of the disciple being possessed by the "spiritual form" of the guru or master. His text *Garbage and the Goddess* describes the experiences he and his disciples underwent at his Persimmon, New York ashram from March to July, 1974. While Free John describes normal everyday living as being "possessed by the most insidious daemonic force in the universe" (229:51), one would hardly suspect it from the following descriptions of, as he calls it, "life in God."

Perhaps Free John is correct: "True wisdom is the capacity for perfect madness" (231:1). We cite several descriptions by different individuals who encountered this phenomenon of mass possession as described in Free John's *Garbage and the Goddess*. (The descriptions are reminiscent of the mass Shaker possessions in the 1840s and related spiritistic incidents; [219:75–83])

> The most significant thing about this event is that contrary to the usual beliefs, even of traditional spirituality, the Guru *literally* enters and transforms. It is a kind of possession. It is God-Possession. Bubba animates this body. (229:151)

> People were screaming and howling and weeping, emitting strange grunts and snarls, their bodies jerking, writhing, and assuming yogic mudras. (229:72).

> I felt utterly possessed, my body was possessed, and my hands started to move, and I couldn't control them. I had no control at all. My face started taking on expressions. (229:263)

> My body wasn't mine. I didn't even *feel* my body as mine. There was only this sensation I've had before in Bubba's Presence, the feeling that this body is being used. . . . I went in and at first I was totally out of my mind. I was screaming for a long time. . . . I was making very strange sounds. . . . It is God-possession. It is God totally taking over your form. (229:282–283, 285)

> I was so insane I didn't know what was happening at all. (229:66)

> Last night I was led to this spontaneous experience of conducting the Force, and I felt possessed, really possessed. Then suddenly I wasn't my body any more. (229:312)

Other gurus also describe the phenomena of possession of the disciple:

Rudrananda.

> There are times when the psychic system of the teacher will seem to control the student. He will feel possessed by his teacher. There is nothing to fear from this. It is only a stage of growth through which he [the student] is passing. (208:103)

Sri Chinmoy.

> If you remain calm and quiet and allow your spiritual Guide to enter into you, you will become flooded with Peace. This kind of tuning in is not

only a valid and correct practice, but is *essential* for one who has placed himself under the guidance of a spiritual Master. (233:113, emphasis added)

Rajneesh.

Whenever a master wants to help you, cleanse your energy channels, your passage [kundalini spinal passage], if it is blocked, he simply possesses you. He simply descends into you. . . . If the disciple is really surrendered, the master can possess him immediately. (234:68)

Merging with "Ultimate Reality"

Almost all forms of meditation have a similar goal. Our own study of meditative systems and occultism has convinced us that the end result of meditation is a goal similar or identical to many forms of occultic self-transformation. Other researchers have made similar conclusions based on their own detailed research. Most meditation systems, despite different external characteristics, all seek to attain the same end state: a psychic merging with "ultimate reality."

This supposed ultimate reality is usually defined either as a merging into the "One" (an impersonal God such as the Hindu *Brahman*) or as "merging" into the "void," as in Buddhist *Nirvana*, or their equivalent in various forms of Western occultism. In all cases, the end result is the same: the destruction of the individual personality, which, after all, was only an illusion.

Dr. Daniel Goleman has studied meditation systems extensively. He teaches courses on meditation at Harvard, is a committed Buddhist with a Hindu guru, Neem Karoli Baba—the guru that Ram Dass made famous in his multi-million selling text *Be Here Now* (639).

In Goleman's *The Varieties of the Meditative Experience*, we discover that (Biblical meditation aside), almost all forms of meditation are strikingly similar. For example, he discusses a dozen different meditative systems which are representative of all varieties of meditation in general. Goleman observes that it was a remark by Joseph Goldstein that "all meditation systems either aim for One or Zero—union with God or emptiness" which became a type of guideline in his research (442:xix).

Nevertheless, despite outer differences between these systems, all of them are potentially harmful due to their anti-Christian world view, occultic techniques and openness to spiritistic elements.

For example, in examining these different systems, "At this [their] most universal level, all meditation systems are variations on a single process for transforming consciousness. The core elements of this process are found in every system, and its specifics undercut ostensible differences among the various schools of meditation" (442:106).

While it is true that "the meditator's beliefs determines how he interprets and labels his meditation experiences," nevertheless, "all [systems] seem to refer to a single state [of consciousness] with identical characteristics. These many terms for a single state come from Theravadan Buddhism, raja yoga, Sufism, [the] Kabbalah, kundalini yoga, Zen, and TM, respectively" (201:112).

Regardless of the system of meditation employed, they all aim at the same end state: a radical (occultic) transformation of the individual and how he perceives himself and the world. Dr. Goleman concludes:

> The literature of every Meditation system describes an altered state. . . . Virtually every system of Meditation recognizes the awakened state as the ultimate goal of meditation. . . .
>
> Each path labels this end state differently. But no matter how diverse the names, these paths all propose the same basic formula in an alchemy [transformation] of the self: the diffusion of the effects of Meditation into the meditator's waking, dreaming and sleep states. At the outset, this diffusion requires the meditator's effort. As he progresses, it becomes easier for him to maintain prolonged meditative awareness in the midst of his other activities. As the states produced by his Meditation meld with his waking activity, the awakened state ripens. When it reaches full maturity, it lastingly changes his consciousness, transforming his experience of himself and his universe. (201:115–118)

Indeed, in every major and most minor meditative systems this transformation of personal identity and perception of the universe is achieved principally along occultic, non-Christian lines and at the expense of Biblical truth.

Having now examined the characteristics and goals of most meditation as it is practiced today, there is little doubt that most meditation systems should be classified as occultic training. To view them as positive health practices is simply a delusion.

Potential Dangers

Spirit-possession is not the only danger of meditation. There are several studies in the literature showing the possible physical and psychological harm that can occur from meditation training (e.g., 217). Significantly, these consequences mirror those effects produced by occultic practices in general.

A symposium report by a number of authorities, some of whom practice meditation, "Spiritual and Transpersonal Aspects of Altered States of Consciousness" comments: "Recently the 'fringe benefits' of meditation regarding health, vitality, and cognitive functioning have been broadcast, and increasing numbers of people practice meditation for these purposes. . . . [But] there are many dangers in this journey" (216:62–63). One authority observes, "There can arise a clear vision of the dissolution of the self from moment to moment, and this often leads to a realm of fear and terror, and a kind of inner death" (400:153).

In "Psychiatric Complications of Meditation Practice," Mark Epstein, M.D., and Jonathan Leiff, M.D., discuss some of the potential hazards. Leiff is a graduate of Yale College and the Harvard Medical School and is currently with the Boston University School of Medicine. Epstein is a psychiatrist at Cambridge Hospital, Harvard Medical School. He wrote his undergraduate thesis on Theravadin Buddhist psychology and has practiced *Vipassana* meditation for over a decade. Unfortunately, both authors observe a certain lack of awareness on the part of the public concerning meditation hazards:

> What has not been made clear, however, is the range of side effects of meditative practices that may present to the clinician as psychological disturbance. Some of these complications have already been noted by Western health professionals, others are only too well known within the meditative traditions. The most obvious misuses of Meditation were hinted out by early psychoanalytic investigators, while the more subtle abuses and psychological crises of the advanced practitioner have traditionally been handled by the Meditation teacher. (213:137)

The above cited conclusions are based on the authors' ten years of experience observing literally "hundred of meditators." They note that "practitioners of meditation, often swimming in the rhetoric of transformation, may fail to recognize the regressive nature of much of their experiences" (213:139). After a long discussion of the psychiatric complications noted in the literature, they conclude with a significant observation: "Meditation may be conceptualized as a developmental process that may produce side effects anywhere along the continuum. Some of the side effects may be pathological in nature while some may be temporary distractions or hindrances," and they ask, "How can innocuous side effects of meditation be differentiated from debilitating ones?" (213:144–145).

The point is they cannot be differentiated. One who meditates takes risks with his bodily health, his mental health, and his spiritual health, as research and the traditional and critical literature demonstrates (e.g., ref. 214; 215; 224).

The following characteristics of experiences were reported at the deeper levels of a particular form of Buddhist *Vipassana* meditation, but are not unique to it. They include spontaneous movements, experiencing dramatic "energy flows," unusual breathing, dream and time changes, out of the body experiences, psychic phenomena, etc.

The "spontaneous movement" category included such things as "much twitching," "involuntary jerks," "violent shaking," "spontaneous yoga stretching," "jerking," "weird faces," "drooling," "pain," "arms dancing, head rolling, falling over," "violent shakes," "loosening," "arms flapping like wings," etc. (215:41–45).

Meditators described other experiences, including loss of body awareness, the body disappearing, leaving the body, the head detaching itself, the body growing huge, LSD-like visions, hallucinations, visions of Buddha, etc. Almost half of those completing student questionnaires reported "especially dramatic mood swings." These included huge releases of anger, "screaming mind trips," depression, fantastic mood swings, "turbulence of mind," "days of acute anxiety, depression," "violent crying," restlessness, hellishness, etc. (215:47–49).

Frankly, it is hardly surprising that one hears of meditation-induced casualties: The very process of meditation is *designed* to radically dismantle the divinely-instituted functions of human perception—by deliberately inducing altered states of consciousness which teach us that fantasy is reality and vice versa. If one refuses to play by the rules, one might expect to encounter problems. Many of the horrors experienced by committed meditators are also revealed by Tal Brooke, perhaps the former leading Western disciple of India's premier guru, Sathya Sai Baba. Before receiving his graduate degree in religion from Princeton University, Brooke wrote *Riders of the Cosmic Circuit* (111), a little known but urgently needed exposé unveiling much Eastern practice for what it really is: a form of metaphysical satanism. But the power of the book also lies in documenting the hazards of many Eastern paths, including the radical breakdown of personal morality, suicides, and insanity (e.g. 111:140–154, 190–202).

Profoundly regressive states of consciousness are one reason why there exists a current state of confusion over just what constitutes so-called "enlightenment"—how to properly evaluate it and distinguish it or its components from psychopathology (madness or insanity). Experiences of "enlightenment" and mental illness are often so similar that even some new agers have expressed bafflement at the correspondence.

Properly evaluating the relationship between enlightenment and psychopathology is a difficult task for some people. The reason is simple. In a large number of meditative traditions what we commonly define as mental illness in the West is actually a sign or component of "enlightenment" in the East. Many Eastern gurus often teach that periods of insanity are an actual *indication* of spiritual enlightenment! This is why it is called "divine madness." Rajneesh quaintly remarks that many of his disciples are going to become zombies, and all to the good:

> You be a Zombie. Be a perfect Zombie. . . . This is what is happening: catalepsy. . . . This is going to happen to many. Don't be afraid when it happens. . . . You become idiotic. . . . And [it is] good, because it will destroy the past. . . . That is the whole meaning of sannyas and discipleship: That your past has been completely washed away—your memory, your ego, your identity—all has to go. (385:11)

Meher Baba teaches that the insane of India (the *Masts*, described as those who in the West would be treated in mental hospitals) are in various stages of spiritual evolution, from elementary stages to advanced ones. They are mad precisely because they are so spiritually committed to God (244:137–139). Baba calls them "God-intoxicated" ones. In the words of biographer and disciple C. B. Purdom:

> They are in a state of mental and physical disorder because their minds are overcome by strong spiritual energies that are far too much for them, forcing them to renounce the world, normal human habits and customs, and civilized society, and to live in a condition of chaos. They are psychological cases beyond the reach of psychoanalysis, because their condition is too advanced and obscure for any known procedures. Their minds are in some way shattered and their brains cannot fully function. Only a spiritual Master, says Baba, who is aware of the divine spirit that possesses them, which causes them to be unfit for normal society, can be of any help to them, and even his help reaches them with difficulty as they are virtually

> shut off from human contact. They are in the world but not of it. In Baba's terms they are 'God-intoxicated souls'. (244:137)

Significantly, they became mad from meditative practices and during some of these practices "by sudden contact with a highly advanced spiritual being" (244:137). Regardless, it is a supposedly a "divine spirit that possessed them which causes them to be unfit for normal society" (244:137).

The famous Ramakrishna experienced insanity while undertaking his duties as a priest in the temple of Kali and also at many other times. He would experience a "divine delirium" and see demonic creatures emerging from him. For him, the truly enlightened soul often acts, in his words, "like a madman" (241:405, cf. p. 548).

Biographer Romain Rolland describes part of Ramakrishna's experiences:

> He was no longer capable of performing the temple rites. In the midst of the ritual acts he was seized with fits of unconsciousness, sudden collapses and petrifactions, when he lost the control of the use of his joints and stiffened into a statue. . . . Minute drops of blood oozed through his skin. His whole body seemed on fire. . . . He became the Gods himself. . . . He was the great monkey {god}, Hanuman.
>
> The legion of Gods swooped upon him like a whirlwind. He was torn in pieces. He was divided against himself. His madness returned tenfold. He saw demoniac creatures emerging from him. . . . He remained motionless, watching these manifestations issue from him. . . . He felt madness approaching. . . . Two years went by in this orgy of mental intoxication and despair. (242:36–37,41)

On his own path to enlightenment, Gopi Krishna "passed through almost all the stages of different, mediumistic, psychotic, and other types of mind; [and] for some time I was hovering between sanity and insanity" (243:124). Da Free John extolls the "divine madness" of his own gurus, Nityananda, Muktananda, and Rudrananda:

> True yogis are living forceful beings. They are madmen, absolutely mad—and absolutely dangerous. . . . Look at Nityananda—he severed heads all his life. . . . Those who came to him . . . were wiped out, torn apart. . . . My experience with people like Rudi, Muktananda, Nityananda, and others was like this: I would be sitting in my house in New York by myself, and this force would enter me, it would practically break my neck, and my body and mind would be taken over. And I would walk around as Nityananda, as Rudi, as Muktananda, literally. . . . These wildmen served that process [of enlightenment]. (399:275 cf. 398:256–258)

Such stories could be multipled ad nauseum. This modern penchant for the reinterpretation of insanity as spirituality is illustrated in books such as those edited by consciousness researchers Stanislav and Christina Grof, e.g., *Spiritual Emergency: When Personal Transformation Becomes a Crisis* and *The Stormy Search for the Self*. Chapter titles from *Spiritual Emergency* include such items as "When Insanity Is a Blessing: The Message of Shamanism" (337:77–97). The introduction to the book informs us that pathological states of consciousness, when "properly understood and treated supportively" can "be healing and have very beneficial effects on the people who experience them" (337:X).

❧ ❧ ❧

All of this illustrates the deep spiritual confusion of our time. Meditation today is almost universally seen as a positive path bringing physical health and spiritual wholeness. Unfortunately, many of those who suffer from such an interpretation have little knowledge of either the spiritual (occult) tradition behind meditation or the dynamics of spiritual warfare.

Therapeutic Touch

Definition: Therapeutic Touch is a form of psychic healing stressing the manipulation of alleged body energies (e.g., *prana*).

Founders: Dolores Krieger and Dora Kunz.

How Does It Claim to Work? Therapeutic Touch claims to work by channeling (psychic transfer) the therapist's supposed *prana* into the patient. Practitioners claim that this prods the patient's own life energies toward healing.

Scientific Evaluation: Discredited.

Occultic Potential: Psychic healing; spiritism; developing psychic powers; occultic self-transformation; use of occult meditation; and altered states of consciousness.

Major Problem: Therapeutic Touch appears so innocent and is sufficiently accepted within the nursing profession that many people refuse to classify it as a form of psychic healing.

Biblical/Christian Evaluation: Practices that are occultic or potentially occultic should be avoided.

Potential Dangers: Occultic influences.

TWENTY

THERAPEUTIC TOUCH

A cover story for *Time* magazine noted that one of the most popular new age "medical" techniques is Therapeutic Touch (254:64). According to *Psychology Today* "an estimated twenty to thirty thousand nurses practice the form of mental healing called Non-Contact Therapeutic Touch, or NCTT" (275:28).

But the twenty to thirty thousand figure is probably low. The co-originator of the method, Dolores Krieger, Ph.D., R.N., has personally taught the practice to at least ten thousand nurses. Furthermore, approximately 80 percent of those to whom Dr. Krieger teaches the technique proceed "to incorporate Therapeutic Touch into their health care practices" (60:3). In turn, hundreds of these nurses have become teachers themselves, teaching hundreds of others. Thus, a more accurate figure would probably be forty to fifty thousand nurses. This constitutes a small but significant percentage of the entire nursing profession (see introduction; 431).

Therapeutic Touch has also influenced the field of Christian nursing. In fact, discernment concerning this and other new age techniques is so marginal that the *Journal of Christian Nursing* felt it necessary to run a three-part series critiquing such practices (255:23–26; 256:30–34; 257:16–21).

Scores and perhaps hundreds of hospitals employ Therapeutic Touch teams for use in their treatment programs:

> There are now many such Therapeutic Touch teams in hospitals around the country—Boston, New York City, Austin, Tucson, San Francisco, and Portland, OR, to name but a few. In some hospitals, Therapeutic Touch is used for

> its relaxation effect before the administration of anesthesia. It is also used in cardiac units previous to the insertion of cardiac pacemakers and it is used on apprehensive patients who are to have dental procedures. (60:147)

Therapeutic Touch has been the subject of numerous Ph.D. dissertations and a variety of books have been published such as: *Therapeutic Touch: A Book of Readings* (258) and Dora Kunz' *Spiritual Aspects of the Healing Arts* (45).

Scientific and other research on the practice has been conducted and published in major journals such as *Nursing Research* (1981, 1986), *The Journal of Continuing Education in Nursing* (1979), *Topics in Clinical Nursing* (1979, 1980), *American Journal of Nursing* (1976, 1979), RN (1980) as well as in several parapsychological journals, e.g., *Journal of the American Society for Psychical Research* (1965) and *Psychoenergetic Systems* (1976).

The practice of Therapeutic Touch was first taught at the graduate level at New York University, a scientifically prestigious institution and the largest private university in the United States. The course was titled "Frontiers in Nursing: The Actualization of Potential for Therapeutic Human Field Interaction." This was the first class of its kind in the United States within a fully accredited nursing curriculum for the master's degree (60:vii). Having been taught at such a prestigious university, the course gained credibility and has spread to at least fifty (277:432) and perhaps as many as one hundred universities around the country.

Why is Therapeutic Touch so popular? The popularity of Therapeutic Touch results from four factors: (1) its seeming effectiveness; (2) its appearance as a safe, natural technique; (3) its acceptance within the nursing profession and use in scores of hospitals; and (4) among Christians, the superficial similarity to the Biblical practice of laying on of hands.

Therapeutic Touch has gained wide support because those who use it claim that it is simple to learn, safe, and more importantly, it *works*. Dr. Krieger observes "on a purely pragmatic basis, therapeutic touch works, and therein lies its value" (60:90) and "the safety level of Therapeutic Touch for both healer and healee has been excellent, and this accounts for much of its enthusiastic acceptance" (60:147–148).

The Nature of Therapeutic Touch

Dolores Krieger was taught this Therapeutic Touch technique by occultist Dora Kunz, the current president of the Theosophical Society. She confesses, "I had been taught the technique of laying-on of hands by Kunz . . . " (295:28; cf. 81:182–183, 6:22).* Because she learned the technique from Kunz, Dolores Krieger dedicated her book, *The Therapeutic Touch: How to Use Your Hands to Help or to Heal*, to her (60:ii, viii).

In the introduction, Dr. Krieger not only confesses her great indebtedness to Kunz for the development of the technique, she also describes the occultic background of Kunz. Krieger observes that "she . . . was born with a unique ability to perceive subtle energies around living beings. From the time she was a child, she studied the function and control of these energies under the tutelage of [leading theosophist] Charles W. Leadbeater, one of the great seers [occultists] of the twentieth century" (60:4). Krieger also describes her and Kunz' involvement with Oskar Estebany, a Hungarian medium who believes that "he [is] a channel for the spirit of Jesus the Christ" who gives him healing powers (60:6).

Significantly, Dora Kunz is herself a spiritist who looks to "invisible intelligences," "angels," and theosophy's "Ascended Masters" for inspiration and guidance (276:340).

What all this means is that Dolores Krieger was taught an occult method of healing by Dora Kunz, a spiritist trained personally by one of the most famous occultists of the twentieth century. What Kunz had learned about healing as an occultist and spiritist she taught to Dolores Krieger.

But her training under Kunz was not the only source for the development of Therapeutic Touch. Dr. Krieger also studied yoga, *Ayurvedic* medicine (which incorporates Hindu occultism applied to medicine), occultic *Tibetan* Medicine (97), Chinese medicine (19; see chapter 9), and related practices.

It was from such occultic Eastern sources that Krieger came to believe in such things as *prana* and the Hindu *chakra* system. She explains, " . . . that prana [psychic energy] can be transferred from one individual to another, may not be so readily apparent to us unless we have gotten into the *practice* and literature of hatha yoga, tantric yoga, or the martial arts of the Orient" (60:13, emphasis added). Citing Leadbeater's text *The Chakras*, she notes that "the Aruvedic literature describes these *chakras* as agents for the

---

* The Theosophical Society is an occult organization begun by medium Helena P. Blavatsky in the nineteenth century. It stresses the development of psychic powers, occult practices such as astrology and yoga, spirit contact, and Eastern methods of meditation and healing.[317].

transforming of universal energies, as they become available to our bodies, to levels which can be used by human beings" (60:46).

Thus, Therapeutic Touch was developed as a result of one occultist, Dora Kunz, teaching a method of psychic healing to a willing student named Dolores Krieger. Krieger's additional research into Eastern mystical traditions and the occult refined the practice. Because what Dolores Krieger really learned was a form of psychic healing, Therapeutic Touch should be labeled as such and not passed off as scientific medicine or a form of true divine spiritual healing.

Therapeutic Touch claims to work by channeling psychic energies from nurse to patient. By the alleged transfer of *prana* (psychic energy) from the healer to the patient, the practitioner thinks he/she can stimulate the patient's own *prana* toward healing. Krieger confesses,

> The act of healing, then, would entail the channeling of this energy flow by the healer for the well being of the sick individual. . . . The healer projects this energy, *prana*, for the use [healing] of another person. . . . The expertise [of the healer] lies in the healer's ability to *direct* energies, and that is what you must learn if you would play the role of healer. . . . The functional basis of Therapeutic Touch lies in the intelligent direction of significant life energies from the person playing the role of healer to the healee (the ill person). (60:13, 17, 23)

Janet Macrae, Ph.D., R.N., is adjunct professor of nursing at New York University and teaches workshops on Therapeutic Touch throughout the country. In her "Therapeutic Touch as Meditation" she asserts:

> The practice of Therapeutic Touch is based on the idea of an energy transfer. . . . During the process of Therapeutic Touch the practitioner, with a clear, focused intent, channels life energy through himself or herself to the patient. He or she also helps the patient to assimilate the energy by releasing congestion and balancing disharmonious rhythms. Thus the practitioner, through regular practice, must develop a sensitivity to the subtle energy which surrounds and interpenetrates the physical body. Borelli (1981) has written that this sensitivity to very subtle stimuli is a central characteristic of both Therapeutic Touch and meditation. (417:286, 273)

In other words, the nurse or health professional who wishes to practice Therapeutic Touch "must develop a sensitivity" to occultic ("subtle") energies. This is why Dr. Macrae observes that "It is becoming obvious that Therapeutic Touch is not only a technique for helping to alleviate suffering but is also a vehicle or means of self-transformation" (417:272). In fact, she views Therapeutic Touch as an actual form of (occultic) meditation (417:275–80).

Occultic Influences

No one should doubt that Therapeutic Touch is really an occult practice; unfortunately, its occult nature is usually hidden by scientific associations and use in respected medical facilities. Thus, it is often discussed in a scientific context with a scientific veneer and is used in many hospitals and health centers throughout the country as an accepted adjunct to traditional methods of treatment.

Like most psychic healing, the process also *appears* entirely innocent. Indeed, these two facts—its acceptance in hospitals and its innocent appearance—are the very reasons so many people have a difficult time accepting the practice as a form of psychic healing.

Most of the Christian nurses responding to a critique co-authored by Dr. Weldon in the *Journal of Christian Nursing* (JCN) were in favor of the practice even after reading the critique! Correspondence with the editor of the *Journal* revealed that, "The responses I printed on the Letters to the Editor page were typical of those we received responding to the article on Therapeutic Touch. I think nurses are so accustomed to thinking Therapeutic Touch is a good thing that they simply don't know how to think critically about it" (261:1).

But one wonders, if evangelical Christian nurses cannot detect an occultic practice, how can other health professionals and laymen who are not even cognizant of the categories of spiritual warfare do so? Consider two typical responses:

> I am concerned that the narrow perspective from which Therapeutic Touch was critiqued will lead JCN readers to assume [it] is off-limits for Christian nurses. One does not have to be an Eastern mystic to practice Therapeutic Touch. The Christian church has practiced laying on of hands for centuries. Also research studies done by nurses using accepted research methods have shown the positive effects of Therapeutic Touch on client well-being. I would hate to see this promising technique thrown out. (260:39)
>
> I am a Christian and I not only participate in holistic nursing activities, I practice and teach Therapeutic Touch. Was it oversight or did the au-

> thors of "Holistic Healing and Therapeutic Touch" deliberately leave out Delores Krieger's most important message? She emphasizes that you must do Therapeutic Touch with compassion and love. When I am dealing with patients who are dying, does it really matter if Therapeutic Touch or my voice affords them relaxation and pain relief? . . . I have [no] awareness of an occult or Satanic emphasis in [Therapeutic Touch]. . . . (260:39)

But only a few short years ago, the entire process of training in Therapeutic Touch would have been termed the training of psychic healers. In fact, there is little doubt that the practice of Therapeutic Touch is laying the groundwork for the acceptance of more traditional psychic healers in our hospitals.

We believe Therapeutic Touch should be considered a form of psychic healing, and to begin we will show how Dr. Krieger teaches her method of Therapeutic Touch. The method is taught through carefully controlled exercises where one learns to "sense" or "feel" subtle psychic energies. The nurse or health practitioner must learn to develop specific meditative techniques and to enter altered states of consciousness by a process of "centering" as a means to become psychically sensitive. As one disciple noted, "By the seventh week of class, I was convinced that centering myself altered my state of consciousness" (60:122).

Meditation and altered states of consciousness are so crucial to the technique of Therapeutic Touch that Krieger confesses, "I sometimes refer to Therapeutic Touch as a yoga of healing" (60:37). In fact, the technique does not appear to work unless one enters meditative, altered states of consciousness: e.g., "I failed to center myself and thereby failed to help my friend" (60:123).

Dowsing, itself a spiritistic activity (259), is another method used to teach the nurse that he/she can contact psychic energy and to learn to direct it (60:30–34). Thus, in teaching therapeutic touch, "a kind of dowsing rod will be used to demonstrate this field pattern [of psychic energy] . . ."(60:30).

The point is this: The techniques for teaching Therapeutic Touch involve the same methods used traditionally for the training of psychic healers—using meditation, altered states of consciousness, and other means to sensitize a person to the psychic realm.

In essence, Krieger trains nurses and other health practitioners to become psychically "sensitive" so they can examine the alleged energy field of the healee "for differences in the quality of energy flow" (60:35). Why is the "energy flow" important? Because as is true for many other forms of new age medicine, most illnesses are seen as a "blockage" of this energy. Thus, part of the goal is to find:

> A blockage in the meridians through which the *chi*, or vital energy, flows through the body. . . . When one feels this sense of congestion during the Assessment [examination or diagnosis] of Therapeutic Touch, it feels as though there is no movement in the energy field in that particular area of the person. (60:53)

Therefore, like other psychic healers, the Therapeutic Touch healer must mobilize and direct his or her own supposed psychic energy, placing it directly into the patient for healing. By directing their own energy into the patient, the practitioners of Therapeutic Touch can supposedly help "unblock" the patient's energy and thereby promote healing: "The conscious direction by the healer of his or her excess body energies [will] assist the healee to repattern his or her own energies" (60:36). This process of allegedly unblocking the energy is soothingly termed "unruffling" the field.

According to Krieger, what brings about healing is, (1) the ability of the healer to direct psychic energy into the person, and (2) that person's own recuperative system responding appropriately to the released energy. In other words, the healer is one who accelerates the healing process by psychically unblocking the energy obstruction of the healee, permitting the patient's own body to heal itself (60:17).

As in other forms of psychic healing, in Therapeutic Touch the patient can actually *feel* the psychic energy being transmitted into them. Consider the response of one of Dolores Krieger's patients, "I always know when Dee [Dolores Krieger] is working on me. I can tell exactly where her hands are from the deep heat that is generated inside my body, and I can feel the energy flow she transmits to me" (60:9). But again such a description is indistinguishable from that which occurs in psychic/spiritistic healing in general (see chapter 13).

In essence, there is little doubt that Therapeutic Touch is a form of psychic healing. But this presents us with a major problem. Genuine psychic healing is accomplished through spiritistic power (6:29–190). This is why anyone who examines the standard works by psychic healers cannot help but observe the connections that exist between Therapeutic Touch and traditional psychic healing accomplished through the power of the spirit world.

As two examples we could mention psychic Lawrence LeShan's *The Medium, the Mystic and the Physicist* (296) or channeler Barbara Brennan's *Hands of Light: A Guide to Healing Through the Human Energy Field* (47), which stresses the importance of contact with spirit guides and their healing abilities.

But even with all of the above information many people have refused to consider Therapeutic Touch as a form of psychic healing, perhaps because the practice looks so innocent. What additional proof can we offer that Therapeutic Touch is really a form of psychic healing and not a scientific practice or a form of true spiritual healing as claimed?

We have just seen that the method of teaching Therapeutic Touch involves the same components as found in the teaching of psychic healing in general. Seven additional characteristic associations Therapeutic Touch has with the practice of psychic healing convince us that it is proper to consider Therapeutic Touch as a form of psychic healing.

First, Dora Kunz, who instructed Dr. Krieger in developing Therapeutic Touch, freely confesses she is a psychic healer and that the practice she taught Krieger was a form of psychic healing (279:213–261, 289–305). Second, there is little doubt that Dr. Krieger herself is also a psychic healer (60:91). What method of healing would psychic healers teach if not psychic healing?

Third, altered states of consciousness are essential for the effective working of Therapeutic Touch (60:35–41) and yet these altered states are notorious for fostering spirit contact (see chapter 10). Krieger confesses "that there are various states of consciousness to be experienced during Therapeutic Touch. For instance, I have noted that I have had experiences in five different modes or states of consciousness during the Assessment [diagnosis]" (60:69). One example, the "fifth" state of consciousness is experiencing an extremely deep level of one's being "where it is possible for one facet of an individual's personality to be in dialogue with another facet, and it is from that depth [of consciousness] that the Assessment [diagnosis] arises" (60:70). But this description is reminiscent of psychic healers who claim to diagnose by a "dialogue" with their "higher self," archetypal consciousness, or some other euphemisms for what may really be a spirit entity.

In her article, "High Order Emergence of the Self During Therapeutic Touch," Dr. Krieger confesses:

> A core phase of Therapeutic Touch, which appears to be at the heart of this high-order emergence of the deep structures of self, is an act of center-

> ing, which begins the healing process. Centering is a sustained act of interiority in which the healer turns her attention within, towards the innermost reaches of her consciousness of self. In the very act itself she enters into a qualitatively different state of consciousness and of quietude. She maintains this centered state throughout the other stages of Therapeutic Touch as she attempts to assess the healee's problem and then go on to help or to heal that condition. Thus, this centered state of consciousness is maintained throughout the healing experience. . . .
>
> Over time this cultivation of mindfulness can enter significantly into the individual's life style, for centering introduces a meditative quality into the background of one's activities of daily living. Slowly one begins to realize that that state "belongs" to oneself, that one is "really" part of that Reality. . . . (418:265)

Again, this description by Krieger is little different than that supplied by innumerable mediums (such as Barbara Brennan mentioned above) who describe how their own spirit guides help them in assessing the patient's condition and the long-term effects such practices can have in their lives.

Fourth, like all methods of spiritistic or psychic healing, Therapeutic Touch develops psychic abilities. Dr. Krieger admits that the practice of Therapeutic Touch commonly produces "a significant change in lifestyle taking, on the average, two to three weeks of continued use of Therapeutic Touch" and that the most frequent development encountered is telepathic abilities:

> Most frequently the change is based on an increased use of natural [i.e. psychic] faculties—faculties that our culture usually allows to lie dormant within us. One such faculty is that which we have called telepathy. This faculty does not announce itself dramatically; rather, it appears unobtrusively and touches one's life in small, frequently routine ways. . . . What is interesting about the person who is deeply into Therapeutic Touch is that these incidents occur frequently. . . . (60:70)

This is why Dr. Krieger informs us that,

> it should not come as a surprise that he or she [the practitioner of Therapeutic Touch] is going to succeed in developing latent [psychic] abilities in communication. . . . It is because the interaction between healer and healee can become so highly personalized that I call it a yoga of healing. Through it, one learns to develop many latent human [psychic] abilities; as in yoga, the expert practice of Therapeutic Touch demands concentration. . . . It is an effort so constant that it can become a way of life. (60:71)

The mention of yoga in conjunction with the practice of Therapeutic Touch is more than incidental. Yoga itself is an occult practice which develops psychic abilities. Viewing Therapeutic Touch as a form of yoga is indeed appropriate, as even practitioners have confessed. Janet Macrae, Ph.D., R.N, in her "Therapeutic Touch as Meditation" observes that it is most appropriate to "look at Therapeutic Touch within the context of the most comprehensive yogic system, that of Patanjali. . . . [If we do so] we can then find aspects of the eight limbs [branches] of this [yoga] within the one act of Therapeutic Touch" (417:282). She also discusses how it can be viewed as a meditative process itself:

> This quality of non-attachment is characteristic of both meditation and Therapeutic Touch. . . .
>
> Therapeutic Touch can thus be seen as a synthesis of concentrative and insight techniques. The essence of meditation, however, is not the particular technique we use, but the quality of being which the technique helps us to unfold. As Naranjo (1971) has emphasized, . . . meditation is concerned with the development of a presence, a modality of being. . . .
>
> In the case of Therapeutic Touch, this meditative presence would transform both the patient and the practitioner.
>
> A meditative action, such as Therapeutic Touch, is performed in a completely focused manner. . . .
>
> Spiritually, the practitioner becomes attuned to the universal healing power and channels this energy to the patient. . . . The hands are extremely useful in directing the energy. . . .
>
> In my own practice, I have observed that the most effective treatments are those in which the practitioner does not think about the effect but is completely involved in the treatment process itself. . . .
>
> The practitioner reaches deeper levels of being and integration in the process of opening the self as a channel for the universal life energy.
>
> The experience of the unity of all things and the experience of self-identity are both necessary for facilitating healing (Kunz and Peper, 1983) and both develop through the meditative process. Here again, we see how the practice of Therapeutic Touch, as meditation, itself evokes from within the practitioner those qualities which are necessary. (417:275–278)

Fifth, Dr. Krieger encourages her students to practice other forms of occult activity often found in conjunction with psychic healers. One important component of Therapeutic Touch, for example, is for the nurse or practitioner to become deeply involved in the exploration of their own psyche. How does Dr. Krieger recommend they accomplish such an exploration? Dr. Krieger endorses very particular methods: "There are several ways of doing this, but I find that the recording of dreams, the drawing of mandalas [for visualization techniques], and divination by means of consulting the *I-Ching* most useful" (60:80). Krieger also recommends intuitive symbolism, *mantras*, *yantras*, and color therapy (60:80–88, 124–126).

Sixth, additional evidence that Therapeutic Touch is a form of psychic healing can be seen from Krieger's own recommended teaching strategies. In her article, "High-Order Emergence of the Self During Therapeutic Touch," she refers to certain "reliable teaching strategies by which a person can learn to play the role of healer" (418:263). But when we examine the books which recommend these "reliable teaching strategies," what do we discover? We discover books by mediums, psychic healers, and spiritists: e.g., medium Harry Edwards' *A Guide to Spirit Healing* (297), psychic Lawrence LaShan's *The Medium, the Mystic, and the Physicist*, (296) and spiritist Yogi Ramacharaka's *The Science of Psychic Healing* (49) (418:271).

The seventh and final reason Therapeutic Touch should be considered a form of psychic healing is seen in the description practitioners give of powerful energy flowing through them. They do not produce this energy; they are merely vehicles through which this energy flows and is transferred. Consider the comments by those who actually use Therapeutic Touch. The fact that many of them become "channels" for an energy which they freely confess lies outside of them is significant. Why? Because once again, the descriptions they give concerning their own healing attributes are indistinguishable from those given by channelers, psychic healers, and spiritistic mediums when they are "healing" people.

> I am aware of . . . energy coming through me. (60:98)
>
> I can feel the transfer of energy . . . and I *know* it's flowing . . . my hands get hot. (60:99)

In her article, "High-Order Emergence of the Self During Therapeutic Touch," Dr. Krieger supplies additional comments by her students:

> When I am healing I feel as though I am a conduit sending appropriate energies for healing or peace or love. The source of these energies does not seem to originate within me, but rather I seem to tap into it. (418:267)
>
> When I am doing Therapeutic Touch, I identify as a healer of universal mind-energy, an extension for a universal force of which I, myself, am only a small facet but, nevertheless, a connecting link for healing power and a loving power of consciousness. (418:267)

> I am an instrument of my God, the creative source of all energy. I only clear myself for the flow and allow the healing energy to do its work. The healee seems to take it and use it as is needed and desired. (418:267)

In response to the question, "What sense of identity have you; that is, what role do you perceive yourself enacting" while using Therapeutic Touch, many students respond with statements like the following:

> During healing, I try to remember to be a channel, and sometimes I am, because the energy I feel surprises me. (60:107)
>
> As being a human channel. (60:107)
>
> A channel. (60:107)
>
> Being a vehicle through which energy can go. (60:108)
>
> A channel, definitely. . . . I am certain that it is not 'I' who does it. . . . I am an aligned channel. . . . (60:108, emphasis added)

Other comments by students learning the procedure are also reminiscent of the experiences of channelers, mediums, and psychic healers:

> I go into a sense of oneness with God, the universe and the healee. As long as I stay in that space, I'm not much aware of what else is going on around me. (418:266)
>
> An "inner voice" speaks when or if a connection with the healee is made. I am learning to listen better as that (inner voice) is the "me" that knows. (60:99)
>
> Increased sensitivity to situations that can't be explained. Many telepathic instances. . . . There has been a high rate of telepathic information that now significantly influences my evaluative processing and perhaps my cognitive processing as well. (418:268)
>
> Time seems irrelevant. (418:269)
>
> Time seems to become timeless. (418:269)
>
> I am aware of an inner dialogue in my head. . . . I sensitize myself to that and "listen" very carefully to its cues. (418:269)

Now consider the following description of a student's experience with Therapeutic Touch from start to finish, again indistinguishable from the experience of channelers and psychic healers:

> After consciously deciding that I do indeed desire to help, I assess my own energy field in order to determine whether I have the needed energy to do so. If so, I go deeper into the centering process, which somehow has already begun during the period of self-assessment. A different or altered state of consciousness occurs, which seems to make necessary adjustments in my field [energy] boundaries.

> Primarily guided by my hands (which in turn are guided by my whole field), I begin to will or think and direct energy towards the healee with the intention of facilitating a free flow of energy throughout his or her entire field.
>
> Most often, I find that I "give" and direct energy through my left hand. . . . I have had the experience a few times of using both hands to transmit the energy.
>
> Time perception is definitely altered; there is a speeding up or timelessness about it. . . . What has always amazed me is the sudden and definite STOP! that comes unmistakably and is unannounced.
>
> As soon as I get the message to stop, I do just that, saying: "OK, that's it!" and saying it in such a way that it really seems to carry with it my last spurt of energy to the other person's field. (60:126–127)

Other students report an "increase in the energy fields" while using dowsing rods; how the Therapeutic Touch technique of "centering altered my state of consciousness" and the discovering of a "co-existing [spiritual] reality" (60:119–125).

Those who believe that Therapeutic Touch is not a form of psychic, spiritistic healing need to seriously reassess their thinking.

Scientific Evaluation

Therapeutic Touch, according to preliminary scientific testing, claims to have an indirect impact on the patient's blood components, brain waves, and elicits a generalized relaxation response (60:116). However, almost all of the research has been criticized for having methodological flaws. In their "Therapeutic Touch: Is There a Scientific Basis for the Practice?" researchers Clark and Clark conclude, "In the final analysis the current research base supporting continued nursing practice of Therapeutic Touch is, at best, weak. Well-designed, double blind studies have thus far shown transient results (Grad, 1961), no significant results (Randolph, 1980), or are in need of independent replication (Grad, 1963)" (419:294).

The National Institute of Health recently awarded major research grants for studying Therapeutic Touch at NYU Medical Center to try and determine exactly what does occur.

But the fact that occult techniques using spiritistic powers can have psychological effects on humans should not be surprising. This has been happening among mediums, spiritistic channelers, psychics, yogis, and gurus for thousands of years. There is little doubt spirit influence or possession can cause dramatic physical, physiological, and psychological changes as demonstrated in Tal Brooke's *Riders of the Cosmic Circuit: . . . Gods of the New Age* (111) and other literature (141, 178). And we are convinced, in many cases, that this is what we are dealing with, no matter how innocuous and helpful Therapeutic Touch appears to the uninformed.

Unfortunately, it is often the physicians themselves who are most uninformed. Margaret L. McClurr, executive director of Nursing at New York University Medical Center, observes, "Most of our doctors don't even know about the technique" and "they tolerate it because it can't do any harm. They're satisfied that we never use it as a replacement for traditional nursing and medical practices" (275:30). Furthermore,

> Most doctors who [do] know about NCTT [Non Contact Therapeutic Touch] are cautiously awaiting the results of this [new] research, but many patients don't want to wait. "I can't think of a single instance where one of our doctors has ordered NCTT," McClure reports, "but about ten percent of our nurses offer it on their own initiative. The patients keep asking for it." (275:30)

Potential Dangers

The fact that Therapeutic Touch is done by those in the caring professions whom we tend to trust, such as nurses; the fact that it *appears* as an entirely innocuous procedure; and the fact that it "works" should not blind us to the fact that none of these are sufficient reasons for accepting it as a legitimate medical practice.

We must know *why* it works, and our conclusion is that when it *does* work, it works either on the basis of principles unrelated to the theory, such as psychological principles (e.g., the well known "placebo effect") or through spiritist power. (see chapter 4)

It should be obvious by now that Therapeutic Touch is a form of psychic healing. Co-author Dr. Weldon has documented the dangers of psychic healing in his *Psychic Healing: An Exposé of an Occult Phenomenon* (6:149–208). There is no need to replicate these findings here; nevertheless, a word of caution is in order.

The practice of Therapeutic Touch is similar to that carried out by mediums and spiritists in both its method and results. This means that many nurses who use Therapeutic Touch could be engaging in a form of spiritistic healing without even knowing it. Because it is well documented that spiritist healing is dangerous, Therapeutic Touch should be avoided.

Indeed, what is of particular concern is the attempt to use this technique on children and even babies. Krieger observes that, "Babies respond very well to Therapeutic Touch" (60:18).

If Krieger herself admits her ignorance as to what is occurring in Therapeutic Touch, then logically even she could not rule out the possibility of spiritistic power and control. She confesses, "There are still too many questions left unanswered to develop a theory [of how it works] unencumbered by guess work" (144:90) and, "The deeper one studies the dynamics of healing, the more one is impressed by how little we really know about the healing act" (144:20). As to why the dowsing rods operate in the energy matrix they do, "I don't know why this happens" and "there is much that I do not understand about this strange occurrence" (144:33–34).

❧ ❧ ❧

Unfortunately, the Biblical practice of laying on of hands and similar methods attempting to give physical comfort to patients cannot in any manner be equated with Therapeutic Touch. When Christian nurses are taught and practice in the Kunz-Krieger manner, they are engaging in a form of psychic healing. In addition, they inadvertently lend support to the Eastern occult philosophy of these psychic healers as well as to an occult practice itself.

Neither these manipulations of alleged psychic energies or an occultic philosophy will help a nurse's patients in the manner they hope to. This is why we find it difficult to believe that a dedicated Christian nurse who is truly knowledgeable about Therapeutic Touch, and not just mesmerized with its surface appeal, could continue the practice in good conscience.

Therapeutic Touch was developed by Dora Kunz, a psychic and the current president of one of the most profoundly occultic and anti-Christian societies in America, The Theosophical Society. Dolores Krieger, its co-developer and popularizer, is also psychic.

Scientific studies have failed to confirm that Therapeutic Touch works on any known scientific or medical principles. Krieger herself admits that she is uncertain how it works, yet the techniques of Therapeutic Touch are indistinguishable from the techniques practiced by spiritistic healers.

Because Therapeutic Touch is fundamentally an occultic practice, and not a scientific one, it is dangerous and should be avoided by any thinking person. In this era of unprecedented occult revival, we must be careful indeed about what we endorse.

CONCLUSION

THE THREAT OF NEW AGE MEDICINE

We began this book by noting with Norman Cousins that many Americans don't know how to think about health and illness. We will conclude it by showing that the issue of health and illness is only the tip of the iceberg.

New age medicine involves more profound matters than most people realize. The issue is not merely physical health and illness, scientific medicine versus quackery, or the moral responsibility of health practitioners to provide safe and effective health treatment. If we think of new age medicine only on a "physical" level, we misunderstand the more fundamental issue. New age medicine is basically a spiritual issue with spiritual implications and consequences.

Studies in diverse fields relating to demonism such as missiology, cults, and occult counseling, reveal that occultic practices can harm people spiritually. Christians are not immune from these hazards. The works of Drs. Kurt Koch, Merrill Unger, Fred Dickason, and many others prove this (refs. 123–126, 351–353; 396). Let us give you two illustrations known to the authors.

A nurse and missionary among the Nduga people of Mapnduma in Irian Jaya, Indonesia, had won numerous awards for her medical work in training nationals and in setting up health clinics. Two years ago she suffered an attack of dengue fever, an infectious tropical disease, forcing her to come home on furlough. After an entire year of medical treatment she returned to the mission field, still weak, with a "heaviness" over her but supposedly recovered because medical tests revealed nothing wrong.

Six months later, however, she had a relapse forcing her home again. Chronic fatigue and other problems proved intractable. The best efforts of a tropical disease specialist and several other physicians proved fruitless. She was prayed over many times but also to no avail.

Finally, a pastor she happened to encounter suspected a heretofore unaddressed spiritual cause of her problems. During counseling he asked her whether she had ever used alternate medicine. She explained that as a health conscious nurse, when normal medical means did not help, it was her practice to turn to alternate health-care: naturopathy, homeopathy, acupuncture, reflexology, and other new age techniques. After counseling concerning the nature and implications of these methods, the missionary forsook them and before the Lord confessed her involvement in such practices as sin. As a result of confession and forsaking these activities, her oppression, chronic fatigue, and other medical problems vanished, and she returned to the mission field in good health.

Let us give one more illustration before we offer our final analysis. A Christian man was in the hospital. A group of Christian men went to pray over him, but he was restless, spiritually oppressed, and unable to find peace with God. No amount of prayer or counsel would help this man's spiritual condition. Someone noticed he wore a Masonic ring. Counsel as to the nature of Masonry (249) and the man's repentance bore no fruit until the man also removed his Masonic ring. This simple act produced a dramatic change in his spiritual condition. He went from a state of depression and spiritual oppression to one of peace and reconciliation with God. Incidents such as these are not unique; scores of related events are chronicled in the writing of those who counsel in the area of occult oppression (refs. 123–126; 351–353).

But what is their meaning? What could a Masonic ring have to do with one's spiritual condition? How could visiting an acupuncturist or homeopathist produce intractable physical problems that would not respond to medical treatment? Why the dramatic, physical, and spiritual changes over seemingly insignificant actions such as confession and renunciation or removing a symbolic ring?

Obviously, these were not insignificant actions. They were necessary actions to break the power of spiritual forces; even "small" things may be significant when it comes to spiritual realities. Over twenty years of studying Biblical demonology and its cultural manifestations have proven to the authors that certain "laws" operate in the spiritual world just as they do in the physical world. Dr. Kurt Koch observes the following after forty-five years of counseling thousands of occultly oppressed: For deliverance from demonic powers, all paraphernalia associated with one's occult involvement must be destroyed, occult friendship broken, and confession and renunciation must occur—otherwise deliverance may not be had:

> Magical books and occult objects carry with them a hidden band. Anyone not prepared to rid himself of this ban will be unable to free himself from the influence of the powers of darkness. . . . Sometimes when one asks a person to destroy his occult objects, one meets with a lot of resistance, especially if the articles are also extremely expensive works of art. Yet even the little figures made out of precious stones which often originate from heathen temples have to be destroyed if the owner finds he cannot free himself from his occult oppression. . . . Mediumistic contacts and friendship must [also] be broken. . . .
>
> Occultly oppressed people should, in fact, make an open confession of every single hidden thing in their lives in order to remove the very last foothold of the enemy. . . .
>
> In counseling the occultly oppressed, a prayer of renunciation is . . . of great significance. The question is why? Every sin connected with sorcery is basically a contract with the powers of darkness. By means of sorcery the arch enemy of mankind gains the right of ownership over a person's life. The same is true even if it is only the sins of a person's parents or grandparents that are involved. The devil is well acquainted with the second commandment which ends, "For I the Lord your God am a jealous God, visiting the iniquity of the fathers upon the children to the third and fourth generation of those who hate me." The powers of darkness continue to claim the right of ownership although quite often the descendants remain completely unaware of the fact, perhaps since they have had no contact with sorcery themselves. . . .
>
> In praying a prayer of renunciation the person cancels Satan's right both officially and judicially. . . . Although modern theologians ridicule the whole idea, the devil is in earnest. Hundreds of examples could be quoted to show how seriously he takes the matter. (123:90, 92–93, 100)

The Scripture reveals that God is a jealous God. His love for His people is zealous and pure and requires that they cling to Him alone; double-mindedness in spiritual matters cannot be blessed (James 1:6–8). Consider the following Scriptures:

> Or do you think that the scripture speaks to no purpose. "He jealously desires the spirit which He has made to dwell in us?" (James 4:5, NASB)

> You shall have no other gods before me. You shall not make for yourself an idol in the form of anything in heaven above or on the earth beneath or in the waters below. You shall not bow down to them or worship them; for I, the Lord your God, am a jealous God, punishing the children for the sin of the fathers to the third and fourth generation of those who hate me, but showing love to thousands who love me and keep my commandments. (Exodus 20:3–6, NIV)

> Do not worship any other god, for the LORD, whose name is Jealous, is a jealous God. (Exodus 34:14; cf. Deuteronomy 4:24; Joshua 24:19; Zechariah 8:2, NIV)

> I am jealous for you with a godly jealousy. I promised you to one husband, to Christ, so that I might present you as a pure virgin to him. But I am afraid that just as Eve was deceived by the serpent's cunning, your minds may somehow be led astray from your sincere and pure devotion to Christ. (2 Corinthians 11:2 NIV)

The above Scriptures reveal that God takes a person's spiritual walk seriously. The problem with Christian involvement in new age medicine is that it can easily compromise the purity of a person's spiritual life.

One particular form of disobedience that God has warned against is idolatry, a practice characteristically associated with the powers of darkness (e.g., Psalm 106:34–39; 1 Corinthians 10:14, 20). Because God knows the consequences of idolatry—revealed so profoundly throughout Old Testment history and in anthropological studies—He has warned that those who practice it will suffer its consequences.

In essence, this is the fundamental reality of new age medicine—it is a form of idolatry. Only this can explain its spiritual philosophy and consequences:

> They exchanged the truth of God for a lie, and worshiped and served created things rather than the Creator—who is forever praised. Amen. (Romans 1:25, NIV)

Why do we say new age medicine is a form of idolatry? Simply because its practices reflect an underlying religious philosophy which promotes a false god—new age practices consistently underscore variations on new age pantheism. When one involves himself in practices whose philosophy is idolatrous, practices which lead one away from the one true God and into the realm of false gods and demonic spirits, can we be surprised there may be consequences?

On the one hand, when we sin ignorantly God understands, is merciful, and may blunt the consequences of our sin (Numbers 15:22–29; 1 Timothy 1:12–13; Luke 12:48; 23:34).

On the other hand, ignorance of the law is not an excuse to break it, and the consequences may not be blunted (Ephesians 4:18). Further, willful sin is even more likely to bring consequences and God's discipline (1 Samuel 15:23).

God lamented in Hosea, "My people are destroyed from lack of knowledge" (Hosea 4:6, NIV). The "lack of knowledge" that had destroyed His people was a lack of knowledge concerning God and His ways (Hosea 4:1–6). As a result, they turned to other gods, and their idolatrous practices became a snare and delusion. Because they did not know the true God, they became the prey of false gods—even while thinking that their lifestyle was pleasing to God.

Often times we need to be reminded that spiritual warfare exists (Ephesians 6:10–18). When God's people do not make knowledge of Him a priority, and His glory preeminent, given the fact of spiritual warfare, is it really surprising some are led astray by false practices and deceitful spirits or that there are consequences to such deception?

> The Spirit clearly says that in later times some will abandon the faith and follow deceiving spirits and things taught by demons. (1 Timothy 4:1, NIV)

> Be self-controlled and alert. Your enemy the devil prowls around like a roaring lion looking for someone to devour. (1 Peter 5:8, NIV)

> Put on the full armor of God so that you can take your stand against the devil's schemes. For our struggle is not against flesh and blood, but against the rulers, against the authorities, against the powers of this dark world and against the spiritual forces of evil in the heavenly realms. (Ephesians 6:11–12, NIV)

No one who has experienced severe pain, or pain of any type, enjoys it. And yet pain is one of the necessary accompaniments to a fallen world. It teaches us to avoid things that are dangerous to our health. Without it, we would engage in activities that could injure or destroy us.

The same holds true in the area of spirituality. The reasons there are consequences for sin and idolatry is to help admonish people about healthy spiritual living. Consider the following Scriptures warning about the consequences of idolatry and false spirituality:

> The sorrows of those will increase who run after other gods. (Psalm 16:4, NIV)
>
> Many are the woes of the wicked, but the LORD's unfailing love surrounds the man who trusts in him. (Psalm 32:10, NIV)
>
> If you ever forget the LORD your God and follow other gods and worship and bow down to them, I testify against you today that you will surely be destroyed. (Deuteronomy 8:19, NIV)
>
> For rebellion is like the sin of divination, and arrogance like the evil of idolatry. . . . (1 Samuel 15:23, NIV)
>
> They will turn to other gods and worship them, rejecting me and breaking my covenant. And when many disasters and difficulties come upon them, this . . . will testify against them, because it will not be forgotten by their descendants. (Deuteronomy 31:20–21, NIV)
>
> Therefore, my dear friends, flee from idolatry. . . . The sacrifices of pagans are offered to demons, not to God, and I do not want you to be participants with demons. (1 Corinthians 10:14, 20, NIV)
>
> Dear children, keep yourselves from idols. (1 John 5:21, NIV)
>
> The rest of mankind that were not killed by these plagues still did not repent of the work of their hands; they did not stop worshiping demons, and idols of gold, silver, bronze, stone and wood—idols that cannot see or hear or walk. (Revelation 9:20, NIV)

The bulk of this text has revealed that the major issue of new age medicine is fundamentally a spiritual one. Christians are to flee practices which are false, which promote idolatry, lies, and pagan gods, and which lead men astray and harm people spiritually. In essence, to fail to recognize the spiritual implications of new age medicine is to fail to understand new age medicine.

What may we conclude from our study of this topic? We may conclude the following:

1. Physically, as a whole, new age medicine uses highly questionable techniques which are scientifically unfounded. This means new age

medicine is quackery. As a recent article in the *Journal of Pharmacy Technology* observed, practices like acupuncture, auriculotherapy, biofeedback, chiropractic, herbal medicine, homeopathy, hypnosis, iridology, and naturopathy "have been promoted without adequate scientific evidence to support their usefulness or safety" (403:67).

2. Spiritually, new age medicine is permeated with spiritistic influence and occult philosophy; this means it is both physically and spiritually dangerous. Again, new age medicine is ultimately idolatry. The spirits who reveal themselves in new age medical techniques can be shown to be evil spirits, or what the Bible refers to as demonic beings (chapter 6). God strictly warns against involvement with them in Deuteronomy 18:9–12 and other Scriptures.

Then, new age medicine is either quackery or occultic. It is dangerous to any person's physical health because it is quackery. It is dangerous to any person's spiritual health because it is occultic, idolatrous, and demonic. This means that those who trust in new age medical procedures risk both their physical and spiritual health.

But the quest for physical health is not the final issue in any person's life. Good health is precious, but it is not the ultimate gift. Even if new age medicine could cure all illness, in the end everyone dies. So what is the final purpose in life?

The purpose of life is to inherit eternal life. The purpose of life is to know and honor the one true God. Jesus said, "And this is eternal life, that they may know Thee, the only true God, and Jesus Christ whom Thou hast sent" (John 17:3, NASB). The ultimate gift is the gift of eternal life by God's gracious forgiveness of our sins through Christ's death on the Cross.

Jesus taught that the very purpose He came to this earth was to pay the divine penalty for our sins. He testified, "Just as the Son of Man did not come to be served, but to serve, and to give His life as a ransom for many" (Matthew 20:28, NIV), and "For God so loved the world, that He gave His only begotten Son, that whoever believes in Him should not perish but have eternal life" (John 3:16, NASB).

He warned, "For what does it profit a man to gain the whole world, and forfeit his soul?" (Mark 8:36, NASB).

Each of us must choose to either receive this gift and inherit eternal life, or to reject this gift and inherit eternal misery and separation from God.

> And the witness is this, that God has given us eternal life, and this life is in His Son. He who has the Son has the life; he who does not have the Son of God does not have the life. (1 John 5:11–12, NASB)

> Whoever believes in the Son has eternal life, but whoever rejects the Son will not see life, for God's wrath remains on him. (John 3:36, NIV)

All who wish to come to Christ and have their sins forgiven may do so by praying the following prayer:

> Dear God, I now turn from my sins. I ask Jesus Christ to enter my life and be my Lord and Savior. I realize that this is a serious decision and commitment, and I do not enter into it lightly. I believe that on the cross Jesus Christ died for my sins, then rose from the dead three days later. I now receive Him into my life, as my Lord and Savior. Help me to live a life that is pleasing to You. Amen.

If you have prayed this prayer, we encourage you to write us at The John Ankerberg Show for help in growing as a Christian. Begin to read a modern, easy-to-read translation of the Bible such as the New International or New American Standard Versions. Start with the New Testament, Psalms, and Proverbs and then proceed to the rest of the Scriptures. Learning basic Christian doctrine is also crucial. We highly recommend J. I. Packer's *God's Words* and *Knowing God* (389). Finally, find a church where people honor the Bible as God's Word and Christ as Lord and Savior. Tell someone of your decision to follow Christ and begin to grow in your new relationship with God by talking with Him daily in prayer.

We can do no better than to close this text with the following statement from the book of Nehemiah. By God's faithfulness, the Israelites had just returned to their land after the Babylonian capitivity. The people of Israel reminded themselves that God's judgment had come upon their nation because of their idolatrous and occultic practices, practices that God had warned them about (Deuteronomy 18:9–12). On a day of pennance the leaders of the people recalled both God's unbounded mercy and His unerring justice. As they remembered their history prior to the captivity from which they had just returned, they produced one of the most beautiful prayers reflecting God's grace and power anywhere in the Old Testament:

> But you are a forgiving God, gracious and compassionate, slow to anger and abounding in love. Therefore you did not desert them, even when they cast for themselves an image of a calf and said, "This is your god, who brought you up out of Egypt," or when they committed awful blasphe-

> mies. . . . But they were disobedient and rebelled against you; they put your law behind their backs. They killed your prophets, who had admonished them in order to turn them back to you; . . .
>
> You warned them to return to your law, but they became arrogant and disobeyed your commands. They sinned against your ordinances, by which a man will live if he obeys them. Stubbornly they turned their backs on you, became stiff-necked and refused to listen. For many years you were patient with them. By your Spirit you admonished them through your prophets. Yet they paid no attention, so you handed them over to the neighboring peoples.
>
> But in your great mercy you did not put an end to them, or abandon them, for you are a gracious and merciful God. Now therefore, O our God, the great, mighty and awesome God, who keeps his covenant of love, do not let all this hardship seem trifling in your eyes—the hardship that has come upon us, upon our kings and leaders, upon our priests and prophets, upon our fathers and all your people, from the days of the kings of Assyria until today. In all that has happened to us, you have been just; you have acted faithfully, while we did wrong.
>
> Our kings, our leaders, our priests and our fathers did not follow your law; they did not pay attention to your commands or the warnings you gave them. Even while they were in their kingdom, enjoying your great goodness to them in the spacious and fertile land you gave them, they did not serve you or turn from their evil ways. (Nehemiah 9:17b, 18, 26, 29–35, NIV).

Thankfully, the people of Nehemiah's day consecrated themselves anew "to obey carefully all the commands . . . of the Lord our God" (Nehemiah 10:29, NIV). America in the 1990s may face the most critical decision of its history. The question remains for each of us, and our nation: To whom will we give our allegiance?

Bibliographic Notes

(Note: References in the text are keyed to this section. The system includes a number for a title listed below and then, if needed, corresponding page numbers for each title. For example, the reference listed within the text as 8:23 would refer to page 23 of Pedro Chan's Finger Acupressure*)*

1. Paul C. Reisser, Teri K. Reisser, John Weldon, *New Age Medicine: A Christian Perspective on Holistic Health*, Downers Grove, IL: InterVarsity, 1988.
2. Samuel Pfeifer, M.D., *Healing at Any Price?*, Milton Keynes, England: Word Limited, 1988.
3. Douglas Stalker, Clark Glymour, eds., *Examining Holistic Medicine*, Buffalo, NY: Prometheus Books, 1985.
4. Jane D. Gumprecht, *Holistic Health: A Medical and Biblical Critique of New Age Deception*, Moscow, ID: Ransom Press, 1986.
5. Clifford Wilson, John Weldon, *Psychic Forces and Occult Shock*, Chattanooga, TN: Global Publishers, 1987.
6. John Weldon, Zola Levitt, *Psychic Healing: An Exposé of an Occult Phenomenon*, Chicago, IL: Moody Press, 1982.
7. Iona Teeguarden, *Acupressure Way of Health: Jin Shin Do*, Tokyo, Japan: Japan Publications, 1978.
8. Pedro Chan, *Finger Acupressure*, New York, NY: Ballantine Books, 1978.
9. Mary Austin, *The Textbook of Acupuncture Therapy*, New York, NY: ASI Publishers, Inc., 1978.
10. Denis Lawson-Wood, Joyce Lawson-Wood, *The Incredible Healing Needles*, New York, NY: Samuel Weiser, Inc., 1975.
11. Hiroshi Motoyama, Yasuo Yuasa, eds., "How to Measure and Diagnose the Function of Meridians," *Research for Religion and Parapsychology*, Tokyo, Japan: The International Association for Religion and Parapsychology, volume 1, number 2, September, 1975.
12. Hiroshi Motoyama, *The Ejection of Energy from the Chakra of Yoga and Meridian Points of Acupuncture*, Tokyo, Japan: The Institute for Religious Psychology, 1975.

13. Hiroshi Motoyama, Yasuo Yuasa, eds., "Do Meridians ("Keiraku") Exist, and What Are They Like? *Research for Religion and Parapsychology*, Tokyo, Japan: The International Association for Religion and Parapsychology, February, 1975.
14. William A. McGarey, M.D., *Acupuncture and Body Energies*, Phoenix, AZ: Gabriel Press, 1974.
15. Ilza Veith, trans., *The Yellow Emperor's Classic of Internal Medicine* (Huang Ti Nei Ching Su Wen), Berkeley: University of California Press, 1972, new edition.
16. Felix Mann, *The Meridians of Acupuncture*, London: William Heinemann Medical Books Limited, 1974.
17. Andrew Weil, *Health and Healing: Understanding Conventional and Alternative Medicine*, Boston, MA: Houghton Mifflin, 1983.
18. Hiroshi Motoyama, *Chakra, Nadi of Yoga and Meridians, Points of Acupuncture: Points Where the Western Medicine, the Chinese Medicine and the Indian Yoga Meet Each Other*, Tokyo, Japan: The Institute of Religious Psychology, 1972.
19. Manfred Porkert, *The Theoretical Foundations of Chinese Medicine: Systems of Correspondence*, Cambridge, MA: The MIT Press, 1974.
20. John F. Thie, *Touch for Health: A Practical Guide to Natural Health Using Acupuncture, Touch and Massage*, Marina del Ray, CA: DeVorss and Company, 1973.
21. John Diamond, *BK—Behavioral Kinesiology: The New Science for Positive Health Through Muscle Testing—How to Activate Your Thymus and Increase Your Life Energy*, San Francisco, CA: Harper and Row, 1979.
22. Elmer and Alyce Green, *Beyond Biofeedback*, San Francisco, CA: Delacorte Press, 1977.
23. Corinne Heline, *Healing and Regeneration Through Color*, La Canada, CA: New Age Press, Inc., 1976.
24. T. M. Clement, Jr., *A Warning to Christians Regarding the Origins and Principles of Chiropractic*, Moses Lake, WA: T.M. Clement, Jr., 1986.
25. *Atlas Orthogonal Chiropractic*, N. D., N. P. Obtained from Robb Chiropractic Clinic, Madison, WI: 1987.
26. D. D. Palmer, *Textbook of the Science, Art, and Philosophy of Chiropractic for Students and Practitioners*, Portland, OR: Portland Printing House, 1910.
27. Consumers Union, "Chiropractors: Healers or Quacks?" in *Health Quackery: Consumers Union's Report on False Health Claims, Worthless Remedies, and Unproved Therapies*, the editors of Consumer Reports Books, New York, NY: Holt Rinehart Winston, 1980.
28. B. J. Palmer, *The Bigness of the Fellow Within*, Spartanburg, SC: Sherman College of Straight Chiropractic, 1949.
29. B. J. Palmer, *Answers*, Davenport, IA: Chiropractic Fountain Head, 1952.
30. Chittenden Turner, *The Rise of Chiropractic*, Los Angeles, CA: Powell Publishing, 1931. See ref. 428.
31. B. J. Palmer, *The Philosophy of Chiropractic*, 5th Edition, Davenport, IA: The Palmer School of Chiropractic Publishers, 1920.
32. Clyde H. Reid, *Dreams: Discovering Your Inner Teacher*, Minneapolis, MN: Winston Press, 1983.
33. Jane Roberts, *Seth: Dreams and Projection of Consciousness*, Walpole, NH: Stillpoint, 1986.

34. Harmon H. Bro, *Edgar Cayce on Dreams*, New York, NY: Warner, 1968.
35. Herbert Robert, M.D., *Art of Cure by Homeopathy: A Modern Textbook*, reprint, New Dehli, India: B. Jain Publishers, 1976.
36. James Tyler Kent, *Lectures on Homeopathic Philosophy*, Richmond, CA: North Atlantic Books, 1979.
37. H. J. Bopp, M.D., *Homeopathy*, Down, North Ireland: Word of Life Publications, 1984.
38. Samuel Hahnemann, *Organon of Medicine*, 6th Edition, reprint, New Dehli, India: B. Jain Publishers, 1978.
39. Samuel Hahnemann, *The Chronic Diseases, Their Peculiar Nature and Their Homeopathic Cure—Theoretical Part*, trans., Louis H. Tafel, New Dehli, India: Jain Publishing Company, 1976.
40. Bernard Jensen, *The Science and Practice of Iridology: A System of Analyzing and Caring for the Body Through the Use of Drugless and Nature-Cure Methods*, Provo, UT: BiWorld Publishers, Inc., 1952.
41. A. LaDean Griffin, *Eyes: Windows of the Body and the Soul*, Provo, UT: BiWorld Publishers, Inc., 1978.
42. Theodore Kriege, *Fundamental Basis of Iris Diagnosis: A Concise Textbook*, trans., A.W. Priest, London: L. N. Fowler, 1975.
43. Kathryn Davis Henry, *Medical Astrology: Physiognomy and Astrological Quotations*, Privately published, 1978.
44. John Ankerberg, John Weldon, *Astrology: Do the Heavens Rule Our Destiny?* Eugene, OR: Harvest House Publishers, 1989.
45. Dora Kunz, ed., *Spiritual Aspects of the Healing Arts*, Wheaton, IL: Quest/Theosophical Publishing House, 1985.
46. Alberto Villoldo and Stanley Krippner, *Healing States: A Journey into the World of Spiritual Healing and Shamanism*, New York, NY: Fireside/Simon and Schuster, Inc., 1987.
47. A. Barbara Brennan, *Hands of Light: A Guide to Healing Through the Human Energy Field*, New York, NY: Bantam Books, 1988.
48. George W. Meek, ed., *Healers and the Healing Process*, Wheaton, IL: Quest/Theosophical Publishing House, 1977.
49. Yogi Ramacharaka, *The Science of Psychic Healing*, reprint, Chicago, IL: Yogi Publication Society, 1937.
50. C. Norman Shealy, *Occult Medicine Can Save Your Life*, New York, NY: Bantam, 1977.
51. C. Norman Shealey, M.D., Caroline M. Myss, *The Creation of Health: Merging Traditional Medicine with Intuitive Diagnosis*, Walpole, NH: Stillpoint Publishing, 1988.
52. Arthur Guirdham, *The Psyche in Medicine: Possession, Past Lives, Powers of Evil in Disease*, Jersey, Channel Islands, Great Britain: Neville Spearman, 1978.
53. Douglas Baker, *Esoteric Healing*, vol. 3, part 1 of *The Seven Pillars of Ancient Wisdom: The Synthesis of Yoga, Esoteric Science and Psychology*, Herts., England: Douglas Baker, n.d.
54. Douglas Baker, *Esoteric Healing*, vol. 3, part 2 of *The Seven Pillars of Ancient Wisdom: The Synthesis of Yoga, Esoteric Science and Psychology*, Herts., England: Douglas Baker, 1976.

55. Tom Valentine, *Psychic Surgery*, Chicago, IL: Henry Regnery Company, 1973.
56. David V. Tansley, *Radionics and the Subtle Anatomy of Man*, Devon, England: Health Science Press, 1976.
57. Christopher Hills, *Supersensonics: The Science of Radiational Paraphysics*, vol. 3, Boulder Creek, CA: University of the Trees Press, 1975.
58. Michael Harner, *The Way of the Shaman: A Guide to Power and Healing*, New York, NY: Bantam, 1986.
59. Jeanne Achterberg, *Imagery in Healing: Shamanism and Modern Medicine*, Boston, MA: New Science Library/Shambhala, 1985.
60. Dolores Krieger, *The Therapeutic Touch: How to Use Your Hands to Help or to Heal*, New York, NY: Prentice Hall, 1986.
61. Victor Beasley, *Your Electro-Vibratory Body: A Study of the Life Force as Electro-Vibratory Phenomena*, Boulder Creek, CA: University of the Trees Press, 1978.
62. Aubrey T. Westlake, *The Pattern of Health: A Search for a Greater Understanding of the Life Force in Health and Disease*, Boulder, CO: Shambhala, 1973.
63. Jack Schwarz, *Human Energy Systems: A Way of Good Health Using Our Auric Fields*, New York, NY: E. P. Dutton, 1980.
64. Virginia Maclvor, Sandra LaForest, *Vibrations: Healing Through Color, Homeopathy and Radionics*, New York, NY: Samuel Weiser, 1979.
65. Mary Coddington, *In Search of the Healing Energy*, New York, NY: Warner/Destiny Books, 1978.
66. Lynn Sereda, *Outward Bound: The Spiritual Basis of the New Age Self-Integrative Therapies*, Vancouver, Canada: Light-House Publications, 1977.
67. Bernard Gunther, *Energy Ecstasy and Your Seven Vital Chakras*, Los Angeles, CA: The Guild of Tutors Press, 1978.
68. Thelma Moss, *The Body Electric: A Personal Journey into the Mysteries of Parapsychological Research, Bioenergy and Kirlian Photography*, Los Angeles, CA: J. P. Tarcher, 1979.
69. Edward Russell, *Design for Destiny: Science Reveals the Soul*, Suffolk, Great Britain: Neville Spearman, 1978.
70. Victor R. Beasley, *Dimensions of Electro-Vibratory Phenomena*, Boulder Creek, CA: University of the Trees Press, 1975.
71. J. G. Gallimore, *The Handbook of Unusual Energies*, Mokelumne, CA: Health Research, 1976.
72. Corinne Heline, *Occult Anatomy and the Bible*, La Canada, CA: New Age Press, n.d.
73. George J. Feiss, *Mind Therapies, Body Therapies: A Consumers Guide*, Millbrae, CA: Celestial Arts, 1979.
74. W. Edward Mann, Edward Hoffman, *The Man Who Dreamed of Tomorrow: A Conceptual Biography of Wilhelm Reich*, Los Angeles, CA: J. P. Tarcher, 1980.
75. W. Edward Mann, *Orgone, Reich and Eros: Wilhelm Reich's Theory of Life Energy*, New York, NY: Touchstone/Simon and Schuster, 1973.
76. Ann Hill, ed., *A Visual Encyclopedia of Unconventional Medicine*, New York, NY: Crown Publishers, 1979.
77. Arthur C. Hastings, James Fadiman, James S. Gordon, eds., *Health for the Whole Person: A Complete Guide to Wholistic Medicine*, Boulder, CO: Westview Press, 1980.

78. Richard Grossinger, *Planet Medicine: From Stone Age Shamanism to Post-Industrial Healing*, Garden City, NY: Anchor Press/Doubleday, 1980.
79. David S. Sobel, ed., *Ways of Health: Wholistic Approaches to Ancient and Contemporary Medicine*, New York, NY: Harcourt Brace Jovanich, 1979.
80. Berkeley Holistic Health Center, *The Holistic Health Handbook: A Tool for Attaining Wholeness of Body, Mind, and Spirit*, Berkeley, CA: And/Or Press, 1978.
81. Leslie J. Kaslof, *Wholistic Dimensions in Healing: A Resource Guide*, Garden City, NY: Dolphin/Doubleday, 1978.
82. Uma Silbey, *The Complete Crystal Guidebook: A Practical Path to Personal Power, Self-Development and Healing Using Quartz Crystals*, New York, NY: Bantam, 1987.
83. DaEl Walker, *The Crystal Healing Book*, Pacheco, CA: The Crystal Company, 1988.
84. Julia Lorusso, Joel Glick, *Healing Stoned: The Therapeutic Use of Gems and Minerals—A New Work Dealing with Gemstone Energies*, Miami Shores, FL: Mineral Perspectives, 1978.
85. George Frederick Kunz, *The Curious Lure of Precious Stones*, reprint, New York, NY: Dover, 1971.
86. William Jarvis, "Chiropractic: A Skeptical View," *The Skeptical Inquirer*, Fall, 1987.
87. Stephen Barrett, "Homeopathy: Is It Medicine?" *The Skeptical Inquirer*, Fall, 1987.
88. Leonard Pellettiri, ed., *Journal of Holistic Health*, San Diego, CA: Association for Holistic Health/Mandala Society, 1975–1976.
89. ———, *Journal of Holistic Health*, San Diego, CA: Association for Holistic Health/Mandala Society, 1977.
90. Michael Gosney, ed., *Journal of Holistic Health*, vol. 3, San Diego, CA: Association for Holistic Health/Mandala Society, 1978.
91. ———, *Journal of Holistic Health*, vol. 4, San Diego, CA: Association for Holistic Health/Mandala Society, 1979.
92. Anastas Harris, ed., *Journal of Holistic Health*, vol. 5, San Diego, CA: Association for Holistic Health/Mandala Society, 1980.
93. ———, *Journal of Holistic Health*, vol. 6, San Diego, CA: Association for Holistic Health/Mandala Society, 1981.
94. Alice DeBolt, Shelby Shapiro, eds., *Journal of Holistic Health*, vol. 7, San Diego, CA: Association for Holistic Health/Mandala Society, 1982.
95. ———, *Journal of Holistic Health*, vol. 9, San Diego, CA: Association for Holistic Health/Mandala Society, 1984.
96. The Edgar Cayce Foundation and the A.R.E. Clinic, *Proceedings: A Symposium on Varieties of Healing*, 6th Annual Medical Symposium, Phoenix, AZ: The Edgar Cayce Foundation, 1973.
97. Rechung Rinpoche, Jampal Kunzang, *Tibetan Medicine*, Berkeley, CA: University of California Press, 1976.
98. Walter Addison Jayne, *The Healing Gods of Ancient Civilizations*, reprint, New Hyde Park, NY: University Books, 1962.
99. C. W. Leadbeater, *Vegetarianism and Occultism*, Wheaton, IL: Theosophical Publishing House, 1972.
100. W. B. Crow, *The Occult Properties of Herbs*, New York, NY: Samuel Weiser, 1976.

101. Robert B. Tisserand, *The Art of Aromatherapy: The Healing and Beautifying Properties of the Essential Oils of Flowers and Herbs*, New York, NY: Inner Traditions International, Ltd., 1977.
102. Ralph Whiteside Kerr, *Herbalism Through the Ages*, vol. 30, San Jose, CA: Supreme Grand Lodge of AMORC, Inc., Rosecrucian Library, 1977.
103. John White, ed., *Kundalini Evolution and Enlightenment*, Garden City, NY: Anchor/Doubleday, 1979.
104. David Conway, *Magic: An Occult Primer*, New York, NY: Bantam, 1973.
105. Doreen Irvine, *Freed from Witchcraft*, Nashville, TN: Thomas Nelson, 1973.
106. Raphael Gasson, *The Challenging Counterfeit*, Plainfield, NJ: Logos, 1970.
107. Johanna Michaelsen, *The Beautiful Side of Evil*, Eugene, OR: Harvest House, 1975.
108. Victor H. Ernest, *I Talked with Spirits*, Wheaton, IL: Tyndale, 1971.
109. John Ankerberg, John Weldon, *The Facts on Spirit Guides*, Eugene, OR: Harvest House, 1989.
110. Ben Alexander, *Out from Darkness: The True Story of a Medium Who Escapes the Occult*, Joplin, MO: College Press Publishing, 1986.
111. Tal Brooke, *Riders of the Cosmic Circuit: Rajneesh, Sai Baba, Muktananda . . . Gods of the New Age*, Batavia, IL: Lion, 1986. Available from SCP, P.O. Box 4308, Berkeley, CA 94702.
112. Dana Ullman, Stephen Cummings, "The Science of Homeopathy," *New Realities*, Summer, 1985.
113. Elizabeth Philip, MiMi Tandler, "New Age Health: An Introduction to Homeopathy, Radionics and the Healing Touch," *Frontiers of Science*, January/February, 1981.
114. Consumer Reports, "Homeopathic Remedies," *Consumer Reports*, January, 1987.
115. Mantak Chia, *Chi Self-Massage: The Taoist Way of Rejuvenation*, Huntington, NY: Healing Tao Books, 1986.
116. Garabed Paelian, *Nicholas Roérich*, Agoura, CA: The Aquarian Educational Group, 1974.
117. Martin Gardner, "Water with Memory? The Dilution Affair: A Special Report," *The Skeptical Inquirer*, Winter, 1989. See also ref. 404.
118. John Ferguson, *An Illustrated Encyclopedia of Mysticism and the Mystery Religions*, New York, NY: Seabury Press, 1977.
119. R. Michael Miller, Josephine M. Harper, *The Psychic Energy Workbook: An Illustrated Course in Practical Psychic Skills*, Wellingborough, Northamptonshire: Aquarian Press, 1986.
120. Karl Sabbagh, "The Psychopathology of Fringe Medicine," *The Skeptical Inquirer*, volume 10, number 2, Winter, 1985–86.
121. Lewis Jones, "Alternative Therapies: A Report on an Inquiry by the British Medical Association," *The Skeptical Inquirer*, Fall, 1987.
122. David Conway, *Magic: An Occult Primer*, New York, NY: Bantam, 1973.
123. Kurt Koch, *Occult Bondage and Deliverance*, Grand Rapids, MI: Kregel Publishers, 1970.
124. ———, *Demonology Past and Present*, Grand Rapids, MI: Kregel Publishers, 1973.
125. ———, *Between Christ and Satan*, Grand Rapids, MI: Kregel Publishers, 1962.

126. ———, *Christian Counselling and Occultism*, Grand Rapids, MI: Kregel Publishers, 1982.
127. Stanislav Grof, Christina Grof, eds., *Spiritual Emergency: When Personal Transformation Becomes a Crisis*, Los Angeles, CA: J. P. Tarcher, 1989.
128. Merrill Unger, *Biblical Demonology: A Study of the Spiritual Forces Behind the Present World Unrest*, Wheaton, IL: Scripture Press, 1971.
129. Tom and Carole Valentine, *Applied Kinesiology: Muscle Response in Diagnosis Therapy and Preventive Medicine*, Rochester, VT: Healing Arts Press, 1987.
130. See refs. 270–273, 275, 291–295, 317 and Merrill Unger, *Demons in the World Today*, Wheaton, IL: Tyndale, 1973; Merrill Unger, *The Haunting of Bishop Pike*, Wheaton, IL: Tyndale, 1971; Merrill Unger, *What Demons Can Do to Saints*, Chicago, IL: Moody, 1977; also, Carl A. Raschke, "Satanism and the Devolution of the 'New Religions'," *SCP Newsletter*, Fall 1985; Carl A. Raschke, *The Interruption of Eternity: Modern Gnosticism and the Origins of New Religious Consciousness*, Chicago, IL: Nelson-Hall, 1980; John Warwick Montgomery, *Principalities and Powers*, Minneapolis, MN: Bethany, 1973; Gary North, *Unholy Spirits: Occultism and New Age Humanism*, Ft. Worth, TX: Dominion, 1986; John Weldon, *The Hazards of Psychic Involvement: A Look at Some Consequences*, unpublished mss., 1986; John Weldon and Zola Levitt, *Psychic Healing*, Chicago, IL: Moody Press, 1982; Johanna Michaelson, *Like Lambs to the Slaughter: Your Child and the Occult*, Eugene, OR: Harvest House, 1989; Ted Schwarz and Duane Empey, *Satanism: Is Your Family Safe?*, Grand Rapids, MI: Zondervan, 1988; M. Lamar Keene, *The Psychic Mafia: The True and Shocking Confessions of a Famous Medium*, New York, NY: St. Martin's Press, 1976.
131. John Weldon, *Hazards of Psychic Involvement*, unpublished mss., 1988.
132. John Ankerberg and John Weldon, *The Facts on Spirit Guides*, Eugene, OR: Harvest House Publishers, 1988. (Earlier title, *The Facts on Channeling*).
133. Andrija Puharich, *Uri*, New York, NY: Bantam, 1975, p. 112; Robert Leichtman, M.D., "Clairvoyant Diagnosis," *Journal of Holistic Health*, 1977, p. 40; Robert Leichtman, *Eileen Garrett Returns*, pp. 46–48 and *Edgar Cayce Returns*, pp. 50–52, Columbus, OH: Ariel Press, 1978, 1980; D. Kendrick Johnson, the *From Heaven to Earth*, series; and Robert Leichtman, Carl Japikse, *The Art of Living*, vol. 4, Columbus, OH: Ariel 1984, p. 78.
134. *Chattanooga News-Free Press*, Chattanooga, TN, April 29, 1990.
135. Monty Kline, *Christian Health Counselor*, Bellvue: WA; March, April, 1988.
136. "Health and Spirituality: An Interview with Dr. Bernard Jensen," *Rays from the Rose Cross*, May, 1978.
137. Dr. Randolph Stone, *The Mystic Bible*, Punjab, India: Radha Soami Satsang Beas, 1977.
138. Alice Bailey, *The Unfinished Autobiography*, New York, NY: Lucis Publishing Co., 1976.
139. Mike Samuels, M.D., Hal Bennett, *Spirit Guides: Access to Inner Worlds*, New York, NY: Random House, Inc., 1974.
140. James Hastings, ed., *Hastings Encyclopedia of Religion and Ethics*, vol. 4, New York, NY: Charles Schribner's Sons, n.d.

141. John Warwick Montgomery, ed., *Demon-Possession*, Minneapolis, MN: Bethany, 1976; cf. Malachi Martin, *Hostage to the Devil: The Possession and Exorcism of Five Living Americans*, New York, NY: Bantam, 1977; T. K. Oesterreich, *Possession: Demonical and Other Among Primitive Races, in Antiquity, the Middle Ages and Modern Times*, Secaucus, NJ: Citadel, 1974.
142. Doreen Irvine, *Freed from Witchcraft*, Nashville, TN: Thomas Nelson, 1978.
143. M. Scott Peck, *People of the Lie*, New York, NY: Simon and Schuster, 1983.
144. C. S. Lewis, *The Screwtape Letters*, New York, NY: McMillan, 1971.
145. John Warwick Montgomery, *Principalities and Powers*, Minneapolis, MN: Bethany, 1973.
146. Erika Bourguignon, ed., *Religion, Altered States of Consciousness and Social Change*, Columbus, OH: Ohio State University Press, 1973.
147. Machaelle Small Wright, *The Perelandra Garden Workbook: A Complete Guide to Gardening with Nature Intelligences*, U.K.: Perelandra Ltd./Jefferson, VA: Perelandra, 1987.
148. Evelyn deSmedt, et.al., *Life Arts: A Practical Guide to Total Being—New Medicine and Ancient Wisdom*, New York, NY: St. Martin's Press, 1977.
149. Marilyn Ferguson, *The Aquarian Conspiracy: Personal and Social Transformation in the 1980s*, Los Angeles, CA: J. P. Tarcher, Inc., 1980.
150. Keith Crim, ed., *Abingdon Dictionary of Living Religions*, Nashville, TN: Abingdon, 1981.
151. Robert W. Loftin, "Auras: Searching for the Light," *The Skeptical Inquirer*, Summer, 1990.
152. Victor Herbert, Steven Barrett, *Vitamins and "Health" Foods: The Great American Hustle*, Philadelphia, PA: George F. Stickley Company, 1981.
153. Marcus Bach, *The Chiropractic Story*, Los Angeles: De Vorss, 1968.
154. Barbara A. Goosen, "Touch Me, Heal Me," *Psychic*, November/ December, 1976.
155. Kurt Koch, *The Devil's Alphabet*, Grand Rapids, MI: Kregel Publications, 1969.
156. Dean C. Halverson, Kenneth Wapnick, "A Matter of Course: Conversation with Kenneth Wapnick," *Spiritual Counterfeits Journal*, volume 7, number 1, 1987.
157. Dean C. Halverson, "Seeing Yourself as Sinless," *SCP Journal*, volume 7, number 1, 1987.
158. Frances Adeny, *Re-visioning Reality: A Critique of a Course in Miracles, SCP Newsletter*, volume 7, number 2, 1981.
159. Brian Van Der Horst, "Update on 'A Course in Miracles'," *New Realities*, volume 3, number 1, August, 1979.
160. *New Realities*, volume 1, number 1, 1977.
161. Gerald Jampolsky, *Teach Only Love*, New York, NY: Bantam, 1983.
162. Gerald Jampolsky, *Good-Bye to Guilt: Releasing Fear Through Forgiveness*, New York, NY: Bantam, 1985.
163. *A Course in Miracles, Volume 2: Workbook for Students*, Huntington Station, New York, NY: Foundation for Inner Peace, 1977.
164. James Bolen, "Interview: William N. Thetford, Part 1 *New Realities*, volume 6, number 1, July/August, 1984.
165. James Bolen, "Interview: William N. Thetford, Part 2 *New Realities*, volume 6, number 2, September/October, 1984.

166. *A Course in Miracles, Volume 3, Manual for Teachers*, Huntington Station, New York, NY: Foundation for Inner Peace, 1977.
167. *A Course in Miracles, Volume 1: Text*, Huntington Station, New York, NY: Foundation for Inner Peace, 1977.
168. e.g., the editors of *Psychic* magazine, *Psychics: In-depth Interviews*, New York, NY: Harper and Row, 1972.
169. Joan Windsor, *Dreams and Dreaming: Expanding the Inner Eye—How to Attune Your Mind-Body Connection Through Imagery, Intuition and Life Energies*, New York, NY: Dodd Mead, 1987.
170. Shirley MacLaine, *Dancing in the Light*, New York, NY: Bantam, 1985.
171. Karen Schultz, "Bach Flower Remedies," *New Age Journal*, January, 1978.
172. Bernard Jensen, *Iridology: Science and Practice in the Healing Arts*, Provo, UT: BiWorld Publishing, Escondido, CA: Iridologists International, 1982.
173. E. M. Oakley, "Iridology: Your Eyes Reflect Your Health," *New Realities*, volume 1, number 3.
174. Allie Simon, David M. Worthen, John A. Mitas, "An Evaluation of Iridology," *Journal of the American Medical Association*, September 28, 1979.
175. Jessica Maxwell, "What Your Eyes Tell You About Your Health," *Esquire*, January, 1978.
176. Jerry A. Green, Steven Markell, "The Health Care Contract: A Model for Sharing Responsibility," *Somatics: Magazine-Journal of the Bodily Arts and Sciences*, subsection in Jerry A. Green, "Holistic Practitioners Unite! It's Time to Learn to Fly," *Somatics: Magazine-Journal of the Bodily Arts and Sciences*, Spring/Summer, 1982.
177. In Margaret Gaddis, "Teachers of Delusion" in Martin Ebon, ed., *The Satan Trap: Dangers of the Occult*, Garden City, NY: Doubleday, 1976.
178. Nandor Fodor, *An Encyclopedia of Psychic Science*, Secaucus, NJ: The Citadel Press, 1966.
179. Joseph Millard, *Edgar Cayce: Mystery Man of Miracles*, Greenwich, CT: Fawcett, 1967.
180. Association for Research Enlightenment, ARE Circulating File, *Truth*, Virginia Beach, VA: n.d.
181. ———, ARE Circulating File, *Reincarnation*, Part I, Virginia Beach, VA: n.d.
182. ———, ARE Circulating File, *Planetary Sojourns in Astrology*, Virginia Beach, VA: n.d.
183. ———, ARE Circulating File, *The Occult*, Virginia Beach, VA: n.d.
184. ———, ARE Circulating File, *Oneness of Life and Death*, Virginia Beach, VA: n.d.
185. ———, ARE Circulating File, *Jesus the Pattern and You*, Virginia Beach, VA: n.d.
186. *Oxford American Dictionary*, New York, NY: Avon, 1982.
187. Swami Muktananda, *Play of Consciousness*, New York, NY: Harper and Row, 1978.
188. Da Free John, *Garbage and the Goddess*, Lower Lake, CA: Dawn Horse Press, 1974.
189. Personal conversation with Dr. Jane Gumbrecht (ref. 4) who had a nurse practitioner relay this information to her.
190. Hugh Lynn Cayce, "The Variety of Healings," in ref. 96, p. 5.
191. William Rodarmor, "Acupuncture Comes of Age in America," *Yoga Journal*, March-April, 1986.
192. *The San Francisco Chronicle*, October 14, 1976.
193. Richard Foster, *Celebration of Discipline*, New York, NY: Harper and Row, 1978.

194. Michael Murphy, Steven Donovan, "A Bibliography of Meditation Theory and Research, 1931–1983," *The Journal of Transpersonal Psychology*, volume 15, number 2, 1983.

195. Haridas Chaudhuri, *Philosophy of Meditation*, New York, NY: Philosophical Library, 1974.

196. Cited by Stanley Krippner in *Song of the Siren*, San Francisco, CA: Harper and Row, 1975.

197. Karlis Osis, et.al., "Dimensions of the Meditative Experience," *The Journal of Transpersonal Psychology*, volume 5, number 2, 1973.

198. Roger Walsh, "A Model for Viewing Meditation Research," *The Journal of Transpersonal Psychology*, volume 14, number 1, 1982.

199. Roger N. Walsh, et.al., "Meditation: Aspects of Research and Practice," *The Journal of Transpersonal Psychology*, volume 10, number 2, 1978.

200. Roger Walsh, "Initial Meditative Experiences, Part One," *The Journal of Transpersonal Psychology*, volume 9, number 2, 1977.

201. Daniel Goleman, *The Varieties of the Meditative Experience*, New York, NY: E. P. Dutton, 1977.

202. Gertrude Schmeidler, "The Psychic Personality," *Psychic*, March/April, 1974.

203. John White, "What Is Meditation," *New Realities*, September/October 1984.

204. Patricia Mischell, *Beyond Positive Thinking: Mind Power Techniques*, Englewood Cliffs, NJ: Prentice-Hall, 1985.

205. Stanley Krippner, Leonard George, "Psi Phenomena Related to Altered States of Consciousness," in Benjamin B. Wolman, Montague Ullman, eds., *Handbook of States of Consciousness*, New York, NY: Van Nostrand Reinhold Co., 1987.

206. Anthony Norvell, *The Miracle Power of Transcendental Meditation*, New York, NY: Barnes and Noble, 1974.

207. Frances Clark, "Exploring Intuition: Prospects and Possibilities," *The Journal of Transpersonal Psychology*, volume 5, number 2, 1973.

208. Rudi (Swami Rudrananda), *Spiritual Cannibalism*, Woodstock, NY: Overlook Press, 1978.

209. Chogyam Trungpa, "An Approach to Meditation," *The Journal of Transpersonal Psychology*, volume 5, number 1, 1973.

210. Roger Walsh, et.al., "Meditation: Aspects of Research and Practice," *The Journal of Transpersonal Psychology*, volume 10, number 2, 1978.

211. Doris H. Buckley, *Spirit Communication for the Millions*, Los Angeles, CA: Sherbourne Press, 1967.

212. Ruth Montgomery, *A World Beyond*, New York, NY: Coward McCann and Geoghegan, 1971.

213. Mark D. Epstein, Jonathan Leiff, "Psychiatric Complications of Meditation Practice," *The Journal of Transpersonal Psychology*, volume 13, number 2, 1981.

214. Komilla Thapa, Vinida Murphy, "Experiential Characteristics of Certain Altered States of Consciousness," *The Journal of Transpersonal Psychology*, volume 17, number 1, 1985.

215. Jack Kornfield, "Intensive Insight Meditation: A Phenomenological Study," *The Journal of Transpersonal Psychology*, volume 11, number 1, 1979.

216. Mary Jo Meadow, et.al., "Spiritual and Transpersonal Aspects of Altered States of Consciousness," *The Journal of Transpersonal Psychology*, volume 11, number 1, 1979.
217. Among them are Leon Otis, *Adverse Effects of Meditation*, Menlo Park, CA: Stanford Research Institute, 1979; J. A. Fahmy and H. Fledulisu, "Yoga Induced Attacks of Acute Glaucoma," *Acta Ophthalmologica*, 51, 80–84 1973, ; J. Hassett, "Meditation Can Hurt," *Psychology Today*, volume 12, number 6, 125–126; 1978; A. Lazarus, "Psychiatric Problems Precipitated by Transcendental Meditation," *Psychological Reports*, volume 39, number 2, 601–602; 1976; B. O'Regan, "Mind/Body Effects: The Physiological Consequence of Tibetan Meditation," *Newsletter of the Institute of Noetic Sciences*, volume 10, number 2, 1982.
218. Taken from the 1985–86 *Catalogue* of the Palmer College of Chiropractic-West, Sunnyvale, CA.
219. Slater Brown, *The Heyday of Spiritualism*, New York, NY: Pocket Books, 1972.
220. College of Physicians and Surgeons of the Province of Quebec, *The New Physician*, September, 1966.
221. David Tansley, "The Body Temple of Man," *Human Dimensions*, Spring, 1974.
222. Personal statement given to author, May, 1988.
223. Swami Muktananda, *Play of Consciousness*, New York, NY: Harper and Row, 1978.
224. A critique is found in John Weldon, Zola Levitt, *The Transcendental Explosion*, Irvine, CA: Harvest House Publications, 1975.
225. Maharishi Mahesh Yogi, *On the Bhagavad Gita*, Baltimore, MD: Penquin, 1974.
226. Paul Hawken, *The Magic of Findhorn*, New York, NY: Bantam, 1976.
227. Herbert H. Koepf, *What Is Bio-Dynamic Agriculture?*, Springfield, IL: Biodynamic Farming and Gardening Assoc., 1976.
228. Anthroposophical Society in America, *Directory of Activities and Services*, New York, NY: Rudolf Steiner Information Center, n.d.
229. Da Free John, *Garbage and the Goddess*, Lower Lake, CA: Dawn Horse Press, 1974.
230. Sita Wiener, *Swami Satchidananda*, San Francisco, CA: Straight Arrow Books, 1970.
231. Da Free John, *A New Tradition*, Clear Lake, CA: The Laughing Man Institute, 1980.
232. Swami Bakta Vishita, *Genuine Mediumship*, npp: Yoga Publication Society, 1919.
233. Sri Chinmoy, *Yoga and the Spiritual Life: The Journey of India's Soul*, Jamaica, NY: Agni Press, 1974.
234. Yarti, Swami Anand, comp., *The Sound of Running Water, a Photo-Biography of Bhagwan Shree Rajneesh and His Work, 1974-1978*, Poona, India: Rajneesh Foundation, 1980.
235. Swami Muktananda, *Siddha Meditation: Commentaries on the Shiva Sutras and Other Sacred Texts*, Oakland, CA: Siddha Yoga Dham of America, 1975.
236. Sai Baba, *Sathya Shivam Sundaram, Part Three*, Whitefield, Bangalore, India: Sri Sathya Sai Publication and Education Foundation, 1972.
237. Sanathann Sarathi, ed., *Sathya Sai Speaks*, volume 1X, Tustin, CA: Sri Sathya Sai Baba Book Center of America, 1975.
238. Bhagwan Shree Rajneesh, *The Mustard Seed*, San Francisco, CA: Harper and Row, 1975.

239. Douglas Shah, *The Meditators*, Plainfield, NJ: Logos, 1975.
240. Os Guinness, *The Dust of Death*, Downers Grove, IL: InterVarsity, 1973.
241. Mahendranath Gupta, *The Gospel of Sri Ramakrishna*, New York, NY: Ramakrishna-Vivekananda Center, 1977.
242. Romain Rolland, *The Life of Ramakrishna*, volume 1, Calcutta, India: Advaita Ashrama, 1979.
243. Gopi Krishna, *The Awakening of Kundalini*, New York, NY: E. P. Dutton, 1975.
244. C. B. Purdom, *The God-Man: The Life, Journeys and Work of Meher Baba*, London: George Allen and Unwin, Ltd., 1964.
245. Betty Morales, "Homeopathy and Acupuncture," *Let's Live*, January, 1983.
246. Mary Carpenter, "Homeopathic Chic," *Health*, March, 1989.
247. Letter from Annick Sullivan with a copy of personal testimony re: the benefits of homeopathy.
248. Translation from French of an interview with Dr. Desmichelle, M.D., honorary president of the Centre Homeopathique De France, *Elle* Magazine, April, 1988.
249. John Ankerberg, John Weldon, *The Secret Teachings of the Masonic Lodge*, Chicago, IL: Moody Press, 1990.
250. Rosalyn Bruyere, *Wheels of Light: A Study of the Chakras*, Sierra Madre, CA: Bon Productions, 1989.
251. Ann Nietzke, "Portrait of an Aura Reader," Part I, *Human Behavior*, February, 1979; Part II, *Human Behavior*, March, 1979.
252. See D. Stalker, C. Glymour, "Quantum Medicine" in Ref. 3:107–125; Tom Napier, "Quantum Theory and Psi: Grasping at Quantum Straws," *The Skeptical Inquirer*, volume 10, number 2, Winter 1986–1987; cf. Martin Gardner, "Parapsychology and Modern Physics," *The Skeptical Inquirer* volume 7, number 1, p. 37.
253. Jeffrey Mishlove, *The Roots of Consciousness: Psychic Liberation Through History, Science and Experience*, New York, NY: Random House, 1975.
254. Otto Friedrich, "New Age Harmonies," *Time*, December 7, 1987.
255. Paul C. Reisser, Teri K. Reisser, John Weldon, "Holistic Healers and Therapeutic Touch," *Journal of Christian Nursing*, Spring 1980. (This series was excerpted from *New Age Medicine*, Ref. 1.)
256. ———, "Holistic Health and Psychic Healers," *Journal of Christian Nursing*, Summer, 1986.
257. ———, "What Holistic Healers Believe," *Journal of Christian Nursing*, Winter, 1986.
258. M. Borelli, P. Heidt, eds., *Therapeutic Touch: A Book of Readings*, New York, NY: Springer, 1981.
259. Ben G. Hester, *Dowsing: An Exposé of Hidden Occult Forces*, 1982. Rev.ed., available from the author 4883 Hedrick Ave. Arlington, CA. 92505, 1984.
260. Reader's Forum, *Journal of Christian Nursing*, Summer, 1986.
261. Letter from Ramona Cass, editor, *JCN*, July 23, 1986.
262. Robert A. Bradly, "The Need for the Academy of Parapsychology and Medicine," *The Varieties of Healing Experience: Exploring Psychic Phenomenon in Healing*, Los Altos, CA: Academy of Parapsychology and Medicine, 1971.
263. Robert R. Leichtman, the "From Heaven to Earth" series, Columbus, OH: Ariel Press, 1978–1990.

264. W. B. Crow, *Precious Stones: Their Occult Power and Hidden Significance*, New York, NY: Samuel Weiser, 1977.
265. Carlos Castaneda, *The Teachings of Don Juan: A Yaqui Way of Knowledge*, New York, NY: Simon and Schuster/Touchstone, 1974.
266. Michael Harner, ed., *Hallucinogens and Shamanism*, New York, NY: Oxford, 1973.
267. Harold A. Hansen, *The Witches Garden*, Santa Cruz, CA: Unity Press, 1978.
268. Peter Tompkins, Christopher Bird, *The Secret Life of Plants*, New York, NY: Avon, 1974.
269. Ambrose A. Worrall, Alga N. Worrall, *Explore Your Psychic World*, New York, NY: Harper and Row, 1970.
270. Katinka Matson, *The Psychology Today Omnibook of Personal Development*, New York, NY: William Morrow, 1977.
271. 1981 Yearbook, *World Book Encyclopedia*, 412.
272. Norma Meyer, *The Daily Breeze*, Torrance, CA, Sept. 5, 1982, in ref. 3, p. 178.
273. Jake Page, "Dilutions of Grandeur," *American Health*, November, 1988.
274. "Paracelsus," *Encyclopedia Britannica*, Macropedia, volume 13, 1978, p. 982.
275. Elizabeth Stark, "Healing Hands," *Psychology Today*, July/Aug. 1989.
276. Dora Kunz, "Viewpoint," in *The American Theosophist*, December, 1978; See also December, 1976, 342–343.
277. Leah Wallach, "Healing Touch," in Peter Tyson, ed., *The Omni Book of Psychology*, New York, NY: Zebra Books, 1986.
278. Ralph Lee Smith, *At Your Own Risk: The Case Against Chiropractic*, New York, NY: Trident, 1969.
279. Dora Kunz, Erik Peper, "Fields and Their Clinical Implications," in ref. 45.
280. Arthur Guirdham, *A Foot in Both Worlds*, London: Neville Spearman, 1973.
281. Sri Chinmoy, *Meditation: Man-Perfection in God-Satisfaction*, Jamaica, NY: Agni Press, 1985.
282. Deane Shapiro, Roger Walsh, eds., *Meditation: Classic and Contemporary Perspectives*, New York, NY: Aldine, 1979.
283. Bhagwan Shree Rajneesh, *The Book of the Secrets, Volume 1: Discourses on Vigyana Bhairava Tantra*, New York, NY: Harper Colophon, 1977.
284. Swami Rudrananda, *Spiritual Cannibalism*, New York, NY: Quick Fox, 1973.
285. Dave Hunt, *America: The Sorcerer's New Apprentice*, Eugene, OR: Harvest House, 1989.
286. Johanna Michaelson, *Like Lambs to the Slaughter: Your Child and the Occult*, Eugene, OR: Harvest House, 1989.
287. Jon Klimo, *Channeling: Investigations on Receiving Information from Paranormal Sources*, Los Angeles, CA: J. P. Tarcher, 1987.
288. Sanaya Roman and Duane Packer, *Opening to Channel: How to Connect with Your Guide*, Tiburon, CA: H. J. Kramer, Inc., 1987.
289. Robin Westen, *Channelers: A New Age Directory*, New York, NY: Perigree Books, 1988.
290. Kathryn Ridall, *Channeling: How to Reach Out to Your Spirit Guides*, New York, NY: Bantam Books, 1988.

291. Robert Leichtman, "Clairvoyant Diagnosis: Developing Intuition and Psychic Abilities in the Diagnostic Process," *The Journal of Holistic Health*, San Diego, CA: Mandala Society, 1977.
292. John Ankerberg, John Weldon, *The Facts on Spirit Guides*, Eugene, OR: Harvest House, 1988.
293. John White, ed., *Kundalini Evolution and Enlightenment*, Garden City, NY: Anchor, 1979.
294. John Weldon, "Eastern Gurus in a Western Milieu: A Critique from the Perspective of Biblical Revelation," Ph.D. Dissertation, Pacific College of Graduate Studies, Melbourne, Australia, 1988.
295. Dolores Krieger, "Therapeutic Touch and Healing Energies from the Laying-On of Hands," *Journal of Holistic Health*, number 1, San Diego, CA: Mandala Society, 1975–1976.
296. Lawrence LeShan, *The Medium, the Mystic and the Physicist: Toward a General Theory of the Paranormal*, New York, NY: Ballantine, 1975.
297. Harry Edwards, *A Guide to Spirit Healing*, London: Spiritualist Press, 1955.
298. William Vrooman, "Dowsing for Health: Mental and Spiritual Bodies of Human and Non-Human Entities," *The American Dowser*, November, 1977.
299. Ram Dass, *Be Here Now*, Boulder, CO: Hanuman Foundation, 1978.
300. Kurt Koch, *Occult ABC*, Grand Rapids, MI: Kregel, 1980. Retitled *Satan's Devices*.
301. W. Brugh Joy, *Joy's Way*, Los Angeles, CA: J. P. Tarcher, 1979.
302. J. P. Moreland, *Christianity and the Nature of Science: A Philosophical Investigation*, Grand Rapids, MI: Baker, 1979.
303. Poll results may be obtained by contacting the Gallup and Roper organizations. For Greeley's results contact the National Opinion Research Center at the University of Chicago. The popular press usually publishes their results; e.g., Robert Lindsay, "Spiritual Concepts Drawing a Different Breed of Adherent," *New York Times*, September 29, 1986; *National and International Religion Report*, July 4, 1988.
304. John Ankerberg, John Weldon, *The Facts on the New Age Movement*, Eugene, OR: Harvest House, 1988.
305. *Webster's Third New International Dictionary*, unabridged, Springfield, MA: Merriam Webster, 1981.
306. Glen Hultgren, "Christian Chiropractors Association Board of Directors Establishes a Policy on Innate," *The Christian Chiropractor*, August, 1988.
307. See the February, March, and October, 1987, and the February, April, August, and October, 1988, issues of *The Christian Chiropractor*.
308. John N. Moore, *How to Teach Origins (Without ACLU Interference)*, Midford, MI: Mott Media, 1983.
309. Norman Cousins, "A Nation of Hypochondriacs," *Time*, International Version, June 18, 1990.
310. Steven Findlay, "Health Guide: Body," *U.S. News and World Report*, June 18, 1990.
311. Walter D. Glanze, ed., *The Mosby Medical Encyclopedia*, New York, NY: New American Library, 1985.
312. Roderick E. McGrew, *Encyclopedia of Medical History*, New York, NY: McGraw-Hill, 1985.

313. *The American Medical Association Encyclopedia of Medicine*, New York, NY: Random House, 1989.
314. *Fishbein's Illustrated Medical and Health Encyclopedia*, New York, NY: H. S. Stuttman Co., 1977.
315. Shafica Karagulla, *Breakthrough to Creativity: Your Higher Sense Perception*, Santa Monica, CA: DeVorss and Co., 1972.
316. David Akstein, "Terpsichoretrancetherapy: A New Hypnopsychotherapeutic Method," *The International Journal of Clinical and Experimental Hypnosis*, volume 21, number 3, 1973.
317. John Weldon, *A Critical Encyclopedia of Modern American Sects and Cults*, unpublished (This ms. covers seventy groups and is eight thousand pages in length); cf. Robert S. Ellwood, *Religious and Spiritual Groups in Modern America*, in ref. 454, p. 12.
318. Malachi Martin, *Hostage to the Devil: The Possession and Exorcism of Five Living Americans*, New York, NY: Bantam, 1979.
319. Douglas Stalker, Clark Glymour, "Quantum Medicine," in ref. 3.
320. J. C. Cooper, *Taoism: The Way of the Mystic*, New York, NY: Samuel Weiser, Inc., 1977.
321. Gersham Stein, "What Is Chiropractic?", *Your Jerusalem*, June, 1990.
322. Mike Warnke, *The Satan Seller*, Plainfield, NJ: Logos, 1972.
323. American Chiropractic Assocation, "Master Plan Definitions," ratified by the House of Delegates, June, 1964, amended June, 1979, and June, 1989, p. Bii.
324. For example, Norman L. Geisler, William E. Nix, *A General Introduction to the Bible*, Chicago, IL: Moody, 1986; Rev. Rene Pache, *The Inspiration and Authority of Scripture*, Chicago, IL: Moody Press, 1969.
325. Brian Inglis, Ruth West, *The Alternative Health Guide*, New York, NY: Alfred A. Knopf, 1983.
326. American Chiropractic Association, "Master Plan Definition," section D–10, D–11, under "Diagnosis" and "Subluxation Definition," n.d.
327. I. Mark Breth, "Our Members Speak: Putting Innate into Perspective," *The Christian Chiropractor*, August, 1988.
328. Emanuel Swedenborg, *The True Christian Religion Containing the Universal Theology of the New Church*, volume 2, standard edition, New York, NY: Swedenborg Foundation, 1972.
329. "Empowering Message from Genesis, a Universal Teacher," and "Applying Universal Principles for Spiritual Fitness," in *The Stillpoint Catalogue*, Walpole, NH: Fall/Winter, 1987–88.
330. See Edmond Gruss, "God Calling: A Critical Look at a Christian Best Seller," Personal Freedom Outreach Newsletter, volume 6, number 3, (P. O. Box 26062, St. Louis, MO. 63136); Arnold's text and *Oahspe* are much more blatantly anti-Christian.
331. Each issue of *Shaman's Drum* lists a "Resources Directory," with numerous workshops, retreats, shaman centers, shaman counseling, etc.
332. Strephon Kaplan-Williams, *Jungian-Senoi Dreamwork Manual*, Novato, CA: Journey Press, 1988.
333. Timothy White, "An Interview with Luisah Teish, Daughter of Oshun," *Shaman's Drum*, Spring, 1986.

334. Geoffrey Ahern, *Sun At Midnight: The Rudolf Steiner Movement and the Western Esoteric Tradition*, Wellingborough, Northamptonshire: The Aquarian Press, 1984.
335. C. W. Leadbeater, *Man Visible and Invisible*, reprint, Wheaton, IL: Theosophical, 1969.
336. cf. Ken Wilbur, *The Spectrums of Consciousness* and *The Atman Project: A Transpersonal View of Human Development*, Wheaton, IL: Theosophical, 1977, 1985; Ken Wilbur, *No Boundary: Eastern and Western Approaches to Personal Growth*, Boston, MA: Shambala, 1979; John White, ed., *What Is Enlightenment?*, Los Angeles, CA: J. P. Tarcher, 1984; Douglas and Barbara Dillon, *An Explosion of Being: An American Family's Journey into the Psychic*, West Nyack, New York, NY: Parker, 1984.
337. Stanislav Grof, Christina Grof, eds., *Spiritual Emergency*, Los Angeles, CA: J. P. Tarcher, 1989.
338. John White, ed., *Frontiers of Consciousness*, New York, NY: Avon, 1975.
339. Porter Shiner, "Unwind and DeStress," Part One, *Prevention*, July, 1990.
340. Vincent Buranelli, *The Wizard from Vienna*, New York, NY: Coward, McCann, and Geoghegan, 1975.
341. Rudolf Steiner, "How We Can Help Our Dead," *The Christian Community Journal*, volume 7, 1953, p. 48; Rudolf Steiner, lecture, "The Dead Are with Us," London: 1945.
342. Rudolf Steiner, "The Relationship Between the Living and the Dead," *Journal for Anthroposophy*, Autumn, 1978.
343. Rudolf Steiner, *Building Stones for an Understanding of the Mystery of Golgotha*, London: Rudolf Steiner Press, 1972.
344. Russell S. Worrall, "Iridology: Diagnosis or Delusion," 167–180, in ref. 3.
345. Helena P. Blavatsky, *Isis Unveiled*, Wheaton, IL: Theosophical 1972, cf. vol. 2, pp. 1–52.
346. Jane Roberts, *The Nature of Personal Reality: A Seth Book*, New York, NY: Bantam, 1978.
347. Oliver Wendell Holmes, "Homeopathy," ref. 3, pp. 221–243.
348. John Ankerberg, John Weldon, *Do the Resurrection Accounts Conflict and What Proof Is There Jesus Rose from the Dead?*, Chattanooga, TN: Ankerberg Theological Research Institute, 1990.
349. See e.g., Wendell R. Bird, *The Origin of Species Revisited*, 2 volumes, New York, NY: Philosophical Library, 1989; A.E. Wilder-Smith, *The Creation of Life: A Cybernetic Approach to Evolution*, San Diego, CA: Creation-Life, 1970; Charles Thaxton, et. al., *The Mystery of Life's Origin: Reassessing Current Theories*, New York, NY: Philosophical Library, 1984.
350. James C. Whorton, "The First Holistic Revolution: Alternative Medicine in the Nineteenth Century," in ref. 3, pp. 29–48.
351. C. Fred Dickason, *Demon Possession and the Christian*, Chicago, IL: Moody Press, 1987.
352. Merrill Unger, *What Demons Can Do to Saints*, Chicago, IL: Moody Press, 1977.
353. ———, *Demons in the World Today*, Wheaton, IL: Tyndale, 1972., cf. his *Biblical Demonology*, Wheaton, IL: Scripture Press, 1971.
354. Sri Chinmoy, *Astrology the Supernatural and the Beyond*, Jamaica, NY: Agni Press, 1973.
355. Sri Chinmoy, *Conversations with the Master*, Jamaica, NY: 1977.

356. Paul Reisser, Teri Reisser, John Weldon, *The Holistic Healers*, Downer's Grove, IL: InterVarsity, 1982; expanded and republished in 1988, see ref. 1.
357. For an excellent discussion of systematic theology in popular form, see J. I. Packer *God's Words*. For a defense of theology as a rational truth-seeking discipline, see Augustus H. Strong, *Systematic Theology: A Compendium*, Old Tappan, NJ: Revelle, 1976; prolegomena, 1–51; and Charles Hodge, *Systematic Theology*, Grand Rapids, MI: Eerdmans, 1981, volume 1, Introduction, 1–190.
358. Eugene M. Klaaren, *Religious Origins of Modern Science*, Grand Rapids, MI: Eerdmans, 1977.
359. Henry Morris, *Men of Science Men of God*, San Diego, CA: Creation Life, 1982.
360. e.g., Ken Wilbur, ed., *The Holographic Paradigm and Other Paradoxes: Exploring the Leading Edge of Science*, Boulder, CO: Shambhala, 1982; cf. Martin Gardner, "Guest Comment: Is Realism a Dirty Word?" *American Journal of Physics*, March, 1989, p. 203; Martin Gardner, *Science: Good, Bad and Bogus*, 1982; Daisie Radner, Michael Radner, *Science and Unreason*, Belmont, CA: Wadsworth, 1982; Milton Rothman, "Myths About Science . . . And Belief in the Paranormal," *The Skeptical Inquirer*, volume 14, number 1, Fall, 1989; also Amaury de Riencourt and Michael Talbot, in ref. 361.
361. See ref. 319; Fritjof Capra, *The Tao of Physics*, Berkeley, CA: Shambhala, 1975, 300–307; Amaury de Riencourt, *The Eye of Shiva: Eastern Mysticism and Science*, New York, NY: William Morrow and Co. 1981; Michael Talbot, *Mysticism and the New Physics*, New York, NY: Bantam, 1981.
362. William Broad, Nicholas Wade, *Betrayers of the Truth: Fraud and Deceit in the Halls of Science*, New York, NY: Simon and Schuster, 1982; Alexander Kohn, *False Prophets: Fraud and Error in Science and Medicine*, New York, NY: Basil Blackwell, 1986.
363. Nigel Davies, *Human Sacrifice in History and Today*, New York, NY: William Morrow, 1981; see also, refs. 111; 396.
364. R. Hooykaas, *Religion and the Rise of Modern Science*, Grand Rapids, MI: Eerdmans, 1972.
365. R. E. D. Clark, *Science and Christianity: A Partnership*, Omaha, NE: Pacific Press Publishing, 1972.
366. John Ankerberg and John Weldon, *The Case for Jesus the Messiah: Incredible Prophecies That Prove God Exists*, and *Do the Resurrection Accounts Conflict and What Proof Is There That Jesus Rose from the Dead?*, Chattanooga, TN: Ankerberg Theological Research Institute, 1989–90.
367. Pierre Huard, Ming Wong, *Oriental Methods of Mental and Physical Fitness: The Complete Book of Meditation, Kinesitherapy and Martial Arts in China, India and Japan*, trans., Donald N. Smith, New York, NY: Funk and Wagnalls, 1977.
368. See ref. 455; and Charles T. Tart, *On Being Stoned: A Psychological Study of Marijuana Intoxication*, Palo Alto, CA: Science and Behavior Books, 1971, 195–196, 204–206, passim.
369. John Lilly, *The Scientist: A Novel Autobiography*, New York, NY: J. B. Lippincott, 1978.
370. Illustrations can be found in the following magazines: *The Journal of Transpersonal Psychology*; *Revision*; *The Common Boundary*; *Shaman's Drum*; *Parapsychology Review*; and others.

371. R. C. Zaehner, *Zen, Drugs, and Mysticism*, New York, NY: Random House/Vintage, 1974.

372. Arnold M. Ludwig, "Altered States of Consciousness" in Charles Tart, ed., *Altered States of Consciousness*, Garden City, NY: Doubleday/Anchor, 1972.

373. Elsa First, "Visions, Voyages and New Interpretations of Madness" in John White, ed., *Frontiers of Consciousness*, in ref. 338.

374. Kenneth Ring, "A Transpersonal View of Consciousness: A Mapping of Farther Regions of Inner Space," *Journal of Transpersonal Psychology*, 1974, no. 2.

375. Lynn Andrews, *Jaguar Woman and the Wisdom of the Butterfly Tree*, San Francisco, CA: Harper and Row, 1986.

376. John White, ed., *What Is Enlightenment?: Exploring the Goal of the Spiritual Path*, Los Angeles, CA: J. P. Tarcher, 1984.

377. Benjamine B. Wolman, Montague Ullman, eds., *Handbook of States of Consciousness*, New York, NY: Van Nostrand Reinhold Co., 1986.

378. The editors of *Psychic* magazine, *Psychics: In Depth Interviews*, New York, NY: Harper and Row, 1972, cf. Arthur Ford's autobiography, *Unknown but Known: My Adventure into the Meditative Dimension*, New York, NY: Harper and Row, 1968.

379. See Merrill Unger, *The Haunting of Bishop Pike*, Wheaton, IL: Tyndale, 1971.

380. M. Lamar Keene, *The Psychic Mafia*, New York, NY: St. Martins, 1976.

381. Carl Wickland, *Thirty Years Among the Dead*, reprint, Van Nuys, CA: Newcastle, 1974.

382. Ted Schwarz, Duane Empey, *Satanism*, Grand Rapids, MI: Zondervan, 1988.

383. SUNY at Stoney Brook University Hospital, "Lyme Disease: Symptoms, Treatment and Care," brochure, n.d.; "Lyme Disease in the U.S.: A Primer for Patients, *Emergency Decisions*, June, 197, 31–32; "Tiny Tick, Big Worry," *Newsweek*, May 22, 1989, 66–72.

384. Raymond J. Corsini, ed., *Handbook of Innovative Therapies*, New York, NY: John Wiley, 1981. (This book discusses some 250 therapies.)

385. Bhagwan Shree Rajneesh, "God Is a Christ in a Christ," *Sannyas*, May/June, 1978.

386. Martin Gumpert, *Hahnemann: The Adventurous Career of a Medical Rebel*, New York, NY: L. B. Fisher, 1945.

387. The Church of the New Jerusalem (Swedenlogianiam), chapter from ref. 317; cf. Walter Martin, *Kingdom of the Cults*, revised, Minneapolis, MN: Bethany, 1975, pp. 513–526.

388. Letter from Paul Reisser, M.D., August 31, 1990.

389. J. I. Packer, *God's Words* and *Knowing God*, Downer's Grove, IL: InterVarsity, 1981 and 1978.

390. "Kundalini Casualities," *The New Age Journal*, March, 1978.

391. Gordon Boals, "Toward a Cognitive Reconceptualization of Meditation," *The Journal of Transpersonal Psychology*, volume 10, number 2, 1983.

392. E. S. Gallegos, "Animal Imagery, the Chakra System and Psychotherapy," *The Journal of Transpersonal Psychology*, volume 15, number 2, 1983.

393. Kirk Bottomly, Jim French, "Christians Meditate Too!" *Yoga Journal*, May/June, 1984.

394. Karlis Osis, Edwin Bokert, "ESP and Meditation," *Journal of the American Society for Psychical Research*, January 1971.

395. Herbert Benson, *The Relaxation Response*, New York, NY: William Morrow, 1975.

396. John Weldon, John Ankerberg, *The Facts on the Occult*, Eugene, OR: Harvest House, 1991.

397. We examined the last forty issues of the *Journal of Transpersonal Psychology* from 1969. This revealed that Eastern and occult forms of meditation have great importance to transpersonal psychologists.

398. Franklin Jones [Da Free John], *The Method of the Siddhas*, Los Angeles, CA: The Dawn Horse Press, 1973.

399. Da Free John, *No Remedy: An Introduction to the Life and Practices of the Spiritual Community of Bubba Free John*, Lower Lake, CA: The Dawn Horse Press, 1976.

400. Roger N. Walsh, Frances Vaughan, eds., *Beyond Ego: Transpersonal Dimensions in Psychology*, Los Angeles, CA: J. P. Tarcher, 1980.

401. Henry Morris, *The Biblical Basis for Modern Science*, Grand Rapids, MI: Baker, 1984. Morris observes:

> Modern science actually grew in large measure out of the seeds of Christian theism. It is absurd to claim, as modern evolutionists often do, that one cannot be a true scientist if he believes in creation. . . . Most of the great founders of science believed in creation and, indeed, in all the great doctrines of Biblical Christianity.
>
> Men such as Johann Kepler, Isaac Newton, Robert Boyle, David Brewster, John Dalton, Michael Faraday, Blaise Pascal, Clerk Maxwell, Louis Pasteur, William Thompson (Lord Kelvin), and a host of others of comparable stature were men who firmly believed in special creation and the personal omnipotent God of creation, as well as believing in the Bible as the inspired Word of God and in Jesus Christ as Lord and Savior. . . .
>
> Many recent scientists, even though they themselves are not creationists, are still willing to recognize the Christian, creationist origin of modern science. (p. 29)

In appendix 1 of this book he lists over sixty great scientists with the scientific disciplines they established (antiseptic surgery, calculus, chemistry, electrodynamics, hydraulics, oceanography, thermodynamics, vertebrate paleontology, etc.) or their notable inventions or discoveries (law of gravity, actuarial tables, Pasteurization, scientific method, telegraph, etc.). In his *Men of Science—Men of God* (ref. 359), he supplies brief biographies and testimonies of these same men.

402. Eligio Stephen Gallegos, Teresa Rennick, *Inner Journeys: Visualization in Growth and Therapy*, Wellingborough, Northamptonshire: Turnstone Press, Ltd., 1984.

403. Merlin V. Nelson, "Health Professionals and Unproven Medical Alternatives," *Journal of Pharmacy Technology*, March/April, 1988, 60–69; the following methods "have been promoted without adequate scientific evidence to support their usefulness or safety": acupuncture, auriculotherapy, biofeedback, cellular therapy, chiropractic, herbal medicine, homeopathy, hypnosis, iridology, naturopathy, nutrition quackery, etc. Extensive references.

404. Wallace I. Sampson, "When Not to Believe the Unbelievable," and Elie A. Shneour, "The Benveniste Case: A Reappraisal," in *The Skeptical Inquirer*, volume 14, number 1, Fall, 1989, 90–95.

405. Varro E. Tyler, Virginia M. Tyler, "Modern Herbalism—A Dr. Jekyll or Mr. Hyde?" Proceedings of the Fourth National Herb Growing and Marketing Conference, July 22–25, 1989. San Jose, CA. In this journal:

> "Purdue University scholars examine what they call "paraherbalism," pseudo-scientific twisting of true herbalism. In contrast to the wise use of safe and effective herbs and the scientific study and testing of herbs ("true herbalism"), paraherbalism is marked by ten tenets. Among them: the medical establishment is in a conspiracy to discourage use of herbs; natural and organic herbs are superior to synthetic drugs; whole herbs are more effective than their isolated constituents; anecdotal testimonials are highly significant. Urges attention and support for "positive and hopeful side of modern herbalism" for the continued benefit of humankind." (406:208)

406. Kendrick Frazier, "Articles of Note," *Skeptical Inquirer*, volume 14, number 2, Winter, 1990.
407. "Meet Professor Bruce L. Johnson," *Brethren Biblical Institute News*, September, 1989, volume 5, number 2, North Fort Meyers, FL 33918.
408. Thomas C. Chalmers, "Scientific Quality and the Journal of Holistic Medicine," in ref. 3.
409. Daisie Radner, Michael Radner, "Holistic Methodology and Pseudoscience," in ref. 3.
410. Petr Skrabanek, "Acupuncture: Past, Present, Future," in ref. 3.
411. Brian H. Butler, "Applied Kinesiology," in ref. 76.
412. George J. Goodheart and Walter H. Schmitt, "Applied Kinesiology" in ref. 81.
413. Edmund S. Crelin, "Chiropractic," in ref. 3.
414. Sandy Newhouse, John Amoedo, "Native American Healing," in ref. 80.
415. *Webster's New Twentieth Century Dictionary*, 2nd Ed., 1978.
416. *Webster's Third New International Dictionary*, 1981.
417. Janet Macrae, "Therapeutic Touch as Meditation," in ref. 45.
418. Dolores Krieger, "High-Order Emergence of the Self During Therapeutic Touch," in ref. 45.
419. Philip E. Clark, Mary Jo Clark, "Therapeutic Touch: Is There a Scientific Basis for the Practice?" in ref. 3.
420. Eva Maria Herriot, "Life Changing Network" Chiropractic," *Yoga Journal*, September/October, 1990.
421. Eva Maria Norlyk, "Beyond Bones: A New Chiropractic System Strives to Align Body and Soul," *East West Journal*, December, 1989.
422. Varro E. Tyler, "Hazards of Herbal Medicine," in ref. 3.
423. Harris L. Coulter, "Homeopathy," in ref. 81.
424. Wyrth Post Baker, "Homeotherapeutics," in ref. 81.
425. Rajneesh, "Energy," *Sannyas*, Rajneesh Foundation International, number 1; January/February, 1978. See ref. 426.
426. See the kundalini issue, *Sannyas*, Rajneesh Foundation International, number 2, 1976; also Rajneesh, "Suicide or Sannyas," *Sannyas*, number 2, 1978.
427. Joseph F. Kett, *The Formation of the American Medical Profession: The Role of Institutions, 1780–1860*, New Haven, CT: Yale University Press, 1968.

428. See The National Council Against Health Fraud, Inc., Loma Linda, CA, "Position Paper on Chiropractic," February 14, 1985
429. Brooks Alexander, "Compromise and Vulnerability: Why the New Age Gets into the Church," *SCP Newsletter*, volume 15, number 1, 1990.
430. Marie Spengler and Brian Van Der Horst, "The Inner-Directeds," *New Realities*, volume 3, number 6, 1980.
431. Nursing texts authored by professors and leaders in nursing having an emphasis on new age methods and/or psychic healing include Barbara Blattner, *Holistic Nursing*, (1981); Patricia Randolf Flynn, *Holistic Health: The Art and Science of Care*, (1980); Barbara Dossey, et. al., *Holistic Nursing: A Handbook for Practice*, (1988); Cathie Guzetta, Barbara Dossey, *Cardio-vascular Nursing: Bodymind Tapestry* (1984), endorsed by the American Association of Critical Care Nurses; Jean Watson,*Nursing: Human Science and Human Caring* (1988); Margaret Newman, *Health As Expanding Consciousness*, (1986). *Topics in Clinical Nursing*, is now *New Age Nursing* Magazine. See Sharon Fish, "Nursing's New Age," *SCP Newsletter*, volume 14, number 3, 1989.
432. Susan M. Williams, "Holistic Nursing," in ref. 3, p. 24–33; see ref. 431.
433. Robert Pollack, Edward Kravitz, *Nutrition in Oral Health and Disease*, Philadephia, PA: Lea & Febiger, 1985.
434. Terence Hines, "High-Flying Health Quackery," *The Skeptical Inquirer*, Summer, 1988.
435. Benjamin F. Miller, Claire Brackman Keane, *Encyclopedia and Dictionary of Medicine, Nursing and Allied Health Care*, 3rd ed., Philadelphia, PA: W. B. Sanders, 1983.
436. *Webster's Medical Desk Dictionary*, Springfield, MA: Merriam Webster, 1986.
437. *Dorland's Illustrated Medical Dictionary*, 27th ed., Philadelphia, PA: W. B. Sanders, 1988.
438. John Keel, *UFO's: Operation Trojan Horse*, New York, NY: G. P. Putnams, 1970.
439. George Ohsawa, *Acupuncture and the Philosophy of the Far East*, Boston, MA: Tao Books and Publications, Inc., 1973.
440. Glenn Hultgren, "Applied Kinesiology," *The Christian Chiropractor*, October, 1988.
441. Marilyn Ferguson, ed., *The Brain-Mind Bulletin*, October 26, 1981.
442. As told by his friend Colin Wilson, in *Mysteries*, New York, NY: G. P. Putnam's Sons, 1978.
443. Herward Carrington, *Your Psychic Powers and How to Develop Them*, reprint, Van Nuys, CA: Newcastle, 1975.
444. Simeon Edmunds, *Hypnosis: Key to Psychic Powers*, New York, NY: Samuel Weiser, 1972.
445. Stephen N. Shore, "Quantum Theory and the Paranormal: The Misuse of Science," *The Skeptical Inquirer*, Fall, 1984.
446. George Vithoulkas, "Homeopathy," in ref. 80.
447. Daisie Radner, Michael Radner, "Holistic Methodology and Pseudoscience," in ref. 3.
448. Russell S. Worrall, "Iridology: Diagnosis or Delusion," p. 167–180, ref. 3.
449. Russell S. Worrall, "Pseudoscience: A Critical Look at Iridology," *Journal of the American Optometric Association*, October, 1984.
450. Norma Meyer, *The Daily Breeze*, Torrance, CA, Sept. 5, 1982, in ref. 3, p. 178.

451. William Johnston, *Silent Music: The Science of Meditation*, New York, NY: Harper & Row, 1975.

452. Dave Hunt, T.A. McMahon, *The Seduction of Christianity*, Eugene, OR: Harvest House, 1984.

453. Theosophy in ref. 317, cf. Martin, in ref. 387, p. 246–61.

454. Robert S. Ellwood, *Religious and Spiritual Groups in Modern America*, Englewood Cliffs, NJ: Prentice-Hall, 1973.

455. Michael Harner, "The Sound of Rushing Water," in Michael Harner ed., *Hallucinogens and Shamanism*, in ref. 266.

456. Anonymous.

457. Statement from Daniel Bowden, M.D., of Chattanooga, TN, September 15, 1990.

458. From copyrighted material supplied by Dr. Jarirs, October 5, 1990.

459. Haridas Bhattacharyya, ed. *The Cultural Heritage of India, vol. 4, The Religions* Calcutta, The Ramakrishna Mission Institute of Culture, 1969.

460. John Ankerberg and John Weldon, *When Does Life Begin? and Thirty-Nine Other Tough Questions on Abortion*, Brentwood, TN: Wolgemuth & Hyatt, 1990.

461. e.g. Walter Martin, Norman Klann, *Jehovah of the Watchtower*, Chicago, IL, Moody, 1974, in ref., pp. 91–104, cf., Joel Stephen Williams, *Ethical Issues in Compulsory Medical Treatment: A Study of Jehovah's Witness and Blood Transfusion*, Waco, TX: Baylor University, Ph. D. dissertation 1987, p. 116; Walter R. Martin, Norman Klann, *The Christian Science Myth*, p. 151–171, Grand Rapids, MI: Zondervan, 1962.

462. Position paper on acupuncture released in 1991 by the National Council Against Health Fraud, Loma Linda University School of Medicine, Loma Linda, CA. At press this was being considered for publication by Postgraduate Medicine.

463. Alan Horrilleur, *The Family Guide to Homeopathy*; D. Clausen, trans., Virginia: Health and Homeopathy Publishing, 1986.

INDEX

A

B

L

M

N

O

P

T

U

V

W

Y

About the Authors

John Ankerberg is host of the nationally televised, award-winning "The John Ankerberg Show" carried on more than thirty-nine thousand outlets every week in all fifty states. The show offers an opportunity for discussion and debate on widely varying topics, bringing together Christian and non–Christian religious leaders and leading secular authorities. Mr. Ankerberg has personally researched and hosted many debates on new age themes including one on new age medicine. He has a B.A. degree from the University of Illinois, M.A. and M. Div. degrees from Trinity Seminary, and has completed most of the requirements for a doctorate degree from Bethel Theological Seminary. John Ankerberg is also the co-author of fifteen books.

John Weldon is an honors graduate in sociology from California State University, San Diego, and has a master's degree in Christian Apologetics from the Simon Greenleaf School of Law in Anaheim, California, (summa cum laude); the M. Div. and D. Min. degrees from Luther Rice Seminary in Atlanta, Georgia; and a third masters issued jointly with William Carey International University, Pasadena, California, and Pacific College of Graduate Studies, Melbourne, Australia. His thesis for Pacific College involved a study of psychic healing. He also has the Ph.D in comparative religion, with an emphasis on Eastern religion from the latter institution.

Dr. Weldon has studied alternate religious movements and phenomena in depth for twenty years. He is co-author of *New Age Medicine*, (InterVarsity, 1988,) the *Facts on the New Age Movement*, (Harvest House, 1988), and *Psychic Healing*, (Moody, 1984), as well as fifteen additional books related to new age themes. He is working on a ten-volume critique of the new age movement and finishing an eight-thousand-page theological and critical analysis of seventy of the new religions. He is senior researcher for The John Ankerberg Show.

The typeface for the text of this book is *Goudy Old Style*. Its creator, Frederic W. Goudy, was commissioned by American Type Founders Company to design a new Roman type face. Completed in 1915 and named Goudy Old Style, it was an instant bestseller. However, its designer had sold the design outright to the foundry, so when it became evident that additional versions would be needed to complete the family, the work was done by the foundry's own designer, Morris Benton. From the original design came seven additional weights and variants, all of which sold in great quantity. However, Goudy himself received no additional compensation for them. He later recounted a visit to the foundry with a group of printers, during which the guide stopped at one of the busy casting machines and stated, "Here's where Goudy goes down to posterity, while American Type Founders Company goes down to prosperity."

Substantive Editing:
Michael S. Hyatt

Copy Editing:
Cynthia Tripp

Cover Design:
Steve Diggs & Friends
Nashville, Tennessee

Page Composition:
Xerox Ventura Publisher
Printware 720 IQ Laser Printer

Printing and Binding:
Maple-Vail Book Manufacturing Group
York, Pennsylvania

Cover Printing:
Strine Printing
York, Pennsylvania